Achieving Ethical Competence for Public Service Leadership

Achieving Ethical Competence for Public Service Leadership

Terry L. Cooper and Donald C. Menzel, Editors

M.E.Sharpe
Armonk, New York
London, England

Library of Congress Cataloging-in-Publication Data

Achieving ethical competence for public service leadership / edited by Terry L. Cooper and
Donald C. Menzel.
   p. cm.
  Includes bibliographical references and index.
  ISBN 978-0-7656-3245-6 (hardcover : alk. paper)—ISBN 978-0-7656-3246-3 (pbk. : alk. paper)
  1. Civil service ethics—United States. 2. Government executives—Professional ethics—
United States. 3. Civil service ethics. 4. Government executives—Professional ethics.
  I. Cooper, Terry L., 1938– II. Menzel, Donald C.

JK468.E7A62 2013
172′.2—dc23
                                        2012026131

Printed in the United States of America
The paper used in this publication meets the minimum requirements of
American National Standard for Information Sciences
Permanence of Paper for Printed Library Materials,
ANSI Z 39.48-1984.

IBT (c) 10   9   8   7   6   5   4   3   2   1
IBT (p) 10   9   8   7   6   5   4   3   2   1

In memory of Rebecca Catherine Menzel . . . almost 21!

28 March 1991–10 March 2012

DCM

Contents

Preface   ix

1.   In Pursuit of Ethical Competence
     Terry L. Cooper and Donald C. Menzel   3

Part I. Ethical Competence and Leadership   **25**

2.   A New Definition and Conceptualization of Ethical
     Competence
     Annelies De Schrijver and Jeroen Maesschalck   29

3.   From Ethical Competence to Ethical Leadership
     Leonie Heres and Karin Lasthuizen   51

4.   Ethical Competence in Business Leadership
     Diane L. Swanson   71

**Part II. Pedagogical Approaches and Methods
       to Achieve Ethical Competence**   **91**

5.   Developing Ethical Competence: An Integrated Pedagogical
     Method
     Richard M. Jacobs   95

6   Advancing Ethical Competence Through Pedagogy
     Carole L. Jurkiewicz   131

Part III. Ethical Competence Within and Across Professions   **155**

7.   Ethical Competence in Social Work
     Frederic G. Reamer   163

8. Ethical Competence and Professionalism
in Public Administration
Jeremy F. Plant   189

9. Ethical Competence for Public Service Lawyers
Robert N. Roberts   218

10. Ethical Competence in Nonprofit Organizations: A Human
Resources Perspective
Barbara S. Liggett   242

Part IV. Conclusion   **273**

11. The Road Ahead
Donald C. Menzel and Terry L. Cooper   275

Index   283
About the Editors and Contributors   293

Preface

This book has its intellectual roots in a debate and question that are both old and new: How do we know when we, and others, are capable of acting with integrity and have confidence that our behavior meets the highest standards of our profession? In other words, what does it mean to become ethically competent and to know when that has happened or is happening? A complicated question? Maybe, but it is a very important one. It is time to face up to the challenge of achieving ethical competence for public service leadership.

Our motives for undertaking this volume are several. First, the National Association of Schools of Public Affairs and Administration (NASPAA) has moved full force toward adopting competency-based standards applicable to master's degree granting programs in public affairs and administration. NASPAA does not seek to determine what competence is or is not, but it does hold member schools responsible for cultivating, training, and teaching certain competencies (i.e., specific skills, traits, knowledge, and attitudes that are identified as leading to a state of competence). Although there is no universal exam for the field of public administration similar to those in law (the bar exam) or medicine (medical board exams), it follows that schools successful in producing these characteristics (competencies) will turn out students who have achieved some level of competence sufficient to be considered competent in practice. This approach will surely strengthen professional management in governmental and nonprofit organizations throughout the United States and abroad. Managerial competence in subfields—fiscal and budgetary analysis, human resources, planning, the legal environment, and so on—likely will be more agreeable to the development of measureable competency-driven standards than is the case for ethics. The result could be a diminishment of ethics education and learning. We believe this volume takes a first step toward preventing such an unwelcome outcome.

A second motive for this project is the belief that while competency-driven workplaces are necessary and valuable, our understanding of the ethics culture of the workplace is often ignored or taken for granted in too many organizations. Thus the pursuit of ethical competence must go beyond the individual. We believe that the discussion of ethical competence in the pages of this volume is also relevant to the task of strengthening the ethical culture of the workplace.

The contributing authors in this volume were challenged to think widely and creatively about ethical competence—how it might be achieved and how ethical competence contributes to effective public service leadership. We charged them with "taking off the gloves" and venturing into territory where few others in our discipline have traveled. As the discerning reader will surely discover, the contributors accepted this charge with energy and enthusiasm.

Moreover, the chapter authors are fully aware that the discussion launched several years ago at NASPAA's conference and expanded upon in the chapters here is by no means the definitive word on ethical competence. However, the editors believe that an important milestone has been reached, and that it can be built upon in the years ahead by those who believe that ethical competence is so very important in ensuring a bright future in public governance. While much of the content in the chapters that follow is germane to public service in the United States and Europe, we are of the firm belief that our inquiries are relevant to those who advocate ethical public service worldwide.

It might be immodest to stake a claim for creative, if not pioneering, thinking about ethical competence; still, we would challenge readers to move the baton forward. At a minimum, we hope that our effort will motivate others to follow with the intent of pushing the frontier of practice and knowledge ever forward. We are neither at the end of the beginning nor the beginning of the end.

Terminology

The terms *competence*, *competent*, and *competency* are threaded throughout this volume. The editors' understanding of these terms is the following:

Competence is a noun that can be qualified by an adjective; e.g., she has a moderate (or low or high) level of competence to run an organization.

Competent indicates that one has achieved a sufficient level of competence to meet the standards for a profession, practice, craft, or trade. The granting of a license, passing an exam, completing an apprenticeship, receiving an academic degree, or combinations of these typically certifies one's competence.

Competency is a much trickier word that has crept into our vocabulary without much consensus about its meaning; therefore, it is used in various and often conflicting ways. We would prefer to reserve this term for references to sets of specific skills, knowledge, and attitudes that are components of *competence,* including (1) the ability to perceive ethical problems, (2) the possession of ethical analysis skills, (3) a knowledge of ethical theories, (4) an understanding of how organization design encourages or impedes ethical decision making and conduct, (5) the value of strength of character to act on one's ethical conclusions, and (6) a recognition of the impact of positive attitudes toward the importance of ethical conduct, and so on. The most appropriate use of the term in this case would be references to *competencies* that are necessary to have some degree of *competence* and, ultimately, to be deemed *competent* in a profession, practice, craft, or trade. One might use *competency* appropriately to refer to a competency-based approach to ethics training, for example. This word has been overused in recent discourse and more often than not is used inappropriately. All contributors have made an effort to use these terms in a consistent manner.

Acknowledgments

We would like to express our most sincere appreciation to the contributors of this volume for their patience, their goodwill, and most important, their commitment to a quality product. We also would like to acknowledge the insights, constructive criticism, and responsiveness that external reviewers brought to the table to ensure the successful conclusion of this enterprise. An edited volume is by definition the work of many hands and minds. Those reviewers who gave freely of their time and energy include (in alphabetic order): Nancy W. Basinger, University of Utah; Dominic Bearfield, Texas A&M University; Fran Burke, International Integrity; Ralph Dolgoff, University of Maryland; Melvin Dubnick, University of New Hampshire; Elaine Englehardt, Utah Valley University; Rod Erakovich, Texas Wesleyan University; Angela Evans, University of Texas; Charles P. Garofalo, Texas State University; Richard Ghere, University of Dayton; Pamela A. Gibson, Troy University; Gjalt de Graaf, VU University Amsterdam; Karianne Kalshoven, University of Amsterdam; Terry Lamboo, VU University Amsterdam; Steve Maser, Willamette University; Manfred F. Meine, Troy University; Susan Paddock, University of Wisconsin Madison; Suzanne Piotrowski, Rutgers University; Jerry Pops, West Virginia University; David A. Schultz, Hamline University; Jessica Sowa, University of Colorado Denver; Harvey L. White, University of Pittsburgh; Diane Yoder, University of Southern California; and Susan E. Zinner, Indiana University Northwest. Others who provided valuable advice and support include James S. Bowman, Florida State University; Linda F. Dennard, Auburn University; Bruce Jansson, University of Southern California; Nan Kutchner, Tampa, Florida; Joan Pynes, University of South Florida; William L. Richter, Kansas State University; Ellen Rosell, Troy University; Becky Stuteville, Park University; Laurel Terry, Penn State Dickinson School of Law; Linda Treviño, Penn State; Jonathan P. West, University of Miami; Howard Whitton, Australia.

Many thanks to Harry M. Briggs, executive editor of M.E. Sharpe, who had the foresight to recognize the need for and value of a volume that breaks new ground on a difficult but significant subject. His patience, goodwill, and professionalism were much appreciated.

Kay F. Menzel, Don's partner for more than 50 years, served as a valuable critic and listening board during the months that passed as work proceeded on this project. Emmy and Sammy "woof-woof" also helped with time away from the project.

Achieving Ethical Competence for Public Service Leadership

standards, sensitivity to public opinion, and character, have been discussed at length. That orientation has caused many to think and inquire about the normative foundations of administrative ethics identified with constitutional regime values, founding values, bureaucratic ethics, citizenship ethics, social equity, and the public interest.

The cognitive moral development of individuals has been one of the systematic and consistent lines of research based on the initial work of Lawrence Kohlberg (1980) and carried forward in the field of public administration by Debra Stewart and Norman Sprinthall (1994) in their Stewart Sprinthall Management Survey (SSMS), along with Carole Jurkiewicz (2002) and Richard White (1999) using the Defining Issues Test (DIT). That body of empirical research has caused us to consider the importance of developing principled thinking and its relationship to ethical conduct. Moreover, we have written and talked about ethics education and the training of those preparing for public administration careers, in addition to ongoing instruction for those already in practice, who are more likely to cultivate principled thinking.

It is also true that the organizational structure and culture in which administrators make ethical decisions and attempt to carry them out has often been identified as an important influence for better or worse—usually worse. Research by scholars such as Kurt (1935, 1936, 1951), Stanley Milgram (1974, 1983), Philip Zimbardo (2007), and Robert Denhardt (1981) has informed our thinking about the power of organizations to shape both our thinking and our conduct. Also, in the "real world," we have been confronted with numerous cases in which organizational hierarchy has prevented ethical conduct and punished those with the courage to persist. These include the Nazi Holocaust, the disasters involving the *Challenger* and *Columbia* space shuttles, and the torture of prisoners at the Abu Ghraib prison in Iraq. The whistleblower literature is filled with examples of the power of organizations to resist ethical conduct and punish severely those who persist in following their conscience and professional ethical standards.

However, a much less-developed skill and knowledge necessary for ethical competence is what to do about organizational influence on conduct—the prescriptions that should follow a good diagnosis of an organizational problem with ethical implications. That kind of competence should include the following.

1. Knowledge of the Normative Foundations of Public Administrative Ethics

Public affairs and administration students should be required to take a freestanding course devoted primarily to the development of a normative professional ethical perspective that goes beyond skill in analyzing and resolving ethical dilemmas. While the ability to engage in ethical analysis of particular decisions is necessary, it is not sufficient. A place to stand professionally with respect to ethics is also required. Public administration is ultimately a normative field based on the use of administrative power and discretion for the good of a democratic society. Codes of ethics developed by professional associations such as the American Society for Public Administration (ASPA) and the International City/County Management Association (ICMA) are only very small elements in that normative perspective. More extensive work to help students and public service professionals develop clarity about their ethical commitments—commitments rooted in the U.S. Constitution, founding thought, citizenship ethics, social equity, and the public interest—is essential.

2. Thorough Grounding in Organization Theory and Behavior

In order to develop competence that links ethics to the organizational context, knowledge of the structure and culture of organizations is required, along with an understanding of human behavior in organizations. This includes knowledge of the research literature on the effects of (1) structuring organizations more or less vertically, (2) providing for varying amounts of flexibility, (3) using various dissent channels, (4) establishing transparency of various degrees, and (5) encouraging participation in organizational decisions both by members of organizations and by citizens. Also, it is important to understand how structure and culture often collide, resulting in one subverting the other. Organization structure may allow for flexible communication among levels rather than adhering strictly to a chain of command, but if a cultural norm is to never take bad news to the boss (as it is in many organizations), the culture winds up defeating the structural intent. A key question is: How can culture and structure work together to support ethical thinking and conduct?

3. Knowledge of Organization Development and the Design Approach

This is the point at which a normative ethical foundation and an ability to think diagnostically about the effects of organization structure and culture lead logically to a plan for change. How does the organization need to change in order to obstruct ethical conduct less and encourage it more? Students faced with this kind of problem tend to fall back on training of a rather traditional kind as the solution. If the structure has become too rigid, then train those within it to be less so; if the culture is subverting the structure, then train for a change in cultural norms. We really need to go well beyond this simplistic tendency.

Perhaps the design approach as advocated by Caroline Whitbeck (1996) should be drawn on to link ethics at the individual level to the organizational setting. The design approach attempts to look at an ethical problem in its context and determine its causes. If any of those causes are related to the organization, the next step is a diagnosis of the organizational characteristics that are involved. One then seeks to design new structures or redesign old ones; design new cultural norms or redesign old ones. From this perspective, one always acknowledges both the constraints and the opportunities inherent in the given organizational setting. In the same way one would take a parcel of land with its vegetation, size, shape, contours, and any existing structures as a set of constraints and opportunities for designing a building, so one does similarly with organizational structure and cultural norms. Notions of ethical perfection are set aside for the best possible organization, given these conditions. The task then is how to carry out the design or redesign process using research, organization change methods, training, personnel changes, job redefinition, mission revision, strategic planning, and the full array of tools at hand in our field.

A Comprehensive Definition

The previous discussion points to the need for an inclusive definition of *ethical competence.* Donald C. Menzel (2010, 18), writing in *Ethics Moments in Government,* offers one such definition: (1) a commitment to high standards of personal and professional behavior, (2) a knowledge of relevant ethics codes and laws, (3) the ability to engage in ethical reasoning when confronted with challenging ethical situations, (4) the ability to identify and act on public service ethics and values, and (5) a commitment to promoting ethical practices and behaviors in public agencies and organizations (see Figure 1.1). Implicit in this definition is knowledge of the normative foundations of public administrative ethics, grounding in organization theory and behavior (especially knowledge of the structure and culture of organizations and human behavior), and the skill and ability to think diagnostically about the effects of organization structure and culture on ethical conduct. Each of these five competencies is a variable. Any particular professional or candidate for professional status possesses them *more or less.* Judgments about how much competence is sufficient and when one has fallen below the required standard is a matter of collective judgment by a professional community.

Figure 1.1   **Dynamics of Ethical Competence as Envisioned by Menzel**

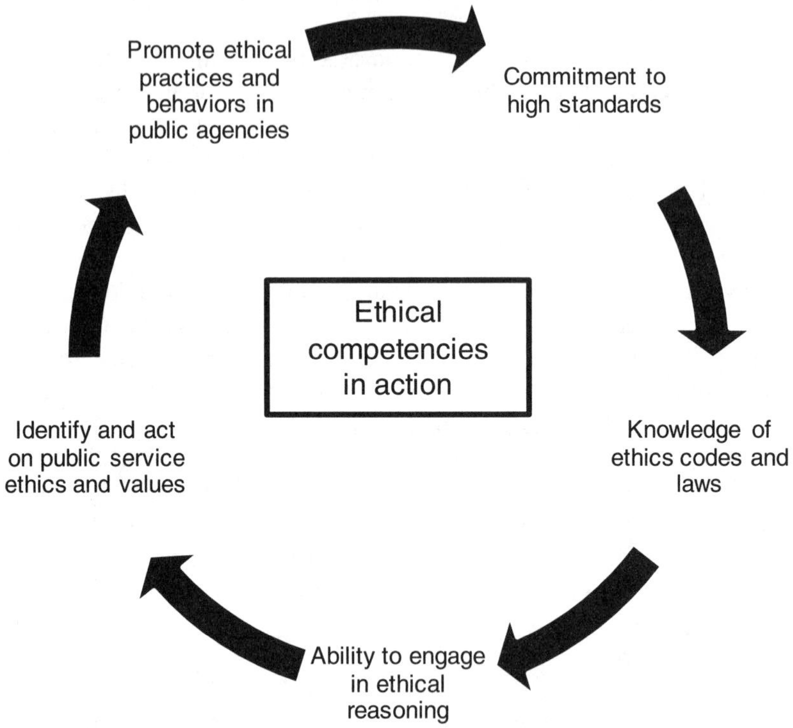

Promote ethical practices and behaviors in public agencies

Commitment to high standards

Ethical competencies in action

Identify and act on public service ethics and values

Knowledge of ethics codes and laws

Ability to engage in ethical reasoning

Source: Adapted from Menzel 2010.

How Does One Achieve a Satisfactory Level of Ethical Competence?

Within the public administration and public affairs graduate program community, public service ethics education should be an essential part of the process of preparing individuals to lead and advance the public interest. Yet considerable disagreement continues about whether ethics courses taught as part of public administration and public affairs programs and in-service ethics programs should focus primarily on "high road"/"integrity-based" or on "low road"/"compliance-driven" ethical competencies. The low road approach puts the emphasis on rules and enforcement. The high road challenges individuals to do the right thing as reflected through their ethical lens on the world. Today, the vast majority of in-service ethics training programs in government focus heavily on low road–type issues involving public corruption, financial conflicts of interest, and public financial disclosure.

These competing approaches bring to mind the famous Carl Friedrich–Herman Finer debate of 1940–41, regarding the question: How can public servants be held accountable to democratically elected leaders? While Friedrich (1940) argued for accountability derived from moral responsibility, Finer (1941) contended that responsible behavior required that administrators conform to rules and enforceable codes of ethics.

In contrast, survey courses in ethics offered as part of graduate programs in public administration and public affairs indicate that the vast majority of university-based public service ethics instructors believe the "primary goal of ethics education is to improve the moral judgment of students" (Hejka-Ekins 1988, 885). As detailed by Goss (1996, 579–580), numerous public service ethics scholars have presented their views regarding which "virtues, ethical characteristics, and attributes" are most desirable in public administrators. Stephen K. Bailey (1964), for example, "suggests optimism, courage, and fairness" as essential virtues for public servants. John Rohr, on the other hand, emphasizes regime values found in the Constitution "or enunciated by the Supreme Court" (Goss 1996, 580). Kathryn Denhardt, according to Goss, "suggests that the moral foundations of public administration consists of three elements: honor, benevolence, and justice" (Goss 1996, 580).

Integrating Approaches

Surprisingly, university-based public service ethics scholars and in-service ethics trainers seem content to operate within their respective spheres of influence. The advocates of compliance-based and integrity-based ethics training seem quite content to preach to the choir and see little value in integrating each other's approach in their respective forms of ethics education. However, a handful of ethics scholars have put forward a fusion approach to ethics education. April Hejka-Ekins (2001) notes that "such an approach to ethics education would combine two curricular areas: (1) understanding legal statutes or agency regulations and the minimum standards . . . and (2) identification of ethical standards and values such as those embodied in the democratic ethos or a professional code of ethics" (84). Carole Lewis and Stuart Gilman (2005, 18) add that a fusion model offers "a two-pronged, systematic approach that incorporates both compliance with formal standards and the promotion of individual ethical responsibility."

How Does Ethical Competence Contribute to Effective Public Service Leadership?

Administrators must do things right, but they also must do right things. Ethics policy, then, matters profoundly in government as it lays the foundation for excellence in public affairs. As Dennis Thompson's (1992) famous paradox stipulates, because other issues are more important than ethics, ethics is more important than any issue. It is a precondition for, and a hallmark of, good government. It follows that the "umbrella profession" of public administration has the duty and privilege of articulating key competencies.

The ICMA, the professional home for more than 8,000 local executive leaders worldwide, recognized the centrality of ethics to leadership in 1923 with the adoption of a Code of Ethics that is often regarded as exemplary. The code prohibits unacceptable conduct and prescribes appropriate behaviors, with a particular emphasis on promoting professionalism in managing the affairs of cities and counties. Above all else, local executives are expected to avoid politics and place public integrity at the center of decision making. Getting the job done with efficiency, economy, and effectiveness are essential *but not sufficient*. Successful local government leaders are expected to get the job done without sacrificing integrity. Indeed, integrity is writ large in ICMA documents. Here is what the ICMA (2008) has in print and calls for in practice:

> Integrity. Demonstrating fairness, honesty, and ethical and legal awareness in personal and professional relationships and activities (requires knowledge of business and personal ethics; ability to understand issues of ethics and integrity in specific situations). Practices that contribute to this core content area are:
>
> - *Personal Integrity*. Demonstrating accountability for personal actions; conducting personal relationships and activities fairly and honestly.
> - *Professional Integrity*. Conducting professional relationships and activities fairly, honestly, legally, and in conformance with the ICMA Code of Ethics—requires knowledge of administrative ethics and specifically the ICMA Code of Ethics.
> - *Organizational Integrity*. Fostering ethical behavior throughout the organization through personal example, management practices, and training (requires knowledge of administrative ethics; ability to instill accountability into operations; and ability to communicate ethical standards and guidelines to others).

The ICMA's commitment to promoting and supporting ethical behavior is unconditional. Nonetheless, their extensive code (2,000 words long with a 3,200-word supplementary "Rules of Procedure for Enforcement") is sometimes perceived as "a set of rules to comply with." One friendly critic (Stone 2010) claims that eight "Principles of Ethical Conduct" are all that are needed:

1. Do my best at work . . .
2. Avoid conflict of interest . . .
3. Speak truth to power . . .
4. Be a good citizen . . .
5. Shun any private gain from public employment . . .
6. Act impartially . . .
7. Treat others the way I would like to be treated . . .
8. Report waste, fraud, and corruption . . .

Leadership Success and Failure

While it very well might seem that successful leaders are people of integrity, there are many cases and examples of successful leaders gone astray. In this section, we present two illustrative cases involving the chief executives of two large counties in Florida.

The Case of Hillsborough County, Florida

Located on the Gulf Coast of Florida with a population of nearly 1.3 million, Hillsborough County is in a metropolitan region of more than 4 million that includes the cities of Tampa, St. Petersburg, and Clearwater. Three professional sports teams call the region home: the Tampa Bay Buccaneers (football), the Tampa Bay Lightening (hockey), and the Tampa Bay Rays (baseball). The county, although urbanized, has a sizeable unincorporated area and a mixed economy of businesses, light industry, shipbuilding, and maintenance along with a deepwater seaport that handles petroleum, phosphates, cargo containers, and cruise ship passengers. Hillsborough is a charter county with the chief administrative officer appointed by a partisan-elected county commission. Republican officeholders have dominated county government in recent years while Democrats have dominated Tampa's strong mayoral system of government.

This case involves a county administrator who climbed the ladder of success over more than 30 years to become its chief executive.[3] Alas, Bailey's (1964) famous dictum that "the higher a person goes on the rungs of power and authority, the more wobbly the ethical ladder" became a reality for her.

What happened? The county established an independent auditor who, among other things, reported that the administrator had given herself and top aides pay raises at a time in which the county was experiencing significant fiscal stress that necessitated cutbacks and layoffs. Moreover, the county's 8,000 employees were asked to take on more work to cope with the downsizing, a recipe for low morale and disgruntlement. The county had in place an unwritten policy to reward employees who engaged in innovative cost-saving measures, which included laying off subordinates. One of the chief executive's top aides nominated her for a reward in recognition of the decision she made to lay off one of her assistant county administrators. Uncertain that she was eligible to participate in the program, she consulted the county attorney, who told her that she was indeed eligible. Therefore, she accepted (some critics would say "gave" herself) a $2,000 salary increase that was determined by a set percentage of her $224,000 annual salary. However, she did not seek approval from the county commission, which was unaware of the policy to adjust her salary. The county charter specifically authorizes the commission to set the pay of the administrator.

As events unfolded, including private interchanges between the auditor and individual members of the commission, the chief executive began to suspect that the auditor was "out to get her." Consequently, she ordered one of her managers to collect all emails involving the auditor, commission, and county attorney relevant to the pay issue. The media began to follow the story and broke the "email snooping" news, as it was called. The administrator admitted that she had collected the email messages but, upon second thought, decided not to read them. The commission's trust in this claim rapidly deteriorated and motivated them to place the administrator, the county attorney, and the auditor on 90 days of paid administrative leave.

As the leave period moved along, the commission struggled with what to do—demote the administrator, fire her and the others with or without cause, wait out an investigation by the state law enforcement agency into whether or not email snooping violated the law and then decide what to do, or strike a deal with the administrator to resign. Firing the administrator without cause would let her walk with more than $500,000 in compensation plus unpaid leave time. Consequently, the commission and the administrator through their lawyers attempted to work out a settlement. As the suspension approached its end, the administrator became more determined to find an arrangement that would let her receive $550,000 or more in severance and benefits. In the meantime, there was considerable stress and distress reported in the media about the ill effects that the situation was having on employee morale, job performance, and the public's negative perception of the imbroglio. The story ends with the auditor losing his job, the administrator fired unceremoniously with cause, and the county attorney reinstated.

This case is replete with ethical breaches, most of which are obvious. Perhaps a less obvious but ever so important breach was the matter of doing what was believed to be in the best interests of the community, and, of course, putting an end to the erosion of public trust and confidence in county government. While it was clearly in the best financial interests of the administrator to stay the course, did she also have an obligation to put the community interest ahead of her personal and professional interests? It would seem so. However, it is fair to say that she felt strongly that she had been victimized, especially by the auditor's reports and behavior. At stake were her sense of fair treatment and justice, her professional reputation, and fiscal considerations, all of which made it difficult to simply steal away into the night. Moreover, her 30-plus years of longevity in county employment meant that she was well known in the community and had many friends and colleagues.

Indeed, she did not steal away. Rather, she embarked on a two-year quest to acquire her severance payout and clear herself of the charges that she abused the public trust and committed an illegal act by accepting a 1 percent pay raise without the authorization of the county commission. A criminal investigation by the Florida Department of Law Enforcement (FDLE) found no evidence that she had violated state law and an administrative law judge ruled that commissioners could not deny her severance pay. Soon thereafter, the Florida Ethics Commission dismissed the charges that she had given herself a secret pay raise (Davis 2012).

It should be noted that past commissions and the professional community had held the administrator in high regard during her six-year tenure as chief executive and years as HR director and assistant county administrator. She had a respected reputation for promoting professional and ethical behavior by county employees. She certainly did nothing illegal as ascertained by the FDLE, nor violated her contract as determined by an administrative law judge—nor did she breech the state's ethics law according to the Florida Commission on Ethics. Did the administrator demonstrate ethical competence? You decide!

The Case of Sarasota County, Florida

Sarasota County is an affluent charter county located on the Gulf Coast, about 70 miles south of Tampa-Hillsborough County. With a highly educated, older population of nearly 380,000 and four incorporated cities, including the well-known community of Venice, the county has enjoyed a strong record of good governance. A five-member county commission that appoints a professional administrator is responsible for overseeing county affairs. The most recent administrator served for 14 years, no small feat in local government management. During those years, he garnered the respect and admiration of the Board of County Commissioners, good government citizen groups, and the local media. He viewed himself as a person with high ethical standards and took pride in the organization's performance in getting the job done at an affordable price. He also took considerable pride in a progressive management style that delegated responsibility to top managers.

The county has a model code of ethics, and the administrator trusted his management team to be exemplars of integrity and performance. He had every reason to feel comfortable with the ethical culture that pervaded the 2,000-member workforce until . . . all hell broke loose: The local newspaper published a story about a 55-year-old project manager in the public works department who had accepted $15,000 in cruises, hotel stays, gift cards, and other kickbacks from a company whose contract he helped supervise.

As the scandal unfolded, other misdeeds were alleged. County supervisors were reported to "piggyback" contracts—that is, opt for the same deal another local government had with a company, thus allowing county managers to avoid putting contracts out to bid. Procurement managers also practiced "change orders," where a contract is bid for specific terms only to be altered at points along the way, with extra work and pay added. The "change orders" practice allowed favored companies to come in at unrealistically low bids. Topping off the string of procurement problems was the fact that administrators and supervisors could use county-issued credit cards to purchase products that would ordinarily be put out to bid if they exceeded $10,000. In other words, credit cards could be used to "break" a payment into several parts if their sum exceeded the $10,000 limit.

The administrator was shocked to learn of these practices. He said to himself, "Frankly, either I have failed personally or I feel abandoned by the entire management team, in the sense that my business and personal ethics appear to have not been translated into the culture of at least one operation." What should I do, he mused? Should I clean house by firing a number of managers? Should I accept responsibility and resign? Should I fashion a memo to my top managers admonishing them to "fix the problems or resign"?

Faced with an ever-widening probe by the local media, one commissioner urged the administrator to fix it. "Ultimately he's accountable for his employees' action and we as a board are accountable for his actions and the public's trust. I would now suggest that all are in jeopardy."

The administrator took the commissioner's advice seriously and acted quickly by drafting a memo to his top managers that said, among other things:

> These last two weeks have been the most uncomfortable ones of my 36-year career in public service. I am appalled by what I learned as a result of the now named John Doe incident, and that in fact I keep learning as new stuff seems to be revealed to me every day.

A month later the administrator resigned. In his letter of resignation, he said: "I take responsibility as the leader of the organization when such things happen." A termination agreement was reached, which one newspaper reporter declared, enabled the administrator to walk away "with hugs and smiles" and with a severance payout of a lump sum equivalent to his annual salary and benefits for one year (estimated at $265,833).

Case Implications

These cases point to three important conclusions. First, experienced administrators can develop "ethical blind spots" that can tarnish a long, successful career. Can it be that well-intentioned, ethically minded public managers are capable of engaging in unintended unethical behavior? Can there be a gap between intended and actual ethical behavior that is caused by conditions and circumstances that bound our ethicality? "Bounded ethicality," Max H. Bazerman and Ann E. Tenbrunsel explain, "comes into play when individuals make decisions that harm others and when that harm is inconsistent with these decision makers' conscious beliefs and preferences" (2011, 5).

One explanation for ethical blind spots or gaps between what we should do and what we actually do is lack of awareness. That is, psychologically, "our minds are subject to bounded ethicality, or cognitive limitations that can make us unaware of the moral implications of our decisions" (Bazerman and Tenbrunsel 2011, 30). There are "aspects of everyday work life—including goals, rewards, compliance systems, and informal pressures—[that] can contribute to *ethical fading*, a process by which ethical dimensions are eliminated from a decision" (30).

If the administrators in one or both of these cases developed ethical blind spots that may have contributed to ethical fading in their organizations, the awareness dimension of ethical competence clearly failed them.

The second conclusion drawn from these cases is that becoming ethically competent is a lifelong pursuit of a goal that may always be difficult and challenging to reach. Does this mean that the pursuit of ethical competence is in vain or that one is hopelessly doomed to failure? No. Rather, it suggests that the journey may be long and very difficult.

A third perhaps faulty conclusion can be drawn from the Hillsborough case. Namely, if an act is not illegal it is ethical. This low bar standard is all too often accepted as defining sufficient ethical competence. This is an unacceptable conclusion.

As these cases point out, no high-ranking government administrator is too big or important to fail. As you reflect on these cases and their implications for ethical competence, you might ask yourself, how would I have avoided falling off the ethical ladder? There is, of course, no magic wand that you can wave to ensure that you stay on the ethical pathway. But with sensitivity and due diligence day in and day out in your workplace, you can go a long way toward achieving ethical competence for public service leadership.

The Challenge of Collaborative Leadership

Typically, administrative leadership is viewed as taking place within highly structured bureaucratic organizations of the modern, industrial age. Roles and duties are well specified in the hierarchy. Much change in this model has taken place over the past several decades, although few would contend that bureaucratic organizations have altogether vanished. Rather, the flattening of organizations, both in the private and public sectors, has proceeded in spurts. The postmodern era has arrived, and it is replete with networks, collaboration, and partnerships aided and abetted by new age information technology and communications. "Collaborative public management, managing across boundaries, leveraging networks, and governance through networking are contemporary concepts that characterize a near-tsunami sweeping across recent public administration literature," write Wright, Stenberg, and Cho (2011). Moreover, the interconnectedness of problems, the regionalization and globalization of solutions, and the decrease in government resources have emphasized the need to move increasingly from government to governance as an inclusive process and from hierarchy to networks (Maak and Pless 2006, in Van Wart 2011). "This requires that leaders have a new worldview, different competencies and additional tools" (Van Wart 2011).

The ethical challenges and competencies required to exercise effective collaborative leadership are surely different and perhaps more complicated than those of the past. Van Wart (2011) describes the ethics-leadership connection from three perspectives. First is the ethical leadership model with a "focus on moral management at a more transactional level and ethical standards at the organizational level." Put in question format, the model asks, "What do leaders do to support ethical and moral behavior, and what do they need to do in order to make sure that organizations themselves are ethical?" A second perspective emphasizes servant leadership, "which focuses more on supporting followers via participation, empowerment, and development." Spiritual leadership, he asserts, is a more recent version of servant leadership, with an emphasis on membership and calling to balance transformational needs with a focus primarily on the organization. In other words, spiritual leadership seeks to blend and balance the emotive needs of the individual (e.g., sense of belonging, respect, confidence, prestige) with the leadership vision of the purpose and mission of the organization. The third perspective is authentic leadership, with a focus on self-awareness, honesty, and transparency. "How can leaders have integrity in a multifaceted world?" he asks (2011).

The currency of the collaborative public manager is trust. He cannot lead in a collaborative environment without this currency. Trust means placing oneself in harm's way, providing the opportunity for others, including organizational and professional colleagues, to inflict harm in some manner. It makes sense, then, that people choose to trust others who possess high ethical standards and integrity. Trust is often said to be the "glue" that holds organizations together. It might also be said that ethical behavior and integrity are the ingredients that build and sustain trust.

Ethical Competence and Leadership

At the outset of this chapter it was noted that becoming ethically competent is a lifelong process. There are no assurances that one's feet are on solid ethical ground because of one's education, training, or professional engagement with colleagues. Indeed, some argue that learning ethics can be achieved only through life experiences, a "feet-by-the-fire" trial. While we do not dismiss this argument out of hand, we believe that education and professional engagement can make a difference. Moreover, we believe that one can acquire a level of ethical competence that is essential for leadership that serves the public interest. Still, we recognize that the path to becoming ethically competent is seldom straight, and any number of blind alleys will likely be difficult to avoid.

The traveler on the path to ethical competence has a responsibility to do the right thing, but she also has a responsibility to exercise ethical leadership, a topic about which much more needs to be known. Joanne B. Ciulla, writing in the second edition of *Ethics, the Heart of Leadership* (2004), notes: "Given the central role of ethics in the practice of leadership it's remarkable that there has been little in the way of sustained and systematic treatment of the subject by scholars. A literature search of 1,800 article abstracts from psychology, business, religion, philosophy, anthropology, sociology, and political science yielded only a handful of articles that offered any in-depth discussion of ethics and leadership." Ciulla further laments that "the state of research on leadership ethics is similar to the state of business ethics 20 years ago. For the most part, the discussion of ethics in the leadership literature is fragmented; there is little reference to other works on the subject, and one gets the sense that most authors write as if they were starting from scratch."

Linda K. Treviño and colleagues (2003) share Ciulla's assessment, asserting that the leadership literature has made little mention of the ethical dimension of leadership. Indeed, Treviño and her study team sought to overcome this deficit in part with a qualitative investigation of executive ethical leadership in corporate America. They conducted semi-structured interviews with 20 senior executives and 20 corporate ethics/compliance officers representing medium- to large-sized American companies. Their principal objective was to develop a more nuanced understanding of ethical leadership, one that reaches beyond the conventional wisdom that traits such as honesty and integrity are all that matter. Indeed, they concluded that ethical leadership is much more. It includes:

- Being people-focused—ethical leaders "care about people, respect people, develop their people, and treat people right."
- Engaging in visible ethical actions and traits—"ethical leaders are *role models* of ethical conduct who lead by example and who *walk the ethical talk.*"
- Setting ethical standards and accountability—"they *set standards and expectations* regarding appropriate and inappropriate conduct, . . . *create and institutionalize values,* . . . practice *values-based management,* . . . use *rewards and punishments* to hold people *accountable to standards,* . . . [and] *do not tolerate ethical lapses.*"
- Having broad ethical awareness—"ethical leaders have broad ethical awareness and concerns that include, but extend beyond, bottom-line interest to include the good of the organization and the community."
- Engaging in decision-making processes—processes that emphasize such principles as the golden rule and employ fairness criteria. (Treviño, Brown, and Hartman 2003)

The themes and competencies identified by Treviño and colleagues for ethical leadership in corporate America have equal merit for ethical leadership in public service. And, we would add, it is just as important for leaders to "talk the walk" as it is to "walk the talk." It is important for ethical leaders to talk about the ethical dimensions of what they are doing, including ethical quandaries they face and how they think through them.

Conclusion

As this chapter suggests, ethical competence for public service leadership can be defined in several ways. Perhaps that is how it should be, given that those in pursuit of public service careers bring many occupational backgrounds and educational experiences to the task. While much of our attention in this book focuses on public administrators who occupy positions of authority in governmental and nonprofit agencies, others such as lawyers, planners, social workers, engineers, health and medical personnel, financial specialists, information technology managers, policy analysts, and business administrators should be equally engaged in advancing the public interest.

We cannot define competence apart from a set of specific competencies—skills, knowledge, and abilities required to do things measured against a standard. Competencies would then be personal skills that reflect proficiency in:

1. identifying ethical problems and the issues that emerge from them,
2. reasoning about the principles involved in the problem and issues,
3. arriving at a decision that can be defended based on public service principles, and
4. balancing organization development and design to move organizations toward structures and cultures that are supportive of ethical conduct.

Rules and codes are just one kind of moral standard against which these skills can be measured. There are also overarching ethical principles such as fairness and respect for others that may be used to critique the rules and codes. Competence is not one state of being, but a variable. One can be more or less competent. At some point, a profession must decide whether particular persons who seek admission to its ranks are competent *enough*, and whether its members have demonstrated adequate competence in particular situations.

We believe a concerted effort should be made to identify and incorporate specific competencies in the education and training of all who enter public service. The chapters that follow offer many suggestions and propose a foundation for achieving this goal.

Notes

This chapter draws in part from essays presented at a roundtable on "Becoming Ethically Competent" held at the 2009 Conference of the National Schools of Public Affairs and Administration. Participants included James S. Bowman, Florida State University; Terry L. Cooper, University of Southern California; Kathryn Denhardt, University of Delaware; Carole L. Jurkiewicz, Louisiana State University; Manfred F. Meine, Troy University; Donald C. Menzel, Northern Illinois University; Jeremy Plant, Penn State University Harrisburg; and James H. Svara, Arizona State University.

1. There are a growing number of edited volumes that focus in part on ethical competencies and public service leadership (see West and Berman 2004; Cox 2009; Richter and Burke 2007).

2. This section was drawn from Manfred F. Meine in his paper "To Be or Not to Be: The Issue of Ethical Competence," presented at the 2009 Conference of the National Schools of Public Affairs and Administration.

3. This case is drawn from newspaper accounts published in the *Tampa Tribune* and *St. Petersburg Times* from March 2010 through June 2010.

References

Bailey, Stephen K. 1964. Ethics and the public service. *Public Administration Review* 24(4) (December): 234–243.

Bazerman, Max H., and Ann E. Tenbrunsel. 2011. *Blind Spots: Why We Fail to Do What's Right and What to Do About It.* Princeton, NJ: Princeton University Press.

Berghofer, Desmond. 2003. *The Ethical Competence Framework.* Vancouver, British Columbia: Institute for Ethical Leadership. http://www.ethicalleadership.com/EthicalCompetenceFramework.htm (accessed August 26, 2012).

Bowman, James S., Jonathan P. West, and Marcia A. Beck. 2010. *Achieving Competencies in Public Service: The Professional Edge,* 2d ed. Armonk, NY: M.E. Sharpe.

Ciulla, Joanne B. 2004. Leadership ethics: Mapping the territory. In *Ethics, the Heart of Leadership,* 2d ed., ed. J.B. Ciulla, 3–26. Westport, CT: Praeger.

Cooper, Terry L. 2012. *The Responsible Administrator,* 6th ed. San Francisco: Jossey-Bass.

Cox, Raymond W., ed. 2009. *Ethics and Integrity in Public Service: Concepts and Cases.* Armonk, NY: M.E. Sharpe.

Davis, Brittany Alana. 2012. Bean cleared by ethics panel. *Tampa Bay Times.* July 28, p. 1B.

Denhardt, Robert B. 1981. *In the Shadow of Organization.* Lawrence, KS: Regents Press of Kansas.

Eriksson, S., G. Hegelsson, and A.T. Hoeglund. 2007. Being, doing, and knowing: Developing ethical competence in health care. *Journal of Academic Ethics* 5: 207–216.

Finer, Herman. 1941. Administrative responsibility in democratic government. *Public Administration Review* 1: 336–350.

Friedrich, Carl Joachim. 1940. Public policy and the nature of administrative responsibility. *Public Policy* 1: 5–20.

Goss, Robert P. 1996. A distinct public administration ethics? *Journal of Public Administration Research and Theory* 6(4): 573–597.

Hejka-Ekins, A. 1988. Teaching ethics in public administration. *Public Administration Review* 48(5): 885–891.

———. 2001. Ethics in in-service training. In *Handbook of Administrative Ethics,* 2d ed., ed. T.L. Cooper, 79–103. New York: Marcel Dekker.

International City/County Management Association (ICMA). 2008. Practices for effective local government management: Point 17. http://icma.org/main/bc.asp?bcid=120&hsid=11&ssid1=2495&t=0 (accessed July 23, 2012).

Jurkiewicz, Carole L. 2002. The influence of pedagogical style on students' level of ethical reasoning. *Journal of Public Affairs Education* 8(3): 263–274.

Kavathatzopoulos, Iordanis. 2002. Ethical competence training for individuals and organizations. In *Moral Leadership in Action: Building and Sustaining Moral Competence in European Organizations,* ed. H. Von Weltzien Hoivik, 293–303. Cheltenham, UK: Edward Elgar.

Kohlberg, Lawrence. 1980. *The Meaning and Measurement of Moral Development.* Worcester, MA: Clark University Press.

Lewin, Kurt. 1935. *A Dynamic Theory of Personality,* New York: McGraw-Hill.

———. 1936. *Principles of Topological Psychology.* New York: McGraw-Hill.

———. 1951. *Field Theory in Social Science: Selected Theoretical Papers.* D. Cartwright (ed.). New York: Harper & Row.

Lewis, Carol W., and Stuart C. Gilman. 2005. *The Ethics Challenge in Public Service,* 2d ed. San Francisco: Jossey-Bass.

Light, Paul. 1999. *The New Public Service.* Washington, DC: Brookings Institution Press.

Menzel, Donald C. 2007. *Ethics Management for Public Administrators: Building Organizations of Integrity.* Armonk, NY: M.E. Sharpe.

———. 2010. *Ethics Moments in Government: Cases and Controversies.* Boca Raton, FL: CRC Press.

Milgram, Stanley. 1974. The dilemma of obedience. *Phi Delta Kappan* 55(9): 603–606.

———. 1983. *Obedience to Authority: An Experimental View.* New York: HarperCollins.

Richter, William L., and Frances Burke, eds. 2007. *Combating Corruption/Encouraging Ethics,* 2d ed. Lanham, MD: Rowman and Littlefield.

Stewart, Debra W., and Norman A. Sprinthall. 1994. Moral development in public administration. In *Handbook of Administrative Ethics,* ed. T.L. Cooper. New York: Marcel Dekker.

Stone, Bob. 2010. A wallet-sized code of ethics in governing. *Governing,* May 5.

Svara, James H. 2007. *The Ethics Primer for Public Administrators in Government and Nonprofit Organizations.* Sudbury, MA: Jones and Bartlett.

Thompson, Dennis. 1985. The possibility of administrative ethics. *Public Administration Review* 45(5): 555–561.

———. 1992. Paradoxes of government ethics. *Public Administration Review* 52(3): 254–259.

Treviño, Linda Klebe, Michael Brown, and Laura Pincus Hartman. 2003. A qualitative investigation of perceived executive ethical leadership: Perceptions from inside and outside the executive suite. *Human Relations* 56(1): 5–37.

Van Wart, Montgomery. 2011. Changing dynamics of administrative leadership. In *The State of Public Administration,* ed. Donald C. Menzel and Harvey L. White. Armonk, NY: M.E. Sharpe.

Virtanen, Turo. 2000. Changing competences of public managers: Tensions in commitment. *International Journal of Public Sector Management* 13(4): 333–341.

West, Jonathan P., and Evan M. Berman, eds. 2006. *The Ethics Edge,* 2d ed. Washington, DC: ICMA Press.

Whitbeck, Caroline. 1996. Ethics as design: Doing justice to moral problems. *Hastings Center Report* 26(3): 9–16.

White, Richard. 1999. Are women more ethical? Recent findings on the effects of gender upon moral development. *Journal of Public Administration Research and Theory* 9(3): 459–471.

Wright, Deil S., Carl W. Stenberg, and Chung-Lae Cho. 2011. Historic relevance confronting contemporary obsolescence? Federalism, intergovernmental relations, and intergovernmental management. In *The State of Public Administration: Issues, Challenges, and Opportunities,* ed. Donald C. Menzel and Harvey L. White. Armonk, NY: M.E. Sharpe.

Zimbardo, P. 2007. *The Lucifer Effect: Understanding How Good People Turn Evil.* New York: Random House.

Part I

Ethical Competence and Leadership

So what does it mean to be a competent, ethical person? This straightforward question does not beget a straightforward answer, as Annelies De Schrijver and Jeroen Maesschalck are quick to point out in Chapter 2. They take the reader on a definitional and conceptual journey that charts new territory. After sorting through the conceptual haze surrounding the terms *competence* and *ethical,* they put forward a definition of *ethical competence* as "the cluster of knowledge, skills, and attitudes and abilities [often referred to as KSAs] as an underlying characteristic of employees that is causally related to ethical performance in a job." This definition, they readily admit, is quite broad but can be operationalized in observable and measurable KSAs.

Thus the authors devise a conceptual framework that has the potential to demystify ethical competence and, more important, creates a platform upon which students, practitioners, and academic investigators can stand to discover and advance public service leadership. Their framework integrates James Rest's (1986) widely embraced (although not without its critics) Four-Component Model of ethical decision making with KSAs. A 12-cell matrix provides the intersection between Rest's stages, which involve rules and standards, moral sensitivity, moral reasoning, and moral motivation and character, with the knowledge, skills, and attitudes and abilities. Each row and corresponding cells, contend De Schrijver and Maesschalck, represent subcompetencies. The authors are careful to point out that while the framework structures the different components of ethical competence, it does not offer a step-by-step process model of ethical decision making. The subcompetencies are logically arranged, not causally arranged. Furthermore, they assert that ethical competence should be viewed within the context of the entire framework, not in terms of a specific level. The result can lead to the ability to differentiate between competence and incompetence.

Have De Schrijver and Maesschalck taken us to a new threshold in our understanding of ethical competence? Do they offer us a roadmap, however unfinished, to demystifying the secret of achieving ethical competence to advance public service leadership? Perhaps. Readers will have to reach their own conclusions about this. Still, De Schrijver and Maesschalck have pushed the envelope of understanding and are convinced that "both theory and empirical research indicate that the idea of *ethical competence* is distinctive enough to merit its own conceptualization, operationalization, and measurement." Moreover, they observe that much empirical research on ethical decision making already uses instruments that measure ethical competence—the measurement process is just not recognized as such. In addition, the authors hold out the promise that the concept of competence in the field of administrative ethics may yield a "large body of practice-oriented knowledge and expertise that could be very useful." Competence-based management is increasingly drawn by public and private sectors to get the job done in an efficient, effective, economical, and equitable manner.

Despite the promise offered in the pursuit of ethical competence, De Schrijver and Maesschalck are cautious to note that their framework needs further operationalization into measurement instruments that allow the testing of hypotheses involving ethical competence.

While we may have some difficulty in agreeing on what constitutes ethical competence within and among professions, as suggested in Chapter 1, there is little question that we know it when we see it. Might the same be said about leadership? Perhaps. Certainly the extensive literature on and about leadership suggests that we know a great deal about a subject that all too often seems elusive. Leonie Heres and Karin Lasthuizen tackle the hard-to-describe qualities of ethical leadership in Chapter 3. They offer a review of theoretical and empirical research on ethical leadership with an eye toward providing "important insights" on the key aspects required for ethical competence.

Heres and Lasthuizen identify and discuss three key attributes of ethical leadership. The first is the moral character of the leader. Ethical leaders have strong moral values and are highly principled and concerned with doing the right thing. They also demonstrate moral courage in the face of external pressures, adversity, or risks. The second attribute is the ability to build a strong relationship with followers through behavior that indicates support, trust, respect, openness, and loyalty toward followers. This relationship is reciprocated by followers through constructive behavior and a sense of commitment that deters behavior detrimental to the leader or the group. The third attribute of ethical leadership is placing ethics at the forefront of the leadership agenda—that is, ethical leaders "walk the talk" and "talk the walk." The leader's ethical decisions and actions must be sufficiently visible and salient to be noticed against a noisy organizational backdrop—one that sometimes obscures why ethical matters are so important. The leadership agenda must also include "holding people accountable for their conduct and consistently reinforcing ethical standards through reward and discipline," Heres and Lasthuizen assert. Unethical behavior should be punished. Failure to do so will only result in more problems related to ethical lapses. Equally important is communicating with followers about ethics. This entails much more than just telling followers what to do or not to do to stay out of trouble. Leaders must clarify norms, expectations, and responsibilities, formulate positive ethical expectations, and give followers feedback about their conduct.

Strong, proactive ethical leadership is not an end in itself. Rather, it is a vital means to fostering an organizational culture that supports the work and mission of the organization. In short, it enhances both individual and organizational performances.

Ethical leadership and ethical competence are mutually reinforcing. Ethical leadership studies suggest "ethical competence might be strengthened further by . . . an open and vulnerable attitude when discussing one's own ethical dilemmas and mistakes with others." An ethically competent leader is unafraid to share her shortcomings and misgivings when they arise, as they surely will. Failure by leaders to acknowledge the ethical challenges they face can diminish the "moral person" in the eyes of one's followers.

In Chapter 4, Diane L. Swanson takes a closer look at a meaningful connection between ethical competence and effective leadership in the business environment. She argues that in business leadership, especially in fostering corporate social responsibility, the link is significant. Swanson presents two heuristics of myopic and discovery leadership, neither of which represent actual organizations but are ideal types that can be used to understand why leaders in some firms are capable of striving for social responsibility and those in others are not. *Myopic leadership* takes the form of executive managers "ignoring, suppressing, or denying the role of values in their decisions." This form manifests itself in a variety of ways, such as when "executives discourage employees from including information about stakeholder value-based expectations in official reports, memos, agendas, and other feedback mechanisms." In this case, annual evaluations and promotions are also skewed to reflect the narrow mindset of the executive.

Contrary to myopic leadership is what Swanson labels *discovery leadership*. Executives who practice discovery leadership consciously strive to incorporate values in decision making while encouraging employees to do the same. Formal mechanisms that can be employed in discovery leadership include "company-wide training programs in value detection, analysis, and communication and rewarding employees who demonstrate proficiency in these skills." Furthermore, executives may use ethics hotlines and conduct ethics audits "to assess the effectiveness of ethical codes and practices and identify deviations from established standards so that continuous improvements become possible."

Discovery leadership reaches beyond, indeed far beyond, mere legal compliance with the law, since the law does not always reflect ethical norms. Swanson views ethical competence as value inclusive and, therefore, a necessary ingredient in the practice of discovery leadership in the business sector.

Is discovery leadership in the business world relevant to ethical competence for public service leadership? Yes, Swanson notes. "Although the missions of private and public sectors are distinct, a necessary condition for ethical competence in leadership in both realms can be understood as the ability of executives and administrators to recognize constructive social values and encourage other employees to do the same." As the author concludes, "Public service leaders should not only invoke value-based mission statements and codes of ethics but model value receptivity in their actions as well."

2
A New Definition and Conceptualization of Ethical Competence

Annelies De Schrijver and Jeroen Maesschalck

There is little need to emphasize the importance of ethical decision making and ethical behavior in public administration in this chapter, since numerous scholars have done this before (e.g., Martinez and Richardson 2011; Garofalo 2008; Maesschalck 2005; Bowman et al. 2004). They refer to public trust and confidence in light of a government's legitimacy, to the discretionary power civil servants have, and to the damaging aftermath of scandals. These arguments also apply when assessing the importance of ethical competence in public administration.

Ethical competence has the conceptual potential to combine insights from two research traditions that have developed largely independent of each other: the literature on administrative and business ethics on the one hand and the literature on competence and competency in human resource management and educational sciences on the other. This makes *ethical competence* an attractive, powerful, and promising concept with several advantages for both research and practice. At the same time, the diversity of its background creates significant confusion surrounding the differentiation of the terms *competence, ethical,* and *ethical competence.* In this chapter, we first address that conceptual confusion and then propose the boundary approach (Stoof, Martens, and Bastiaens 2002) as a tool to reach a new and clear definition. We also present an ethical competence framework that operationalizes the definition into empirically meaningful components. The chapter concludes with a discussion of the advantages of using *ethical competence* as a concept.

Defining Ethical Competence

It is useful to distinguish between the two constitutive terms of the concept of *ethical competence* as they originate from distinct research areas, each with its own traditions. *Competence*—as discussed in the fields of human resource management and educational sciences—is the term that defines the

Table 2.1

Variations in Competence Definitions

1.	Level	Individual level or organizational level
2.	Focus	Worker-oriented perspective or work-oriented perspective
3.	Range	General or specific
4.	Related concepts	Competence as a continuum from competent to incompetent; or competence as a position in the continuum from novice to expert
5.	Elements	Knowledge, skills, attitudes, abilities, personality traits, and/or motives

Source: Stoof, Martens, and Bastiaens, 2002.

structure, while *ethical*—as discussed in the fields of business and administrative ethics—gives its content. This section reviews the relevant literature that addresses these two terms separately before examining the overall concept.

Competence as a Concept

Many authors have noted the conceptual vagueness that surrounds *competence* as a concept (e.g., Sampson and Fytros 2008; Delamare Le Deist and Winterton 2005; Boon and van der Klink 2002; Horton 2002; Garavan and McGuire 2001; While 1994). Stoof, Martens, and Bastiaens (2002) argue that competence definitions vary in their (1) level of analysis, (2) focus, (3) range, (4) position to related concepts, and (5) constituting elements (see Table 2.1).

Stoof, Martens, and Bastiaens (2002) criticize the objectivistic approach to competence definitions in the literature and argue that one true definition does not exist; hence, it is not useful to try to reach a consensus about it. Diversity in definitions should not be surprising: Competence is a relative term used in different domains such as human resource management and strategic management as well as in several distinct research traditions such as psychology and educational sciences, each serving different purposes (Nunes, Martins, and Duarte 2007). Consensus is thus both impossible and undesirable; definitional flexibility is a necessity. Stoof, Martens, and Bastiaens therefore suggest a constructivist approach, where the criterion "is not whether the definition is true, but the extent to which the constructed definition has proven to be adequate in the context in which it is used" (2002, 347). They present the boundary approach as a tool to construct that contextual definition. Specifically, when developing a definition for a project, one should consider the specific boundaries of the concept in that particular project based on five central questions along which definitions of competence can vary.

The first question is whether competence is being viewed as an individual-level or an organizational-level trait (Stoof, Martens, and Bastiaens 2002). The latter is also referred to as "core competence" i.e., the cluster of important characteristics of an organization given its strategic goals and competitive advantage (Garavan and McGuire 2001). Individual-level competence, in contrast, refers to the cluster of personal characteristics necessary for effective performance at work by an individual. Although individual-level competence is considered a personal characteristic, it also refers to the organizational work context. Individual-level competence is the subject of literature about education, psychology, and human resource management, while organizational-level competence is mostly addressed in the field of strategic management (e.g., Hamel 1994; Porter 1987). Stoof, Martens, and Bastiaens (2002) work in educational sciences and seem to opt implicitly for the individual-level perspective; the four remaining questions seem relevant only when such a perspective is taken.

The second distinction to be made is whether competence is a personal characteristic or a task characteristic (Stoof, Martens, and Bastiaens 2002). The former focuses on characteristics of the worker, while the latter focuses on work activities (Sandberg 1994). The worker-oriented perspective defines competence as the cluster of knowledge, skills, and attitudes and abilities individuals need to be effective in their jobs. These are often referred to as KSAs. For some authors the "A" refers to attitudes (e.g., Crofts et al. 2010; Horton 2002), while for others the "A" refers to abilities (e.g., Nunes, Martins, and Duarte 2007; Stevens and Campion 1994); some even use attitudes and abilities interchangeably (e.g., Delamare Le Deist and Winterton 2005).

Authors typically do not justify why they choose one concept over another or why they use them interchangeably. We would argue that both concepts have different meanings and that both are important. While an attitude, for us, refers to a way of looking at a specific object, an ability refers to an individual's capacity to do something. Since we believe that both components are valuable, the "A" in KSAs will refer to both attitudes and abilities. Knowledge, skills, and attitudes and abilities are general personal attributes of the worker that can be applied in a variety of work activities (Sandberg 1994). Boyatzis's definition is a clear example of this perspective; he refers to "characteristics that are causally related to effective and/or superior performance in a job" (1982, 23). The work-oriented perspective, on the other hand, defines competence in terms of specific work activity standards. Sandberg clarifies that "they first identify work activities that are central for accomplishing specific work and then transform those activities into personal attributes" (1994, 49). Cheng, Dainty, and Moore, for example, define competence as "the ability to perform activities within an occupation to the standards expected" (2003, 529). Put differently, the worker-oriented perspective focuses on employees' personal attributes as input for effective work performance, while the work-oriented perspective focuses on meeting work demands as an outcome (Horton 2002). The literature often uses the term *competency* for the worker-oriented perspective and the term *competence* for the work-oriented perspective (Delamare Le Deist and Winterton 2005; Boon and van der Klink 2002; Stoof, Martens, and Bastiaens 2002). Yet, in line with the choice made by the editors of this book, we do not follow that distinction here. Instead, we consider the clusters of knowledge, skills, and attitudes and abilities as different *competencies* that, in turn, constitute a person's *competence* (Sampson and Fytros 2008; Eraut 1994).

The third consideration is whether competence is specific or general (Stoof, Martens, and Bastiaens 2002). Specific competence is limited to a specific organization or a task. The competence definition is then only applicable for that specificity. General competence, in contrast, refers to an entire profession, or even all professions (2002).

The fourth question concerns whether competence exists on a continuum that ranges from incompetent to competent, or if it is a specific level on another continuum (Stoof, Martens, and Bastiaens 2002). As for the latter, Dreyfus and Dreyfus (2004) propose a continuum ranging from novice to advanced beginner to competent and proficient to expert.

The fifth question deals with the constituting elements of competence in light of its purpose (Stoof, Martens, and Bastiaens 2002). Some also add motives and personality traits as elements of their definition. When competence is used for training and education purposes, the constituting elements should be teachable (Stoof, Martens, and Bastiaens 2002). When it is used for other purposes, such as recruitment, then these restrictions are not necessary. Sanghi (2004) addresses this issue by distinguishing between surface elements (e.g., knowledge, skills, and attitudes and abilities) and central elements (e.g., personality traits and motives) of competence. The former are considered easier to train and develop than the latter.

As the meaning of competence might vary along the five dimensions, it is important that each author clearly defines *competence* to allow for a correct understanding of her perspective. Such a process is not objective but is the result of normative-prescriptive choices (Eraut 1994). This inherent normativity is featured in two ways. First, it focuses on the selection and description of the specific knowledge, skills, and attitudes and abilities that are considered essential elements of competence. Second, one needs thresholds, standards, and criteria to decide when the presence of these necessary attributes is sufficient to label an individual as competent or not (Eraut 1994).

Ethical as a Concept

The term *ethical* defines the nature of the competence involved. As with *competence,* the abundance of views on ethics leads to a wide array of definitions. Preston indicates that "ethics is concerned about what is right, fair, just or good; about what we ought to do, not just what is the case or what is most acceptable or expedient" (2007, 16). Hence, it follows that ethics is debatable and contestable. Any choice of a definition, therefore, will inevitably imply a normative choice (Maesschalck 2011). Cooper (2006) distinguishes between a normative and a descriptive interpretation of ethics. *Normative* or *prescriptive ethics* provides guiding principles of conduct. The central question is: What is ethically right and what is ethically wrong? *Descriptive ethics,* on the other hand, is concerned with the underlying arguments of people's conduct (Cooper 2006). It is about "describing and predicting what people think, perceive, and do" in contrast to prescriptive ethics, which is about "telling people what they should do" (Warren and Smith-Crowe 2008, 84).

Given that we want to use the concept of ethical competence in both empirical research and as a source for prescription in a public administration context, we would need a definition with both descriptive and normative elements. Specifically, we will draw from the definition of van den Heuvel and Huberts, who define administrative ethics as the generally accepted public values and norms that give direction to the daily practice within the public sector (adapted from van den Heuvel and Huberts 2003, 19). While the definition is essentially descriptive, it of course leaves room for normative ethics in allowing its users to operationalize "generally accepted values and norms" in many different ways. With a definition that is this broad, it will become important to make clear and transparent choices when applying the intended meaning in specific contexts. The remainder of this chapter aims to provide a language that will make these choices transparent.

Ethical Competence as a Concept

The use of *ethical competence* as a concept is on the rise in both theoretical and empirical literature in business and administrative ethics. It is frequently perceived as an individual-level characteristic of an employee. Three types of definitions can be distinguished within this perspective: general definitions, definitions that consist of components based on Rest's (1986) model, and definitions based on KSAs.

First, general definitions do not refer explicitly to the specific structure of *competence* (knowledge, skills, and attitudes and abilities), but instead refer to the contents of *ethical* as a general description of a work approach (e.g.,

Friedman 2007). Karsing, for example, defines ethical competence as "the capability and willingness to adequately and carefully exercise tasks, taking all the relevant interests into account, based on a reasonable appraisal of the relevant facts" (2001, 40, own translation).

Definitions in the second category also refer to the contents of *ethical* without explicitly referring to the specific structure of *competence* (e.g., Boland 2006; Jormsri et al. 2005). Yet they differ from definitions in the first category because they list several specific characteristics that an ethically competent employee possesses. These characteristics are often based on one or more components of Rest's (1986) Four-Component Model. Rest (1986) stated that there are four processes preceding ethical behavior: (1) moral awareness—being sensitive to ethical dilemma situations, (2) moral judgment—being able to judge which behavior is morally right, (3) moral motivation—being motivated to do what is defined as morally right, and (4) moral character—being strong enough to perform the morally right behavior. A case in point is Bowman et al.'s (2004) definition. For these authors, ethical competence consists of "(a) principled moral reasoning, (b) recognition of ethics-related conflicts, (c) refusal to do something unethical, and (d) application of ethical theory" (2004, 26).

The third category refers to definitions that also use Rest's (1986) model as an inspiration (e.g., Whitton 2007; Falender 2006), but explicitly try to present these in terms of the competence structure. By doing so, these definitions make it much easier than the previous two categories to distinguish between "being ethical" as a desirable characteristic of individual employees on the one hand and "possessing ethical competence" on the other. The interesting debate for this third category becomes which clusters of knowledge, skills, and attitudes and abilities should be considered central for ethical competence. For Menzel, "an ethically competent public manager is (1) committed to high standards of personal and professional behavior, (2) has knowledge of relevant ethics codes and laws, (3) has the ability to engage in ethical reasoning when confronted with challenging situations, (4) is able to identify and act upon public service ethics and values, and (5) promotes ethical practice and behavior in public agencies and organizations" (2010, 18). Other authors refer to different characteristics. Whitton (2007), for example, identifies the following key elements of ethical competence: subject-matter knowledge, reasoning skills, problem-solving skills, advocacy skills, self-awareness and consensus-building skills, and attitudes and commitment.

Kavathatzopoulos and Rigas (1998) provide yet another list of necessary knowledge, skills, and attitudes and abilities an ethically competent person needs. According to these authors, an ethically competent person "must have (a) high ethical awareness, the ability to anticipate ethical problems in real life and to perceive them in time; (b) the cognitive skill to analyze and solve them in an optimal way; (c) the capability to discuss and handle moral problems at group and organizational levels and, together with significant others, formulate ethical principles and guidelines; (d) the power to argue convincingly for preferred actions or decisions made; and (e) the strength to implement controversial decisions" (792).

This discussion leads to two important conclusions. First, not all authors define *ethical competence* in terms of a cluster of knowledge, skills, and attitudes and abilities, even if they see competence as an individual-level characteristic. Second, those definitions that do refer to a cluster of knowledge, skills, and attitudes and abilities, do this implicitly. Additionally, there is no consensus about which of those clusters an employee should possess before earning the title "ethically competent." Moreover, how those clusters and the components of Rest's (1986) model relate to one another is uncertain. We therefore conclude that a conceptual framework is needed—one that structures ethical competence in terms of different aspects of ethics and the different components of competence.

Applying the Boundary Approach to an Ethical Competence Definition

Based on the discussions in the preceding pages, we can now define *ethical competence*. This will be done in two steps. First, the boundary approach to defining competence provides the general structure of the definition. Second, we will augment content by drawing from the definitions of the term *ethical*. We opt to define *ethical competence* broadly to allow for its wide use. The framework presented later will conceptualize ethical competence in more detail.

First, the boundary approach provides five questions that need to be answered when choosing a specific definition of competence in a specific context (Stoof, Martens, and Bastiaens 2002). As for the first question—individual-versus organizational-level competence—an individual-level perspective is chosen because ethical competence of public servants is this book's theme. However, the organizational context of a job in public administration needs to be taken into account. Thus, the second question concerns a choice between the worker-oriented and the work-oriented perspectives. In light of this book's theme, we prefer a worker-oriented perspective. Sound ethical decision making and ethical behavior of public servants requires defining ethical competence as a cluster of knowledge, skills, and attitudes and abilities that should be applied in all work activities, and should not be limited to specific activities as in the work-oriented perspective. The third question implies a choice between a general and a specific competence. Ethical competence can be considered a general competence because each employee is expected to be ethically competent. However, there can be different thresholds for different functions. The fourth question implies a choice for a particular continuum. We opt for a general competence continuum. This allows us to state that two employees are ethically competent, but that one is more competent than the other. The last question concerns the scope of the definition. We prefer a definition that includes only the surface elements of competence (knowledge, skills, and attitudes and abilities). This allows for a broad application in empirical research and human resource management, in contrast to definitions that also include motives and personality traits.

Having chosen a particular structure, we can now fill this with content, i.e., with knowledge, skills, and attitudes and abilities. We opt for a very generic definition because the discussion of ethical competence definitions showed that there is no consensus on the specific KSAs, and because this is consistent with the descriptive definition of *ethics* cited earlier. Not determining which specific KSAs an ethically competent person should have allows us to adapt the operationalization of the concept to different times, different contexts, and different organizational roles.

Ethical competence is thus defined as the cluster of knowledge, skills, and attitudes and abilities as an underlying characteristic of employees that is causally related to ethical performance in a job (based on Boyatzis 1982). The broad formulation of this definition is deliberate; it is intended to be a general definition (cf. the third question of the boundary approach) that applies to public servants in all organizational positions and roles. It is further operationalized in observable and measurable components in the next section.

A Conceptual Framework of Ethical Competence

The ethical competence definition in the previous section needs specification. We therefore present a conceptual framework that structures ethical competence in terms of different aspects of ethics and different components of competence, as can be seen in Table 2.2. The framework merely addresses components of competence as combination of KSAs and relevant areas of ethics; it does not address the degree of knowledge, skills, and attitudes and abilities required. The actual normative thresholds for each cell are left open because this model is designed to be applicable for both research and practice purposes, and for employees at all hierarchical levels, in all functions, and in all types of organizations. The framework thus provides the broad language and structure but, within this language, leaves the choices open. Additionally, role-specific KSAs are not included for the same reason of generalizability,

Table 2.2

Conceptual Framework of Ethical Competence

	Knowledge	Skill	Attitude and ability
Rules and standards	(1) Law, ethics code, rules and procedures	(2) Applying rules	(3) Importance of rules
Moral sensitivity	(4) Position in the organization and society	(5) Defining a situation as an ethical one Seeing different solutions	(6) Empathy Perspective-taking
Moral reasoning	(7) Moral arguments: • rules • consequences for others • consequences for oneself	(8) Using different moral arguments: • rules • consequences for others • consequences for oneself	(9) Attitude of flexibility: • not only rules • not only consequences for others • not only consequences for oneself
Moral motivation and character	(10) Rules and consequences for others are more important than consequences for oneself	(11) Priority to rules and consequences for others in what you choose to do	(12) Autonomy Ego-strength

Source: Based on Rest's Four-Component Model, 1986.

but they can be added to the model by its users. An example in light of this book's theme is ethical leadership responsibility (e.g., Avey, Palanski, and Walumbwa 2011; Brown, Treviño, and Harrison 2005).

The three components that constitute competence (knowledge, skills, and attitudes and abilities, respectively) are set out in the three columns of the ethical competence framework. Inspiration for the four rows (i.e., rules and standards; moral sensitivity; moral reasoning; and moral motivation and character) and for the interpretation of the different cells was drawn from Rest's (1986) Four-Component Model and other authors' ethical competence definitions. Each row is a cluster of KSAs and is therefore a subcompetency.

The first subcompetency represented by the first row in the table refers to "rules and standards." While "simply saying ethical competence means understanding the law and formal rules and applying them uniformly seems to be too simplistic" (Meine 2009, 1), most will agree that rules and standards are indeed an essential aspect of ethical competence. Cell 1 indicates that for an employee to be called ethically competent, she should know the formal rules, guidelines, standards, and regulations, as well as the law and the relevant code(s) of ethics (Whitton 2007; Falender 2006; Kavathatzopoulos, Persson, and Aborg 2002). However, only knowing the rules and standards is not enough. An ethically competent person should also have the skill to apply those rules and standards in specific situations (Whitton 2007; Falender 2006; Kavathatzopoulos 2005), as shown in cell 2. The multiplicity of rules in modern society makes this a difficult task (Eriksson, Helgesson, and Höglund 2007). The importance of the distinction between cell 1 (theoretical knowledge) and cell 2 (the skill to apply it) can be clarified by referring to the difference between "know that" and "know how" (Karsing 2001). Some experienced professionals are able to intuitively apply the rules and standards ("know how"), without really knowing them ("know that"). This can, and probably will, lead to ethical behavior by those professionals, but it will become difficult for them to deal with new and complex situations and to account for their actions (Karsing 2001). Thus, both cells are important and distinct parts of the ethical competence model. The third cell refers to the fundamental attitude that acknowledges the importance of rules and standards in the job context. Such an attitude ensures that employees will actually apply the knowledge and the skills described respectively in cells 1 and 2.

The second subcompetency, "moral sensitivity," refers to component 1 of Rest's (1986) model. Other authors also included this aspect in their ethical competence definition (e.g., Whitton 2007; Falender 2006; Boland 2006; Bowman et al. 2004; Kavathatzopoulos and Rigas 1998). In his description of this component, Rest (1994) actually presents three important aspects: an awareness of the implications of one's actions for others; an awareness of possible solutions and how these might affect others; and empathy and role-taking. Although he does not use the competence terminology, one can easily consider those aspects as the skills (cell 5) and abilities (cell 6) necessary to define a situation as an ethical one. As for the former, an ethically competent person should have the skill to sense when conflicting values are at stake in a situation. Such ethical dilemmas occur, for example, when rules contradict each other or when they clash with values (e.g., loyalty, equality, fairness, and honesty). They might also occur when interests of different groups of people conflict with each other. An ethically competent person not only should be sensitive to those dilemmas but also should be skilled enough to see a variety of solutions and to think about the short- and long-term consequences for oneself and others. However, those skills can only be applied when the individual has the ability to empathize and view a situation from the perspective of others (Pedersen 2009; Podolskiy 2005; Rest 1994; Eisenberg et al. 1991). This ability is referenced in cell 6. Empathy is then understood as the ability to experience vicariously the feelings of other persons, while perspective-taking or role-taking refers to the ability to take another person's point of view (Davis 1983). In addition to these skills (cell 5) and abilities (cell 6), one also needs a knowledge component (cell 4). In order to be ethically sensitive and to empathize with others, a person should indeed have knowledge about his position in society and, more specifically, in a given organization. Public servants, for example, should know that their behavior has an impact on public trust and government's legitimacy. Managers should be aware of their exemplary function and the importance of being both a moral manager and a moral person (Brown, Treviño, and Harrison 2005).

Our operationalization of "moral reasoning" as the third subcompetency is based partially on Rest's (1986) "moral judgment" component. Rest (1986) emphasizes the result of a decision-making process (i.e., the choice for the most morally justifiable course of action) in theoretical terms, but his empirical research—particularly with the Defining Issues Test (Rest 1994)—seems to focus on the reasoning process that precedes that decision and the argumentation used to justify it. Both interpretations are essential parts of the ethical competence framework proposed here. The actual decision is part of the fourth subcompetency (cf. infra cell 11), while the reasoning process fits in subcompetency three (cell 8), and is discussed next.

We now discuss each of the three cells of the moral reasoning subcompetency (i.e., the third row) in turn. First, cell 7 refers to the knowledge that is essential for moral reasoning: Clearly, an ethically competent person must be familiar with different types of moral arguments. We propose to distinguish between three types of arguments that can be relevant in the context of public organizations: (1) arguments that refer to rules and procedures (e.g., "In my actions I have to follow the organizational procedures"), (2) arguments that refer to consequences of actions for others (e.g., "I have to minimize the negative consequences of my behavior for others"), and (3) arguments that refer to consequences for oneself (e.g., "I have to optimize the positive consequences of my behavior for myself"). Thus an ethically competent employee must know and understand these three types of arguments. Second, as seen in cell 8, an ethically competent person also must possess the skill to apply that knowledge in specific situations (Bowman et al. 2004). An employee should be able to choose among the three relevant types of arguments, taking into consideration the different contextual elements of a situation. However, knowledge of the need to combine approaches (cell 7) and the skill to actually combine them in practice (cell 8) are not sufficient. One also needs a more fundamental attitude of flexibility (cell 9): the willingness to accept that there is never only one solution for a problem. An ethically competent person almost automatically approaches a particular situation from different perspectives. She deeply understands that each of the three types of arguments carries particular types of risks. Always adhering to rules and procedures might in some cases lead to adverse results (Whitton 2007). Only taking other people's interests into account is also dangerous, especially in governmental organizations, where equity and lawfulness are essential. Finally, too strong a focus on self-interest, of course, entails considerable risks.

"Moral motivation and character," the fourth subcompetency, merges components 3 and 4 of Rest's (1986) model. It refers to the knowledge, skills, and abilities to make an ethical decision and behave accordingly. While moral reasoning in the third row referred to the capacity to take different positions and understand that this is necessary, "moral motivation and character" now refers to the strength to follow up on that reasoning, choose the *right* ethical decision, and implement that decision in actual behavior. Row three explicitly presents "consequences for oneself" as one of the three types of moral arguments to be considered; row four ("moral motivation and character") shifts the focus, stressing that the other two arguments (i.e., rules and consequences for others) should take priority (Whitton 2007; Rest 1994). Note, however, that this does not necessarily imply that behavior based on egoistic considerations is always unethical. A public servant might, for example, refuse a gift from a citizen not because he thinks that it might affect his neutrality or create a perception of unethical conduct that undermines public trust, but because he fears punishment. Such behavior might be ethical, but it does not demonstrate ethical competence.

The cognitive understanding that rules and consequences for others are more important than egoistic considerations is referred to in cell 10. Cell 11 deals with the actual skill to choose these types of arguments (rules and consequences for others) over egoistic values. Cell 12 identifies the two abilities that are crucial for such behavior to occur: autonomy and ego-strength. Autonomy refers to independent decision making as opposed to decision making based on other people's expectations or judgments (Falender 2006; Kavathatzopoulos, Persson, and Aborg 2002); yet, even autonomy is not enough. One also needs the moral courage to actually implement a difficult decision and deal with the consequences (Bowman et al. 2004; Kavathatzopoulos et al. 2002; Rest 1994). As easy as this may sound, actually refusing to do what colleagues or a supervisor demands requires moral courage (Bowman et al. 2004).

It is useful to make three remarks on the use of this framework. First, the subcompetencies are presented in a logical order rather than a causal order. The model structures the different components of ethical competence; it is not a step-by-step process model of ethical decision making.

Second, the 12 cells are 12 separately required characteristics. A "low" score on one cell cannot be compensated for by a "high" score on another cell. For example, "high" scores on the first 11 cells can never compensate for a lack of autonomous thinking and ego-strength (cell 12). However, some cells might be more important in relation to ethical behavior than others and thus weigh heavier in determining a person's position on the incompetent-competent continuum. This normative choice should be made by the user of the framework based on the context of its use. For example, for a public servant who has much discretionary power, a low score on the knowledge of his position in the organization and society (cell 4) and a high score on the skill to define a situation as an ethical one (cell 5) might be less serious than a high score on cell 4 and a low score on cell 5. Defining a situation as an ethical one is, for this public servant, extremely important, because there are only a few organizational guidelines that will help him shape his behavior. The interpretation of ethical competence as a continuum also implies that individuals can be scored as more or less ethically competent. Yet, lower scores on ethical competence do not necessarily imply unethical behavior; an exact correspondence between ethical competence and ethical behavior does not exist (see next section).

Third, for many purposes it will be necessary to identify thresholds that distinguish between incompetent and competent (or more subtle degrees of competence). These thresholds can vary depending on employees' hierarchical levels, their functions, and the type of organizations in which they work. For example, police officers responsible for victim care might need higher levels of empathy to be considered ethically competent than their colleagues who are responsible for enforcing traffic regulations.

To conclude, ethical competence is the combination of all 12 cells in Table 2.2. Researchers and practitioners can focus on specific rows, or even specific cells, but we would argue that by doing so they do not address all elements of ethical competence as a theoretical concept. Keep in mind that the normative thresholds for each cell can be chosen freely. This implies that, under certain circumstances, researchers and practitioners can set the thresholds for specific cells to zero when they believe the given part of ethical competence is not necessary in that particular context. For example, knowledge of the different types of moral arguments (cell 7) might be expected from an ethically competent public leader but not necessarily from the ethically competent public servants in lower levels of the organization. In that case, cell 7 would still be part of the theoretical concept of *ethical competence,* but it would not be measured; its minimum threshold would be zero.

The Case for Ethical Competence

The previous sections developed a general definition of ethical competence that was then operationalized in a framework with 12 cells. We see at least three arguments in favor of using the concept of *ethical competence.*

First, and most obviously, both theory and empirical research indicate that the idea of ethical competence is distinctive enough to merit its own conceptualization, operationalization, and measurement. Theoretically, *competence* on the one hand and *behavior* (or performance) on the other are indeed two distinct things. Messick explains that competence "refers to what a person knows and can do under ideal circumstances, whereas performance refers to what is actually done under existing circumstances" (1984, 227). This gap implies that other personal and contextual factors—time pressures, practical constraints, and emotions, for example—might disturb this causal link (Oser 1991). Since there is not yet an instrument that measures ethical competence as defined and conceptualized in this chapter, the empirical link between ethical competence and ethical performance cannot be assessed. However, there is empirical work on ethical reasoning that suggests there might be a gap between ethical competence and (un)ethical behavior. An ethically incompetent public servant does not necessarily act unethically all the time, while an ethically competent public servant does not necessarily act ethically all the time. A case in point is the research that involves frequently used standardized questionnaires like Rest's (1994) Defining Issues Test (DIT), Stewart and Sprinthall's (1991) Stewart-Sprinthall Management Survey (SSMS), and Lind and Wakenhut's (1985) Moral Judgment Test (MJT). These tests present respondents with hypothetical ethical dilemmas and ask them what the actor should do. Respondents are then instructed to rate the importance of several moral arguments for their decision-making process. For the scoring of the answers, these tests use Lawrence Kohlberg's (1971) theory of moral development. Although these tests measure only one aspect of ethical competence (i.e., cell 8 in our framework), their relationship with ethical performance is still relevant here. A number of authors have tested the link between these test scores and self-reports of (un) ethical behavior (e.g., Andreoli and Lefkowitz 2009; Harding et al. 2007). The results show that the correlations between ethical reasoning and ethical behavior are significant but moderate (Stewart, Sprinthall, and Kem 2002; White 2001; Thoma et al. 1999; Thoma 1994; Treviño 1992; Krebs et al. 1991).

Second, in empirical research, ethical decision making is often operationalized using instruments that in fact measure ethical competence. Typically, ethical decision-making research is structured on Rest's (1986) Four-Component Model,[1] which includes moral awareness or sensitivity, moral judgment or reasoning, moral intention, and moral behavior (O'Fallon and Butterfield 2005). These components are frequently measured using vignettes.[2] For ethical sensitivity, respondents are asked, for example, to indicate whether they interpret the issue in the vignette as an ethical dilemma or not (e.g., May and Pauli 2002; Singhapakdi, Vitell, and Franke 1999, 27). For moral reasoning, the measurements are diverse. Some present a story in which a person has already acted and respondents then need to evaluate the action in terms of its acceptability, fairness, ethicality, and the like (e.g., May and Pauli 2002; Razzaque and Hwee 2002). Others present vignettes wherein the actor has not yet acted and respondents are asked to identify themselves with the actor and indicate which arguments they would use to justify their actions. In some studies on moral intention, the person in the vignette has already acted and respondents are asked whether they would have acted the same way (e.g., Singhapakdi, Vitell, and Franke 1999; Glover et al. 1997); other moral intention studies present respondents with an open-ended story and ask them to indicate what they would do in this situation (e.g., Ritter 2006; Sims and Keon 1999). In most cases, these vignette studies make abstractions from reality by relying on hypothetical situations instead of real-life observations. As a consequence, what is really measured is not ethical decision making but rather some aspects of ethical competence. Given that these instruments in fact measure ethical competence, one could make a case for considering them as operationalizations of *ethical competence.* This would also allow for thinking more explicitly about all the dimensions and aspects of the concept, for example, by using the framework presented in Table 2.2.

The third argument in favor of explicitly introducing the concept of competence in the field of administrative ethics also brings in a large body of practice-oriented knowledge and expertise that could be very useful. Recent years have seen a growing interest in competency-based management in the public sector (Horton 2002; Hondeghem and Vandermeulen 2000). Many organizations have developed "competency models," defined by Mansfield as "a detailed, behaviorally specific description of the skills and the traits that employees need to be effective in a job" (1996, 7). Those normative lists of characteristics then serve as an important foundation for the recruitment and selection of new employees, as well as for the development and evaluation of the existing staff. This competency-based management approach is often contrasted with traditional personnel management. While the latter focuses on qualification and experience of employees as predictors of work performance, competency-based management takes a much broader perspective by concentrating on the knowledge, skills, and attitudes and abilities employees need to do their job successfully (Horton 2002). It focuses on "learning outcomes, irrespective of the routes of acquisition involved, rather than inputs in terms of time spent in institutions of learning" (Delamare Le Deist and Winterton 2005, 28). Since only the results of the acquisition process matter and not how competence has been acquired, nonqualified employees can be competent, and likewise, qualified employees can be incompetent. This suggests that while ethics courses and practical experience might of course be useful, there are many other factors that contribute to the development of ethical competence. The literature on competency-based management offers numerous suggestions for such competence development. Kak, Burkhalter, and Cooper (2001), for example, argue that different learning strategies should be applied to develop different components of competence. Knowledge can be obtained through theoretical education and in-service training, while role-playing is more effective in learning skills. Attitudes and abilities are more stable than knowledge and skills. They develop over time beginning in childhood and are therefore harder to change through training and education (Kak, Burkhalter, and Cooper 2001). For these components, recruitment might be a more relevant instrument than personnel development.

Conclusion

In this chapter, we have proposed a definition of ethical competence that is formulated in a generic way to allow for usage at different times, in different contexts, and for different purposes. The meaning of the term was further operationalized in a conceptual framework that draws both from the literature on competence and the literature on administrative and business ethics, with an eye toward usefulness in both research and practice. With three columns (referring to the components of competence), four rows (referring to subcompetencies), and thus 12 cells, the framework is rather complex. Nevertheless, we maintain that this complexity is necessary to cover both the competence structure (knowledge, skills, and attitudes and abilities) and the ethical contents (rules and standards, moral sensitivity, moral reasoning, and moral motivation and character). Reducing the complexity of the model would jeopardize important aspects of ethical competence.

The proposed framework is only a first step. The model needs to be further operationalized into measurement instruments. This would then allow for systematic testing of hypotheses in research. There are several avenues for such research. First, research could focus on hypotheses with ethical competence as the dependent variable. Independent variables would then be management instruments and other organizational-level variables such as ethics codes (e.g., Grundstein 2001; Somers 2001), ethics training programs (e.g., Valentine and Fleischman 2004; Jurkiewicz 2002), ethical leadership (e.g., Lasthuizen 2008; Brown and Treviño 2006), or organizational fairness (e.g., De Schrijver et al. 2010; Treviño and Weaver 2001). Second, ethical competence can also be the independent variable, explaining different types of behavioral outcomes such as organizational misbehavior or work performance. Put together, ethical competence might be the mediator variable between organizational-level variables on the one hand and behavioral outcomes on the other. The 12-cell conceptualization would then allow for more subtle hypotheses. The management instruments and other organizational-level variables might vary in their impact on the different cells and subcompetencies of ethical competence, which in turn vary in their impact on different types of behavioral outcomes. For instance, a code of ethics might have a strong impact on subcompetency "rules and standards," while it might have little to no effect on the other three subcompetencies. Likewise, ethics training programs might have an impact on employees' "moral sensitivity" and "moral reasoning" subcompetencies, while organizational fairness and ethical leadership might particularly influence their "moral motivation and character" subcompetency.

The concept of ethical competence as operationalized above also might be useful in the practice of ethics management in public administration, particularly when integrated into broader efforts of competency management. Indeed, knowing which management instruments work on which subcompetencies might help practitioners in building a more balanced and subtle integrity management system. The 12-dimensional concept could also be useful in recruitment, serving as the basis for a multidimensional checklist to aid recruiters in a more nuanced assessment of applicants' ethical competence for particular positions.

Notes

1. Although Rest (1986) states explicitly that the processes (moral awareness, moral judgment, and moral motivation and character) are presented in a logical rather than a causal order, causality is frequently assumed in those models.

2. Another possibility is an in-basket exercise (e.g., Treviño and Youngblood 1990).

References

Andreoli, N., and Joel Lefkowitz. 2009. Individual and organizational antecedents of misconduct in organizations. *Journal of Business Ethics* 85: 309–332.

Avey, James B., Michael E. Palanski, and Fred O. Walumbwa. 2011. When leadership goes unnoticed: The moderation role of follower self-esteem on the relationship between ethical leadership and follower behavior. *Journal of Business Ethics* 98(4): 573–582.

Boland, Kathleen. 2006. Ethical decision-making among hospital social workers. *Journal of Social Work Values and Ethics* 3(1). http://www.socialworker.com/jswve/content/view/27/44/ (accessed November 15, 2010).

Boon, Jo, and Marcel van der Klink. 2002. Competencies: The triumph of a fuzzy concept. Paper presented at Competencies: Fuzzy Concepts to Context, Honolulu, HI, February 27–March 3.

Bowman, James S., Jonathan P. West, Evan M. Berman, and Montgomery Van Wart. 2004. *The Professional Edge: Competencies in Public Service.* Armonk, NY: M.E. Sharpe.

Boyatzis, Richard E. 1982. *The Competent Manager: A Model for Effective Performance.* New York: John Wiley & Sons.

Brown, Michael E., and Linda K. Treviño. 2006. Ethical leadership: A review and future directions. *Leadership Quarterly* 17: 595–616.

Brown, Michael E., Linda K. Treviño, and David A. Harrison. 2005. Ethical leadership: A social learning perspective for construct development and hypothesis testing. *Organizational Behavior and Human Decision Processes* 97: 117–134.

Cheng, Mei-I, Andrew R.J. Dainty, and David R. Moore. 2003. The differing faces of managerial competency in Britain and America. *Journal of Management Development* 22: 527–537.

Cooper, Terry L. 2006. *The Responsible Administrator: An Approach to Ethics for the Administrative Role,* 5th ed. San Francisco: Jossey-Bass.

Crofts, J.F., T.J. Draycott, R. Fox, L.P. Hunt, D. Siassakos, and D. Winter. 2010. More to teamwork than knowledge, skill, and attitude. *BJOG: An International Journal of Obstetrics & Gynaecology* 117: 1262–1269.

Davis, Mark H. 1983. Measuring individual differences in empathy: Evidence for a multidimensional approach. *Journal of Personality and Social Psychology* 44: 113–126.

De Schrijver, Annelies, Karlien Delbeke, Jeroen Maesschalck, and Stefaan Pleysier. 2010. Fairness perceptions and organizational misbehavior: An empirical study. *American Review of Public Administration* 40: 691–703.

Delamare Le Deist, François, and Jonathan Winterton. 2005. What is competence? *Human Resource Development International* 8: 27–46.

Dreyfus, Hubert L., and Stuart F. Dreyfus. 2004. The ethical implications of the five-stage skill-acquisition model. *Bulletin of Science, Technology, and Society* 24: 251–264.

Eisenberg, Nancy, Cindy L. Shea, Gustavo Carlo, and George P. Knight. 1991. Empathy-related responding and cognition: A "chicken and the egg" dilemma. In *Handbook of Moral Behavior and Development,* Vol. 2: *Research,* ed. W.M. Kurtines and J.L. Gerwirtz, 63–88. Hillsdale, NJ: L. Erlbaum.

Eraut, Michael. 1994. *Developing Professional Knowledge and Competence.* London: Falmer.

Eriksson, S., G. Helgesson, and A.T. Höglund. 2007. Being, doing, and knowing: Developing ethical competence in health care. *Journal of Academic Ethics* 5: 207–216.

Falender, Carol. 2006. Ethics and supervision in the practicum and internship. Paper presented at the 114th Conference of the American Psychological Association, New Orleans, LA.

Friedman, Andrew. 2007. *Ethical Competence and Professional Associations.* Bristol, UK: Professional Association Research Network.

Garavan, Thomas N., and David McGuire. 2001. Competencies and workplace learning: Some reflections on the rhetoric and the reality. *Journal of Workplace Learning* 13: 144–163.

Garofalo, Charles. 2008. With deference to Woodrow Wilson: The ethics-administration dichotomy in American public service. *Public Integrity* 10: 345–354.

Glover, Saundra H., Minnette A. Bumpus, John E. Logan, and James R. Ciesla. 1997. Reexamining the influence of individual values on ethical decision making. *Journal of Business Ethics* 16: 1319–1329.

Grundstein, R. 2001. A strategy for formulation and implementation of codes of ethics in public service organizations. *Journal of Public Administration* 24: 461–678.

Hamel, Gary. 1994. The concept of core competence. In *Competence-Based Competition,* ed. Gary Hamel and Aime Heene, 11–33. Chichester, UK: John Wiley & Sons.

Harding, Trevor S., Matthew J. Mayhew, Cynthia J. Finelli, and Donald D. Carpenter. 2007. The theory of planned behavior as a model of academic dishonesty in engineering and humanities undergraduates. *Ethics & Behavior* 17: 255–279.

Hondeghem, Annie, and Filip Vandermeulen. 2000. Competency management in the Flemish and Dutch civil service. *The International Journal of Public Sector Management* 13: 342–353.

Horton, Sylvia. 2002. The competency movement. In *Competency Management in the Public Sector: European Variations on the Theme*, ed. Sylvia Horton, Annie Hondeghem, and David Farnham, 1–16. Amsterdam, the Netherlands: IOS Press.

Jormsri, P., W. Kunaviktikul, S. Ketefian, and A. Chaowalit. 2005. Moral competence in nursing practice. *Nursing Ethics* 12(6): 582–594.

Jurkiewicz, Carole L. 2002. The influence of pedagogical style on students' level of ethical reasoning. *Journal of Public Affairs Education* 8: 263–274.

Kak, Neeraj, Bart Burkhalter, and Merri-Ann Cooper. 2001. Measuring the competence of healthcare providers. *Quality Assurance Projects* 2: 1–28.

Karsing, Edgar D. 2001. *Morele competenties in organisaties* [Moral competency in organizations]. Assen, the Netherlands: Van Gorcum.

Kavathatzopoulos, I. 2005. Making ethical decisions in professional life. In *How Professionals Make Decisions*, ed. H. Montgomery, R. Lipshitz, and B. Brehmer, 277–288. Mahwah, NJ: L. Erlbaum.

Kavathatzopoulos, I., J. Persson, and C. Aborg. 2002. Individual learning and organizational change for ethical competence in the use of information technology tools. In *The Transformation of Organisations in the Information Age: Social and Ethical Implications,* ed. Simon Rogerson, Jose Alvaro Assis Lopes, Terrel Ward Bynum, and Isabel Alvarez, 383–390. Lisboa, Portugal: Universidade Lusiada.

Kavathatzopoulos, I., and G. Rigas. 1998. A Piagetian scale for the measurement of ethical competence in politics. *Educational and Psychological Measurement* 58: 791–803.

Kohlberg, Lawrence. 1971. Stages of moral development. In *Moral Education,* ed. C.M. Beck, B.S. Crittenden, and E.V. Sullivan, 23–92. Toronto, Ontario, Canada: University of Toronto Press.

Krebs, Dennis L., Sandra C.A. Vermeulen, Jeremy I. Carpendale, and Kathy Denton. 1991. Structural and situational influences on moral judgment: The interaction between stage and dilemma. In *Handbook of Moral Behavior and Development,* Vol. 2: *Research,* ed. W.M. Kurtines and J.L. Gerwirtz, 139–169. Hillsdale, NJ: L. Erlbaum.

Lasthuizen, Karin. 2008. *Leading to Integrity: Empirical Research into the Effects of Leadership on Ethics and Integrity.* Amsterdam, the Netherlands: Vrije Universiteit Amsterdam.

Lind, George, and R. Wakenhut. 1985. Testing for moral judgment competence. In *Moral Development and the Social Environment: Studies in the Philosophy and Psychology of Moral Judgment and Education,* ed. G. Lind, H.A. Hartmann, and R. Wakenhut, 79–105. Chicago: Precedent Publishing.

Maesschalck, Jeroen. 2005. *Een ambtelijk integriteitsbeleid in de Vlaamse overheid* [An integrity policy in the Flemish government]. Leuven, Belgium: Steunpunt Bestuurlijke Organisatie Vlaanderen.

———. 2011. Integriteit en integriteitsbeleid [Integrity and integrity policy]. In *Handboek bestuurskunde* [Handbook of public administration], ed. A. Hondeghem, W. Van Dooren, D. Vancoppenolle, B. Verschure, and S. Op de Beekck, 1–27. Bruges, Belgium: Vanden Broele.

Mansfield, Richard S. 1996. Building competency models: Approaches for HR professionals. *Human Resource Management* 35: 7–18.

Martinez, James Michael, and William Donald Richardson. 2011. *Administrative Ethics in the Twenty-First Century.* New York: Peter Lang.

May, Douglas R., and Kevin P. Pauli. 2002. The role of moral intensity in ethical decision making: A review and investigation of moral recognition, evaluation, and intention. *Business Society* 41: 84–117.

Meine, Manfred F. 2009. To be or not to be: The issue of ethical competence. Paper presented at the National Association of Schools of Public Affairs and Administration, Crystal City, VA, October 15.

Menzel, D.C. 2010. *Ethics Moments in Government: Cases and Controversies.* Boca Raton, FL: CRC Press.

Messick, Samuel. 1984. The psychology of educational measurement. *Journal of Educational Measurement* 21: 215–237.

Nunes, Francisco, Luis Martins, and Henrique Duarte. 2007. Competency management in European Union public administrations. Survey commissioned by the Portuguese EU Presidency, EUPAN Human Resources Working Group. December.

O'Fallon, Michael J., and Kenneth D. Butterfield. 2005. A review of the empirical ethical decision-making literature: 1996–2003. *Journal of Business Ethics* 59: 375–413.

Oser, Fritz K. 1991. Professional morality: A discourse approach (The case of the teaching profession). In *Handbook of Moral Behavior and Development,* Vol. 2: *Research,* ed. W.M. Kurtines, and J.L. Gerwirtz, 191–227. Hillsdale, NJ: L. Erlbaum.

Pedersen, Lars Jacob Tynes. 2009. See no evil: Moral sensitivity in the formulation of business problems. *Business Ethics: A European Review* 18: 335–348.

Podolskiy, Oleg. 2005. Moral competence of contemporary adolescents: Technology-based ways of measurement. PhD dissertation, Albert-Ludwigs-Universität Freiburg im Breisgau, Germany.

Porter, Michael E. 1987. From competitive advantage to corporate strategy. *Harvard Business Review* 65: 43–59.

Preston, Noel. 2007. *Understanding Ethics,* 3d ed. Sydney, Australia: The Federation Press.

Razzaque, Mohammed Abdur, and Tan Piak Hwee. 2002. Ethics and purchasing dilemma: A Singaporean view. *Journal of Business Ethics* 35: 307–326.

Rest, J.R. 1986. *Moral Development: Advance in Theory and Research.* New York: Praeger.

———. 1994. Background: Theory and research. In *Moral Development in the Professions: Psychology and Applied Ethics,* ed. James R. Rest and Darcia Narvaez, 1–25. Hillsdale, NJ: L. Erlbaum.

Ritter, Barbara A. 2006. Can business ethics be trained? A study of the ethical decision-making process in business students. *Journal of Business Ethics* 68: 153–164.

Sampson, Demetrios, and Demetrios Fytros. 2008. Competence models in technology-enhanced competence-based learning. In *Handbook on Information Technologies for Education and Training,* 2d ed., ed. H.H. Adelsberger Kinshuk, J.M. Pawlowksi, and D. Sampson, 155–178. Berlin, Germany: Springer-Verlag.

Sandberg, Jörgen. 1994. Competence—The basis for a smart workforce. In *Training for a Smart Workforce,* ed. Rod Gerber and Colin Lankshear, 47–53. London: Routledge.

Sanghi, Seema. 2004. *The Handbook of Competency Mapping: Understanding, Designing and Implementing Competency Models in Organizations.* New Delhi: Response Books.

Sims, Randi L., and Thomas L. Keon. 1999. Determinants of ethical decision making: The relationship of the perceived organizational environment. *Journal of Business Ethics* 19: 393–401.

Singhapakdi, Anusorn, Scott J. Vitell, and George R. Franke. 1999. Antecedents, consequences, and mediating effects of perceived moral intensity and personal moral philosophies. *Journal of the Academy of Marketing Science* 27: 19–36.

Somers, M.J. 2001. Ethical codes of conduct and organizational context: A study of the relationship between codes of conduct, employee behavior, and organizational values. *Journal of Business Ethics* 30: 185–195.

Stevens, Michael J., and Michael A. Campion. 1994. The knowledge, skill, and ability requirements for teamwork: Implications for human resource management. *Journal of Management* 20: 503–530.

Stewart, Debra W., and Norman W. Sprinthall. 1991. Strengthening ethical judgment in public administration. In *Ethical Frontiers in Public Management,* ed. James S. Bowman, 243–260. San Francisco: Jossey-Bass.

Stewart, Debra W., Norman W. Sprinthall, and Jackie D. Kem. 2002. Moral reasoning in the context of reform: A study of Russian officials. *Public Administration Review* 62: 282–297.

Stoof, Angela, Rob L. Martens, and Theo J. Bastiaens. 2002. The boundary approach of competence: A constructivistic aid for understanding and using the concept of competence. *Human Resource Development Review* 1: 345–365.

Thoma, Stephen. 1994. Moral judgment and moral action. In *Moral Development in the Professions: Psychology and Applied Ethics,* ed. James R. Rest and Darcia Narvaez, 199–211. Hillsdale, NJ: L. Erlbaum.

Thoma, Stephen J., Darcia Narvaez, James Rest, and Pitt Derryberry. 1999. Does moral judgment development reduce to political attitudes or verbal ability? Evidence using the defining issues test. *Educational Psychology Review* 11: 325–341.

Treviño, Linda Klebe. 1992. Moral reasoning and business ethics: Implications for research, education, and management. *Journal of Business Ethics* 11: 445–459.

Treviño, Linda Klebe, and Gary R. Weaver. 2001. Organizational justice and ethics program follow-through: Influences on employees' harmful and helpful behavior. *Business Ethics Quarterly* 11: 651–671.

Treviño, Linda Klebe, and Stuart A. Youngblood. 1990. Bad apples in bad barrels: A causal analysis of ethical decision-making behavior. *Journal of Applied Psychology* 75: 378–385.

van den Heuvel, J.H.J., and L.W.J.C. Huberts. 2003. *Integriteitsbeleid van gemeenten* [Integrity policy of municipalities]. Utrecht, the Netherlands: Lemma.

Valentine, Sean, and Gary Fleischman. 2004. Ethics training and businesspersons' perceptions of organizational ethics. *Journal of Business Ethics* 52: 391–400.

Warren, Danielle E., and Kristin Smith-Crowe. 2008. Deciding what's right: The role of external sanctions and embarrassment in shaping moral judgments in the workplace. *Research in Organizational Behavior* 28: 81–105.

While, Alison E. 1994. Competence versus performance: Which is more important? *Journal of Advanced Nursing* 20: 525–531.

White, Richard D. 2001. Do employees act like they think? Exploring the dichotomy between moral judgment and ethical behavior. *Public Administration Quarterly* 25: 391–412.

Whitton, Howard. 2007. Developing the "ethical competence" of public officials—A capacity-building approach. *Viesoji Politika ir Administravimas* 21:49–60.

3

From Ethical Competence to Ethical Leadership

Leonie Heres and Karin Lasthuizen

As asserted throughout this volume, being ethically competent entails more than just being a virtuous person or doing the right thing in a given situation. In the first chapter of this book, Cooper and Menzel (2013) argue that ethical competence should also include the active promotion of ethics within an organization. In other words, ethically competent people also provide ethical leadership. But what exactly does it mean to "provide ethical leadership"? And precisely how is ethical leadership related to ethical competence?

In this chapter, we begin with a discussion of what ethical competence entails and how it relates to ethical leadership. Then we take a closer look at what ethical leadership is and what it can achieve. We close with a reflection on what the ethical leadership literature offers in further developing our understanding of ethical competence.

Achieving Ethical Competence

Ethical competence may be defined in various ways; we have yet to reach a consensus on what it means to be ethically competent. Nevertheless, there is a common denominator in the definitions offered in the literature—namely, that ethical competence *at the very least* encompasses a set of knowledge, skills, and attitudes and abilities that enable a person to adequately deal with moral challenges and make decisions and behaviors that meet high ethical standards. Larkin (1999, 307), for instance, notes that ethical competence entails both the ethical capacity and moral reasoning of a person: "The former would represent the theoretical basis of learned knowledge of [bio]ethics, law, and customs. The latter would be reflected in the ability to solve practical ethical dilemmas through independent reasoning grounded on considered deliberation." Likewise, for nursing practice, Jormsri et al. (2005, 586) define ethical competence as "the ability or capacity of persons to recognize their feelings as they influence what is good or bad in particular situations, and then to reflect on these feelings, to make their decision, and to act in ways that bring about the highest level of benefit for patients." Other definitions, such as those offered by Kavathatzopoulos and Rigas (1998), Bowman and colleagues (2004), and Menzel (2010), make references to similar characteristics.

While these definitions provide us with a general understanding of what ethical competence entails, it raises the question of when a person can and cannot be considered ethically competent. In the words of Cooper and Menzel (2013, xx), "How does one achieve a satisfactory level of ethical competence?" The answer to this question requires a clarification of what we mean by "satisfactory," as well as a recognition of the fact that terms like *ethics, morality,* and *integrity* are by their very nature subjective and dynamic constructs. What is ethical to some may not be considered so by others, and a decision can be seen as more or less ethical depending on the specific circumstances and zeitgeist. As Six, Bakker, and Huberts (2007) have argued, what is ethical and what is not depends on the moral values, norms, rules, and obligations that are considered valid by the professional and societal context in which an actor operates. Thus we consider it the task of the organization and its respective members, the sector, *and* the profession to specify what constitutes a "satisfactory" level of ethical competence. Even more so, we believe it to be the role of the broader (international) society, government, clients, and citizens as they develop laws and regulations and support, condone, or reject certain behaviors or outcomes. Even though we may not be able to provide a clear-cut threshold here that distinguishes the ethically competent from the ethically incompetent, we can and should try to identify the specific knowledge, skills, and attitudes and abilities that are needed for ethical competence.

Understanding Ethical Competence and Ethical Leadership

The notion of *ethical competence* has considerable conceptual overlap with the concept of *ethical leadership.* As the overview presented later in this chapter illustrates, both ethical leadership and ethical competence are based firmly in a person's ability to make sound ethical decisions and behave in a normatively appropriate manner. As such, studies on the knowledge, skills, and attitudes and abilities that are key to ethical leadership can provide useful insight into what is needed to achieve ethical competence.

Still, there are specific features of ethical leadership that distinguish it from ethical competence. While ethical competence is generally ascribed to a person (or other type of actor), ethical leadership is more relational and reputational in nature. Ethical leadership is, to an important extent, in the eye of the beholder. Those who are not perceived as ethical leaders are simply less likely to influence the ethical decision making and behavior of others (Brown and Treviño 2006; Treviño, Hartman, and Brown 2000). Ethical leadership therefore goes beyond a leader's mere ethical competence; it necessitates that one also has a *reputation* for being ethically competent. In contrast, ethical competence is much less dependent on whether other people notice it or not.

Another, and perhaps even more important, distinction between ethical competence and ethical leadership has to do with the notion of motivating others to become ethically competent. As mentioned before, most definitions and discussions of ethical competence focus on the knowledge, skills, and attitudes and abilities that allow a person to deal with moral challenges and exhibit ethical decisions and behaviors. Thus ethical competence does not *necessarily* include the active promotion of ethical decision making and behavior among followers. In the case of ethical leadership, however, actively and deliberately promoting ethics among others is precisely what scholars consider to be its core defining and distinguishing feature (see Brown, Treviño, and Harrison 2005; Brown and Treviño 2006; Huberts, Kaptein, and Lasthuizen 2007). Without active promotion of ethics, ethical leadership cannot exist. For ethical competence, on the other hand, such a statement is far less obvious.

The boundaries between the ethical competence and ethical leadership concepts are blurring, though. Cooper and Menzel (2013, 9), for instance, argue that an ethically competent person also "promote[s] ethical practices and behaviors in public agencies and organizations" and "has a responsibility to exercise ethical leadership." Such assertions imply that ethical leadership should be considered an aspect of ethical competence. A person should be considered ethically competent if he is able to stimulate others' ethical competence. But does the ability to promote ethical practices among others really attest to one's own *ethical competence*? Or is it more a sign of one's *leadership* competence? In our view, one can be a very ethically competent person without possessing good leadership skills. Incorporating *ethical leadership* into the concept and definition of *ethical competence* leads to conflation and confusion between the two concepts and makes it more difficult to delineate precisely how ethical leadership contributes to ethical competence and vice versa.

Ethical competence, we believe, is best understood as a necessary—albeit not sufficient—aspect of a person's ethical leadership. A person can be ethically competent without being an ethical leader, but not an ethical leader without being ethically competent. Ethical competence is the basis from which the leader can build and maintain a reputation for being a moral person. It provides the ethical leader with the necessary credibility and allows the leader to become an effective ethical role model to followers. Ethical competence is required to communicate convincingly and from one's own experience about the struggles involved in dealing with ethical dilemmas and the means by which sound moral judgments can be made: It is the "practice what you preach" factor that infuses leaders' words with power, strength, and credibility and gives them the moral authority to discipline others. Without ethical competence, leadership that professes ethics and integrity is hypocriti-cal, and followers will likely view these phony proclamations of ethicality as the superficial "window dressing" it is (Treviño, Hartman, and Brown 2000). Such hypocritical leadership is unlikely to be successful in the long term: Just consider the case of Ken Lay, chief executive officer of the now-defunct Houston-based energy company Enron, who had repeatedly professed his commitment to ethics and propagated it throughout the company. Lay didn't practice what he preached, and in the end his fraudulent actions led to the organization's downfall.

As a vital part of a person's ethical leadership, ethical competence is part of a self-reinforcing cycle. In this chapter, we will show that ethical leadership is a key factor in developing, improving, supporting, and reinforcing the ethical competence of *others*. Furthermore, ethical leadership is an important compo-nent in determining whether the boundary conditions for ethical competence are met; without those conditions, ethical performance cannot be achieved. In a way, then, ethical competence and ethical leadership are part of an ongoing process wherein ethically competent people can become ethical leaders who develop the ethical competencies of their followers; these followers, in turn, may go on to become ethical leaders one day, and so on. . . . To gain a fuller understanding of how this cyclical process works (i.e., how ethical leadership is based on the ethical competence of the leader and how ethical leadership in turn helps build the ethical competence of others), we next provide an overview of the main features and mechanisms of ethical leadership.

What Makes an Ethical Leader?

Ethical leadership generally is defined as "the demonstration of normatively appropriate conduct through two-way communication, reinforcement, and decision making" (Brown, Treviño, and Harrison 2005, 120). As this defini-tion implies, the primary objective of ethical leadership is to cultivate ethical decision making and behavior among followers, and it is this explicit focus on promoting and managing ethics that distinguishes ethical leadership, both conceptually and empirically, from other leadership styles such as transfor-mational or authentic leadership (see Brown, Treviño, and Harrison [2005] and Brown and Treviño [2006] for a more extensive discussion). For this chapter, we derive three essential components of effective ethical leadership from the literature (see Figure 3.1). The first, which prevailing research and theory often refer to as the "moral person" component of ethical leadership (cf. Treviño, Hartman, and Brown 2000), concerns the leader's moral values

Ethical Role Modeling

Role modeling ethical behavior is widely acknowledged as a critical factor in ethical leadership (e.g., Berman, West, and Cava 1994; Kakabadse, Korac-Kakabadse, and Kouzmin 2003; Lasthuizen 2008; Loe, Ferrell, and Mansfield 2000; Menzel 2007; Treviño et al. 1999). To an important extent, behavior is learned by watching the behavior of significant others and imitating that behavior if it is shown to have desirable outcomes (Bandura 1977, 1986). As Brown and colleagues (2005) note, leaders' high prestige, status, and power makes them particularly attractive role models. Thus, Jurkiewicz (2006, 247) argues, whether the influence is intentional or unintentional and exercised formally or informally, followers have a tendency to align their ethical orientations with those of their leaders. Indeed, leaders' decision making and behavior give strong moral cues to followers (Cooper 2006; Menzel 2007) and set the ethical tone of an organization (Grojean et al. 2004). Furthermore, role modeling ethical behavior is essential for effective reinforcement and communication on ethics: It conveys the underlying principles that leaders themselves adhere to and thereby directly attests to the credibility of the leader (Dineen, Lewicki, and Tomlinson 2006; Heres and Lasthuizen 2012). If leaders lack such credibility, their words simply lose power (Simons 1999). Take a look at the case of the Hillsborough county administrator discussed in Chapter 1. The moment she chose to authorize her own pay raise and spend public resources in ways that were clearly not in the best interest of the community they were meant to serve, she lost her moral authority and hence any ethical leadership reputation she may have had.

Although closely intertwined with the "moral person" component discussed earlier, ethical role modeling entails more than having the right traits and behaving in a normatively appropriate manner. Of course, prerequisites for being an ethical role model include embodying moral virtues such as honesty and trustworthiness, possessing a genuine sense of caring and consideration for others, and behaving ethically (Weaver, Treviño, and Agle 2005). However, ethical role modeling additionally requires that the leader's ethical decisions and actions are sufficiently visible and salient to be noticed by followers "against an organizational backdrop that is often ethically neutral at best" (Brown and Treviño 2006, 597). An ethical leader thus makes sure that her ethical conduct is distinctive, consistent, and prevalent so that it stands above "normal" leadership behaviors (Bandura 1986; Brown, Treviño, and Harrison 2005). This does not imply, though, that ethical leaders focus exclusively on making big moral gestures. Ethical role modeling extends to all types of behavior, whether it concerns major events and dilemmas (e.g., choosing to discontinue relations with a questionable client even though it has grave financial ramifications) or relatively mundane, day-to-day issues (e.g., arriving on time for a meeting) (Heres and Lasthuizen 2012; Weaver, Treviño, and Agle 2005).

Reinforcement

A second element that is crucial to being considered a "moral manager" is holding people accountable for their conduct and consistently reinforcing ethical standards through reward and discipline. In this respect, ethical leadership is certainly not "soft" leadership (Johnson 2005); it requires a certain strictness of discipline (Lamboo, Lasthuizen, and Huberts 2008). The underlying idea is fairly straightforward: People are more likely to refrain from unethical behavior when that behavior will result in punishment, especially when the punishment outweighs the reward that one would get from engaging in the unethical behavior (Ball, Treviño, and Sims 1994; Kaptein and Wempe 2002; Treviño 1992). If unethical behavior—intentionally or not—is ignored, condoned, facilitated, or even rewarded, it will be perceived as acceptable behavior and, more than likely, will continue in the future (Ashforth and Anand 2003; Carlson and Perrewe 1995; Sims and Brinkman 2002). Conversely, rewarding behavior that supports and upholds ethical standards can foster ethical decision making and behavior and help create a stronger ethical culture (Grojean et al. 2004; Treviño and Youngblood 1990).

Still, some scholars argue against an overreliance on rewards and punishment. Baucus and Beck-Dudley (2005) suggest that relying too heavily on rewards and punishment may actually lower the level of moral reasoning used by followers. Similarly, Roberts (2009) and Paine (1994) suggest a strong focus on rules and compliance can inhibit the moral imagination of followers, lower their ethical expectations, and provide them with a justification for overlooking the broader moral implications of their behavior or that of the organization.

Ethical leaders use reinforcement in various degrees and employ both formal as well as informal sanctions. For instance, as Grojean et al. (2004) argue, ethical conduct can be included in the criteria for distribution of financial rewards such as base pay raises, bonuses, and incentives. Caution is warranted, though, as too much emphasis on formal, material rewards might lead people to sacrifice the overall desired outcomes for the sake of the rewarded behavior (Bartol and Locke 2000). In this respect, it is important to note that informal reinforcements by the leader and peers may be even more effective than formal ones (Treviño 1992). Informal rewards such as recognition, trust, respect, increased discretion and autonomy, and greater status and power are potent incentives for followers to engage in ethical behavior (Grojean et al. 2004). Likewise, the threat of informal punishments may deter unethical behavior (Treviño 1992).

In dealing with reports of unethical behavior, ethical leaders always treat the parties involved with respect and maintain a sense of justice and conscientiousness as the charges are explored. In doing so, ethical leaders cultivate an atmosphere where followers feel safe enough to report problems and deliver bad news (Heres and Lasthuizen 2012; Kaptein and van Reenen 2001; Walumbwa and Schaubroeck 2009). Moreover, ethical leaders remain thorough and fair in the process of investigating transgressions and, if necessary, punishing the individual(s) involved (Heres and Lasthuizen 2012). The punishments that they give match the transgression and are consistent with what others in similar situations have received (Ball, Treviño, and Sims 1994). As a result, the punishment is more likely to get support from followers—even from those directly involved (Ball, Treviño, and Sims 1994). And because ethical leaders apply a fair and balanced amount of authority in each situation, they prevent resentment and cynicism while sending a clear message that ethical lapses are not tolerated (Ball, Treviño, and Sims 1994; Johnson 2005; Treviño, Brown, and Hartman 2003).

Lessons learned from ethical leaders' reinforcement go beyond the individuals being rewarded or punished; rather, reinforcement has a broader symbolic function. It motivates other followers to pay close attention to the behaviors that leaders reward and discipline (Brown, Treviño, and Harrison 2005; Cooper 2006; Mayer et al. 2009; Treviño 1992). Lamboo, Lasthuizen, and Huberts (2008) note that reinforcement is a very effective means of communicating norms to a wider audience. Therefore, ethical leaders make sure their sanctioning is visible to a broad range of followers (Cooper 2006; Treviño, Hartman, and Brown 2000). Research also points to the benefit of openly discussing such reinforcement, suggesting leaders might consider informing followers of ethics-related incidents, with an emphasis on the constructive and just features of the consequences and measures taken to remedy the situation (Ball, Treviño, and Sims 1994; Treviño 1992). This allows for learning to occur in the broader organizational community and is necessary to "uphold . . . the value of conformity to shared norms and maintain the perception that the organization is a just place where wrongdoers are held accountable for their actions" (Treviño et al. 1999, 139).

Communication about Ethics

Ethical leaders communicate with their followers about ethics (e.g., Brown, Treviño, and Harrison 2005). This third feature of the "moral manager" component entails much more than just telling followers what to *not* to do (Brown

2007). It concerns highlighting the ethical dimension of specific decisions, tasks, and situations (De Hoogh and Den Hartog 2008; Enderle 1987), clarifying norms, expectations, and responsibilities (De Hoogh and Den Hartog 2008; Lamboo, Lasthuizen, and Huberts 2008), providing guidance on the appropriate course of action (Grojean et al. 2004; Van den Akker et al. 2009), formulating positive ethical expectations (Brown 2007), explicating how tasks contribute to achieving socially responsible goals (Piccolo et al. 2010), and giving feedback to followers about their (un)ethical conduct (Grojean et al. 2004). Additionally, ethical leaders make ethics salient by being transparent about their own decision-making processes. This includes publicly sharing information about the alternatives considered, the respective implications these alternatives would have, the process of decision making, and the principles and justifications behind the final decision made (De Hoogh and Den Hartog 2008; Grundstein-Amado 1999; Treviño, Brown, and Hartman 2003; Van Wart 2005). In that sense, ethical leaders again function as important role models by talking about ethics themselves and by being open and honest about their own ethical dilemmas and decisions. They show that it is safe, acceptable, and even desirable to talk about ethics-related issues (Driscoll and McKee 2007).

Obviously, communication is as much about how a message is conveyed as it is about its actual content. Scholars have been skeptical of relying too heavily on codes of conduct (Rhode 2006) and communicating the "values of the organization . . . through formal presentations or the distribution of laminated cards" (Paarlberg and Perry 2007, 405). Instead, organizational stories and myths are considered more fruitful venues for transmitting messages about ethics (Driscoll and McKee 2007; Grojean et al. 2004). Telling appealing stories about critical events of ethical and unethical behavior or about heroic leaders relays the fundamental values, standards, and assumptions of the organization. The key figures described in these stories can become ethical role models for the audience, especially newcomers in the organization, and that role model's behavior may become ingrained in the shared cognitions of organization members about what a prototypical leader is (Grojean et al. 2004). The use of storytelling may also guard ethical leaders from being perceived as talking about ethics in too much of a sermonizing way (Treviño, Hartman, and Brown 2000). To be optimally effective, stories and myths should be communicated to followers at all levels in written as well as verbal form and, where possible, face-to-face (Driscoll and McKee 2007).

What Does Ethical Leadership Achieve?

Empirical research indicates that ethical leadership can have numerous positive outcomes. At the very least, ethical leadership seems to deter followers from behavior that is detrimental to the leader, the group, or the organization at large. For instance, ethical leadership is shown to limit followers' counterproductive behavior (Avey, Palanski, and Walumbwa 2010; De Hoogh and Den Hartog 2008; Mayer et al. 2009). Similarly, followers of ethical leaders are less inclined to commit unethical acts (Chou et al. 2010) and, accordingly, display fewer behaviors that violate ethical norms and values (Mayer et al. 2012; Treviño, Brown, and Hartman 2003). In more concrete terms, ethical leadership can decrease instances of manipulation, fraud, cheating, bullying, or misuse of financial resources (Khuntia and Suar 2004; Lasthuizen 2008). The effect that ethical leadership has on such unethical behavior goes above and beyond the effect of other, more general, leadership styles that lack a specific ethical focus (Brown, Treviño, and Harrison 2005; Lasthuizen 2008).

Empirical research reveals that different elements of ethical leadership have different effects on different types of unethical behavior. Lasthuizen's study (2008) indicates that role modeling ethical behavior is especially effective in minimizing unethical conduct that relates to interpersonal relationships within the organization, including bullying, sexual harassment, or gossiping about colleagues. But when it comes to unethical behaviors that concern organizational resources—e.g., misuse of working hours for private purposes, falsely calling in sick, carelessness in the use of organizational resources—it is essential that a leader is strict and reinforces behavior through rewards and punishments. Finally, being open to discussing ethical dilemmas and clarifying ethical norms seems most effective in reducing the occurrence of discrimination against outside stakeholders and favoritism (see also Huberts, Kaptein, and Lasthuizen 2007).

In addition, ethical leadership has many positive side effects. Multiple studies show that ethical leadership elicits beneficial behaviors from followers that go beyond their formal job descriptions. Ethical leaders are able to evoke such extra-role behaviors because they compel followers to take a broader ethical perspective on things and become more empathic (Kalshoven 2010; Neubert, Wu, and Roberts 2010). Ethical leadership makes followers feel like they have more control over their jobs and their work is more meaningful (Piccolo et al. 2010). As a result, followers tend to take more initiative, put in extra effort, display more altruism, and show more willingness to help others with work-related problems (Avey, Palanski, and Walumbwa 2010; De Hoogh and Den Hartog 2008; Mayer et al. 2009; Toor and Ofori 2009). They have a better work attitude and are more dedicated to and involved in their work (Brown, Treviño, and Harrison 2005). Also, followers of ethical leaders exhibit greater self-efficacy (Walumbwa et al. 2011), less uncertainty (Chou et al. 2010), and more optimism about the future (De Hoogh and Den Hartog

2008). In the end, ethical leadership thus improves the overall performance of followers (Khuntia and Suar 2004; Walumbwa et al. 2011).

Ethical leadership also affects followers' relationships with the leader, the team, and the broader organization. For example, ethical leadership cultivates trust not only in the leader but also among coworkers (Den Hartog and De Hoogh 2009). And ethical leaders are able to lessen interpersonal conflicts between followers (Mayer et al. 2012; Mayer et al. 2009). Followers show more commitment to and identification with the organization (Den Hartog and De Hoogh 2009; Kalshoven 2010; Khuntia and Suar 2004; Treviño et al. 1999; Walumbwa et al. 2011). Moreover, followers are more satisfied with leaders they see as ethical (Brown, Treviño, and Harrison 2005; see also Parry and Proctor-Thomson 2002). Perhaps most notably, though, followers consider ethical leaders to be more effective leaders in general (Brown, Treviño, and Harrison 2005). To conclude, then, ethical leadership appears to be beneficial for more than just ethics; it is also seems to be a good overall leadership strategy.

What Ethical Leadership Tells Us About Ethical Competence

We hope this chapter shows the potential value and usefulness of the ethical leadership literature in further developing our understanding of ethical competence. To illustrate, the discussion first indicates that ethical leaders are necessarily ethically competent people. As such, studies on ethical leadership provide us with important insights on key ethical competencies. Among these are moral courage, the ability to recognize and acknowledge the moral implications of decisions and behaviors, and the ability to weigh different perspectives, principles, and needs in a fair and transparent manner in order to reach a morally acceptable decision. At the same time, ethical leadership studies have identified certain knowledge, skills, and abilities and attitudes that contribute to ethical competence but at first glance are perhaps not as evident. For instance, ethical competence may not necessarily require "ethical heroism" or complete infallibility; rather, ethical leadership studies suggest that a person's ethical competence might be strengthened further by (1) possessing an open and vulnerable attitude when discussing one's own ethical dilemmas and mistakes with others, (2) taking accountability for one's actions and acknowledging mistakes, and (3) having the ability to turn mistakes into valuable learning experiences.

Second, the literature on ethical leadership highlights the importance of external influences and group-level processes both in developing one's ethical competencies and in translating ethical competence into ethical performance. As Cooper and Menzel note in the first chapter of this book (2013), we must recognize that ethical competence is a "lifelong process" and not something that is achieved once and for all after reaching adulthood, finishing college, or participating in a one-time career-related ethics training session. Followers also develop their ethical knowledge, skills, and attitudes by observing the behaviors that are role modeled around them, by looking at what is punished and what is rewarded by the leaders of the organization, and by discussing ethical issues with others. Leaders and peers continuously influence one another, as well as the ethical culture of the organization in general, which in turn shapes the day-to-day ethical performance of both leaders and followers (Lasthuizen 2008; Mayer et al. 2010; Mayer, Kuenzi, and Greenbaum 2010; Neubert, Wu, and Roberts 2010).

Finally, this overview shows how ethical competence, as a crucial element in sustainable ethical leadership, makes an important contribution to effective public service leadership. Leaders who are ethically competent, who build strong relationships with their followers, and who actively promote ethics are able to raise the ethical standards in public decision making and behavior to ever-higher levels. As such, ethical leaders can limit the occurrence of counterproductive and unethical behaviors within their organizations—more so than leaders who do not exhibit such a clear concern for ethics in their leadership (e.g., Brown, Treviño, and Harrison 2005; De Hoogh and Den Hartog 2008; Huberts, Kaptein, and Lasthuizen 2007; Lasthuizen 2008; Mayer et al. 2009). Ethical leadership (and hence ethical competence) improves the ethical performance of and within the organization and protects individuals, organizations, and society at large from the detrimental effects of ethical lapses (Bull and Newell 2003; Cooper 2001; Della Porta and Mény 1997; Heidenheimer and Johnston 2002). In general, ethical leadership makes for more effective public service leadership by improving the overall performance within the organization (Khuntia and Suar 2004; Walumbwa et al. 2011). Public service managers who develop high levels of ethical competence and are able to translate that competence into effective ethical leadership thus hold much promise.

Conclusion

In this chapter, we discussed the relationship between ethical leadership and ethical competence. We argued that while ethical competence is an important component of ethical leadership, we must caution against conflating the two concepts. Ethical leadership *inherently* necessitates a deliberate and visible effort to guide others in developing their ethical competencies. Ethical competence, however, is much less contingent upon its visibility to or its dissemination among others. Being ethically competent, therefore, is not the same as being an ethical leader; it is a mere first—albeit critical—step in the process of becoming an ethical leader.

If we truly wish to develop effective public service leaders for the future and build organizations with a strong moral grounding, we shouldn't stop at developing our leaders' ethical competence. Instead, we should teach our leaders to think beyond their own ethical dilemmas, decisions, and conduct and provide them with the knowledge and tools that allow them to become the moral stewards of their organization. We should teach them how to strengthen their relationship with followers, build trust, cultivate respect, and gain moral authority. We should teach them about the importance of other people's perceptions of the behavior that they model, about the symbolic function of even the smallest sanctions or compliments, and about the inadvertent effects of "doing nothing" and condoning questionable behaviors. We should teach them how to engage others in discussions about ethics and how to make their ethics message heard. In other words, we should teach them to move from ethical competence to ethical leadership.

References

Aronson, E. 2001. Integrating leadership styles and ethical perspectives. *Canadian Journal of Administrative Sciences/Revue Canadienne des Sciences de l'Administration* 18(4): 244–256.

Ashforth, B.E., and V. Anand. 2003. The normalization of corruption in organizations. *Research in Organizational Behavior* 25: 1–25.

Avey, J.B., M.E. Palanski, and F.O. Walumbwa. 2010. When leadership goes unnoticed: The moderating role of follower self-esteem on the relationship between ethical leadership and follower behavior. *Journal of Business Ethics* 98(4): 573–582.

Avolio, B.J., and W.L. Gardner. 2005. Authentic leadership development: Getting to the root of positive forms of leadership. *Leadership Quarterly* 16(3): 315–338.

Ball, G.A., L.K. Treviño, and H.P. Sims. 1994. Just and unjust punishment—Influences on subordinate performance and citizenship. *Academy of Management Journal* 37(2): 299–322.

Bandura, A. 1977. *Social Learning Theory.* New York: General Learning Press.

———. 1986. *Social Foundations of Thought and Action: A Social Cognitive Theory.* Englewood Cliffs, NJ: Prentice Hall.

Bartol, K.M., and E.A. Locke. 2000. Incentives and motivation. In *Compensation in Organizations: Current Research and Practice,* ed. S.L. Rynes and B. Gerhart. San Francisco: Jossey-Bass.

Baucus, M.S., and C.L. Beck-Dudley. 2005. Designing ethical organizations: Avoiding the long-term negative effects of rewards and punishments. *Journal of Business Ethics* 56(4): 355–370.

Berman, E., J. West, and A. Cava. 1994. Ethics management in municipal governments and large firms—Exploring similarities and differences. *Administration & Society* 26(2): 185–203.

Bowman, J.S., J.P. West, E.M. Berman, and M. Van Wart. 2004. *The Professional Edge: Competencies in Public Service.* New York: M.E. Sharpe.

Brown, M.E. 2007. Misconceptions of ethical leadership: How to avoid potential pitfalls. *Organizational Dynamics* 36(2): 140–155.

Brown, M.E., and L.K. Treviño. 2006. Ethical leadership: A review and future directions. *Leadership Quarterly* 17(6): 595–616.

Brown, M.E., L.K. Treviño, and D.A. Harrison. 2005. Ethical leadership: A social learning perspective for construct development and testing. *Organizational Behavior and Human Decision Processes* 97(2): 117–134.

Bull, M.J., and J.L. Newell. 2003. *Corruption in Contemporary Politics.* Basingstoke, UK, and New York: Palgrave Macmillan.

Caldwell, C. 2009. Identity, self-awareness, and self-deception: Ethical implications for leaders and organizations. *Journal of Business Ethics* 90(3): 393–406.

Caldwell, C., S.J. Bischoff, and R. Karri. 2002. The four umpires: A paradigm for ethical leadership. *Journal of Business Ethics* 36(1–2): 153–163.

Carlson, D.S., and P.L. Perrewe. 1995. Institutionalization of organizational ethics through transformational leadership. *Journal of Business Ethics* 14(10): 829–838.

Chou, L.-F., C.-J. Tseng, H.-C.D. Yeh, and Y.-M. Chiang. 2010. Perceived environmental uncertainty, sales performance, and unethical intention: Leadership matters? Paper presented at the Academy of Management Meeting, Montréal, Canada.

Cooper, T.L. 2006. *The Responsible Administrator: An Approach to Ethics for the Administrative Role,* 5th ed. San Francisco: Jossey-Bass.

———, ed. 2001. *Handbook of Administrative Ethics,* 2d ed. New York: Marcel Dekker.

Cooper, T.L., and D.C. Menzel, eds. 2013. *Achieving Ethical Competence for Public Service Leadership.* Armonk, NY: M.E. Sharpe.

Cropanzano, R., and M.S. Mitchell. 2005. Social exchange theory: An interdisciplinary review. *Journal of Management* 31(6): 874–900.

Davis, A.L., and H.R. Rothstein. 2006. The effects of the perceived behavioral integrity of managers on employee attitudes: A meta-analysis. *Journal of Business Ethics* 67(4): 407–419.

De Hoogh, A.H.B., and D.N. Den Hartog. 2008. Ethical and despotic leadership, relationships with leader's social responsibility, top management team effectiveness and subordinates' optimism: A multi-method study. *Leadership Quarterly* 19(3): 297–311.

Della Porta, D., and Y. Mény. 1997. *Democracy and Corruption in Europe.* London: Pinter.

Den Hartog, D.N., and A.H.B. De Hoogh. 2009. Empowering behaviour and leader fairness and integrity: Studying perceptions of ethical leader behaviour from a levels-of-analysis perspective. *European Journal of Work and Organizational Psychology* 18(2): 199–230.

De Schrijver, A., K. Delbeke, J. Maesschalck, and S. Pleysier. 2010. Fairness perceptions and organizational misbehavior: An empirical study. *American Review of Public Administration* 40(6): 691–703.

Dineen, B.R., R.J. Lewicki, and E.C. Tomlinson. 2006. Supervisory guidance and behavioral integrity: Relationships with employee citizenship and deviant behavior. *Journal of Applied Psychology* 91(3): 622–635.

Dobel, J.P. 1999. *Public Integrity.* Baltimore, MD: Johns Hopkins University Press.

Driscoll, C., and M. McKee. 2007. Restorying a culture of ethical and spiritual values: A role for leader storytelling. *Journal of Business Ethics* 73(2): 205–217.

Enderle, G. 1987. Some perspectives of managerial ethical leadership. *Journal of Business Ethics* 6(8): 657–663.

Gini, A. 1997. Moral leadership: An overview. *Journal of Business Ethics* 16(3): 323–330.

Grojean, M., C. Resick, M. Dickson, and D. Smith. 2004. Leaders, values, and organizational climate: Examining leadership strategies for establishing an organizational climate regarding ethics. *Journal of Business Ethics* 55(3): 223–241.

Grundstein-Amado, R. 1999. Bilateral transformational leadership—An approach for fostering ethical conduct in public service organizations. *Administration & Society* 31(2): 247–260.

Heidenheimer, A.J., and M. Johnston. 2002. *Political Corruption: Concepts and Contexts*. New Brunswick, NJ: Transaction Publishers.

Heres, L., and K. Lasthuizen. 2012. What's the difference? Ethical leadership in public, hybrid, and private sector organisations. *Journal of Change Management* 12(4): 44–466..

Hoekstra, A., A. Belling, and E. van der Heide. 2008. A paradigmatic shift in ethics and integrity management within the Dutch public sector? Beyond compliance—A practitioners' view. In *Ethics and Integrity of Governance: Perspectives Across Frontiers*, ed. L.W.J.C. Huberts, J. Maesschalck, and C.L. Jurkiewicz. Cheltenham, UK: Edward Elgar.

Huberts, L.W.J.C., M. Kaptein, and K. Lasthuizen. 2007. A study of the impact of three leadership styles on integrity violations committed by police officers. *Policing: An International Journal of Police Strategies & Management* 30(4): 587–607.

Johnson, K.W. 2005. The role of leadership in organizational integrity and five modes of ethical leadership. *Ethical Leadership,* EPIC-Online.net, June 20, 1–9. http://www.ethicaledge.com/Components%20of%20Ethical%20Leadership%20July%2001.pdf (accessed July 24, 2012).

Jormsri, P., W. Kunaviktikul, S. Ketefian, and A. Chaowait. 2005. Moral competence in nursing practice. *Nursing Ethics* 12(6): 582–594.

Jurkiewicz, C.L. 2006. Soul food: Morrison and the transformative power of ethical leadership in the public sector. *Public Integrity* 8(3): 245–256.

Kakabadse, A., N. Korac-Kakabadse, and A. Kouzmin. 2003. Ethics, values, and paradox: Comparison of three case studies examining the paucity of leadership in government. *Public Administration* 81(3): 477–508.

Kalshoven, K. 2010. *Ethical Leadership Through the Eyes of Employees*. Amsterdam, the Netherlands: University of Amsterdam.

Kaptein, M. 2003. The diamond of managerial integrity. *European Management Review* 21(1): 99–108.

Kaptein, M., and P. van Reenen. 2001. Integrity management of police organizations. *Policing: An International Journal of Police Strategies & Management* 24(3): 281–300.

Kaptein, M., and J. Wempe. 2002. *The Balanced Company: A Theory of Corporate Integrity*. Oxford, UK: Oxford University Press.

Kavathatzopoulos, I., and G. Rigas. 1998. A Piagetian scale for the measurement of ethical competence in politics. *Educational and Psychological Measurement* 58(5): 791–803.

Khuntia, R., and D. Suar. 2004. A scale to assess ethical leadership of Indian private and public sector managers. *Journal of Business Ethics* 49(1): 13–26.

Lamboo, M.E.D., K. Lasthuizen, and L.W.J.C. Huberts. 2008. How to encourage ethical behavior: The impact of police leadership on police officers taking gratuities. In *Ethics and Integrity of Governance: Perspectives Across Frontiers,* ed. L.W.J.C. Huberts, J. Maesschalck, and C.L. Jurkiewicz. Cheltenham, UK: Edward Elgar.

Larkin, G.L. 1999. Evaluating professionalism in emergency medicine: Clinical ethical competence. *Academic Emergency Medicine* 6(4): 302–311.

Lasthuizen, K.M. 2008. *Leading to Integrity: Empirical Research into the Effects of Leadership on Ethics and Integrity.* Amsterdam, the Netherlands: Vrije Universiteit.

Loe, T.W., L. Ferrell, and P. Mansfield. 2000. A review of empirical studies assessing ethical decision making in business. *Journal of Business Ethics* 25(3): 185–204.

Mahsud, R., G. Yukl, and G. Prussia. 2010. Leader empathy, ethical leadership, and relations-oriented behaviors as antecedents of leader-member exchange quality. *Journal of Managerial Psychology* 25(6): 561–577.

May, D.R., A.Y.L. Chan, T.D. Hodges, and B.J. Avolio. 2003. Developing the moral component of authentic leadership. *Organizational Dynamics* 32(3): 247–260.

Mayer, D.M., K. Aquino, R. Greenbaum, and M. Kuenzi. 2012. Who displays ethical leadership, and why does it matter? An examination of antecedents and consequences of ethical leadership. *Academy of Management Journal* 55(1): 151–171.

Mayer, D.M., T. Kosalka, C. Moore, and R. Folger. 2010. Why are followers of ethical leaders more ethical? The mediating role of moral disengagement. Paper presented at the Academy of Management Meeting, Montreal, Canada.

Mayer, D.M., M. Kuenzi, and R. Greenbaum. 2010. Examining the link between ethical leadership and employee misconduct: The mediating role of ethical climate. *Journal of Business Ethics* 95(1): 7–16.

Mayer, D.M., M. Kuenzi, R. Greenbaum, M. Bardes, and R. Salvador. 2009. How low does ethical leadership flow? Test of a trickle-down model. *Organizational Behavior and Human Decision Processes* 108(1): 1–13.

Menzel, D.C. 2007. *Ethics Management for Public Administrators: Building Organizations of Integrity.* Armonk, NY: M.E. Sharpe.

———. 2010. *Ethics Moments in Government: Cases and Controversies.* Boca Raton, FL: CRC Press.

Michie, S., and J. Gooty. 2005. Values, emotions, and authenticity: Will the real leader please stand up? *Leadership Quarterly* 16(3): 441–457.

Moorman, R.H., and S. Grover. 2009. Why does leader integrity matter to followers? An uncertainty management–based explanation. *International Journal of Leadership Studies* 5(2): 102–114.

Murphy, P.E., and G. Enderle. 1995. Managerial ethical leadership: Examples do matter. *Business Ethics Quarterly* 5(1): 117–128.

Neubert, M.J., D.S. Carlson, K.M. Kacmar, J.A. Roberts, and L.B. Chonko. 2009. The virtuous influence of ethical leadership behavior: Evidence from the field. *Journal of Business Ethics* 90(2): 157–170.

Neubert, M.J., C. Wu, and J. Roberts. 2010. The influence of ethical leadership and regulatory focus on employee outcomes. Paper presented at the Academy of Management Meeting, Montreal, Canada.

O'Connell, W., and M. Bligh. 2009. Emerging from ethical scandal: Can corruption really have a happy ending? *Leadership* 5(2): 213–235.

Paarlberg, L.E., and J.L. Perry. 2007. Values management: Aligning employee values and organization goals. *American Review of Public Administration* 37(4): 387–408.

Paine, L.S. 1994. Managing for organizational integrity. *Harvard Business Review* 72(2): 106–117.

Parry, K.W., and S.B. Proctor-Thomson. 2002. Perceived integrity of transformational leaders in organisational settings. *Journal of Business Ethics* 35(2): 75–96.

Piccolo, R.F., R. Greenbaum, D.N. Den Hartog, and R. Folger. 2010. The relationship between ethical leadership and core job characteristics. *Journal of Organizational Behavior* 31(2–3): 259–278.

Popper, M., and O. Mayseless. 2003. Back to basics: Applying a parenting perspective to transformational leadership. *Leadership Quarterly* 14(1): 41–65.

Resick, C.J., P.J. Hanges, M.W. Dickson, and J.K. Mitchelson. 2006. A cross-cultural examination of the endorsement of ethical leadership. *Journal of Business Ethics* 63(4): 345–359.

Rhode, D.L., ed. 2006. *Moral Leadership. The Theory and Practice of Power, Judgment, and Policy.* San Francisco: Jossey-Bass.

Roberts, R. 2009. The rise of compliance-based ethics management: Implications for organizational ethics. *Public Integrity* 11(3): 261–277.

Simons, T.L. 1999. Behavioral integrity as a critical ingredient for transformational leadership. *Journal of Organizational Change Management* 12(2): 89–104.

Sims, R.R., and J. Brinkman. 2002. Leaders as moral role models: The case of John Gutfreund at Salomon Brothers. *Journal of Business Ethics* 35(4): 327–339.

Six, F.E., F.G.A. Bakker, and L.W.J.C. Huberts. 2007. Judging a corporate leader's integrity: An illustrated three-component model. *European Management Journal* 25(3): 185–194.

Storr, L. 2004. Leading with integrity: A qualitative research study. *Journal of Health Organization and Management* 18(6): 415–434.

Toor, S.U.R., and G. Ofori. 2009. Ethical leadership: Examining the relationships with Full Range Leadership Model, employee outcomes, and organizational culture. *Journal of Business Ethics* 90(4): 533–547.

Treviño, L.K. 1992. The social effects of punishment in organizations. A justice perspective. *Academy of Management Review* 17(4): 647–676.

Treviño, L.K., M.E. Brown, and L.P. Hartman. 2003. A qualitative investigation of perceived executive ethical leadership: Perceptions from inside and outside the executive suite. *Human Relations* 56(1): 5–37.

Treviño, L.K., L.P. Hartman, and M.E. Brown. 2000. Moral person and moral manager: How executives develop a reputation for ethical leadership. *California Management Review* 42(4): 128–142.

Treviño, L.K., G.R. Weaver, D.G. Gibson, and B.L. Toffler. 1999. Managing ethics and legal compliance: What works and what hurts. *California Management Review* 41(2): 131–151.

Treviño, L.K., and S.A. Youngblood. 1990. Bad apples in bad barrels: A causal analysis of ethical decision-making behavior. *Journal of Applied Psychology* 75(4): 378–385.

Van den Akker, L., L. Heres, F.E. Six, and K. Lasthuizen. 2009. Ethical leadership and trust: It's all about meeting expectations. *International Journal of Leadership and Organizational Studies* 5(2): 102–122.

Van Wart, M. 2005. *Dynamics of Leadership in Public Service: Theory and Practice.* Armonk, NY: M.E. Sharpe.

Walumbwa, F.O., D.M. Mayer, P. Wang, H. Wang, K. Workman, and A.L. Christensen. 2011. Linking ethical leadership to employee performance: The roles of leader-member exchange, self-efficacy, and organizational identification. *Organizational Behavior and Human Decision Processes* 115(2): 204–213.

Walumbwa, F.O., and J. Schaubroeck. 2009. Leader personality traits and employee voice behavior: Mediating roles of ethical leadership and work group psychological safety. *Journal of Applied Psychology* 94(5): 1275–1286.

Weaver, G.R., L.K. Treviño, and B. Agle. 2005. "Somebody I look up to": Ethical role models in organizations. *Organizational Dynamics* 34(4): 313–330.

corporate social performance research.[3] According to these classifications, *corporate social responsiveness* refers to how business organizations and their agents can interact with and manage their stakeholder environments, whereas *corporate social responsibility* accentuates the moral obligations that business has to society (Frederick 1987). The latter goes to the nature of the social contract, discussed earlier.

Specifically, corporate social responsiveness involves the detection of and responses to stakeholder issues by public affairs specialists and other organizational agents charged with external affairs management. Influenced by the work of Ackerman and Bauer (1975), this research focuses on the behavioral patterns and tools that enable firms to respond to social concerns. Managerial in tone and quintessentially pragmatic, inquiry into responsiveness examines company procedures (social auditing and social scanning techniques, for example) as the means by which organizations can react to or anticipate social expectations, many of which are embodied in public policy as indications of important community values (Preston and Post 1975). Compared to responsibility, responsiveness is more forward looking, action oriented, and malleable, because it is based on the premise that corporations have the capacity to anticipate and adapt to environmental factors. It is this capacity that makes it important to understand the internal decision processes that make responsible corporate social performance possible (Swanson 1995). Responsiveness and responsibility are interrelated in that responsiveness can be shaped or triggered by stakeholder expectations of business responsibilities, some of which were described earlier. Another way to think about this relationship is that responsibility is marked by the moral overtones of social obligations, whereas responsiveness exemplifies a "how to" mentality (Frederick 1987). To summarize, responsiveness provides the means for responsible corporate performance, understood as beneficial social impacts.

In terms of ideal typing, Swanson's (1999; 2008) two heuristics of value-myopic and value-receptive discovery leadership, described next, do not represent actual leaders of specific organizations. Nor do they constitute full-fledged theories. Rather, they are systems of pure logic that can be used as contrasting points of reference for theory development that incorporates the executive mindset as a driver of ethical competence in the pursuit of responsible social performance. Since ideal types can be used to incorporate the individual, organizational, and societal levels of analysis, this form of modeling is used to personify executive leadership in terms of organizational dynamics and societal impacts. Two vastly different models of leadership are implied. On the one hand, an executive's failure to recognize the importance of values in decision making, referred to as *value myopia,* connotes an organization that will systematically neglect social concerns. In contrast, an executive's ability to be receptive to values, referred to as *discovery leadership,* suggests an organization capable of attuning to social concerns. Put differently, discovery points to the potential that executives have to lead their firms in a quest for responsible social performance, portrayed as value attunement. In reality, of course, organizations can be expected to exhibit degrees of neglect and attunement, just as executive decision making can be viewed on a continuum between value myopia and value receptivity.

Before the potential of value attunement is detailed, its antithesis—neglectful social performance—is given.

Value-Myopic Leadership: The Inevitability of Neglectful Social Performance

The overarching proposition in the case of myopic leadership is that when executive managers exhibit myopia by ignoring, suppressing, or denying the role of values in their decisions, then whole organizations will eventually lose touch with stakeholder expectations of responsibility. These value-based expectations are often articulated in the language of rights and justice such as calls for firms to respect consumers' right to safety and provide just compensation when defective products cause harm. Figure 4.1 illustrates how value myopia and organizational neglect go hand in hand, given the mediating effects of two fundamental aspects of organizational life—the formal chain-of-command structure and the informal culture.

The logic of this model is as follows: Executives who exhibit myopia use formal and informal means (either consciously or unconsciously) to encourage other employees to follow suit and suppress an awareness of value information in decision processes. As Figure 4.1 shows, this dynamic gets played out in the formal (hierarchical) and informal (cultural) organization. In terms of the formal organization, executives can promote organizational value myopia by using their official authority to set a narrow range for employee decision making along the chain of command. Practically speaking, this means that executives discourage employees from including information about stakeholder value-based expectations in official reports, memos, agendas, and other feedback mechanisms. It also means that annual performance reviews are not structured to reward employees for incorporating values in their decisions. Therefore, promotions will go to those who imitate or go along with myopia. Over time, the range of discretion for subordinate decision making gets aligned with the narrow value premises set on the higher level of administration (Simon 1957). Adapting Weick's (1969) terminology, the variety of value information in the environment gets reduced as subordinates select, retain, and enact the narrow mindset of the executive.

Figure 4.1   **Executive Value Myopia and the Inevitability of Neglectful Corporate Social Performance**

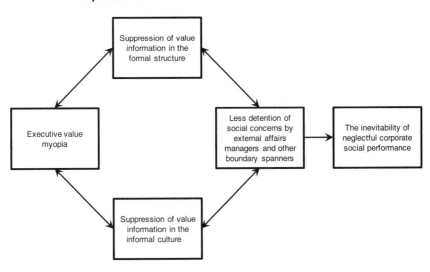

Source: Adapted from Orlitzky and Swanson (2006), based on Swanson (1999).

In terms of the informal organization, executives can also signal a tacit approval of myopia by using certain cultural mechanisms. For instance, they can mentor sycophants who convey only desired information to them and ignore or shun employees who give fuller accountings (see Schein 1992). They can also encourage stories, legends, and myths that celebrate myopia, such as elevating rhetoric that promotes a narrow focus on profits or managerial power prerogatives instead of a broader appreciation for social concerns.

The upshot of these mechanisms and signals in the formal and informal organization is that myopic decision making gets replicated among employees. When boundary-spanning employees, such as external affairs specialists, align with such shortsightedness, they fail to communicate important information about the social environment to senior managers and others in the organization. This undermines the very task they are supposed to carry out. The two-way arrows in Figure 4.1 show that the dynamic is self-perpetuating: Employees develop a reluctance to convey social concerns to the executive who signaled disinterest in the first place. Executive and organizational myopia inevitably align as the executive proclivity to downplay or ignore values gets played out as a chronic tendency for an organization to neglect social concerns (see Scott and Hart 1979). Eventually this sluggish or inert type of organization loses touch with its host environment, and neglectful corporate social performance becomes the norm.

To reiterate, myopia is an exaggerated model of pure logic that is designed to be a point of reference for theory development. To illustrate how neglect can be used as a benchmark for understanding corporate social performance, consider the longstanding controversy that surrounded Nestlé's sales of infant formula in global markets. For decades this firm faced social opposition to its marketing of infant formula in developing countries. Critics, including the World Health Organization, claimed that unsanitary water and low rates of literacy rendered the sale of the product unsafe in those countries, since the potential for sickness or death among infants was a distinct possibility (Sethi 1994). Eventually Nestlé became the target of intense pressure from stakeholders determined to force the firm to comply with an international code aimed at restricting such sales. This controversy may be seen as a clash between managers seeking profits or maintaining power prerogatives on the one hand and external stakeholders striving to protect the most vulnerable consumers on the other. It appears that Nestlé executives adopted a myopic mindset, referencing narrow company objectives to the detriment of broader community values, notably a respect for the sanctity of infant life (Swanson 1999).

In other words, Nestlé appeared to exhibit neglect instead of striving for attunement by engaging critics in a timely, constructive dialogue. By adhering rigidly to original plans, the top executive failed to direct public affairs specialists to detect early signs of the problem and identify other options. The controversy might have been averted in its early stages if executives had decided to treat the infant formula not as a food product but as a health care product, dispensing it by prescription through pharmacies in developing countries (Husted 2000). A precedent for this kind of reevaluation already existed in that pharmaceutical companies such as Abbott Laboratories had successfully responded to stakeholder concerns by treating infant formula as a prescription product where warranted by the risk of infant death (Austin and Kohn 1990). The external affairs specialists at Nestlé should have made this information known to the chief executive officer for full consideration. That Nestlé was initially unable to re-envision its identity as a food company suggests that executive management failed to take compelling stakeholder concerns into account. Such receptivity to stakeholder concerns is especially important when corporations operate globally in host countries where cultural conditions differ from those in the home country. In such cases, myopia may lead to charges of human rights violations and battles with critics that can tarnish a firm's reputation and call its legitimacy into question.

The bottom line is that neglect represents a violation of the social contract that imputes legitimacy to corporations—legitimacy that is earned and kept only by enhancing the greater good through the generation of social benefits value-attuned crisis management involves not only swift responsiveness and effective communication but also the kind of organizational learning that can help minimize or prevent future crises.

In this way, discovery leadership can serve as an exemplar for directing a firm to keep community interests in mind. According to Figure 4.2, this means creating value receptivity that continually informs decision processes in the formal and informal organization. This discovery orientation stands in marked contrast to the recalcitrant culture of neglect that fails to detect, much less act on, social concerns. British Petroleum has been accused of such recalcitrance by failing to detect and address safety problems and respond to community concerns sufficiently in the wake of the disastrous gas explosion and massive oil spill in the Gulf of Mexico in 2010 (Lustgarten 2012; Mauer 2010). A poll conducted by Gallup in 2012 suggests that the public has not forgiven British Petroleum for this disaster (Sauter and Frohlich 2012). As this case aptly demonstrates, corporate conduct involves huge stakes for society, which underscores the importance of ethical competence in executive leadership, modeled here as value-attentive decision making.

Some Implications for Research and Practice

To recap, discovery can serve as a point of reference for understanding how important it is for executives to be adept at value-inclusive decision making. Conversely, value myopia helps explain why social control, such as the extensive pressure exerted on Nestlé, becomes necessary in the first place. As a theoretical perspective, attunement typifies organizational decision making that is open-ended and dynamic instead of closed-ended and focused on static objectives to be measured at a single point in time. Admittedly, attunement is less developed than neglect (Swanson 1999). After all, it is easier to model a closed system than an open one; that is, it is easier to explain how organizations lose touch with society for want of relevant information about that society than it is to account for the plethora of information about the social environment that becomes available when organizations engage in a search-and-discovery mode. Given this state of affairs, receptivity can be viewed as a necessary but insufficient condition for ethical competence in business leadership. A better understanding of the possibilities for attunement awaits more research.

Notably, future research needs to account for the variety of values at stake in organizational decision making and instances where trade-offs seem apparent.[4] This inventory would necessarily include those values that are unlikely to advance attunement. For instance, power aggrandizing and empire building are managerial values that can come at the cost of economizing while decreasing employee morale and public trust (Frederick 1995; Jackall 1989). Moreover, stakeholder values themselves may come into conflict, as when activists want firms to purchase expensive safety equipment that, at least in the short term, may diminish the profits available for dividend payments to shareholders. To complicate matters, many stakeholders maintain that profits should not be gained at the cost of basic human rights. Such situations call for a complementary perspective on public policy that protects fundamental human rights while keeping the greater good in mind. Although striving for attunement may improve businesses' ability to self-regulate, it does not replace the necessity of social control as a means of refereeing value trade-offs and granting priority to the norms of civil society. In fact, public policy can strive to protect community interests while leveling the playing field for executives facing unavoidable tradeoffs between economizing and other important values.[5] The point is that a theory of attunement would be incomplete without explicating a role for public policy.

At the same time, attunement theorizing for international business cannot be tethered rigidly to the particulars of public policy. Transnational corporations increasingly operate in global environments where rules for business lack uniformity (Windsor 2006). Faced with inevitable ethical dilemmas, discovery executives may seek to work voluntarily with public interest groups as well as other firms to establish acceptable norms of conduct, such as those crafted by the Fair Labor Association and Council on Economic Priorities that target humane working conditions in developing countries. Similarly, Social Accountability International strives to improve working conditions by prohibiting child labor, discrimination, abusive discipline, and forced labor and protecting workers' freedom of association, collective bargaining rights, and compensation (Carroll and Buchholtz 2006). Indeed, that the Academy of Management has collaborated with the United Nations Global Compact to explore the use of management knowledge to lead positive change worldwide underscores the role top managers can have in driving responsible social performance in global markets where protections of human rights are inadequate (see AoM 2006). Future research on the attunement prototype should track such developments in order to ascertain value-based emerging standards for international business and the role that executive managers can play in shaping and responding to them, keeping in mind that voluntary codes of ethical conduct are meaningful only to the extent that executives strive actively and openly to enforce them. That said, corporate officers have reported that codes of ethics can yield several benefits, including legal protection, increased company loyalty, reductions in briberies and kickbacks, improved product quality, increased productivity, and enhanced consumer goodwill (ERC 1990).

Using discovery as a benchmark for responsible leadership has many implications for practice. In terms of hiring, boards could screen executive candidates for value receptivity, bearing in mind that one survey designed to tap this construct found that those executives who reported a favorable attitude toward values also scored high on a personality trait that denotes an individual's inclination to be cooperative, friendly, altruistic, tender-minded, and trusting (Orlitzky, Swanson, and Quartermaine 2006). This finding suggests that it is important for top managers to consider others in decision making—a capability that might be measured by testing for their level of moral reasoning (Weber and Green 1993). Another board-level initiative could be to establish committees that reflect a focus on social responsibility, including crisis management, public affairs, and employee relations. As part of this effort, a permanent ombudsperson could report to the board so that stakeholder concerns have a legitimate and fair hearing in the absence of direct representation (Ray 2005). Executive compensation should then be designed to reward the chief executive for overseeing and improving such practices. The board also should ensure that the company's code of ethics is up to date and that executive pay is tied to advancing it in tangible ways. Flattening organizational structure could be another initiative to improve corporate social performance, since large bureaucratic organizations with tall chain-of-command structures tend to produce decision making that is slow to react to novel information (Frederick 1995; Jackall 1989). The corollary is that attuned responsiveness may prove more likely in organizations with flatter structures (Swanson 1999; see also Halal 1994), a possibility that awaits further research.

Boards of directors may also want to consider the educational backgrounds of executive candidates. There is some evidence that value myopia increases with the amount of business coursework taken (AISIB 2002; Orlitzky, Swanson, and Quartermaine 2006). By implication, it may be wise to screen executive candidates for educational backgrounds that include coursework in business ethics or corporate social responsibility. Because such courses constitute a distinct minority in the business school curriculum (Willen 2004), those executives with strong educational training in these subjects might possess a distinct advantage in directing their firms toward attuned social performance.

Finally, given the theme of this book, it is relevant to point out that the advantages of discovery leadership should hold for public service administrators, too. The ideal of a constructive partnership between business and society calls for a discovery mindset in both sectors. Although the missions of private and public sectors are distinct, a necessary condition for ethical competence in leadership in both realms can be understood as the ability of executives and administrators to recognize constructive social values and encourage other employees to do the same. Similar to private-sector firms, public service organizations need to be responsive to constituents' concerns rather than break faith with their social contract by succumbing to the inertia of myopia and neglect. Since avoiding such inertia depends on the effective and efficient communication of value information in decision processes, flattening hierarchical structures in public service organizations may enhance value-informed decision making, just as it is expected to do in business counterparts; so, too, might compensating public service administrators for their ability to create and manage attuned organizations. According to discovery theorizing, public service leaders should not only invoke value-based mission statements and codes of ethics but model value receptivity in their actions as well. Education aimed at developing such competence requires coursework that conveys the importance of value receptivity and the mechanisms for creating and sustaining an organization capable of socially attuned responsiveness.

Conclusion

This chapter has portrayed value-discovery decision making as a necessary condition for ethical competence in business leadership. Discovery leadership means that an executive is willing to factor values into his or her decisions while encouraging other employees to do the same. Consequently, an organization is rendered more capable of recognizing and responding to value-based social expectations of responsible conduct.

Notes

1. This chapter is informed by and extends the author's previous research on socially responsible business leadership (see especially Swanson 1995, 1999, 2008). The 1999 article was awarded "Best Article in Business and Society" in 2001 by the International Association for Business and Society in association with *California Management Review.*

2. Technically, there is a difference between ethics and values. The first refers to philosophical ideas regarding right and wrong conduct (e.g., deontology, utilitarianism, rights-based ethics) and the second to social science understandings of what people prize or hold dear (e.g., security, safety, teamwork). The reason this distinction is not made in this chapter is because the difference between myopia and receptivity hinges on the executive's ability to factor information about social concerns into his decisions. These concerns amount to value preferences that are also expressed in the language of ethics. For instance, when consumers claim the right to safe products, they are essentially indicating that they value safety.

3. A fuller accounting of corporate social performance models is given in Swanson (1995). These static classifications of business and society topics (corporate social responsibility, corporate social responsiveness, and corporate social performance) include those by Carroll (1979), Sethi (1975), Wartick and Cochran (1985), and

Wood (1991). For a longitudinal perspective on corporate social performance topics, see Frederick (1987).

4. Frederick's (1995) theory of business values could be used to extend attunement theorizing as he lays out three major value systems relevant to business and also accounts for the variety of values that can be held by individual managers, employees, and external stakeholders.

5. A cautionary note is that corporations in the United States increasingly exert influence on government in the form of political advocacy, which includes lobbying legislators and contributing financially to their election campaigns (Carroll and Buchholtz 2006). Moreover, in light of the Citizens United v. Federal Trade Commission U.S. Supreme Court decision in 2010, the government may not ban political spending by corporations in candidate elections (Liptak 2010). The danger is that such political advocacy can result in legislation that favors narrow business interests at the expense of the greater good. In terms of corporate social performance, it is important to keep in mind that responsibility does not simply mean that corporations respond to the laws that they help shape (Frederick 1987).

References

Abrams, F. 1951. Management's responsibilities in a complex world. *Harvard Business Review* (May): 29–34.

Academy of Management (AoM). 2006. AoM + UN: Business as an agent of world benefit. *IMD Newsletter* (June): 16. http://division.aomonline.org/im/assets/Newsletters/AOM_JUN06.pdf.

Ackerman, R.W., and R.A. Bauer. 1975. *The Social Challenge to Business*. Cambridge, MA: Harvard University Press.

Aspen Initiative for Social Innovation Through Business (AISIB). 2002. *Where Will They Lead? MBA Student Attitudes About Business & Society*. New York: Aspen ISIB.

Austin, J.E., and T.O. Kohn. 1990. *Strategic Management in Developing Countries: Case Studies*. New York: Free Press.

Bailey, K.D. 1994. *Typologies and Taxonomies*. Belmont, CA: Sage.

Berg, I., and M.N. Zald. 1978. Business and society. *Annual Review of Sociology* 4: 115–143.

Carroll, A.B. 1979. A three-dimensional model of corporate social performance. *Academy of Management Review* 4: 497–505.

Carroll, A.B., and A.K. Buchholtz. 2006. *Business & Society: Ethics and Stakeholder Management*. Mason, OH: Thomson South-Western.

Collins, D. 1988. Adam Smith's social contract: The proper role of individual liberty and government intervention in the 18th century. *Business & Professional Ethics Journal* 7: 120–146.

Committee for Economic Development (CED), Research and Policy Committee. 1971. *Social Responsibilities of Business Corporations: A Statement on National Policy*. New York: Committee for Economic Development.

Corporate Responsibility Magazine. 2011. *Corporate Responsibility's* 100 best corporate citizens listing—Mission: Advancing accountability. www.thecro.com/files/CR%20Magazine%20Corporate%20Citizen%20Methodology%202011.pdf (accessed April 29, 2011).

Davis, K. 1964. The public role of management. Evolving concepts in management. Proceedings of the 24th Annual Academy of Management, Chicago, IL.

Donaldson, T. 1989. *The Ethics of International Business*. New York: Oxford University Press.

Doomen, J. 2005. Smith's analysis of human actions. *Ethic@: An International Journal for Moral Philosophy* 4(2): 111–122.

Drucker, P.F. 1968. *The Age of Discontinuity: Guidelines to Our Changing Society*. New York: Harper & Row.

Epstein, E.M. 1987. The corporate social policy process: Beyond business ethics, corporate social responsibility, and corporate social responsiveness. *California Management Review* 29: 99–114.

Ethics Resource Center (ERC). 1990. *Creating a Workable Company Code of Ethics*. Washington, DC: Ethics Resource Center.

Fombrun, C.J. 1996. *Reputation: Realizing Value from the Corporate Image*. Boston: Harvard Business School Press.

Frederick, W.C. 1987. Theories of corporate social performance. In *Business and Society: Dimensions of Conflict and Cooperation*, ed. S.P. Sethi and C. Falbe, 142–161. New York: Lexington Books.

———. 1995. *Values, Nature, and Culture in the American Corporation*. New York: Oxford University Press.

———. 2006. *Corporation, Be Good! The Story of Corporate Social Responsibility*. Indianapolis, IN: Dog Ear Publishing.

Freeman, R.E. 1984. *Strategic Management: A Stakeholder Approach*. Marshfield, MA: Pitman.

Friedman, M. 1970. The social responsibility of business is to increase its profits. *New York Times Magazine,* September 13, pp. 33, 122–126.

Grover, L.P. 2003. Whistleblowers: A rare breed. *Strategic Finance* (August): 51–53.

Halal, W.H. 1994. From hierarchy to enterprise: Internal markets are the new foundation of management. *Academy of Management Executive* 8: 559–565.

Husted, B. 2000. A contingency theory of corporate social performance. *Business & Society* 39: 24–48.

Jackall, R. 1989. *Moral Mazes: The World of Corporate Managers*. New York: Oxford University Press.

Jones, T.M. 1983. An integrative framework for research in business and society: A step toward the elusive paradigm? *Academy of Management Review* 8: 559–564.

Liptak, A. 2010. Justices, 5–4, reject corporate spending limit. The *New York Times*, January 21. http://www.nytimes.com/2010/01/22/us/politics/22scotus.html?pagewanted=all (accessed September 1, 2012).

Lustgarten, A. 2012. A stain that won't wash away. Editorial. The *New York Times,* April 19. http://www.nytimes.com/2012/04/20/opinion/a-stain-that-wont-wash-away.html?pagewanted=all (accessed September 1, 2012).

Mauer, R. 2010. BP has a history of safety failures. *Anchorage Daily News,* May 8. http://www.adn.com/2010/05/08/1269786/bp-has-a-history-of-safety-faults.html (accessed May 3, 2011).

Mitroff, I., with G. Anagnos. 2001. *Managing Crises Before They Happen: What Every Executive and Manager Needs to Know About Crisis Management*. New York: AMACOM.

Narveson, J. 2008. Social contract theory. In *Encyclopedia of Business Ethics and Society*, ed. R.W. Kolb, 1948–1955. Thousand Oaks, CA: Sage.

Near, J.P., M.P. Miceli, and T.C. Jensen. 1983. *Variables Associated with the Whistle-Blowing Process*. Working Paper Series 83–11, 5. Columbus: Ohio State University, College of Administrative Sciences.

Orlitzky, M., and J.D. Benjamin. 2001. Corporate social performance and firm risk: A meta-analytic review. *Business & Society* 40: 369–396.

Orlitzky, M., F.L. Schmidt, and S.L. Rynes. 2003. Corporate social and financial performance: A meta-analysis. *Organization Studies* 24: 403–441.

Orlitzky, M., and D.L. Swanson. 2006. Socially responsible human resource management: Charting new territory. In *Human Resource Management Ethics*, ed. J.R. Deckop, 13–31. Greenwich, CT: Information Age Publishing.

———. 2008. *Toward Integrative Corporate Citizenship: Research Advances in Corporate Social Performance*. London: Palgrave Macmillan.

Orlitzky, M., D.L. Swanson, and L.K. Quartermaine. 2006. Normative myopia, executives' personality, and preference for pay dispersion: Toward implications for corporate social performance. *Business & Society* 45: 149–177.

Perrow, C. 1986. *Complex Organizations: A Critical Essay,* 3d ed. New York: Random House.

Porter, M.E., and M.R. Kramer. 2002. The competitive advantage of corporate philanthropy. *Harvard Business Review* (December): 57–68.

Posner, B., and W.H. Schmidt. 1984. Values and the American manager: An update. *California Management Review* (Spring): 202–216.

Preston, L.E., and J.E. Post. 1975. *Private Management and Public Policy*. Englewood Cliffs, NJ: Prentice Hall.

Ray, D.M. 2005. Corporate boards and corporate democracy. *Journal of Corporate Citizenship* 20: 93–105.

Saiia, D.H., A.B. Carroll, and A.K. Buchholtz. 2003. Philanthropy as strategy: When corporate charity "begins at home." *Business & Society* 42: 169–201.

Sauter, M. G. and T. C. Frohlich. 2012. America's most hated industries. *MarketWatch*, April 30. http://articles.marketwatch.com/2012-08-30/industries/33493247_1_industries-negative-image-positive-response (access September 1, 2012).

Schein, E.H. 1992. *Organizational Culture and Leadership,* 2d ed. San Francisco: Jossey-Bass.

Scott, W.G., and D.K. Hart. 1979. *Organizational America*. Boston: Houghton Mifflin.

Selznick, P. 1957. *Leadership in Administration*. New York: Harper & Row.

Sethi, S.P. 1975. Dimensions of corporate social performance: An analytical framework. *California Management Review* 17(3): 58–64.

———. 1994. *Multinational Corporations and the Impact of Public Advocacy on Corporate Strategy: Nestlé and the Infant Formula Controversy*. Norwell, MA: Kluwer.

Simon, H. 1957. *Administrative Behavior*. New York: Macmillan.

Swanson, D.L. 1995. Addressing a theoretical problem by reorienting the corporate social performance model. *Academy of Management Review* 20: 43–64.

———. 1999. Toward an integrative theory of business and society: A research strategy for corporate social performance. *Academy of Management Review* 24: 506–521.

———. 2008. Top managers as drivers for corporate social responsibility. In *The Oxford Handbook of Corporate Social Responsibility*, ed. A. Crane et al., 227–248. Oxford: Oxford University Press.

Swanson, D.L., and R.J. Paul. 2002–2003. Violations of ethical expectations: The toxicity of organizational pain and some remedies. *Journal of Individual Employment Rights* 10: 25–39.

Turban, D.B., and D.W. Greening. 1997. Corporate social performance and organizational attractiveness to prospective employees. *Academy of Management Journal* 40: 658–673.

Waddock, S. 2002. *Leading Corporate Citizens: Vision, Values, Value Added.* New York: McGraw-Hill.

Wartick, S., and P. Cochran. 1985. The evolution of the corporate social performance model. *Academy of Management Review* 10: 758–769.

Weber, J., and S. Green. 1993. Principled moral reasoning: Is it a viable approach to promote ethical integrity? *Journal of Business Ethics* 10: 325–333.

Weber, M. 1922/1947. *The Theory of Social and Economic Organization.* Trans. A.H. Henderson and T. Parsons. New York: Oxford University Press.

Weick, K.E. 1969. *The Social Psychology of Organizing.* Reading, MA: Addison-Wesley.

Willen, L. 2004. Kellogg denies guilt as b-schools evade alumni lapses. *Bloomberg,* March 8. http://www.cba.ksu.edu/archives/41/kellogg.pdf (accessed July 27, 2012).

Windsor, D. 2006. Corporate social responsibility: Three key approaches. *Journal of Management Studies* 43: 93–114.

Wood, D. 1991. Corporate social performance revisited. *Academy of Management Review* 16: 691–718.

Part II

Pedagogical Approaches and Methods to Achieve Ethical Competence

While the pursuit of ethical competence can lead to many different paths, there is one that holds out considerable promise—formal education, typically at the graduate level, in social work, business, law, public administration, and other fields. No generic course of study straddles professional fields' study and practice, yet there is reason to believe that certain commonalities exist, including (1) ethical awareness and sensitivity, (2) analytical reasoning, (3) knowledge of ethical thought, and (4) practice/experience that often involves immersion in cases that approximate reality.

In Chapter 5, Richard M. Jacobs explores an integrated pedagogical method that provides a systematic learning experience for students enrolled in a graduate program that awards a master's degree in public administration (MPA). He describes in considerable depth just how important it is for an instructor to foster a classroom culture that introduces normative foundations of ethical thought. He notes that public administration students, perhaps much like those who study business management or social work, often come to ethics courses motivated to learn about concrete matters—developing budgets, supervising others, building teams, analyzing problems, and more. Few, however, are grounded in knowledge of ethical thought or normative frameworks such as virtue theory and consequentialism or deontological thought involving duty and/or principle. Thus the instructor is challenged with the following question: How can I cultivate a classroom culture wherein students will learn to appreciate the normative foundations of ethical thought that will prove relevant for public administration practice? Jacobs contends that Aristotle actually formulated a model that does this—a "practical" mindset. That is, ethical decision making integrates two elements: (1) theories about the good, and (2) what actually works in practice. According to Jacobs, "success in teaching ethics" follows if instructors model for their students how to make "practical decisions represent[ing] a prudent mixture of theory and skill," in much the same way that "highly regarded physicians, lawyers, engineers, artists, teacher and, yes, public administrators, make decisions."

To foster the development of this "practical" mindset, Jacobs suggests that instructors assign "mini-case" presentations, requiring students to apply ethical theory to the dilemmas that arise in the workplace and then formulate solutions to those dilemmas. This integrated methodological approach connects directly with one definition of ethical competence offered in Chapter 1 (Menzel 2010, 18). According to this definition, ethical competence requires:

1. a commitment to high standards of personal and professional behavior;
2. the knowledge of relevant ethics codes and laws;
3. a refined capacity to engage in ethical reasoning when confronted with challenging ethical situations;
4. the ability to identify and act on public service ethics and values; and
5. the competence to promote ethical practices and behaviors in public agencies and organizations.

For those students who possess little or no knowledge of ethical thought or normative frameworks, Jacobs believes this integrated pedagogical approach "prepares [them] for the journey of continuous learning that will constitute their practice of public administration ethics." A tall order? Perhaps. But this approach holds out considerable promise, as instructors intentionally assist students in developing greater ethical competence. The goal is for students to be able to resolve new dilemmas that emerge as they immerse themselves in professional practice. Equally important from Jacobs's perspective, students will begin to stand for something—namely, the ethical principles that support the difficult and often complicated leadership decisions that are surely ahead.

Carole L. Jurkiewicz, the author of Chapter 6, outlines a different yet complementary approach to pedagogy that can advance ethical competence for public service leadership. Ethical competence, she asserts, is rooted in one's level of moral development, moderated by pedagogical influence. Drawing on the pioneering work of Lawrence Kohlberg's stages of moral development and ethical reasoning, she contends that "we can move forward in defining behavioral elements that constitute observable ethical competence."

Kohlberg's model contains six stages, with stages four (Social System and Conscience), five (Social Contract and Individual Rights), and six (Universal Ethical Principles) containing the qualities intrinsic to ethical reasoning that comports with the foundational principles of public service ethics. The sixth stage, however, is so uncommon in a populace that "it is not realistic to expect this level of ethicality in establishing a competence framework for public administrators." Stages four and five, then, become the focal point of her pedagogical framework.

The next step in building a framework is the identification of five key factors in educating for ethical competence. These factors include:

1. an understanding of moral philosophy and moral arguments.
2. the ability to distinguish ethical issues separate from a management or resource issue.
3. the ability to logically reason in seeking a solution to ethical problems.
4. an understanding of one's own ethical framework and value system, and the recognition that others may not share that system.
5. the ability to perform ethically in an environment where pressures to do otherwise may be considerable.

Each factor is then linked to an assessment measure such as a D.I.T. (Defining Issues Test) score, a case study in testing, or some other measure. The author further specifies her pedagogical framework by providing a matrix that shows how topics that an ethics course might encompass are linked to one of the five competence factors.

Jurkiewicz recognizes that the pursuit of ethical competence does not take place in a vacuum but is interconnected with one's organizational environment. Leaders establish a climate in which ethical values are salient or, all too often, missing. Thus the strength of the ethical climate can be pointed to as a surrogate indicator of the leader's ethical competence. She identifies a set of organizational characteristics (e.g., transparency, rewards, trust) that define the nature of the organizational culture and, in turn, the "ethical competence of the administrator."

"Ethical competence can be defined, taught, and measured," she states plainly and vigorously—noting that much empirical research over the past two decades has so demonstrated. While a solid foundation has been put into place for explicating pedagogical measures, much more work remains to be done. Jurkiewicz offers readers "a starting place from which [they] can move forward."

5

Developing Ethical Competence
An Integrated Pedagogical Method

Richard M. Jacobs

This volume introduces into discussion the concept of *ethical competence* with the goal of developing it in students pursuing college degrees in public affairs and administration. Whether ethical competence exists and can be taught are substantive issues yet to be resolved. But, assuming that ethical competence does exist, this chapter describes a method for teaching it, an "integrated pedagogical method" constructed upon Menzel's (2010) five attributes of ethical competence. Instructors can implement or adapt this method during the first half of a public administration ethics course to cultivate a classroom culture wherein students acquire knowledge of the foundations of public administration ethics and begin to incorporate attributes of ethical competence in their own worldviews. This formation of mind and character prepares students to analyze and resolve case studies during the second half of the course. Case study experience, in turn, will further solidify those foundations, providing students multiple opportunities to exemplify the attributes of ethical competence as they endeavor to resolve some complicated dilemmas associated with public administration practice.

This chapter first describes the classroom culture in which this method unfolds, providing ideas about and examples of how instructors might navigate the challenges they will inevitably encounter and, in doing so, introduce students to the normative foundations of ethical thought. The chapter then describes four classroom activities instructors can implement to inculcate greater cognitive complexity in students as they relate the normative foundations of ethical thought to some straightforward dilemmas arising in their workplaces. The discussion closes by identifying three markers of success offering evidence that students are prepared to engage profitably in case study analysis.

More substantively, it is in this classroom culture and through these activities and projects that those who teach public administration ethics challenge their students to reflect upon the attributes of ethical competence. To the degree these attributes influence a student's ability to deliberate and then formulate principled resolutions to the cases analyzed, they may very well be taking root in each student's character. Yet, as laudable a pedagogical achievement as that may be, all of that effort is preparatory. After all, the long-term goal is that students will continue to evidence ethical competence in their professional practice—years and decades after having completed the course—as they think ethically, make ethical decisions, and build organizational cultures that encourage their followers to be characterized by ethical competence.

Cultivating a Classroom Culture That Emphasizes Ethical Competence

I began formulating this integrated pedagogical method more than 20 years ago, when I was asked to develop and teach a graduate leadership ethics course for the Master of Public Administration (MPA) program at Villanova University. I was asked to undertake this challenge because I had studied philosophy during my undergraduate years and, at the time, was teaching a well-regarded graduate course in the philosophy of education.

As Aristotle observed in the *Nicomachean Ethics* (in *The Pocket Aristotle,* 1958 ed.; his treatise on cultivating happiness through good and right living), ethics is the most practical of philosophical endeavors. I began formulating this new course by considering the very practical matter of outcomes—the attributes of character—I hoped would evidence themselves in students as the course unfolded. These outcomes generally included behaviors like: (1) a commitment to high standards of personal and professional behavior; (2) the knowledge of relevant ethics codes and laws; (3) a capacity to engage in ethical reasoning when confronted with challenging ethical situations; (4) the ability to identify and act on public service ethics and values; and (5) the competence to promote ethical practices and behaviors in public agencies and organizations. It took 18 years, but I was pleased to read that Menzel had put words to my hoped-for behavioral outcomes in his book *Ethics Moments in Government* (2010, 18).

One place where public administrators should learn about, develop, and exhibit these attributes of character is in public administration classrooms. This idea led me to consider a second practical matter: the culture of the classroom in which this course would be taught. While the culture of this classroom is neither that of the ivory tower nor of the workplace, it is here that ivory tower theories and workplace realities collide. The culture of this classroom, then, would resemble more of a bumper-car collision course of conflicting principles than an intercity autobahn leading students from "here" to "there" as quickly and efficiently as possible.

In the MPA curriculum, nowhere should this collision of ideas evidence itself more so than in a semester-long public administration ethics course, where theories about the "good" collide with practical ideas about "what works." If only because my previous experience with graduate students seeking administration certificates and licenses indicated they were interested in concrete solutions and traversing their courses and programs via that autobahn, I knew the challenge would involve negotiating these collisions. To that end, the classroom culture I would cultivate needed to encourage students to embrace and allow those attributes of ethical competence to transform their minds and character—that is, their thoughts and conduct.

Formulating an approach to achieve this goal required considering a third practical matter: to return to the library to research—"to search anew"—the works of two ancient philosophers, Aristotle and his teacher, Plato. In this "new" reading of their speculations, Aristotle and Plato offered three suggestions to ponder, test, and assess. The suggestions included: (1) implementing a decision-making process that integrates the theoretical and the technical; (2) persisting in questioning what students assert are the "best" solutions; and (3) assisting students in knowing better what they do not know.

Possessing the comfort afforded by retrospective analysis, the advice these two ancient philosophers suggested early in the planning process demonstrated once again, but in an entirely different context and purpose, their incalculable wisdom. The tasks they described have prepared students during the first half of the course for their study of the normative foundations of ethical thought, as well as for the application of these foundations to the practice of public administration ethics. More important, these tasks have also prepared students well to engage in careful analysis and resolution of the ethical dilemmas presented in case studies during the second half of the course.

For the purposes of this volume, attending to these practical matters appears to have led to two outcomes. First, the theoretical and practical foundation supporting the attributes of character associated with ethical competence (Menzel 2010, 18) has been strengthened. Second, students are prepared to enter their chosen profession "ethically competent to provide the leadership needed to advance the public interest" (Cooper and Menzel 2013, p. 3). And, although I hope each semester that my students will continue to evidence ethical competence long after completing the course, that was not something I intended when designing the course, nor did I envision it as part of my job description. No, that is a matter of their personal commitment to demonstrate ethical competence by providing ethical leadership as public administrators and building organizational cultures whose members are also ethically competent.

Let's examine those three suggestions, how I have implemented them to cultivate a classroom culture wherein each student's mind and character is formed, and some evidence indicating how this integrated pedagogical method has achieved the goals for which it was designed.

Implement a Decision-Making Process That Integrates the Theoretical with the Technical

Anecdotal evidence gleaned over the years through teaching leadership ethics and conversing with colleagues who teach public administration courses at a number of universities indicates that many students come to these courses with high expectations. In particular, they expect to learn about concrete matters—for instance, how to avoid differences of opinion and seemingly intractable arguments about what must be done—which they ascribe to successful public administration practice. This decidedly utilitarian objective makes great sense because, after all, a student's primary goal is to learn how to be a successful professional!

This objective presents a particular challenge to those who teach public administration ethics, a challenge best stated in the form of a question: What classroom culture will enable students to appreciate the normative foundations of ethical thought, as well as their relationship to public administration practice, so they are well prepared to analyze case studies? While success requires introducing students to the normative foundations of ethical thought, it also requires strengthening each student's ability to reason ethically. Yet, again, all of this is preparatory, because it will be as each student reasons ethically and then acts ethically that he will provide evidence of those attributes of character associated with ethical competence (Menzel 2010, 18).

Aristotle (384–322 B.C.E.) understood well the general culture associated with classrooms devoted to education in the professions and the idiosyncratic challenges this culture presents to teachers and students. Assigning value to the acquisition of abstract theory *and* technical skill, Aristotle (*Nicomachean Ethics*, in *The Pocket Aristotle,* 1958 ed.) formulated a normative decision-making model that integrates both. It also provides a solid foundation that not only allows students to learn about successful professional practice but also allows their characters to be shaped through what they are learning. To this end, Aristotle modeled for those who teach public administration ethics a "practical" or "practice-oriented" mindset that would serve as a model for their students. After all, a leadership ethics course should introduce students to the theoretical foundations of public administration ethics not simply for the sake of knowing theory but, more substantively, for the sake of providing ethical leadership as public administrators. The goal is for them to think ethically, not simply to think about ethics.

For Aristotle, an ethical decision is one that is "practical," the result of a

Figure 5.1   **Aristotle's Model of Ethical Decision Making**

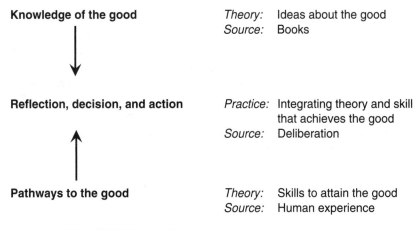

Knowledge of the good	*Theory:*	Ideas about the good
	Source:	Books
Reflection, decision, and action	*Practice:*	Integrating theory and skill that achieves the good
	Source:	Deliberation
Pathways to the good	*Theory:*	Skills to attain the good
	Source:	Human experience

Source: Ethics 1958, II.2, p. 183.

deliberative process that integrates theories about the good, as those abstractions can be contemplated, and what actually works in practice, as those concrete techniques and skills can be learned (see Figure 5.1). This ability to make practical decisions resembles more the stuff of exquisite craftsmanship in a workshop than of careful experimentation in a laboratory and requires great persistence, patience, and practice to develop (Sennett 2008). Success in teaching ethics evidences itself, then, as students learn by observing and responding to the role model provided by the teacher, whose practical decisions represent a prudent mixture of theory and skill. This method is similar to how highly regarded physicians, lawyers, engineers, artists, and, yes, public administrators, make decisions. Again, students are not being prepared for the ideal world but for the world of practice, where public service agencies hopefully are moving toward the ideal and away from its opposite.

More significantly, Aristotle believed success in modeling this practical mindset becomes apparent as students select courses of conduct proceeding "from a firm and unchangeable character" (II.4.187). That is, Aristotle's model was aimed not only at forming each student's mind but also at its taking root in, influencing, and shaping each student's character.

During a public administration ethics course, success can be measured as students learn to make, implement, take personal responsibility for, and then capably defend principled decisions. However, this conduct should also evidence itself one day in their practice as public administrators, extending the lessons first learned when this decision-making process was introduced in the public administration ethics course in the form of some of the typical dilemmas of professional practice.

This pedagogical achievement—the formation of the student's mind *and* character—provides the raíson d'être for a public administration ethics course. Students will learn about ethics and ethical theory, puzzle over questions and probable outcomes, and capably debate and defend solutions proposed. As they identify ethical conduct, begin considering how to act ethically, and deliberate about how they might promote ethical practices and behaviors in public agencies, all of this learning will be reflected in tangible outcomes, particularly as students exhibit those attributes of character associated with ethical competence (Menzel 2010, 18). The goal, then, is for students to develop an internal locus of ethical control that is informed by ethical theory rather than to rely on an external locus of control that is shaped by the force of laws and professional codes of conduct. After all, the aphorism states, "Codes are for criminals and are aimed at compliance." To which it could be added for a public administration ethics course, "Principles are for professionals and are aimed at personal responsibility."

At the same time, all of this learning is for a purpose that ultimately will be assessed one day in the future, long after students complete a public administration ethics course and MPA program. These graduates should distinguish themselves as public administrators whose leadership is informed by professional competence as they capably navigate the organizational terrain, and especially as they competently apply theories of organization, human resources, politics and policy, fiscal affairs, and the like. Even more important, these graduates should display ethical competence, serving as role models who construct organizational cultures that encourage and support ethical competence on the part of their followers.

Temptations to Avoid

To a cultivate a classroom culture and to teach students how they might create an organizational culture promoting these outcomes, Aristotle's model of ethical decision making raises two temptations that public administration ethics course instructors must avoid or surmount.

The first temptation is to introduce students to ethical theory without applying it to public administration practice. While the study of the former is important because students must possess a knowledge base upon which to render principled judgments, this strictly intellectual approach does not encourage students to develop their minds to apply ethical theory in actual practice or to judge whether a theory is germane for resolving the dilemma they are confronting. After all, graduating with a 4.0 GPA from Harvard Medical School does not guarantee that a neophyte physician is a competent neurologist or cardiologist. Nor does graduating with a 4.0 GPA from Vanderbilt's Peabody College of Education and Human Development guarantee that a neophyte educator is a competent teacher, counselor, principal, or superintendent. Why, then, should graduating with a 4.0 GPA from an accredited MPA program guarantee that a neophyte public administrator is competent to fulfill the organizational—if not more so the ethical—responsibilities associated with his profession?

The second temptation is to focus strictly on practical matters—for example, "war stories." While these narratives provide real-life examples of the typical ethical dilemmas that students may confront in professional practice, and experience indicates that students very much enjoy hearing and discussing these stories, this strictly practice-oriented approach does not assist students in honing the intellectual powers they will need if they are to identify the subtle ethics-based principles that oftentimes are shrouded within dilemmas.

Having taught leadership ethics for more than two decades, I have learned that case study analysis should be preceded by both a thoughtful introduction to the ethical foundations of public administration and the application of those foundational elements to students' experiences of professional practice—for example, by relating how they have seen a particular ethical theory evidence itself in a public administrator for whom they have worked or are currently working. These preparatory steps must be taken *before* immersing the students in more in-depth case study analysis because they help sharpen the analytical skills students need if they are to perceive a dilemma, describe the problem, identify the salient ethical principles, identify alternatives and select one, and determine a state of resolution (Cooper 2012, 31).

During the first half of a public administration ethics course, adopting Aristotle's practical mindset and being careful to avoid or surmount these two temptations prepares those who teach public administration ethics to cultivate a classroom culture wherein students learn to integrate theory, technique, and practice. Instructors who follow this advice are better prepared to model ways of balancing theory and technique, making any necessary adjustments as the classroom culture evolves. Lastly, these instructors help students to clarify the foundations of public administration ethics during the second half of the course by applying them to public administration practice through the analysis and resolution of case studies.

For the purposes of this volume, while all of this intellectual and professional development represents a salutary pedagogical achievement, it is insufficient. Those who teach public administration ethics must also be aware that they are implementing Aristotle's normative decision-making process so that each student's character will be "firm and unchangeable" (II.4.187) when one is called upon in the actual public administration practice to resolve complex ethical dilemmas.

How, then, is an instructor to know that one's students are developing this firm and hopefully unchangeable character?

As each semester's leadership ethics course has unfolded, especially during the second half of the term, I see a "strength of character"—Menzel's five attributes of ethical competence (2010, 18)—exhibiting itself in the way students analyze and resolve the cases they are studying as well as in the way they capably defend their oftentimes conflicting resolutions in the "public square" of the classroom. It does take a bit of time for students to become comfortable in expressing their resolutions, and some require additional time to feel comfortable in using principles to defend their resolutions. In other words, as students develop greater familiarity with ethical theory and facility in discussing it, any initial reticence or hesitance gradually dissolves. This is especially true as the more reticent or hesitant students observe their peers engage the instructor as well as one another in thought-provoking discussions where there are no simple, straightforward solutions to a perplexing dilemma.

Persist in Questioning What Students Assert

When formulating the new leadership ethics course, my research also required returning to Aristotle's teacher, Plato (428–347 B.C.E.). In the *Meno*, an early dialogue by Plato (1981b), Socrates—in the role of teacher—persists in asking Meno—in the role of student—some rather challenging questions, personifying a pedagogical method—the *enlenchus*—that reinforces and strengthens the type of intellectual foundation upon which I could implement Aristotle's practical mindset.

This questioning is purposeful. Socrates's intention was to lead Meno to a rather discomforting discovery: Much of what his student presumed to know was much like the knowledge possessed by those Athenian leaders who, Socrates observed, "are no different from soothsayers and prophets. They too say many true things when inspired, but they have no knowledge of what they are saying" (Plato 1981b, 99c87). Learning, then, unfolds only after the teacher has freed the student's intellectual powers from what was constraining them, thus reinforcing and strengthening their ability to differentiate between what Socrates called a "correct" opinion and a "wrong" opinion.

For Socrates, a "correct" opinion is a "true" opinion, one that is supported by objective facts that withstand intense public scrutiny. A "wrong" opinion differs from a correct opinion in two ways, both of which are readily apparent to teachers.

First, *by response*. When challenged about one's correct opinion, a student will utilize the refined intellectual ability to examine objectively and critically the available evidence, endeavoring to judge more accurately what the truth may be. In contrast, when challenged about one's wrong opinion, another student will dogmatically reiterate one's beliefs, feelings, and myths or may be hesitant (or even stubbornly refuse) to enter into this collision course of ideas in the public square of the classroom.

Second, *by awareness*. When challenged about one's correct opinion, a student will evidence awareness that, because the truth is elusive, it is better to question and test what one believes *may* be true. In contrast, when challenged about one's wrong opinion, another student will fail to take into account the fact that truth sometimes is elusive. That is, human beings oftentimes do not possess all of the relevant facts supporting what they assume is true. As a result, human beings are prone to make erroneous decisions and are wrongly believed to support the misguided opinions that back up those decisions.

One important challenge Socrates illuminates through his interactions with Meno arises from the fact that students come to the classroom possessing a wide variety of opinions. Some of those opinions are informed and shaped by family members, peer groups, political parties, social groups, and religious organizations, as well as the culture's zeitgeist, to name but a few. Invoking Socrates's terminology, the problem fueling the challenge for teaching public administration ethics is that students have "tied down" (Plato 1981b) these opinions—whether they are correct or wrong is not relevant—and these opinions provide the foundation supporting their worldviews.

Taking a cue from Socrates, I envisioned cultivating a classroom culture in my leadership ethics course wherein students would voice, examine, and "untie" those opinions. The teacher-student interaction would unfold in a process that is similar to Yankelovich's (1991) seven-stage trajectory—beginning with awareness and ending with responsible judgment—through which public leaders successfully advance a political agenda to a unified public judgment. Using Socrates's *enlenchus*, persistence in questioning provides a tried-and-true method for testing those opinions as students struggle with ethical principles and relevant issues, deliberate about them, and formulate responsible judgments about what the truth *may* be.

Socrates also pointed out that even when his student possessed a correct opinion (as good as that was), this is problematic if his student has not tied down this correct opinion—that is, if Meno could not defend his opinion when challenged. Socrates noted that persistent questioning enables a teacher to assist this particular student—and presumably, the classroom of students once they all possess correct opinions—if they are to develop "knowledge." As Socrates said to Meno:

For true opinions, as long as they remain, are a fine thing and all they do is good, but they are not willing to remain long, and they escape from a [person's] mind, so that they are not worth much until one ties them down by [giving] an account of the reason why. . . . After they are tied down, in the first place they become knowledge, and then they remain in place. That is why knowledge is prized higher than correct opinion, and knowledge differs from correct opinion in being tied down. (Plato 1981b, 98a86)

Using this Socratic lens to reflect upon teaching leadership ethics, I have found many students coming to the first day of class having tied down three wrong opinions: omniscience, reductionism, and immediacy.

Omniscience

At the outset of the course, many students exude a high degree of self-confidence. For some, this confidence is due to the belief that they know more about ethics and ethical decision making than they actually do. What they possess and what fuels this self-confidence is a wrong opinion.

Persistently questioning this belief, it becomes readily apparent that some students feel threatened, their behavior calling to mind Winnicott's description about how people respond to organizational change by grasping hold of those "teddy bears" that have provided security and comfort for so long (1958, 229–242). Some of these students clutch their supposed omniscience with all of their might, quite literally, squeezing the life out of those poor teddy bears! But, persistently questioning their omniscience, students gradually do let go of it and grasp hold of the reasonable idea that there are other, perhaps equally valuable, perspectives for deliberating about these matters.

Persistent questioning also reveals other students who possess sound ethical principles, but do not yet know why those principles are worth defending. For example, some students are completely unaware of the weaknesses associated with their beliefs and, when questioned about these weaknesses, become frustrated. They are not quite sure how to defend what they believe is true because they do not know *why it is true*. Tenacity in persistent questioning has enabled these students to develop the knowledge needed to defend their principles.

One set of students must learn what a correct opinion is. Another set of students must learn to defend their correct opinions. Then, too, if every student is to develop ethical competence, both sets of students must develop *knowledge*—as Socrates defined that term—of the normative foundations of ethical practice. Persistent questioning is a very challenging endeavor!

Reductionism

Two decades of teaching leadership ethics has also taught me that many students come to the course firm in the belief that they will learn things that are not entirely teachable. They expect solutions that will dictate the "right way" for public administrators to make decisions when confronting ethical dilemmas. Further complicating this belief, many students also expect these solutions will affirm much of what they already know, given their omniscience.

Persistent questioning leads these students to discover very early in the course that their study of ethics is opening before them a Pandora's casket of contradictory principles, none of which provides unassailable solutions. This discovery has caused many students to become unsettled both emotionally and intellectually, as the straight and narrow autobahn upon which they have traversed so confidently for so many years is now being transformed into a collision course of conflicting and contradictory principles. Moreover, as these students discover the intellectual complexities that are part and parcel of learning the foundations of public administration ethics, many of those cherished solutions evaporate under the careful scrutiny afforded by persistent questioning. All of this only complicates what these students believe should be a relatively straightforward matter.

Sympathetic to this plight, Socrates provides a role model depicting how teachers might ease their students' discomfort, if only because his student exhibited similar discomfort. Socrates realized that Meno did not yet possess the self-discipline needed to rule himself. As the collision course of ideas in Socrates's classroom caused Meno to experience emotional and intellectual discomfort, Meno made the same U-turn on the autobahn that I have observed students making—namely, Meno attempted to rule Socrates by instructing him! But, wise pedagogue that he was, Socrates responded effectively to Meno and his plight, as the teacher's goal was for his student to overcome his reductionism. Socrates said: "So we must, it appears, inquire into the qualities of something the nature of which we do not yet know. However, please relax your rule a bit for me and agree to investigate whether it is teachable or not by means of a hypothesis" (Plato 1981b, 87e76).

Taking this cue, those teaching public administration ethics can assist students to confront and surmount or to steer around reductionism by restating ethical principles as hypotheses. For example, one might ask, "So, if it is true that what makes the majority happy and doesn't decrease the greatest happiness factor is ethical, then is it ethical for a township manager to order the demolition of a tavern because a fundamentalist Christian preacher and his congregation—who comprise seventy percent of the township's citizens—want it demolished?" Then, to persist in questioning, one can challenge students to test various hypotheses by applying them to dilemmas arising in their workplaces.

Recalling Aristotle's insistence upon integrating theory and technique in practice (in this instance, *technique* being the attributes of character associated with ethical competence and *practice* being the demonstration of those attributes during case study analysis), I developed an exercise in the form of a mini-case worksheet for students to complete as they study the theoretical foundations of public administration ethics. (See Figure 5.3 p. 118 and later discussion of conflicting schools of ethical thought.) The worksheet was designed to achieve four pedagogical objectives: (1) students would demonstrate their knowledge of ethical theories; (2) students would relate those theories to their experience of leaders in the organizations where they have been or currently are employed; (3) students would critically examine the leader's ethical practice from a variety of perspectives; and (4) students would present and defend their analyses in class.

As the study of the normative foundations of public administration ethics unfolds during the first half of the course, each student presents at least one mini-case, depending upon the number of students enrolled as well as theories being studied.

Taken individually, the content of the mini-cases yields evidence of what each student knows—by paraphrasing a theory—as well as how that student is applying and critiquing that knowledge—by evaluating a leader's conduct in the student's workplace. In addition, the discussion generated by these presentations gradually immerses the entire class in ethical discourse. In the early stages, the trajectory of this discourse generally moves from "somewhat guarded" to "spirited" as students near the completion of their study of ethical theory.

In aggregate, this discourse engendered by the mini-cases provides evidence that the integrated pedagogical method has the overall effect of complicating the students' knowledge of the foundations of public administration ethics. In contrast to the first weeks of the course, the mini-case presentations and group discussions as the mid-semester nears reveal the students grappling with conflicts between the ethical principles they have been investigating and the alternative solutions they are proposing and defending. In addition, these mini-cases assist in solidifying the theoretical and experiential base the students will need to analyze full-blown case studies during the second half of the course.

For example, after introducing the worksheets and mini-cases into the first half of the course, students exhibited greater knowledge and self-confidence when presenting their resolutions to the case studies during the second half of the course. Their knowledge and self-confidence become visible when each presenter—playing the role of a public administrator—is scrutinized carefully by the other students who have prepared rebuttals using Cooper's *60 Minutes* and *New York Times* anticipatory scenarios (2012, 37). The intensity in the classroom is palpable when, early on in the semester, the presenter is visibly nervous while announcing the decision and, then, as the presenter explains why this particular decision made sense, sees other students salivating to jump into the fray with rebuttals. This exercise represents well the real world of public administration, especially when dilemmas do not allow for "both/ and" resolutions.

In retrospect, the mini-cases—the worksheets, presentations, and discussions—have met the goals the exercise was designed to achieve. The success of the exercise is apparent in the near elimination of reductionism, especially as students restate ethical principles as hypotheses and as my persistent questioning challenges them to test these hypotheses by applying them to dilemmas arising in their workplaces. Success also has evidenced itself as students generalize those applications to other workplaces through the discourse generated by the mini-cases.

Immediacy

Even though many students come to the study of public administration ethics wanting rote solutions to the complex dilemmas of professional practice, those who teach these courses also know students want them to provide those solutions "*right* here and *right* now." However, developing *knowledge* of public administration ethics, as Socrates personified that term in *The Meno*, require sslowing the pace of the learning process.

The particular pedagogical challenge requires mitigating the power of immediacy so that students will develop the five attributes associated with ethical competence (Menzel 2010, 18). To foster this outcome, Cooper (2012, 31) offers a paradigm: engaging students in the more general analytical process of calming their passions; perceiving the dilemma; describing the problem; identifying the ethical issue; identifying alternatives and selecting one; and determining a state of resolution.

The rationale for slowing the pace of decision making and having students carefully follow Cooper's paradigm is to facilitate their ability to deliberate as well as to render more reasoned and prudent decisions; as happens in public administration practice, "snap" decisions can prove to be wrong decisions. Moreover, good decisions oftentimes prove unpopular with at least some stakeholders or groups of stakeholders. This classroom experience assists students in learning how, as public administrators, they can slow the pace of the process so they will be able to explain and capably defend their decisions in the public square, especially to a skeptical public. More immediately, however, this experience prepares students to be more deliberative during the course's second half, when they analyze cases.

In addition to having students follow Cooper's paradigm, how might instructors assist students to overcome immediacy?

Again, much of it has to do with Aristotle's insistence upon integrating theory and technique in practice. Inviting students to describe how they have come to a solution and using Cooper's paradigm to assess that conclusion slows the pace. So, too, does utilizing Menzel's five attributes of ethical competence to frame questions—for example, asking, What would a public administrator who possesses a commitment to high standards of personal and professional ethics do? Questions like this challenge students to reframe their sometimes glib responses, which, in turn, slows the pace. Presenting an alternative scenario and asking students to debate its efficacy also functions to slow the pace.

This more "reflective practice" stance (Sergiovanni 1986) is the antithesis of what many students believe when they begin the course. It is through this more general analytical process of slowing down the decision-making process that students learn to confront and surmount or steer around their desire for more immediate, rote solutions.

Success in confronting and surmounting these three wrong opinions reinforces and strengthens the theoretical, technical, and practical foundation upon which students can engage in studying the normative foundations of ethical thought, especially as these relate to the dilemmas of public administration practice. Persistence in questioning liberates the students' minds from those intellectual constraints that keep students—just as similar constraints kept Meno—from developing correct opinions and, ultimately, possessing knowledge. At the same time, however, success prepares students for yet another unsettling experience; namely, many come to the realization that they do not know as much about public administration ethics as they thought they did at the outset of the course.

This raises a third pedagogical challenge—to communicate that it is good for students to feel comfortable knowing what they do not know. Why? It is a sign of developing wisdom! But, that does raise the question, Why do so many students assume that successful administrators are omniscient?

Assist Students to Know What They Do Not Know

With the overarching pedagogical goal being to cultivate a classroom culture wherein students develop the attributes of ethical competence as they study the normative foundations of public administration ethics, I discovered early on some "bad news." Students not only possessed those three wrong opinions described above; they also possessed little, if any, exposure to philosophy in general, and ethics in particular.

Even for those few students who have had some limited exposure to these intellectual disciplines, they showed little conversancy with the content or the refined process of deliberation characterizing those who have learned and, thus, have been transformed by these intellectual disciplines into more critical thinkers. Inquiring into this phenomenon a bit, some students have reported forgetting most everything they had allegedly learned. Other students have vaguely remembered "learning something" about philosophical terms like *dilemma, ontological, categorical imperative, deconstructionist, "Cogito, ergo sum," postmodern,* and *Plato's cave,* among others. Exasperated, I told myself: "Forget the persistent questioning! That's going to get you nowhere fast."

Moreover, many students believe the content of ethics is informed by one's religious upbringing, if any, and/or is defined by the dominant culture. Students believing the former do not indicate much awareness of the broad categorical distinctions demarcating religion from philosophy or morality from ethics. Students who believe the latter oftentimes espouse the utilitarian belief that true happiness is achieved by doing "whatever makes me happy so long as it doesn't hurt anyone else."

These two matters present no small pedagogical challenge, as students must be introduced to philosophy in general, and to the normative foundations of public administration ethics in particular. For this reason, the integrated pedagogical method emphasizes the foundations of public administration ethics during the first half of the course. Students are introduced to ethical theory, develop conversancy with ethical theory as they are immersed gradually into ethical discourse and, through the mini-cases, increasingly evidence the attributes of character associated with ethical competence as they are persistently questioned about what should be expected of public administrators.

The good news is that many students possess a keen interest in the subject matter and, as the content of the course unfolds during its first half, they resemble a ShamWow®—the German-made, super-absorbent towel advertised as capable of sopping up to 12 times its weight. As students gradually move beyond any initial hesitance to critique their most cherished feelings, beliefs, and/or childhood myths, and as they become increasingly familiar with the foundations of public administration ethics, they begin to recognize that reasoned responses to persistent questioning is far and away superior to reacting to gut feelings, clutching onto cherished feelings, beliefs, and/or childhood myths, or falling through the trapdoors located within even the simplest dilemmas and through which many otherwise very bright people—including their classmates—have already fallen. Simply put, most students become increasingly wary of responding too quickly and with too little thought to those persistent questions.

In sum, one important lesson for instructors who teach public administration ethics is that during the first half of a public administration ethics course, they need to reinforce and strengthen the foundation upon which their students develop the attributes associated with ethical competence. Instructors cultivate a classroom culture conveying this experience as they (1) implement a normative model of ethical decision making, (2) persist in questioning what students assert unthinkingly with the goal of assisting students to know what they do not know, and (3) introduce students to the intellectual disciplines associated with philosophy and ethics. More important, these activities provide evidence that students are beginning to exhibit ethical competence:

- They identify higher standards of personal and professional conduct.
- They exhibit knowledge of relevant ethical theories.
- They engage in ethical reasoning when confronted with challenging ethical situations.
- They identify and enact public service ethics and values.
- They consider how to promote ethical practices and behaviors in public agencies and organizations. (Menzel 2010, 18)

A body of empirical research suggests that persistent questioning—as ancient a pedagogical tool as it is—encourages MPA students to examine ethical dilemmas from the perspective of a higher stage of ethical reasoning (Jurkiewicz 2002). Students become more critical of their current approach to resolving ethical dilemmas when they are challenged to formulate more ethical solutions.

Four Classroom Activities to Inculcate Greater Cognitive Complexity

A public administration ethics course that aims at developing ethical competence in students while preparing them to engage in case study analysis is neither an introductory philosophy course nor an ethics course. Instead, it is an *applied* ethics course, requiring those teaching the course to implement a variety of classroom activities that introduce students to ethical thought in a way that is concise yet interesting, and perhaps even entertaining as well as provocative.

When I was first considering which classroom activities to implement within the classroom culture I hoped to construct, I kept in mind the desired end—developing ethical competence in students who are pursuing college degrees in public affairs and administration. This end specified four activities: (1) selecting an appropriate textbook that would challenge students to think about ethical theory; (2) engaging students very early in the course in writing a provisional statement of public administration ethics that would identify their current ideas and provide a benchmark for use later in the course; (3) introducing students during the first half of the course to the history and development of ethical thought as well as identifying conflicts between the schools of ethical thought so as to complicate their understanding of ethics and its practice; and (4) critiquing a public administration code of ethics (e.g., the American Society for Public Administration [ASPA], the International City/County Management Association [ICMA]) so that students would possess an external standard against which they would be able to measure their future practice as public administrators.

1. Select an Appropriate Textbook

When selecting the textbook, I had an immediate, short-term goal: to provide students an overview of philosophical ethics in general, and the history and development of ethics and ethical thought along with the principles associated with the schools of ethical thought in particular. The most appropriate textbook would present this content in a way that is accessible to a general audience, provide interesting case examples that apply ethical principles, and balance comprehensiveness with concision, thereby generating interest while drilling down into essentially contested concepts.

One of the many highly regarded and widely used introductory texts for moral philosophy and ethics courses is Rachels's (2011) *The Elements of Moral Philosophy*. This book provides an excellent option, especially for aspiring public administrators at the graduate level. The authors have structured each chapter in a way that seduces an unwary reader into agreeing with the basic principles promulgated by nine schools of ethical thought. The authors then "pull the rug out" from under the reader by introducing the intellectual errors and practical problems associated with each school.

Over the years, this structure has proven particularly effective. As students begin to figure it out, they also learn to pause before agreeing all too quickly with principles when they are first stated and cast in the best light possible. This self-discipline marks an important achievement as students begin, on their own, to conjure up possible alternate solutions and to assess the potential positive and negative implications associated with each solution. The students no longer allow themselves to be unwittingly seduced upon their first read of what appears to be a sound argument, supported by apparently equally sound principles. Instead, students begin to evidence in their classroom discourse a more complicated understanding of the normative foundations of public administration ethics. Then, as students acquire more knowledge, their discourse both inside and outside of class also begins to reflect their inquiring into and deliberation about the substance of the principles asserted (Plato 1981b, 98a86).

It is rather easy to identify which students do *not* read the text. Asking questions about an assigned ethical theory, some students are clueless about the trapdoor upon which they are standing. And, when the lever is pulled through more persistent questioning or when another student does so by pointing out a theory's weakness, those students quickly backtrack. Plus, after experiencing or observing a couple of incidents like this, students realize they will be persistently questioned in ensuing class sessions. They recognize that this classroom culture is one wherein knowledge about ethics is acquired and the intellectual and behavioral foundations of ethical competence are being developed. After all, completing one's assigned work—in this case, reading the text before class—provides the foundation for acquiring the first of Menzel's attributes of ethical competence: a commitment to high standards of personal and professional behavior (2010, 18).

Furthermore, the structure of the Rachels's text provides an antidote to those three wrong opinions many students possess—omniscience, reductionism, and immediacy—by awakening in their minds Ricoeur's (1973a, 1973b) "hermeneutical suspicion." That is, students begin to question what is asserted rather than succumbing to its seductions. Importantly, the hermeneutical suspicion does not inculcate skepticism—the illogical belief that there is no truth; instead, it instills in students the intellectual self-discipline of carefully critiquing what others have asserted in order to determine for oneself what the truth may be. This undoubtedly is an important self-discipline for public administration practice and may very well constitute a sixth attribute of ethical competence.

While this text's brevity is its strength, it is also its weakness, especially for graduate students. However, this weakness can be surmounted by providing supplementary online discussions and commentaries concerning the ethical theories being investigated with applications to public administration practice. Over the past two decades, the end-of-semester course assessment forms have consistently indicated that the webpages are helpful because they provide students more in-depth discussions about the ethical theories and topics being covered in class as well as those ethical theories and topics the authors have discussed all too briefly (e.g., the principle of double effect; intention) or have neglected altogether (e.g., the differences between epistemology and metaphysics; belief, opinion, truth, and Truth; ancient, modern, and postmodern thought). The assessment forms also routinely report that these webpages provide greater context for class discussion and are replete with interesting if not provocative examples specifically related both to the students' lives and to public administration practice.

Students often will come to class with printed copies of online materials, but have they actually read them? One easy assessment device is to hint at some of the supplementary discussion during class. Those who have read the materials respond immediately or volunteer some of the content while discussing other matters. The unprepared students—like deer staring at an automobile's headlights in the dark of night—are very easy to spot.

2. Engage Students in Writing a Provisional Statement of Public Administration Ethics

When designing the new leadership ethics course, I thought it important that students formulate a statement explicating their thoughts concerning public administration ethics. Ideally, this statement could serve one day in the future as a standard against which they could evaluate their professional practice as public administrators.

To that end, I decided to have students formulate a short, three- to five-page essay identifying their current thoughts concerning public administration ethics. Written during the first week of the course, the original essay would become outmoded as the semester progressed, and as students learned the foundations of public administration ethics, they could begin revising their initial statements. Then, at the end of the course, students would write a final five- to seven-page statement of leadership ethics reflecting their best scholarship. Viewing these individual elements as a single project, the initial statement would provide a benchmark against which the final, revised statement could be compared, providing evidence of just how far each student progressed in learning about leadership ethics and what ethical competence requires of public administrators.

Despite their omniscience, it was during the first semester of the course that something surprising emerged when I was grading those initial statements of leadership ethics: Many students had no idea what to include in their essays. To provide assistance, I developed an "Ethics Inventory" tailored specifically to the schools of ethical thought being investigated. The instrument introduces students to the names and principles associated with each school of thought. Concurrently, as students consider the menu of rival principles, the work of completing the instrument challenges them to question and think about what they should include in their first statement of leadership ethics (Figure 5.2).

Designing this inventory was a relatively straightforward endeavor. First,

Figure 5.2   **Three Examples from the Ethics Inventory Instrument**

	(circle one)			
Ethical Theory: Utilitarianism[a]	Agree			Disagree
16. When I am trying to decide what is ethical, I look at the consequences of the alternatives.	1	2	3	4
17. Whatever is best for the majority is the ethical thing to do.	1	2	3	4
18. People deserve credit even if what they try to do works out badly.	1	2	3	4
19. The most important thing in life is to experience pleasure.	1	2	3	4
20. The most important thing in life is to be happy.	1	2	3	4
	(circle one)			
Ethical Theory: The Categorical Imperative[b]	Agree			Disagree
21. When a person attempts to be ethical but things turn out badly, that person deserves credit for trying.	1	2	3	4
22. The ethical thing must be performed for the right reason.	1	2	3	4
23. What is fair for one is fair for all.	1	2	3	4
24. People should always treat one another with respect.	1	2	3	4
25. People should never be used as a means to personal ends.	1	2	3	4
	(circle one)			
Ethical Theory: Social Contract[c]	Agree			Disagree
26. Being ethical means respecting other people's rights.	1	2	3	4
27. Some rights are absolute.	1	2	3	4
28. I possess the right to do whatever I want as long I don't limit the rights of other people.	1	2	3	4
29. Even if they cannot pay for it, people possess the right to health care.	1	2	3	4
30. Education is a fundamental right.	1	2	3	4
31. Animals have rights.	1	2	3	4

Sources:
[a]Rachels 2007, pp. 89–116.
[b]Rachels 2007, pp. 117–140.
[c]Rachels 2007, pp. 141–159.

list the schools of thought in the order they will be investigated during the first half of the course, citing where each school of thought and its principles are found in the textbook or on course webpages. This outline—found in the course syllabus—provides the inventory's basic architecture. Second, in the form of subheadings, state the fundamental principles associated with each school of thought, along with a four-choice Likert scale ranging from "1—I agree" to "4—I disagree" that could be used to score each principle. Four (rather than five) choices forces students to choose sides; similar to a dilemma, there would be no room for "undecideds" here. Upon completing the inventory, the principles with which students agree and disagree the most—the "1s" and the "4s"—provide the basic content for writing the first statement of leadership ethics.

Distributing the Ethics Inventory to students, and even before having the opportunity to explain the inventory and its purpose, students pore over its contents. From their facial expressions, it is clear they are comfortable with some items and puzzled by others. After explaining the inventory and its purpose, students complete it straightaway, with only a few pausing to place their pen or pencil between their lips and to think a bit about what their response should be. I then instruct the students to use the items they agree with most to frame their first statement of leadership ethics and to use the items they disagree with most to provide some sharpness or contrast in their discussion.

The significance of having students revise the initial statement as the course unfolds and write their final statement of leadership ethics at the end of the course typically reveals itself through three outcomes. First, the statement offers a provisional yet comprehensive definition of public administration ethics, demonstrating each student's acquisition of greater ethical sophistication. Second, the statement demonstrates each student's conversancy with ethical principles, as well as ability to apply those principles to public administration practice. This conversancy manifests itself as each student bridges ethical theory with actual problems arising in the workplace. Third, the statement offers evidence of the degree to which each student is considering and implementing Menzel's five attributes of ethical competence (2010, 18).

After handing in their final statements, a few students routinely report a fourth outcome. When composing those statements, these students found themselves having to reject some of the ethical principles they naively accepted early on in the course, as well as other statements they summarily dismissed when completing the ethics inventory and their first statement of leadership ethics.

An examination of the grades assigned to those final statements over the years offers considerable insight into the outcomes for which the project was designed—but in varying degrees. "Within group" variance generally has been high, with several students in each class writing excellent statements (on average, about 30 percent of a class) and a few students writing below average statements (on average, about 20 percent of a class). In contrast, "between group" variance is generally low, as the average grade for the final statement for each class across the years has deviated very little (on average, a B+).

The final statement of leadership ethics each student writes provides evidence of three "markers of success" that will be discussed later.

3. Introduce Students to Conflicting Schools of Ethical Thought

As noted earlier, many students come to the course thinking that religion informs, if not prescribes, the content of ethics. Consequently, one way to spark interest is to begin the course by differentiating between ethics and religion and between principles and morals. While religion and morals provide appropriate content for a theology course, they are not appropriate content for a public administration ethics course. In this regard, Rachels and Rachels's discussion is particularly germane, as the authors carefully and succinctly distinguish between these terms and effectively challenge belief systems and ideologies as the source of ethics (2011, 1–15, 52–67). The recognition tends to be quite helpful in setting up the exploration of the history and development of ethics as well as the conflicts between the schools of ethical thought that the mini-cases elucidate in greater detail. Yet the recognition of these distinctions can be very unsettling for some students.

Because there are more schools of ethical thought than can be covered during one semester, it is necessary to select a sufficient number of schools that provide a comprehensive overview of the foundations of public administration ethics but that conflict sufficiently to inculcate greater cognitive complexity in students. For example, during any semester, natural law theory and utilitarianism, subjectivism and absolutism, social contract and feminist ethics, as well as Rawls's (1999) theory of justice and virtue ethics promote the achievement of this goal. What are the desired outcomes? Once again, through the collision of conflicting principles, students will exhibit greater intellectual self-discipline as they project and evaluate probable outcomes and propose solutions suggested by the rival theories. Then, too, instructors might change the ethical theories studied in any semester to motivate themselves as well as their students to question and think about different theories.

Explicating the history and development of ethics and these various schools of thought during the first half of the course unsettles much of what many students take for granted. This experience gently nudges and sometimes prods them to recognize that they had better think more carefully and critically about ethical principles—that is, assuming they do not want to become or to remain unthinking ideologues and, in the culture of this particular classroom, to hold wrong opinions or cling onto unsupported feelings, beliefs, and/or childhood myths.

That said, this exploration of conflicting principles is not what prepares students directly for case study analysis. Instead, it reinforces and strengthens the foundation of knowledge upon which students begin to apply ethical theory to workplace realities and simultaneously develop the five attributes associated with ethical competence (Menzel 2010, 18). As this foundation is reinforced and strengthened, this integrated pedagogical method prepares students for case study analysis.

For this purpose and as mentioned previously, a mini-case study for each school of ethical thought is assigned. A good mini-case analysis doesn't require writing an essay or paper, preparing a handout, or developing a PowerPoint presentation, although some students may. Instead, a good mini-case analysis provides a paraphrase of each theory's basic principles, applies this paraphrase to a dilemma confronting the leader of an organization where the student presenting the mini-case currently works (or has worked), and offers a principled critique of the theory and/or leadership solution (see Figure 5.3). A good mini-case and the discussion it engenders also provide a culminating activity for the class session where a particular theory is discussed or can serve as a review of that theory at the beginning of the next class session.

More than simply applying ethical theory to common workplace dilemmas, mini-cases challenge students to develop hermeneutical suspicion and inculcate greater cognitive complexity. For example, as students become familiar with an increasing number of ethical theories, this knowledge challenges them to identify how rival theories frame the same dilemma and then propose solutions from a variety of perspectives. In addition, as students identify the divergent principles they can use to justify these solutions, this activity challenges them to reflect a bit more carefully and critically because, like Meno, students are now aware that they know a bit more of what they *do not* know. In short, students are beginning to exhibit wisdom.

As all of this pedagogical effort relates to the purpose of this volume, the mini-cases provide an assessment device to identify the degree to which students are developing Menzel's five attributes of ethical competence (2010, 18). To conduct this assessment, during or after each presentation instructors can ask:

1. How did the presentation reflect a commitment to high standards of personal and professional behavior?
2. How did the presentation exhibit knowledge of relevant ethics codes and laws?
3. How did the presentation demonstrate the ability to engage in ethical reasoning when confronted with challenging ethical situations?
4. How did the presentation reflect the ability to identify and act on public administration ethics and values?
5. How did the presentation promote ethical practices and behaviors in public agencies and organizations?

Likewise, as other students respond to each mini-case presentation, instructors can raise these five questions to conduct an informal assessment of the

Figure 5.3   **An Example of a Mini-Case Worksheet**

Instructions: Translate the "abstract" ethical theory into "concrete" solutions as this theory evidences itself in the workplace. General guidelines include applying the assigned theory to the workplace and providing a critique of the application. The critique should include: what the theory provides that is and is not helpful for thinking about ethical leadership; solutions proposed by other ethical theories that expose the weakness(es) associated with the resolution proposed by the theory; and any other discussion. The presentation should last about five minutes.

Ethical Theory: Utilitarianism

Basic Argument: "Ethical" describes conduct that increases the greatest happiness factor.

Workplace
Application: The Township Manager must present to the Board specific budget that reduce next year's expenses by 7 percent. He wants the Board to make the cuts because he fears alienating Township staff. His basic attitude is, "Keep as many of them as happy as I can." If the Township Manager cuts jobs, many staff members will not be happy, increasing the amount of unhappiness among the staff.

Critique: Isn't the Township Manager responsible for making the "tough decisions" about staffing? Is leadership "success" measured simply by how happy staff members are? Natural law theory asserts "do good, avoid evil." Isn't the "good" making cuts to the staff, regardless of how they may feel about it?

Additional
Discussion: The utilitarian solution makes sense but doesn't solve the dilemma because political interests—Board politics and organizational politics—are involved. How is the Township Manager to know the "good"?

degree to which these students are also developing the five attributes associated with ethical competence. Doing so provides an opportunity to determine whether and what adjustments need to be made to cultivate a classroom culture that better enhances the development of ethical competence in students, especially as each begins to exhibit a firm and unchangeable character when a proposed solution collides with those being proposed by other students.

As students study and apply the schools of ethical thought in the mini-cases, the time is ripe to warn them that attempting to integrate all of these materials the week or night before the final statement is due will present a daunting if not insurmountable task, even for the most gifted students. Simply put, writing the final statement of leadership ethics requires much more time, careful consideration, and attention than is available by "pulling an all-nighter." As the course unfolds, students should be encouraged to incorporate into their statements the new theoretical principles they are studying. Students also should be encouraged to restate their earlier, nascent ideas with greater precision and attentiveness to arguments advanced by the philosophers and ethicists they are studying. Lastly, students should be encouraged to integrate all of this into a more focused, refined, and comprehensive argument.

4. Critique a Public Administration Code of Ethics

Professions have a normative code of ethics, and those who practice a profession are expected to "profess" this code—that is, to use it as a standard against which to make judgments concerning their character and conduct as professionals. At the same time, others can use this code to make judgments concerning the character and conduct of those professionals.

Beyond simply teaching students about the ethical foundations of public administration practice, this integrated pedagogical method familiarizes students with this profession's code of ethics as they access, analyze, and make judgments about what the code states concerning a public administrator's character and conduct. The ASPA and ICMA codes have proven to be helpful in this regard.

Securing a copy of a code of ethics is a challenging aspect of this exercise, in that students must first locate and then successfully navigate a professional organization's webpage. For some, this is a more daunting exercise than might be envisioned; however, this research has the positive outcome of familiarizing students with the organization, its purpose, and its activities, as well as what it offers members. Then, once students access the code and read it, many discover that these codes typically emphasize laws and conduct, not ethical theories and principles. That said, at some point prior to handing in their critiques, students come to realize that some organizations call their codes of conduct a "code of ethics." In most cases, they are genuinely puzzled about why this is so, and some posit a variety of explanations concerning how professional organizations—some of which require training programs to include ethics courses—fail to recognize this difference. Having made this discovery—evidencing knowledge of the foundations of public administration ethics as well as the difference between a code of conduct and code of ethics—students then critique the codes, offering improvements to make them more accurately approximate a code of ethics for public administrators.

Having individuals rather than groups write critiques is important, especially in light of Menzel's second and fourth attributes of ethical competence (that each student demonstrate knowledge of relevant ethics codes and laws, and that each student identify and act on public service ethics and values). The critique consists of two parts: (1) a brief summary of the code, providing evidence of Menzel's second attribute; and (2) a critique of the code that roots its elements more explicitly in ethical theory, providing evidence of Menzel's fourth attribute. A completed critique, in which students have "personalized" the organization's code of ethics rather than simply having indicated that they have read and know its contents, provides evidence—albeit an "ideal" not yet tested in professional practice—of Menzel's first attribute, namely, "a commitment to high standards of personal and professional conduct."

Having woven these four classroom activities into an integrated pedagogical method during the first half of the leadership ethics course, I have noted that students generally evidence a more comprehensive understanding of and insight into the history and development of the foundations of public administration. In addition, the mini-cases reveal the depth of care students take when considering how the foundations of public administration ethics apply to public administration practice. Lastly, students who actively participate in classroom discourse have provided evidence that they are developing the five attributes of ethical competence (Menzel, 2010, 18). To the degree that classroom discourse accurately represents the students' commitments, there is evidence these attributes have begun to take root in their minds and characters.

Markers of Success in Developing Ethical Competence

With the pedagogical objective to cultivate a classroom culture wherein students learn the foundations of public administration ethics, develop ethical competence, and are prepared to engage in case study analysis, attention necessarily turns to assessing outcomes.

Knowing that an evolved sense of ethical competence provides a more demanding standard than that of the generic ethic expected of public administrators (Dorasamy 2010; Thompson 2004; Goss 1996), three "markers of success" can be identified: (1) Students make the transition to more principled reasoning rather than simply responding to feelings; (2) students demonstrate increased sensitivity and responsiveness to contextual variables; and (3) students exhibit courage by beginning to stand *for* something. Note that these three outcomes assume that students already possess *knowledge*—as Plato defined that term (1981b, 98a86)—of the foundations of public administration ethics.

1. The Transition to Principled Reasoning

As students are introduced to and immersed in the world of ethical thought, it does not take long before they identify principles when resolving the mini-cases. If only because an ethical dilemma pits two goods against each other, the ability to identify these principles does not qualify as a marker of success. But, as instructors persistently question students, and as students, in turn, begin to reason more prudently about the principles they have identified, this deliberative process qualifies as a marker of success—students take greater care so as not to fall unwittingly through those trapdoors for which philosophers and ethicists have already proposed viable solutions.

Success also evidences itself as students indicate they are transitioning away from responding to ethical theories and the content of the mini-cases based solely upon how they "feel" and are responding with "principles." For example, it is not unusual early in the course for the discussion of natural law theory—which proscribes certain conduct, like administering chemotherapy, setting a broken arm, engaging in homosexual intercourse, or procuring or providing an abortion—to elicit very strong responses from students. Obviously, students are reacting to the implications of the principle "do good and avoid evil" rather than thinking more critically about it (Rachels, 2011, 58–62). The same goes for the strong feelings elicited during a discussion of utilitarianism that allows certain conduct—like using illegal drugs, engaging in adulterous affairs, or lying—as long as engaging in this conduct does not decrease the "greatest happiness factor" (89–91).

In response to these feeling-based, reactive assertions, Socrates models how to persist in asking questions that will challenge students to deliberate more critically and, then, to offer principles supporting their decisions. That stated, rather than heeding Socrates's advice, I once decided to venture into unchartered terrain by making a statement that caused several students to react in utter disbelief, their slack-jawed faces communicating, "I can't believe he just said that!"

What did I say? I glibly remarked: "I do not particularly care how you feel."

I did not make this statement flippantly, as if thinking and feeling do not interact in the process of making ethical decisions. Instead, I believed this statement would represent an important pedagogical intervention, and for three reasons.

First, it alerted students to intellectual formation and development of cognitive complexity that a public administration ethics course should encourage. After all, feelings are not the primary content of ethics, principles are. My statement drew a line in the sand, instructing students to be more deliberative and to respond more thoughtfully to a concrete application of a principle.

Notwithstanding the salutary benefits of not allowing feelings to overpower reason in the ethical decision-making process, feminist ethicists—Carol Gilligan (1982) and Nel Noddings (1984), in particular—would be extremely critical of this statement and approach. Alert to this critique, I also uttered my "uncaring" statement in the belief that doing so would represent a second significant pedagogical intervention. How so? Feelings are important in the ethical decision-making process, especially when they arise due to cognitive dissonance (Festinger 1957) and, in this way, provide public administrators with a "gut check," an indication that something may be awry and ought to be factored into the decision-making process. The well-honed ability to recognize and demonstrate an appreciation for one's feelings as well as those of various stakeholders and groups *without allowing those feelings to distract attention away from substantive principles* is an important dimension of the practice of public administration ethics. For example, as many township managers have learned from the school of hard knocks, making a decision based solely on one's empathy for an individual or group can lead to all sorts of unintended and very troublesome consequences.

The third reason this statement represented a significant pedagogical intervention is the pervasive opinion—and possibly a fourth wrong opinion students possess—that feelings always trump principles. In contrast, Socrates upset the Athenian elders in Plato's *Apology* (1981a) by teaching their children to question what they were being taught. Thus, my statement should have upset what students typically hold as a self-evident fact (that feelings always trump principles). By directly challenging this belief and engaging students in thinking more critically about it, they begin to engage in more principled reasoning than they might have done otherwise.

As students gradually learn to stop reacting to their feelings by immediately invoking the phrase "I feel . . . ," and learn to replace it with phrases like "I believe . . ." or "The theory argues . . ." or "The theorist maintains . . . ," they show that they are transitioning toward making more principled decisions. Then, as the course progresses and as students consider the dilemmas described in the mini-cases from a variety of ethical theories, they argue various solutions based upon conflicting principles, demonstrating even greater intellectual sophistication and discipline. Not only does all of this complicate the decision-making process, but it also provides evidence that students are developing greater cognitive complexity.

In retrospect, it is interesting—and I must admit, mildly entertaining—to note as the course progresses that after I have said "I do not particularly care how you *feel*," students immediately correct their language, saying "Well, I *feel* that . . . er . . . ummmm . . . I *think* that. . . ." Ditto for other students who sometimes have stopped a classmate midstream when that student has used the word "feel." This verbal jousting has always been "in fun," and everyone laughs—nowhere more so than when students catch me uttering the proscribed "f—" word, "I *feel*. . . ." Then, too, over the years when the course has concluded, a number of students have told me or written on their course assessment forms that this intervention was important in getting them to think more critically. Through the grapevine, I have also heard that some students who have completed the course tell newly matriculating students to prepare themselves to be "shocked," without telling them exactly how and why. In addition, a few alumni who have been invited back to campus to make presentations at MPA colloquia have, at some point during the course of their remarks, joked about my "uncaring" statement and its wisdom for their practice as public administrators. They now "get it." In retrospect, having ventured into that untested terrain of making myself appear not to care about how my students feel has become something of a "rite of passage."

2. An Increased Sensitivity and Responsiveness to Contextual Variables

Getting students to exercise greater prudence—as important as this is—also does not qualify as a marker of success. They must learn to be responsive to contextual variables, because, when called upon to confront dilemmas in professional practice, these variables can conspire in such ways that public administrators implement what Cooper and Menzel call "low road"/"compliance driven" rules (2013, p. 127). Then, too, Aristotle reminds instructors that it is no easy task to account for all of these variables, "but to do this to the right person, to the right extent, at the right time, with the right motive, and in the right way." Aristotle wrote, "that is not for everyone nor is it easy; wherefore goodness is both rare and laudable and noble" (1958, II.195). Isn't that the goal of those who teach public administration ethics—to mentor students who will become public servants and who will exude laudable and noble goodness?

As students begin to analyze the mini-cases, their decisions gradually reveal increasing sensitivity and responsiveness to contextual variables. For example, students raise questions about details concerning the law and its requirements, as well as professional standards, job descriptions, and a leader's intentions. These discussions show a growing awareness of the many ways these variables can exert a potent influence—both pro and con—upon the decision-making process.

Once the study of the ethical foundations of public administration practice is completed, I introduce students to Cooper's (2012) decision-making model to further hone their sensitivity and responsiveness to contextual variables. This model emphasizes the development of "ethical imagination" and accounts for these variables (calling them "contingencies") in three important ways. First, students learn to identify these variables early in the decision-making process by accounting for what their roles and responsibilities require (Cooper

2012, 46–51, 219–223). Second, students complicate their understanding of the dilemma by envisioning multiple resolutions, both pro and con, and formulating principled responses for each resolution, an exercise Cooper calls the "rehearsal of defenses" (26). Third, students select the best resolutions and subject them to rigorous interrogation of the type public administrators would normally expect from investigative reporters or an angry public, what Cooper calls *60 Minutes* and *New York Times* anticipatory scenarios (37). These three activities inculcate in students greater sensitivity and responsiveness to contextual variables for case study analysis, further grounding their study of public administration ethics in organization theory and behavior through what Cooper calls an "organizational design approach" (269–281).

For the purpose of assessing whether students have developed greater ethical imagination, I modified Cooper's model in two ways.

The first modification addresses whether students are moving away from simply "perceiving a dilemma"—an awareness that there is no simple and straightforward resolution to the situation they are confronting—and toward "framing it as a dilemma"—specifying the ethical principles that conflict in this situation. The mini-cases, in particular, focus students upon identifying the salient ethical principles—the specific conflict of goods—involved in and perhaps obscured within each dilemma. This knowledge—the normative foundations of public administration ethics—enables students to generate the insight needed if they are to do something more significant than simply perceive and describe the dilemma.

The second modification involves superimposing Lawrence Kohlberg's (1981) three-level, six-stage theory of moral (ethical) development upon Cooper's model. This modification enables students to assess the stage(s) and/or level(s) of ethical development they and others have attained. Carole Jurkiewicz (2013) concurs, arguing:

> The Kohlberg model of ethical reasoning, and the concomitant approaches to effectively elevating a student's scores in this regard, provide a starting point for asserting that ethicality is a key competency for public service professionals which can be taught and measured. These competencies are most often evidenced in behavior, and these behaviors can serve as an external assessment of ethicality.

Learning to assess the stage(s) or level(s) of ethical development that others have attained makes it possible for students to identify what may be the most appropriate response for particular stakeholders and/or stakeholder groups. In this way, the next generation of public administrators learn to (1) advance their agenda with the objective of making it a "unified public judgment"

(Yankelovich 1991); (2) construct a more ethical organizational culture; and (3) ideally, contribute to the development of a more ethical society.

To facilitate this learning, students apply Kohlberg's theory to the dilemmas raised during the mini-cases and respond to them from Kohlberg's three levels. The exercise prepares students to respond in a similar fashion to the dilemmas emerging later in the case studies, as well as those they will face one day in their public administration practice. Success will evidence itself as students invoke Kohlberg's theory to describe the "levels of ethical leadership" exhibited in proposed solutions to the mini-cases, case studies, and their course projects. But, in terms of the subject of this volume, these behaviors also evidence Menzel's fourth and fifth attributes of ethical competence, "the ability to identify and act on public service ethics and values" and a commitment to "promoting ethical practices and behaviors in public agencies and organizations" (2010, 18).

The integration of these elements into Cooper's model creates a synergy akin to Aristotle's notion of "ethical character." Teachers will note this outcome, in particular, as student discourse in the classroom and course projects brings recognition of Menzel's fifth attribute of ethical competence, "promoting ethical practices and behaviors in public agencies and organizations" (2010, 18). Furthermore, as students prescribe resolutions to ethical dilemmas, these resolutions will highlight the development of ethical imagination that integrates the rational—"I care very much about what you think"—*and* affective dimensions—"Listen to your feelings, but do not let them dictate what you are to do."

As students discuss the mini- cases and engage in case study analyses, they also exhibit Menzel's third and fourth attributes of ethical competence, "the ability to engage in ethical reasoning when confronted with challenging ethical situations" as well as "the ability to identify and act on public service ethics and values" (2010, 18). Teachers will note this achievement as students describe how they are struggling to balance what their minds require with what their hearts demand. This achievement represents the desired end toward which teachers have been directing students from the first day of class.

3. Standing for Something

Teaching students the process of ethical decision making and engaging in it so they think ethically proves inadequate for public administration practice. Why? This particular profession requires communicating one's decisions to followers as well as to a variety of stakeholders and stakeholder groups. Consequently, students must learn to communicate decisions—and the logic behind the making of those decisions—in a timely and appropriate manner. One of best ways to develop this ability, I thought, would be to require students to expose their decision-making process *to* and explore it *in* the light of day.

Public administrators are expected to make tough decisions, as Cooper (2012) rightly notes. But this is not sufficient. To "form a more perfect union," so to speak, public administrators must also forge a consensus concerning those decisions and their implementation, as Yankelovich (1991) explains. Additionally, as these decisions concern the good—and especially the common good—public administrators must exhibit ethical competence by leading others in their organizations and communities to be more deliberative about the conflicting goods and choices that provide the content of the ethical decision-making process.

As most public administrators have experienced, there will always be followers, stakeholders, and stakeholder groups who disagree with just about every decision. But when public administrators are comfortable in exposing their ethical decision-making process to these individuals and groups and exploring it with them, only ideologues and the most stubborn people will fail to appreciate the principles that lead to reasoned and reasonable decisions. In a democratic republic, the body politic is always free to disagree and organize with the goal of overturning decisions and even of dismissing public servants. But, having incorporated knowledge of ethics into the decision-making process and having exposed the principles supporting those opinions to the light of day, public administrators exhibit ethical competence as they courageously advocate and bear personal responsibility for the decisions they have made.

To that end, the analysis of the mini-cases may be crucial. In the face of contrary voices and opposition inside the classroom—sooner for some students and later for others—they begin to stand *for* something, namely, the ethical principles supporting their decisions. Moreover, as they no longer back down or cower when challenged through persistent questioning, they show knowledge of ethical theory as they offer principled rationales to support their decisions. Students also recognize and overcome what Cooper and Menzel call "ethical blind spots" (2013, p. 17). It very well may be that this integrated pedagogical approach promotes the achievement of another outcome: It fosters in students the development of greater self-confidence and poise, especially as they earn the respect of their peers by exhibiting a virtuous character and ethical competence.

When these three markers of pedagogical success evidence themselves, students are well prepared to analyze larger and more intricate case studies. Furthermore, students have successfully transitioned from simply reacting to feelings, as they now carefully consider contextual variables and offer principled reasons to support their decisions. Possessing ethical character, some students will courageously stand for ethical principles in the face of principled opposition. And, having achieved these outcomes in a simultaneously supportive, collaborative, and confrontational classroom culture whose members value principles *and* feelings, students better appreciate how a collaborative approach to ethical decision making improves the process, an especially important aspect of learning for public administration practice.

All of this challenging intellectual work prepares students for the journey of continuous learning that will constitute their practice of public administration ethics. More immediately, however, it prepares them to demonstrate ethical competence when they are called upon to resolve the dilemmas that will emerge in their analysis of case studies during the second half of the course.

Conclusion

This chapter has described an integrated pedagogical method developed and refined over the past two decades to inculcate ethical competence in students pursuing college degrees in public affairs and administration. The purpose for this discussion has been twofold: to explicate this method and to engage those who teach public administration ethics in questioning and thinking about how they might better develop ethical competence in their students. While the "end" of this method is to develop ethical competence in students, there are multiple "means"—like this integrated pedagogical method—to that end. Success, then, requires making a series of choices that gradually—and perhaps imperceptibly—prepare students to engage in case study analysis as they learn to make decisions that reflect a prudent mixture of theory and skill, and for which they accept personal responsibility.

This method is constructed upon three assumptions, the first being that ethical competence does not appear ex nihilo. Neither does it result from wishful thinking. Nor is ethical competence a result of students learning and blindly following "low road/compliance driven" external controls such as codes of conduct, legislation, regulations, or various other accountability schemes designed to prevent misconduct on the part of public administrators (Cooper and Menzel 2013). After all, external controls like these only increase the likelihood that people will become more creative as they invent detours and end runs around those controls and, hence, become even more unethical (Ackroyd and Thompson 1999).

In contrast, this method represents what Cooper and Menzel call a "high road/integrity based" approach, one that intentionally seeks to develop ethical competence in MPA students (2013, p. 127). As those who teach public administration ethics cultivate a classroom culture wherein their students learn about the ethical foundations of public administration practice and develop the attributes of ethical competence (Menzel 2010, 18), students will bring additional intellectual rigor, sophistication, and depth to their analysis of case studies in the classroom and, hopefully, to their practice of public administration beyond the classroom.

A second assumption is that instructors of a public administration ethics course do not create ethical leaders. No, because ethical leaders value being ethically competent, they create themselves. What instructors do is cultivate a classroom culture wherein aspiring public administrators learn the foundations of public administration ethics in a way that enables them to gradually develop and evidence the attributes of character associated with ethical competence as they grapple, first, with the contents of the mini-cases and, second, with case study analysis.

A third assumption is that students have grown up in a culture where the Nike advertisement proclaims, "Just do it." Those who teach public administration ethics cannot succumb to the temptation to "just do it"—the "it" being defined as teaching students what "best practice" prescribes. If instructors were to teach this narrow curriculum, they would be immersing students in the fecund breeding ground of "administrative evil." Such malevolence masks itself in public administrators who perform their jobs as experts do—yes, they "do things right" as that is prescribed by others (Drucker 1967)—but who never question the ends toward which they are directing those efforts (Adams and Balfour 2009), and therefore fail to "do right things," perhaps in the belief that it is wrong to ask questions.

When public administrators "just do it," their conduct is reminiscent of those competent, dependable, and expert train station managers and engineers of the Third Reich who—as proud public servants—kept the trains operating on time. But they never inquired into what would happen once the passengers arrived at destinations like Dachau, Auschwitz-Birkenau, and Treblinka. Worrying about ends, not just the means to those ends, is not satisfactory from an ethical perspective.

When public administrators possess ethical competence, they refuse to "just do it." When asked about *why* they did *what* they did, they do not say with a shrug of the shoulders and a downward glance, "I was just doing my job." No, these public administrators render principled decisions, defend them in the public forum, and do so because they view their work as a vocation through which they uphold, make more concrete, and advance the common good (Weber 1918). These public administrators are not so much worried about compliance as they are about character. They root their decision-making process not so much in a code of conduct and its rules and procedures but in a code of ethics and its principles.

When those who teach public administration ethics fail to possess or, as is more likely the case, when they fail to act upon what ethical competence requires and "just do it," their students may earn professional degrees and certificates. They may even become eminently successful public administrators, as this can be measured quantitatively in terms of professional goal attainment, by doing things right. But when these women and men fail to exhibit ethical competence in the decision-making process and do not build more ethical and democratic organizational cultures, their failure raises a very tough question for these instructors to answer: "Why *was* I there in the first place?"

Cooper and Menzel have noted "a huge gap between classroom instruction and on-the-job realities" (2013, p. 3). Years of experience in using and refining this integrated pedagogical method suggests it has the potential to narrow, or perhaps even eliminate, that gap and to transform public administration into an ethical practice. The means to this outcome begins as those who teach public administration ethics courses form the minds and characters of aspiring public administrators by introducing them to the ethical foundations of public administration and challenging them to develop and to provide evidence of the characteristics associated with ethical competence. More than simply preparing students to engage in case study analysis, those who implement this integrated pedagogical method initiate their students to the continuous and lifelong process of thinking ethically, of making ethical decisions, and of building organizational cultures that form ethical followers who also exhibit ethical competence. In this way, these instructors offer hope that the next generation's public administrators can envision ethical competence as the precondition for and hallmark of professional excellence.

References

Ackroyd, Stephen, and Paul Thompson. 1999. *Organizational Misbehaviour.* Thousand Oaks, CA: Sage.

Adams, Guy B., and Danny L. Balfour. 2009. *Unmasking Administrative Evil,* 3d ed. Armonk, NY: M.E. Sharpe.

Aristotle. 1958. Nicomachean ethics. In *The Pocket Aristotle: Selections from Physics, Psychology, Metaphysics, Nicomachean Ethics, Politics, Poetics*, ed. J.D. Kaplan, 158–274. New York: Washington Square Press.

Cooper, Terry L. 2012. *The Responsible Administrator: An Approach to Ethics for the Administrative Role,* 6th ed. San Francisco: Jossey-Bass.

Donald C., Menzel, 2010. *Ethics Moments in Government: Cases and Controversies.* Boca Raton, FL: CRC Press.

Dorasamy, N. 2010. Enhancing an ethical culture through purpose-directed leadership for improved public service delivery: A case for South Africa. *African Journal of Business Management* 4(1): 56–64.

Drucker, Peter F. 1967. *The Effective Executive.* Burlington, MA: Elsevier-Butterworth Heinemann.

Festinger, Leon. 1957. *A Theory of Cognitive Dissonance.* Stanford, CA: Stanford University Press.

Gilligan, Carol. 1982. *A Different Voice.* Cambridge, MA: Harvard University Press.

Goss, R.P. 1996. A distinct public administration ethics? *Journal of Public Administration Research and Theory* 6(4): 593–597.

Jurkiewicz, C.L. 2002. The influence of pedagogical style on students' level of ethical reasoning. *Journal of Public Affairs Education* 8(4): 263–274.

———. 2013. Advancing ethical competence through pedagogy. In *Achieving Ethical Competence for Public Service Leadership,* ed. Terry L. Cooper and Donald C. Menzel, pp. 131–153. Armonk, NY: M.E. Sharpe.

Kohlberg, Lawrence. 1981. *The Meaning and Measurement of Moral Development.* Cambridge, UK: Oelgeschlager, Gunn and Hain.

Menzel, Donald C., and Terry L. Cooper. 2013. In pursuit of ethical competence. In *Achieving Ethical Competence for Public Service Leadership,* ed. Terry L. Cooper and Donald C. Menzel, pp. 3–23. Armonk, NY: M.E. Sharpe.

Noddings, Nel. 1984. *Caring: A Feminine Approach to Ethics and Moral Education.* Berkeley: University of California Press.

Plato. 1981a. The apology. In *Five Dialogues,* trans. G.M.A. Grube, 23–44. Indianapolis, IN: Hackett Publishing.

———. 1981b. The Meno. In *Five Dialogues,* trans. G.M.A. Grube, 59–88. Indianapolis, IN: Hackett Publishing.

Rachels, James. 2011. *The Elements of Moral Philosophy,* 7th ed. New York: McGraw-Hill.

Rawls, John. 1999. *A Theory of Justice.* Cambridge, MA: Belknap Press of Harvard University of Press.

Ricoeur, Paul. 1973a. The task of hermeneutics. *Philosophy Today* 17(2): 112–128.

———. 1973b. The hermeneutical function of distanciation. *Philosophy Today* 17(2): 129–141.

Sennett, Richard. 2008. *The Craftsman.* New Haven, CT: Yale University Press.

Sergiovanni, Thomas J. 1986. Understanding reflective practice. *Journal of Curriculum and Supervision* 1(4): 353–359.

Thompson, D.F. 2004. *Restoring Responsibility: Ethics in Government, Business, and Healthcare.* New York: Cambridge University Press.

Weber, M. 1918. Politik als beruf [Politics as a vocation]. Lecture. http://www.ne.jp/asahi/moriyuki/abukuma/weber/lecture/politics_vocation.html.

Winnicott, Donald W. 1958. Transitional objects and transitional phenomena. In *Collected Papers: Through Paediatrics to Psychoanalysis,* 229–242. London: Tavistock.

Yankelovich, Daniel. 1991. *Coming to Public Judgment: Making Democracy Work in a Complex World.* Syracuse, NY: Syracuse University Press.

6

Advancing Ethical Competence Through Pedagogy

Carole L. Jurkiewicz

> *No responsibility of government is more fundamental than the responsibility for maintaining the highest standards of ethical behavior by those who conduct the public business. . . . This principle must be followed not only in reality, but in appearance. For the basis of effective government is public confidence, and that confidence is endangered when ethical standards falter or appear to falter.*

—John F. Kennedy

Public-sector competence is rooted in ethical competence. Finance, management, transportation, police protection, and all government operations depend upon the trust of the citizenry to function. The importance of trust, rooted in ethicality, was first noted centuries ago in the original analysis of effective public governance (Machiavelli 1515) and is no less salient today. Trust in the U.S. government has been eroding since the 1972 Watergate scandal, declining by half in 2009 alone (Pew 2010), and is calling into question the competence of all government operations. Yet the public wants confidence in government restored, wants reassurance that tax monies are spent for the good of the whole and that government representatives act for the greater good (Pew 2010); the proposed solution to the decline in trust is a general outcry for ethics education and accountability (Johnson 2007; Kennedy and Malatesta 2010). Dolph and Lycan (2008) go so far as to suggest that failing to provide ethics education is tantamount to educational malpractice. Ethics education through established methodologies has been shown to be effective in preventing unethical behavior (Kohlberg 1981, 1986; Norman, Richards, and Bear 1998; Jurkiewicz and Nichols 2002; Jurkiewicz 2002b) not only for the individual student but also for those whom the student supervises or will supervise into the future (Jurkiewicz 2002b). The persistent questioning of its efficacy is rooted primarily in the ineffective methodologies most often used to teach it (Dolph and Lycan 2008)—that is, tucking it in as a case study within a course on another topic not taught by an ethics expert. This chapter discusses demonstrated methods of effective ethics instruction, along with measures of effective implementation.

The layperson's belief that people instinctively know and agree upon what is right and, therefore, do not need instruction has not been evidenced in fact (e.g., Menzel 1997). Notions of what is right are shaped by a variety of sources, including family and friends, teachers, the media, entertainment, religions, and societal practices; inherent in these beliefs of right or wrong is the key role played by influential others. Both Foucault (1984) and Kohlberg (1976) speak to the power of others to influence ethical standards, with Foucault focusing on the power of authority in general to shape ethics and Kohlberg on the power of individual leaders and social forces to do so. Foucault asserted that normalized values as articulated by those in authority lead to dominant and unquestioned institutional practices, which in turn define acceptable behavior and restrict individual autonomy. He purports it is an involuntary, often unconscious, submission to the power of institutional authority; this view was introduced by Barnard (1946) and expanded upon by Bourdieu (1990) to describe how individuals create and maintain commonplace practices and adopt expected roles even when these practices are oppressive, marginalizing, and contrast with one's previously held ethical beliefs. Kohlberg (1976, 1981, 1986) and Jurkiewicz (2002b), among others, demonstrated that leaders have a profound effect on the ethical standards used by their subordinates in deciding on which action is ethical and which is not. Ethical or unethical behavior is thus learned from those in positions of authority over us. Furthermore, given the increasing number of reported ethical violations, one could surmise that even if people instinctively know what is right, they don't necessarily do what is right. As Hejka-Elkins (1988) and Darley (1996) have demonstrated, individuals are not likely to do what is right in the absence of targeted intervention. While transparency policies are, of course, essential to the advocacy and oversight of administrative ethicality, the discussion here focuses upon teaching how to rationally determine what the right decision is among a set of choices, and instilling the skills to choose that option as the key challenge in achieving ethical competence.

Defining Right

In defining what is right at a societal level, the law offers some assistance, but it is not the sole answer. Laws change and are most often reactionary in nature. Behaviors that were once legal (and therefore ethical, according to that argument) are not so now, such as denying women the right to vote, sanctioning slavery, and turning a blind eye to hate crimes. If ethics were tied only to laws, they could change from one day to the next, and the socially binding element ethics provides would not exist. Additionally, we would be placing those who make laws—namely, politicians—as our moral exemplars, and politicians are the least respected group of professionals in the United States (Rasmussen Reports 2010); certainly, they are not arbiters of morality. Ethical codes attempt to define what is right for a particular group, but even the mafia and gangs abide by codes of conduct they define as ethical (Cummings and Monti 1993; Parker 2007; Schmitz and Christopher 1997; USDOJ 2005, 2008), so in themselves codes at best define who we aspire to be as a member of a society and outline the accepted ethical norms for a particular group (Brown 2007). Further, most individuals abide by a multiplicity of codes that often are in conflict; Joe Doe could be bound by a professional code at work and an unwritten yet socially expected code of conduct in other circumstances such as while attending a bachelor party, playing a competitive sport, or attending a religious service; elements of each of those codes can conflict. No single societal code encompasses all of Joe Doe's behavior (Jurkiewicz 2002a). Social mores offer additional guidance beyond specific codes as to appropriate conduct, but this varies from country to country and across regions in the United States, as well as within many states and across generations (Abramson and Inglehart 2007). Religions can offer codes of conduct as well, but these vary, and there is ample evidence that those who are most dogmatic about their faith are those most likely to behave unethically (e.g., Henle, Giacalone, and Jurkiewicz 2005; Hood et al. 1996; Kohn 1989; Batson et al. 1989; Allport and Ross 1967; Cline and Richards 1965). Philosophy offers some insight, but there remains in the vast majority of the literature an irreconcilable tension between utilitarianism and deontology (e.g., Rawls and Herman 2000).

Certainly, personal directives cannot in themselves be trusted, as evidenced by those who simply want to maximize their own immediate gain above all else, those who exhibit strong biases, as well as the individuals among us with hidden pathologies. The fact is there are no easy answers, but there is a place to start. What can be used as a rubric for instilling ethical competencies are those behaviors one can observe, framed within a system of transparency and accountability that enhances the chance that these behaviors will be evinced. While individual interpretations may vary, general consensus would tend to agree that certain behaviors are ethical whereas others are not, that this consensus shifts in tandem with societal shifts, and that these interpretations usually share the common thread of being advantageous to society as a whole. For instance, lying, thievery, and murder are generally accepted as unethical because such acts can be harmful as a societal norm, although they may confer temporary advantage for an individual and may be socially accepted under particular circumstances (e.g., in defense of one's child or during war).

Ethical Competence

Ethical competence in public administrators is evidenced in managerial decisions and the organizational factors that administrators directly influence (Büngi 2010). At one end of an ethical continuum are satisficing decisions made on the basis of expediency, short-term gain, and involving only those people or elements that are superficially evident; on the other end are decisions focused on long-term outcomes, taking into account the broad spectrum of affected parties, considering possible consequences, and seeking the best possible solution for all (Kohlberg 1976, 1981, 1986). Tolerance of divergent opinions, a high degree of emotional intelligence and adaptability, and the extent to which political gamesmanship is absent from decision making are additional measures of this competence. The amount of transparency in the organization, the degree of organizational commitment on behalf of the leaders' subordinates, the organization or agency's reputation for trustworthiness, the objective resolution of complaints, and the confidence demonstrated in the organization and its leadership are other clear factors.

The most frequently considered determinant of attaining ethical competence is the level of an individual's moral development (Andreoli and Lefkowitz 2009), and it is the basis by which most of the curricula focused on professional ethics education can be evaluated. Kohlberg's stage theory of moral development and ethical reasoning (Kohlberg 1976, 1986) provides a foundation for addressing the components of ethical competence in public service and, thus, what an ethics course in an MPA program might wisely entail. Rather than prescriptive, Kohlberg's model encourages individuals to develop their own ethical reasoning within the parameters of an overall professional and societal rubric, and to think through various options. The model effectively deconstructs ethical competencies into interactionally constructed, logically integrated conceptual structures that frame individual experience (Eddy 1988) and can be operationalized and measured. By examining Kohlberg's theory and the pedagogical methodologies rooted in it, we can move forward in defining behavioral elements that constitute observable ethical competence. While certainly some challenges to Kohlberg's model have been raised (e.g., Baek 2002), it remains the most widely accepted rubric for understanding ethical decision making and has been demonstrated to be applicable cross-culturally (Dolph and Lycan 2008; Kung 1998).

The theory posits a continuum of six stages, ranging from the most elemental decision-making orientation in determining right from wrong, to the most complex. Reviewing the six levels provides an opportunity to target the level of ethical decision making that would constitute ethical competence on behalf of a public administrator. At the lowest level, Heteronomous Morality, an individual determines if something is wrong based upon whether he thinks he is likely to get in trouble for it. While some people do operate at this level of ethical reasoning regardless of chronological age, they do so with an arguable awareness of laws, social mores, customs, and what others around them consider wrong. Moving up a level to Individualism, Instrumental Purpose, and Exchange, ethical reasoning would consist of following rules only when it is of immediate benefit to the individual, where a person acts to attain her own interests and needs and accepts that others will do the same; the quid pro quo would be justified here. The first two stages are classified as egoist (Malloy and Agarwal 2008) in that the motivation is to avoid punishment and seek reward for an individual or a particular organizational unit; success is measured by short-term productivity and cost-effectiveness (Mayer, Davis, and Schoorman 1995). As the incidence of narcissism has increased at a rapid rate in society (Twenge et al. 2008), these modes of ethical reasoning are increasingly witnessed in the population.

The third step in cognitive complexity is the stage wherein individuals define what is right by living up to the expectations of the people closest to them, such family members, close friends, or favored coworkers. Characterized by demonstrating loyalty, gratitude, trust, and concern for others, this third stage is termed Mutual Interpersonal Expectations, Relationships, and Interpersonal Conformity, and it embodies the relationship between authority and values that Foucault (1984) purported. This stage introduces the concept of benevolence (Malloy and Agarwal 2008) aimed at fostering friendships, establishing interpersonal relationships, and developing a kinship bond. Given three factors—the individualistic nature of the reasoning process behind these stages, the relativity of the circumstances that might lead the decision maker to one course of action over another, and the lack of consideration for the public—these approaches could not be supported as the basis of ethical competence for public service professionals.

The fourth stage, Social System and Conscience, is characterized by fulfilling the duties an individual has agreed to accept and upholding laws except under extreme circumstances where they conflict with social duties. Determining what is right here also includes thinking through and choosing actions that positively benefit society, the group, or the institution, thereby extending the concept of benevolence beyond one's immediate personal affiliations to include the goal of group cohesion, public good, and mutual understanding separate from egocentric motivation (Des Jardin 1997; Mayer, Davis, and Schoorman 1995). This, it could be argued, would be the minimum level of ethical competence expected from a public administrator (Badaracco 2006; Jurkiewicz and Massey, Jr. 1998). Ideally, administrators should demonstrate behaviors consistent with the next higher level of ethical reasoning, the Social Contract and Individual Rights level. Inclusive of the concern for duty and benefitting society, this stage would go a step beyond and demonstrate an awareness that people hold a variety of values relative to the groups to which they belong, and that these must be respected insofar as they do not conflict with the general good, or the social contract. Adhering to the standards of this stage would, at times, require doing what is right despite it being unpopular or counter to the majority opinion, but would subjugate short-term individual or group opinions to the rights and good for all into the long-term.

The final stage, Universal Ethical Principles, is the culmination of the stages preceding but goes beyond them in establishing principles that supersede laws, customs, and duties. These principles are *universalizable,* meaning they are thoughtfully considered on an individual basis, not something entered into lightly or adopted from a dogma or a person, and are those the individual wishes all humanity would share; they are absolute and inviolate (Jurkiewicz and Massey, Jr. 1998). These are universal principles of justice, respect for human rights, and the dignity of the individual above all else. Given that less than 2 percent of the population actually attains the final stage, and that only two verifiable methods are known by which individuals can achieve it (Jurkiewicz 2002b), it is not realistic to expect this level of ethicality in establishing a competence framework for public administrators. The first three stages in Kohlberg's model are teleological in approach and justify all means to a particular end, a common thread in ethical violations, while the deontological perspective of stages 4, 5, and 6 focuses on the qualities intrinsic to the decisions themselves, an upholding of principles as the basis of public service ethics. Thus, it can be acknowledged that ethical competence in public administrators is evidenced by stages 4, 5, and 6 of ethical reasoning: Social System and Conscience, Social Contract and Individual Rights, and Universal Ethical Principles. Clearly evident in this rubric is the assertion that ethical competence is not an either/or, absolute factor but a continuum running from none to all. No individual will be found at either end of the continuum, but without ethics instruction the literature suggests most will measure on the lower end of the scale (Kohlberg 1976, 1981, 1986; Jurkiewicz 2002b). Examining stages 4 and 5 in more detail will clarify the pedagogy aimed at teaching and measuring these competencies.

Stage 4: Social System and Conscience

In this stage, individuals establish the basis for determining right and wrong based upon public institutionalized laws (Thoma and Rest 1999). Adherence to such laws is believed to create stability in society and allow for long-term coordination and planning, and should be upheld except when in conflict with social duties. Individual obligations are the fulfillment of both the spirit and the letter of law, and it is anticipated and required that others will act accordingly. In society, each person is expected to do his part as a functional division of labor, and authority should act on behalf of the good of the whole system; the emphasis is on one's fulfillment of duties to society. Rational morality thus affords individuals an accord with one another, a secure foundation from which to describe and assess the moral world in a common voice (Talbot 2000). Morality is therefore viewed as a learned activity, and that progressive evolutionary development in this regard is an adaptive, life-sustaining strategy (Hauser 2006).

Stages 5 and 6: Social Contract and Individual Rights; Universal Ethical Principles

The individual in stage 5 familiarizes herself with public institutionalized laws but also considers the rationality behind the laws to understand whether they are reactionary or genuinely ensure basic rights for all people (Rest 1979). Laws change and generally reflect the will of the people, but they can be unethical, as the earlier examples attest. If laws are fairly made, representing constitutional principles and the most desired set of social arrangements for all, then they establish systems of social cooperation that can guide ethical decision making. The emphasis is on due process, justice, rights, and long-term consequences of establishing societal or legal precedents, as well as the obligation to obey laws and contracts one has freely chosen. The public good here is based on rational calculation of overall utility. Society and those in positions of authority are responsible for establishing a plan of cooperation that minimizes arbitrary inequities and maximizes the stake of each individual in supporting cooperation. The essence of this stage is exemplified in Piaget's (1932/1965) claim that "logic is the morality of thought just as morality is the logic of action."

The stages are, of course, more complex than outlined here, but these core extrapolations enable a discussion of the model as it relates to ethical competence. Stage 6, Universal Ethical Principles, embodies the ultimate values of public service, going a step beyond four and five in establishing the principles a rational society would desire to underpin a system for governing and cooperation. Principles therein are self-determined and supersede laws and social agreements; one demonstrates respect for persons as ends, not means (Jurkiewicz and Massey, Jr. 1998). Again, the difficulty of teaching the orientation toward principle, as it is culturally bound, limits the extent to which it is emphasized here as a reasonable measure of ethical competence. As Kohlberg (1976) concluded, less than 2 percent of the population attains this level; thus, he de-emphasized it in his work on ethical pedagogy. The ethical competencies defined by stages 4 and 5 can, however, be taught and measured.

Teaching Ethical Competence

Moral education as a component of curriculum has been a constant throughout American history, in recent times shifting toward producing educated citizenry and leaders (Dolph and Lycan 2008), and seeking indicators of effectiveness following ethics instruction (e.g., Hartman and Werhane 2009). Increasing interest in developing ethical competence is evidenced in both the growing number of scholarly articles focused on it as well as reports in popular media. The percentage of MPA programs with courses in ethics has increased from 23 percent in 1981 to 39 percent in 1994 (Catron and Denhardt), 60 percent in 1997 (Menzel), 64 percent in 2002 (Jurkiewicz and Nichols), and 74.1 percent in 2011,[1] in addition to those that incorporate ethics into other subject matter courses for which there is no discoverable documentation. The efficacy of teaching ethical competence has been a key challenge for educators, although evidence that it has a measurable impact on behavior has been building over the past decade (e.g., Jurkiewicz 2002b; Hiltebeitel and Jones 1992; Loe and Weeks 2000; Luthar and Karri 2005). Dozens of empirical studies on teaching ethical competence have been published since the 1960s (e.g., Bruce 1998; Menzel 1997), and the most effective teaching approaches in this regard vary little from public administration (e.g., Jurkiewicz 2002b), to business administration (e.g., Bruce and Edgington 2008; Delaney and Sockell 1992), to science (e.g., Bero and Kuhlman 2010), and health (e.g., Musick 1999) professionals. The research identifies five key factors in educating for ethical competence:

1. An understanding of moral philosophy and moral arguments.
2. The ability to distinguish ethical issues separate from a management or resource issue.
3. The ability to logically reason in seeking a solution to ethical problems.
4. An understanding of one's own ethical framework and value system, and the recognition that others may not share that system.

5. The ability to perform ethically in an environment where pressures to do otherwise may be considerable.

Methods of teaching these factors also share consensus across faculties from MPA, MBA, MHA, and other professional programs. A broad range of instructional tools are advocated as most effective, including case analysis; diagnostic tests self-administered by the student and discussed in class; lectures; experiential exercises; and video cases with group discussions (Jurkiewicz and Giacalone 2002). The key concern underpinning efficacy is that ethics instruction includes both theoretical models of ethical reasoning as well as opportunities to apply that knowledge to real-world situations through guided activities (e.g., Shareef 2008). Through this approach, students come to the realization that addressing ethical issues means asking the difficult questions, thoroughly analyzing the choices using substantiated decision-making models, and understanding the context in which these decisions are made along with their potential consequences. Table 6.1 outlines topics a course on ethics might encompass if it included the most effective elements as reported in the literature to date, each matched to the competency it addresses.

The overarching question in ethics education—or any education—is, of course, how one can know if these competencies have been effectively taught. The utility of the five competence factors beyond structuring a pedagogy is the ability to measure students' learning. Table 6.2 presents a matrix that matches each factor to a possible method of measurement that one could expect would result from effective ethics education based upon the research to date.

The call for effective ethics instruction has increased since Watergate, accentuating both the importance of ethics in the public sector and the breadth of corruption that permeates it. Cooper (2006) attests to the growth of interest in administrative ethics in particular since 1980 as evidenced both in the scholarly and professional literature, conference sessions, proliferation of ethics-centered organizations, and in practice. Certainly, the rules, laws, and codes that were put in place to prevent such behavior have not proven effective; if someone wants to engage in unethical behavior, they typically find a way around these deterrents. For those who do want to uphold ethical standards in the workplace, just like those who wish to manage a budget effectively, education is essential. Effective ethics education instills both the motivation to be ethical, the ability to distinguish the ethicality of a situation separate from its legality or politics, and the skills to do what is right. Education heightens awareness of the importance of ethical behavior and the consequences to the individual and the organization of unethical performance (Brudney and Martinez 2010; Norman, Richards, and Bear 1998). The scattershot approach wherein ethics is discussed as an element of a case study in another class, say budget-

Table 6.1

Elements of an Ethics Course Linked to the Five Factors of Ethical Competence

Topic	A	B	C	D	E
Introduction to public service ethics	X	X			
Philosophical modeling	X	X	X	X	
Ethics and law	X	X	X		
Ethical decision making	X	X	X		X
Ethics code		X		X	
Ethics policy		X		X	
Whistleblowing		X	X	X	X
Ethical vs. unethical behavior	X	X		X	
Lying		X		X	
Ethics training in organizations		X	X	X	
Ethics in crises		X	X	X	
The cost of ethics (Ethinomics)	X	X	X	X	
Situational ethics	X	X	X	X	
Ethics and politics		X		X	X
Power and ethics	X	X		X	X
Ethical leadership		X	X	X	X
Organizational evil	X	X		X	X
Moral dilemmas	X	X	X	X	X
Virtues	X	X		X	
Ethics audit		X	X		X
Ethical wills		X		X	
Ethics measures	X	X	X	X	X

Key:
A   Understanding moral philosophy and moral arguments
B   Ability to distinguish moral issues separate from other issues
C   Ability to logically reason regarding resolution of ethical problems
D   Students' enhanced understanding of own and others' ethical frameworks
E   Ability to perform ethically despite pressures

ing, does not impart ethical competencies any more than teaching budgeting as an element of a case study in a course on ethics would establish capacity in budgeting; to expect competence in any field requires a proven course of study taught by an expert (Bowman 1998). Without formal ethics instruction, the student cum administrator is left to either react to ethical issues from an idiosyncratic and usually emotional level, to ignore the issues completely, or to deal with them on a superficial level (Cooper 2006; Bok 1990).

Table 6.2

Measuring the Five Factors of Ethical Competence in Individuals

Competence factor	Assessment measure
Understanding moral philosophy and moral arguments	D.I.T. (see Jurkiewicz, 2002a); Critical Thinking in Ethics (see Curtler 2004)
Ability to distinguish moral issues separate from other issues	Using case studies in testing
Ability to logically reason regarding resolution of ethical problems	Critical Thinking in Ethics (see Curtler 2004); (Schmidt and Hunter 1998)
Students' enhanced understanding of own and others' ethical frameworks	Assigning papers requiring students to outline their moral beliefs; engaging in debate and open discussions in class with professor taking the position of devil's advocate (see Jurkiewicz 2002a)
Ability to perform ethically despite pressures	Experiments can be designed to test this; track students as they move forward in their careers; organizational level measures

Moral reasoning as the foundation of rationally determining the ethical course of action is comprised of a set of abstract concepts that can be examined and evaluated by students through dilemma-based discussions in the classroom, with a professor serving as mediator (Kohlberg 1986). Classroom discussions provide a safe environment to develop ethical competencies by identifying ethical issues as unique from other issues, modeling logical arguments, encouraging diverse perspectives, and providing the tools to separate fact from opinion in reaching a just conclusion (Kennedy and Malatesta 2010; Dolph and Lycan 2008). Facilitating ethical competence in the classroom requires that the student be exposed to questions that encourage him to view an ethical dilemma from the perspective of a higher stage of reasoning. For example, if a student maintains that the right course of action is to follow what others are doing, the instructor would need to ask questions that lead the student to examine both the specific consequences of that approach and entertain alternatives approaches to resolving it (Kohlberg 1969; Jurkiewicz 2002a; Dukerich et al. 1990; Nichols and Day 1982). Such questioning is intended to create dissatisfaction within the student regarding his assumed approach to resolving the ethical dilemma, ultimately challenging him to think of a more effective solution. In fact, individuals without formal ethics education are usually unaware of the ethical problems inherent in the issues they face (Jurkiewicz and Nichols 2002; Kennedy and Malatesta 2010) and therefore are also unable to reason about them effectively.

The classroom atmosphere plays a key role in allowing such learning to take place. It must be characterized by openness, mutual respect, a tolerance of viewpoints, and an emphasis on rational analysis (Kohlberg 1969, 1981, 1986). The instructor should not interject personal views or opinions and should deflect student requests for the "right" answer, instead using questions to help the student arrive at the best solution on her own. Whetten and Cameron (2002) provide a useful set of questions to use in the classroom as a stimulus for ethical development. Figure 6.1 adapts these questions to the public sector and correlates each with an ethical competence central to the Kohlberg model. They can be used as a basis for assessing options in a case discussion, as a reflective tool around which student papers can be developed, or as a method of assessing examples of ethical propriety or malfeasance in the public sector.

The most effective ethics education, as borne out in a broad literature, encompasses four key elements: (1) it includes both philosophical theory and case discussion over the period of a semester; (2) it is a core course taught by a professor with expertise in the field, as opposed to a class discussion led by experts in other areas such as budgeting or finance (e.g., Baetz and Sharp 2004; Dolph and Lycan 2008; Jurkiewicz 2002b); (3) it requires the student to analytically and contextually assess ethical behaviors and outcomes as opposed to providing them with a rubric of what is right and wrong (Ellenwood 2007); and (4) it is integrated and applied to other specific disciplines such as budgeting, human resources, and economics through a class component designed by an ethics expert that can be used by professors in other courses. Instructors should, at a minimum, hold a terminal degree in applied philosophy, organizational behavior, organizational psychology, or a closely related field; as one would expect for professors of economics or budgeting, individuals teaching ethics need more than a layperson's interest or professional experience. They should have a demonstrated research and writing agenda that focuses on applied ethics. Furthermore, they should demonstrate through educational credentials a clear understanding of the public sector. Ideally, the ethics professor is measurably at the highest stages on the Kohlberg scale, in order to introduce increasingly higher levels of reasoning into the class discussion, although of course requiring him to take the test is unrealistic and impractical. Scarily, if ethics is taught by an individual who scores at the first three levels of Kohlberg's model, he can significantly regress the level of ethical reasoning among his students, making them less rather than more ethically competent than when they started the course (e.g., Jurkiewicz 2002b; Kohlberg and Hersh 1977; Kohlberg 1981). For long-term effectiveness, such education needs to be reinforced through professional development (Guskey 1986), perhaps through integrated training initiatives, supplemental conferences or classes, workbooks, and DVD-based discussions.

In addition to elevating one's stage scores using Kohlberg's model (e.g.,

Figure 6.1 **Stimulus Questions for Ethical Development in the Classroom Applied to Decision Alternatives in Group Discussions of Case Studies**

TRANSPARENCY: Would you be embarrassed if your decision became a headline in the local newspaper? Would you feel confident in justifying your actions or decisions to both your coworkers and the public?

UNIVERSALIZABILITY: Would you want to be treated in the same manner?

JUSTICE: Are the dignity and liberty of others preserved by this decision? Is the basic humanity of the affected parties enhanced? Are their opportunities expanded or curtailed?

RIGHTS: Are the rights, welfare, and betterment of minorities and lower-status people given full consideration? Does this decision benefit only those with privilege but without merit?

EGOISM: Is an opportunity for personal gain clouding my judgment? Would I make the same decision regardless of the benefit I may receive from the outcome?

PRINCIPLES: Is this decision or action consistent with my espoused principles? Is it consistent with the highest values to which the public service should aspire? Does it violate the spirit of any organizational policies or laws?

UTILITY: Does the action or decision lead to the greatest good for the greatest number or the least harm to the fewest? How critical is the benefit to society as a whole? Can the harmful effects be mitigated?

SOCIAL CONTRACT: Does the action or decision facilitate the social contract, the bond of common purpose, and encourage pride in the citizens subject to these outcomes?

Source: Adapted from Whetten and Cameron 2002, p. 70.

Jurkiewicz 2002b; Kohlberg 1981), effective ethics pedagogy incorporating the aforementioned elements has resulted in significant relationships between an individual's scores on measures of moral judgment and behavioral outcomes such as delinquency, honesty, and altruism (Blasi 1980; Thoma 1994; Thoma, Rest, and Barnett 1986). Increases in integrity test measures resultant of ethics education have also been shown to be valid predictors of overall job performance (Schmidt and Hunter 1998). A review of studies published between 1996 and 2003 found various measures of moral development and ethical judgment positively correlated higher scores with ethical intentions and behaviors (O'Fallon and Butterfield 2005), meaning students connect theory with action. The Kohlberg model of ethical reasoning, and the concomitant approaches to effectively elevating a student's scores in this regard, provide a starting point for asserting that ethicality is a key competency for public service professionals that can be taught and measured. These competencies are most often evidenced in behavior, and these behaviors can serve as an external assessment of ethicality.

Measuring Ethical Competence

Measurements of ethical competence can occur at the individual level, through direct evaluation, and by proxy at the organizational level by assessing those aspects over which the student has influence. The five competence factors previously identified offer a framework for assessing the efficacy of ethics education. Table 6.2 matches each of these factors with the corresponding method of assessment. In most instances, direct measures of ethical-reasoning levels such as the well-established DIT (see Jurkiewicz 2002b), and assessment measures of critical thinking in ethics (see Curtler 2004) can be used in the classroom to assess the efficacy of ethics instruction at both the theoretical and applied levels. Additionally, using case study analysis as part of an exam, requiring reflective papers, and engaging in classroom debates that have been shown to increase students' levels of ethical reasoning (see Jurkiewicz 2002b) can be used as measurements. To determine whether a student will have the skill and motivation to perform ethically despite pressures to do otherwise, an in-class role-playing exercise can be conducted. For example, the setting could be a government office whereby a student (employee) overhears an offer of kickbacks by a vendor being accepted by the student's supervisor. The student then is asked by her boss to work as a liaison with the vendor, promising her a bonus for the extra work. Knowing she urgently needs the money and would likely be fired for revealing the truth, the class can discuss her potential actions and their consequences using the consequentialist and non-consequentialist, egoist, and justice frameworks. Once the class has considered these possible actions, the next step is for the instructor to facilitate a discussion of how the student in this case might demonstrate ethical competence by emphasizing four components: (1) her ability to outline possible courses of action and to objectively assess how others will be affected by each potential action; (2) the extent to which she can determine which line of action is morally justifiable using principles of logic; (3) a demonstrated motivation to place universalizable values higher than her individual values; and (4) evidence of moral character, defined as ego strength, perseverance, toughness, courage, and strength of conviction (McNeel 1994). This framework, assimilated from Kohlberg (1976, 1981, 1986), suggests that all four components are necessary in measuring ethical competence as an objective set of qualities. For instance, an individual can be morally astute, make good moral judgments, and possess the appropriate values hierarchy, but if the individual is easily distracted, discouraged, or weak-willed, it can lead to moral failure.

A more comprehensive measure of ethical competence, although more difficult, would be to track students as they move forward in their careers, both through surveys and as positive recognition or negative consequences for their ethical performance are publicly revealed. Effective ethics education could be expected to affect administrators' reasoning and subsequent behavior at the conclusion of the course as well as throughout their career, as a component of professional development. This is especially true if the classroom instruction incorporates the multiple cultural viewpoints that students are likely to encounter during their careers (Baek 2002). Increases in integrity test measures post-ethics education have been shown to be valid predictors of overall job performance into the long term (Schmidt and Hunter 1998).

Ethics education affects not only the individual students but those they supervise and the organization of which they are a part. Vershoor (2007) and Jurkiewicz (2009), among others, have substantiated the importance of administrators in having the strongest influence on ethical behavior of employees at work. Leaders establish a climate in which ethical values are salient (Grojean et al. 2004). As Dickson et al. (2001, 208) state, "The leader serves as a role model for his or her subordinates about the type of behaviors that are seen as ethically acceptable and how ethical problems and questions should be addressed. Additionally, the leader provides cues about what is ethical by explicitly rewarding and punishing certain behaviors . In other words leaders may bring out or suppress the tendencies of organizational members to behave in an ethical or unethical fashion." A centuries-old phrase ascribed to the Chinese remains a timely insight into human nature: the fish rots from the head down (Jurkiewicz 2010). The implication is that an unethical leader leads to an organization of unethical followers and, conversely, if an organization's culture is unethical (Jurkiewicz and Grossman 2012), then the problem starts with the leader. A leader establishes the ethical culture of an organization through her actions more so than her words (Jurkiewicz and Brown 2000a 2000b), and is accountable for the culture she thus creates.

As leaders are the primary influencers of the prevailing ethics in an organization, an agency, or a department (Jurkiewicz and Brown 2000a), ethical competence can be measured not only on the individual level but also on the organizational level (Bürgi 2010). As stated earlier, one would not find an ethical leader as the head of an unethical organization, as much as some have tried to maintain an innocence of ignorance, nor would one find an unethical leader at the top of an ethical organization (Mihelič, Lipičnik, and Tekavčič 2010; Brown, Treviño, and Harrison 2005; Grojean et al. 2004; Treviño, Brown, and Hartman 2003; Dickson et al. 2001; Paine 1994; Cyert

Figure 6.2 **Indicators of Administrative Ethical Competence as Measured by Organizational Factors**

- Citizen and employee feedback expresses that they are treated respectfully and valued
- Communication is straightforward and employees/citizens feel honestly informed; gossip and rumor are minimal
- Meets or exceeds legal requirements
- Demonstrates through policies and programs the values the organization espouses
- Addresses ethical dilemmas regularly in meetings and correspondence
- Responds to claims of wrongdoing with respect, in a timely manner, and with transparency
- Resources and opportunities are distributed equitably, inside and outside the organization
- All employees are held to the same standards of moral conduct; absence of favoritism
- Openly transparent in policy and practice
- Rewards ethical behavior
- Implements systems to prevent or minimize harmful behaviors
- Exhibits a culture of trust and commitment
- Low employee turnover and absenteeism; many qualified applicants for advertised positions
- Employees feel empowered and supported
- Training, promotions, and awards tied to ethical performance
- Respects and encourages diverse opinions and viewpoints

1990; Hitt 1990; Bennis and Nanus 1985; Jansen and Von Glinow 1985). The policies, processes, decisions, and reward systems are all influenced directly or indirectly by the leader and therefore serve as proxy measures of their ethicality. Thus, as an inductive measure, Figure 6.2 identifies the indicators of an ethically competent organization, including factors related to resource distribution, policies, programs, and citizen perception.

An organization that exhibits most if not all of these characteristics and one that strives to achieve the remaining factors indicates not only the ethical competence of the administrator, but a leader who facilitates ethical competence in the organization's employees and vendors as well (Gentile 2010; Bazerman 2008; Brown 2007; Brown, Treviño, and Harrison 2005; Khuntia and Suar 2004;) Such organizational-level evocations of a leader's ethical competence have been shown to be consistent across cultures (Baek 2002). Applying both the individual and organizational measures and comparing the two over time would of course be both ultimately informative while practically inhibitive.

Conclusion

At the core of public-sector competence is ethical competence. There is a sentiment connected to those employed in the public sector, a belief that they should embody a set of moral standards referred to as public service values. While the definition of public service values varies, and research indicates that they are no longer values predominant in or unique to the public sector (Bürgi 2010; Ulrich 2008; Sanders 2008; Jurkiewicz, Massey, Jr. and Brown 1998; Wheeler and Brady 1998; Jurkiewicz and Massey, Jr. 1997), the phrase remains a cherished anachronism in our society. The concept of public-sector values embodies the qualities society expects from those who act on behalf of government. Society wants them to be motivated by service, equality, fairness, and altruism; it wants them to be above seeking personal over public good, to set aside politics and personal preference, and to operate with the goal of serving the public. Society wants public-sector employees to be more moral, more ethical than proprietary or nonprofit employees (Dorasamy 2010; Thompson 2004; Goss 1996). While this model may have worked in times past, the reality of today is that crossover employment is near 100 percent, with individuals working in all sectors over the course of their careers. It is unrealistic to think individuals suddenly become more ethical when hired into the public sector, and less so when leaving it (Jurkiewicz 2002a). Given the increased call for advancing ethical behavior in all sectors, what was once a concept known as public service ethics may well be descriptive of the goal of organizational ethics more generally.

Yet the need for public service values is real (e.g., Bozeman 2007). Those in the public sector have power over us that those in other sectors do not, including control of our freedoms, lifestyles, and whether we live or die. Knowing that individuals enter the public sector with basically the same values as those in other sectors, what is needed is training, education, and appropriate oversight policies (Bozeman 2007; Thompson 2004; Jurkiewicz 2002a). Effective techniques for ethics education are thus of vital importance, as are the courses in our MPA programs that teach ethical competence as a required element of the curriculum. As NASPAA (2011) states in its Code of Good Practice, every member program "integrates ethics into the curriculum and all aspects of program operation, and expects students and faculty to exhibit the highest ethical standards in their teaching, research, and service." What research has concluded is that ethical competence can be defined, taught, and measured. Employees want to uphold higher ethical standards in the workplace but often find the biggest impediment to this are the policies to which they are subject, and the organizational culture in which they must participate (Jurkiewicz 2000). Ethics education has a significant impact on their ability to maintain ethicality in the face of pressures to do otherwise (Jurkiewicz 2002b), whereas the lack of ethics education that follows the precepts outlined here leaves decision makers unaware of the ethical dimensions of their choices (Kennedy and Malatesta 2010). It is incumbent upon

MPA programs and those bodies that accredit them to ensure that students with this degree possess ethical competence. A common framework allows for consensus in education, training, organizational policy, and ethical and legal code development. There is a solid foundation, but much work remains to be done in explicating pedagogical measures, developing comprehensive ethics education textbooks, and creating ethical competence measures for the individual and the workplace that can be widely implemented. The discussion here is offered as a summation of where we are and a starting place from which we can move forward.

Note

1. This figure was determined by an analysis of reported curricula on the websites of each of the NASPAA-accredited programs.

References

Abramson, P.R., and R. Inglehart. 2007. Generational replacement and value change in six West European societies. *American Journal of Political Science* 30(1): 1–25.
Allport, G., and M. Ross. 1967. Personal religious orientation and prejudice. *Journal of Personality and Social Psychology* 5: 432–441.
Andreoli, N., and J. Lefkowitz. 2009. Individual and organizational antecedents of misconduct in organizations. *Journal of Business Ethics* 85(3): 309–332.
Badaracco, J.J.L. 2006. Leadership in literature. *Harvard Business Review* 84: 47–55.
Baek, H. 2002. A comparative study of moral development of Korean and British children. *Journal of Moral Education* 31(4): 373–391.
Baetz, M.C., and D.J. Sharp. 2004. Integrating ethics content into the core business curriculum: Do core teaching materials do the job? *Journal of Business Ethics* 51: 53–62.
Barnard, C.I. 1946. Functions and pathology of status systems in formal organizations. In *Industry and Society*, ed. W.F. Whyte, 46–83. New York: McGraw-Hill.
Batson, C.D., K.C. Oleson, J.L. Weeks, S.P. Healy, P.J. Reeves, P. Jennings, and T. Brown. 1989. Religious prosocial motivation: Is it altruistic or egoistic? *Journal of Personality and Social Psychology* 57: 873–884.
Bazerman, M.H. 2008. Evaluating your business ethics: A Harvard professor explains why good people do unethical things. *Gallup Management Journal,* June 12, 1–5. http://businessjournal.gallup.com/content/107527/evaluating-your-business-ethics.aspx.
Bennis, W., and B. Nanus. 1985. *Leadership: The Strategies for Taking Charge.* New York: Harper & Row.
Bero, B., and A. Kuhlman. 2010. Teaching ethics to engineers: Ethical decision making parallels the engineering design process. *Science and Engineering Ethics* 17(3): 597–605.
Blasi, A. 1980. Bridging moral cognition and moral action: A critical review of literature. *Psychological Bulletin* 88(1): 1–45.

Bok, D. 1990. *Universities and the Future of America*. Durham, NC: Duke University Press.
Bourdieu, Pierre. 1990. *The Logic of Practice,* trans. R. Nice. Stanford, CA: Stanford University Press.
Bowman, J. 1998. The lost world of public administration education: Rediscovering the meaning of professionalism. *Journal of Public Affairs Education* 4(1): 27–31.
Bozeman, B. 2007. *Public Values and Public Interest: Counterbalancing Economic Individualism*. Washington, DC: Georgetown University Press.
Brown, M.E. 2007. Misconceptions of ethical leadership: How to avoid potential pitfalls. *Organizational Dynamics* 36(2): 140–155.
Brown, M.E., L.K. Treviño, and D.A. Harrison. 2005. Ethical leadership: A social learning perspective for construct development and testing. *Organizational Behavior and Human Decision Processes* 97(2): 117–134.
Bruce, G., and R. Edgington. 2008. Ethics education in MBA programs: Effectiveness and effects. *International Journal of Management and Marketing Research* 1(1): 49–70.
Bruce, W. 1998. Ethics education in municipal government: It does make a difference. In *Teaching Ethics and Values in Public Administration Programs*, ed. J.S. Bowman and D.C. Menzel, 231–252. Albany: State University of New York Press.
Brudney, J.L., and J.M. Martinez. 2010. Teaching administrative ethics in nonprofit management: Recommendations to improve degrees, certificates, and concentration programs. *Journal of Public Affairs Education* 16(2): 181–206.
Bürgi, J. 2010. A comprehensive model for SMEs: Measuring the dynamic interplay of morality, environment and management systems—Towards continuous improvement. In *Ethics in Small and Medium Sized Enterprises. A Global Commentary*, ed. L. Spence and M. Painter-Morland, 147–171. Dordrecht, the Netherlands: Springer.
Catron, B., and K.G. Denhardt. 1994. Ethics education in public administration. In *Handbook of Administrative Ethics*, ed. T.L. Cooper, 49–61. New York: Marcel Dekker.
Cline, V., and J. Richards. 1965. A factor-analysis study of religious belief and behavior. *Journal of Personality and Social Psychology* 1: 577–592.
Cooper, T.L. 2006. *The Responsible Administrator*. San Francisco: John Wiley & Sons.
Cummings, S., and D.J. Monti. 1993. *Gangs: The Origins and Impact of Contemporary Youth Gangs in the United States*. Albany: State University of New York Press.
Curtler, H.M. 2004. *Ethical Argument: Critical Thinking in Ethics*, 2d ed. New York: Oxford University Press.
Cyert, R.M. 1990. Defining leadership and explicating the process. *Nonprofit Management & Leadership* 1(1): 29–38.
Darley, J.M. 1996. How organizations socialize individuals into evildoing. In *Codes of Conduct,* ed. D.M. Messick and A.E. Tenbrunsel, 13–43. New York: Russell Sage Foundation.
Delaney, J.T., and D. Sockell. 1992. Do company ethics training programs make a difference? An empirical analysis. *Journal of Business Ethics* 11: 719–727.
Des Jardin, J.R. 1997. *Environmental Ethics: An Introduction to Environmental Philosophy.* London: Wadsworth.
Dickson, M.W., D.B. Smith, M.W. Grojean, and M. Ehrhart. 2001. Ethical climate: The result of interactions between leadership, leader values, and follower values. *Leadership Quarterly* 12: 1–21.

Dolph, K., and A. Lycan. 2008. Moral reasoning: A necessary standard of learning in today's classroom. *Journal of Cross-Disciplinary Perspectives in Education* 1(1): 13–19.

Dorasamy, N. 2010. Enhancing an ethical culture through purpose-directed leadership for improved public service delivery: A case for South Africa. *African Journal of Business Management* 4(1): 56–64.

Dukerich, J.M., M.L. Nichols, D.R. Elm, and D.A. Vollrath. 1990. Moral reasoning in groups: Leaders make a difference. *Human Relations* 43: 473–493.

Eddy, P. 1988. Kohlberg and Dewey. *Educational Theory* 38(4): 405–413.

Ellenwood, S. 2007. Revisiting character education: From McGuffey to narratives. *The Journal of Education* 187(3): 21–43.

Foucault, M. 1984. On the genealogy of ethics: An overview of work in progress. In *The Foucault Reader,* ed. P. Rabinow, 340–372. New York: Pantheon.

Gentile, M.C. 2010. Keeping your colleagues honest. *Harvard Business Review* 88(3): 114–117.

Goss, R.P. 1996. A distinct public administration ethics? *Journal of Public Administration Research and Theory* 6(4): 593–597.

Grojean, M.W., C.J. Resick, M.W. Dickson, and D.B. Smith. 2004. Leaders, values, and organizational climate: Examining leadership strategies for establishing an organizational climate regarding ethics. *Journal of Business Ethics* 55(3): 223–241.

Guskey, T. 1986. Staff development and the process of teacher change. *Educational Researcher* 15(5): 5–12.

Hartman, L.P., and P.H. Werhane. 2009. A modular approach to business ethics integration: At the intersection of the stand-alone and the integrated approaches. *Journal of Business Ethics* 90: 295–300. doi:10.1007/s10551-010-0427-z.

Hauser, M.D. 2006. *Moral Minds: How Nature Designed Our Universal Sense of Right and Wrong.* New York: HarperCollins.

Hejka-Elkins, A. 1988. Teaching ethics in public administration. *Public Administration Review* 48(5): 885–891.

Henle, C.P., R.A. Giacalone, and C.L. Jurkiewicz. 2005. The role of ethical ideology in workplace deviance. *Journal of Business Ethics* 56: 219–230.

Hiltebeitel, K.M., and S.K. Jones. 1992. An assessment of ethics instruction in accounting education. *Journal of Business Ethics* 11: 37–46.

Hitt, W.D. 1990. *Ethics and Leadership: Putting Theory into Practice.* Columbus, OH: Battelle Press.

Hood, R., B. Spilka, B. Hunsberger, and R. Gorsuch. 1996. *The Psychology of Religion: An Empirical Approach.* New York: Guilford.

Jansen, E., and M.A. Von Glinow. 1985. Ethical ambivalence and organizational reward systems. *Academy of Management Review* 10(4): 814–822.

Johnson, C.E. 2007. *Ethics in the Workplace: Tools and Tactics for Organizational Transformation.* Thousand Oaks, CA: Sage.

Jurkiewicz, C.L. 2000. The trouble with ethics: Results from a national survey of healthcare executives. *HEC Forum* 12(2): 101–123.

———. 2002a. The phantom code of ethics and public sector reform. *Journal of Public Affairs and Issues* 6(3): 1–19.

———. 2002b. The influence of pedagogical style on students' level of ethical reasoning. *Journal of Public Affairs Education* 8(4): 263–274.

———. 2006. Soul food: Morrison and the transformative power of ethical leadership in the public sector. *Public Integrity* 9(2): 245–256.

————. 2009. Political leadership, cultural ethics and recovery: Louisiana post-Katrina. *Public Organization Review* 9(4): 353–366.

————. 2010. The ethinomics of a leaking Louisiana. *The Public Manager* 39(3): 38–41.

Jurkiewicz, C.L., and R.G. Brown. 2000a. Power corrupts absolutely . . . not. *Public Integrity* 2(3): 195–210.

————. 2000b. The P/E ratio that really counts. *Journal of Power and Ethics* 1(3): 172–195.

Jurkiewicz, C.L., and R.A. Giacalone. 2002. Learning through teaching: Demonstrating ethical applications through a training session and manual development exercise. *Journal of Public Affairs* 8(1): 57–70.

Jurkiewicz, C.L., and D. Grossman. 2012. Evil at work. In *Foundations of Organizational Evil,* ed. C.L. Jurkiewicz, 3–15. Armonk, NY: M.E. Sharpe.

Jurkiewicz, C.L., and T.K. Massey, Jr. 1997. What motivates municipal employees: A comparison study of supervisory vs. non-supervisory personnel. *Public Personnel Management* 26(3): 367–377.

————. 1998. The influence of ethical reasoning on leader effectiveness: An empirical study of nonprofit executives. *Nonprofit Management and Leadership* 9(2): 173–186.

Jurkiewicz, C.L., T.K. Massey, Jr., and R.G. Brown. 1998. Motivation in public and private organizations: A comparative study. *Public Productivity and Management Review* 21(3): 230–250.

Jurkiewicz, C.L., and K.L. Nichols. 2002. Ethics education in the MPA curriculum: What difference does it make? *Journal of Public Affairs Education* 8(2): 103–114.

Kennedy, S.S., and D. Malatesta. 2010. Safeguarding the public trust: Can administrative ethics be taught? *Journal of Public Affairs Education* 16(2): 161–180.

Khuntia, R., and D. Suar. 2004. A scale to assess ethical leadership of Indian private and public sector managers. *Journal of Business Ethics* 49(1): 13–26.

Kohlberg, L. 1969. Stage and sequence: The cognitive-developmental approach to socialization. In *Handbook of Socialization Theory and Research,* ed. D.A. Goslin, 347–480. Chicago: Rand McNally.

————. 1976. Moral stages and moralization: The cognitive-developmental approach. In *Moral Development and Behavior,* ed. T. Lickona, 31–53. New York: Holt, Rinehart & Winston.

————. 1981. *Philosophy of Moral Development.* New York: Harper & Row.

————. 1986. A current statement on some theoretical issues. In *Lawrence Kohlberg: Consensus and Controversy,* ed. S. Modigal and C. Modigal, 485–546. Philadelphia: Falmer.

Kohlberg, L., and R.H. Hersh. 1977. Moral development: A review of the theory. *Theory into Practice* 16(2): 53–59. http://www.jstor.org/stable/1475172 (accessed July 30, 2012).

Kohn, A. 1990. *The Brighter Side of Human Nature: Altruism and Empathy in Everyday Life.* New York: Basic Books.

Kung, H. 1998. *A Global Ethic for Global Politics and Economics.* New York: Oxford University Press.

Loe, T.W., and W.A. Weeks. 2000. An experimental investigation of efforts to improve sales students' moral reasoning. *Journal of Personal Selling and Sales Management* 20: 243–251.

Luthar, H.K., and R. Karri. 2005. Exposure to ethics education and the perception of linkage between organizational ethical behavior and business outcomes. *Journal of Business Ethics* 61: 353–368.

Machiavelli, N. 1515/1984. *The Prince,* trans. D. Donno. New York: Bantam Classics.

Malloy, D.C., and J. Agarwal. 2008. Ethical climate in government and nonprofit sectors: Public policy implications for service delivery. *Journal of Business Ethics* 94(1): 3–21.

Mayer, R.C., J.H. Davis, and F.D. Schoorman. 1995. An integration model of organizational trust. *Academy of Management Review* 20(3): 709–735.

McNeel, S.P. 1994. College teaching and student moral development. In *Moral Development in the Professions: Psychology and Applied Ethics*, ed. J.R. Rest and D. Narvaez, 27–49. Hillsdale, NJ: L. Erlbaum.

Menzel, D.C. 1997. Teaching ethics and values in public administration: Are we making a difference? *Public Administration Review* 57(3): 224–230.

Mihelič, K.K., B. Lipičnik, and M. Tekavčič. 2010. Ethical leadership. *International Journal of Management and Information Systems* 14(5): 31–42.

Musick, D.W. 1999. Teaching medical ethics: A review of the literature from North American medical schools with emphasis on education. *Medicine, Health Care and Philosophy* 2: 239–254.

National Association of Schools of Public Affairs and Administration (NASPAA). 2011. Quality in public affairs education. http://naspaa.org/codeofgoodpractice/index.asp.

Nichols, M.L., and V.E. Day. 1982. A comparison of moral reasoning of groups and individuals on the defining issues test. *Academy of Management Journal* 25: 201–208.

Norman, A., H. Richards, and G. Bear. 1998. Moral reasoning and religious belief: Does content influence structure? *Journal of Moral Education* 27(1): 89–98.

O'Fallon, M.J., and K.D. Butterfield. 2005. A review of the empirical ethical decision-making literature: 1996–2003. *Journal of Business Ethics* 59(4): 375–413.

Paine, L.S. 1994. Managing for organizational integrity. *Harvard Business Review* 72(2): 106–117.

Parker, J. 2007. *Street Gangs: The View from the Street.* Report, June. Los Angeles: Do It Now Foundation.

Pew Research Center. 2010. Distrust, discontent, anger, and partisan rancor: People and their government. Report, April 18. Washington, DC: Pew Research Center. http://pewresearch.org/pubs/1569/trust-in-government-distrust-discontent-anger-partisan-rancor.

Piaget, J. 1932/1965. *The Moral Judgment of the Child*, trans. M. Gabain. New York: Free Press.

Rasmussen Reports. 2010. Americans still regard Congress as least respected profession. CRWE Finance, August 5. http://crwefinance.com/6799/uncategorized/americans-still-regard-congress-as-least-respected-profession/?aidref=A1090565663.

Rawls, J., and B. Herman. 2000. *Lectures on the History of Moral Philosophy*. Cambridge, MA: Harvard University Press.

Rest, J.R. 1979. *Development in Judging Moral Issues*. Minneapolis: University of Minnesota Press.

Sanders, S. 2008. Defining social responsibility: Standard helps clarify a nebulous term. *Quality Progress,* March 6.

Schmidt, F.L., and J.E. Hunter. 1998. The validity and utility of selection methods in personnel psychology: Practical and theoretical implications of 85 years of research findings. *Psychological Bulletin* 124(2): 262–274.

Schmitz, S., and J.C. Christopher. 1997. Troubles in Smurftown: Youth gangs and moral visions on Guam. *Child Welfare* 76(3): 411–428.

Shareef, R. 2008. Teaching public sector ethics to graduate students: The public values/public failure decision-making model. *Journal of Public Affairs Education* 14(3): 285–295.

Talbot, S.E. 2000. *Partial Reason: Critical and Constructive Transformations of Ethics and Epistemology*. Westport, CT: Greenwood Press.

Thoma, S. 1994. Moral judgments and moral action. In *Moral Development in the Professions,* ed. J.R. Rest, and D. Narvaez, 199–212. Hillsdale, NJ: L. Erlbaum.

Thoma, S.J., and J. Rest. 1999. The relationship between moral decision making and patterns of consolidation and transition in moral judgment development. *Developmental Psychology* 35(2): 323–334.

Thoma, S., J.R. Rest, and R. Barnett. 1986. Moral judgment, behavior, decision making, and attitudes. In *Moral Development: Advances in Theory and Research*, ed. J.R. Rest, 133–175. New York: Praeger.

Thompson, D.F. 2004. *Restoring Responsibility: Ethics in Government, Business, and Healthcare*. New York: Cambridge University Press.

Treviño, L.K., M. Brown, and L.P. Hartman. 2003. A qualitative investigation of perceived executive ethical leadership: Perceptions from inside and outside the executive suite. *Human Relations* 56(1): 5.

Twenge, J.M., S. Konrath, J.D. Foster, W.K. Campbell, and B.J. Bushman. 2008. Egos inflating over time: A cross-temporal meta-analysis of the narcissistic personality inventory. *Journal of Personality* 76: 875–901.

Ulrich, P. 2008. *Integrative Economic Ethics: Foundations of a Civilized Market Economy.* New York: Cambridge University Press.

U.S. Department of Justice (USDOJ), National Drug Intelligence Center. 2005. Drugs and gangs: Fast facts. http://www.justice.gov/archive/ndic/pubs11/13157/13157p.pdf.

———. 2008. Appendix B. National-level street, prison, and outlaw motorcycle gang profiles. In *Attorney General's Report to Congress on the Growth of Violent Street Gangs in Suburban Areas.* Report, April. http://www.justice.gov/archive/ndic/pubs27/27612/27612p.pdf.

Vershoor, C.C. 2007. Work-life balance, superior's actions strongly influence ethical culture. *Strategic Finance* 88: 13–16.

Wheeler, G.F., and F.N. Brady. 1998. Do public-sector and private-sector personnel have different ethical dispositions? *Journal of Public Administration Research and Theory* 8(1): 93–115.

Whetten, D.A., and K.S. Cameron. 2002. *Developing Management Skills.* Upper Saddle River, NJ: Prentice Hall.

Part III

Ethical Competence Within and Across Professions

Public service professionals are often educated and trained as social workers, engineers, environmental specialists, medical and health providers, planners, administrators, lawyers, fiscal analysts, and businesspeople, to name several professions. Competence in each of these professions is first and foremost job related or scientific/technical in nature. Civil engineers employed in public transportation agencies must be able to understand and monitor the engineering of roads, highways, bridges, buildings, transportation networks, and more; in addition, they must be able to do their job with the highest ethical standards that are often set by their professional association. Therefore, it is understandable that the common thread of the idea and practice of ethical competence across professional fields is "do no harm." And it is fully understandable that specific standards speak to the context of the profession. City managers, for example, are expected to "do no harm" to their communities in their charge by not jumping from one job to another (unless unusual circumstances exist such a family medical crisis) within two years of taking up their post—so states the International City/County Management Association (ICMA). A brief management tenure is regarded as harmful to the community.

Social Work

Frederic G. Reamer's (see Chapter 7) examination of ethical competence in social work richly describes the many ways in which the social work profession has sought to advance the best interests of the community while protecting individuals, families, and groups from intentional and unintentional harm. As he puts it, the "key to social work's mission is its simultaneous focus on individual well-being in a social context and the well-being of society in general." He documents the decades-long advancement of ethical standards that frame the boundaries of acceptable social work in contemporary society. Social work as a profession has moved from "paternalistic attempts to strengthen the morality or rectitude of the poor whose 'wayward' lives had gotten the best of them" to ethical competence embedded in "robust ethical standards that guide practice, protect the public, and regulate the profession. . . . The evolution of social workers' ethical competence," he asserts, "is one of the most remarkable developments in the profession's history."

Reamer places a great deal of emphasis on the tandem development of ethics codes in social work and the pursuit of ethical competence. One key milestone along the route to code development occurred in 1920, when an experimental code of ethics was published by Mary Richmond that Reamer regards as a major step on the path toward ethical competence. Decades later (1960), the National Association of Social Workers (NASW) in the United States ratified the first prominent social work code of ethics. Among other things, the 1960 code gave precedence to (1) professional responsibility over personal interests and (2) respect for the privacy of clients. In 1996, the NASW overhauled the existing code, an act that Reamer claims constituted "a sea change in social workers' approach to ethics." The need for a much more sophisticated code was prompted by complex and controversial technological developments in health care (e.g., organ transplantation, termination of life support, genetic engineering, and more); the "public's embrace of the language of rights" (women's rights, children's rights, prisoners' rights); and society's growing awareness of widespread abuse by physicians, lawyers, clergy, nurses, pharmacists, and social workers, not to mention public officeholders and the Watergate scandal in the Nixon White House.

One might erroneously conclude from Reamer's account of the evolution of codes that the pursuit of ethical competence in social work is limited entirely to understanding and acting on the latest professional codes along with laws in a given state. Ethical competence involves much more. "Ideally," he contends, "ethical standards are created to help professionals achieve ethical competence by strengthening their ability to identify ethical issues in practice and provide meaningful guidelines to determine what is ethically acceptable and unacceptable behavior." But the author recognizes that ethically competent practitioners can interpret formal ethical standards differently. In other words, there is not necessarily a single correct ethical position on the myriad ethical issues that can confront the social worker. So what is an aspiring ethically competent social worker to do? The answer, according to Reamer: "They must supplement these standards with a conceptually rich, nuanced analysis of pertinent ethical issues and moral judgment that incorporates relevant moral concepts and consultation." Ethical competence is not an end state; rather, it is the recognition that reflects "perpetual growth of knowledge about the moral purposes of the profession and ways to assist people in need."

How then does one grow in knowledge? Four educational and post-educational goals must be pursued. First, social workers must seek ways and means to stimulate the moral imagination in the workplace. They should be encouraged to look actively for moral and ethical issues that are embedded in social work functions. Second, they must obtain knowledge of classic ethical theories and conceptual frameworks and apply them to ethical dilemmas they encounter. This fosters the development of analytical skills. Third, they must acquire a sense of moral obligation and personal responsibility that is wedded to "beliefs about both social work's moral purposes and their own." Fourth, they must develop the ability to respond to ethical controversy and ambiguity. Ethical relativism is not the only realistic option. Instead, "disciplined, principled, and informed discussions of ethical issues can help ethically competent social workers clarify and challenge their own and one another's assertions and conclusions."

Public Administration

Scholars and the practicing community of public administration have wrestled with the issue of ethical competence since Woodrow Wilson proclaimed in 1887 that the field should be based on business principles. Ethical administrators were expected to be "cultured and self-sufficient to act with sense and vigor, and yet so intimately connected with the popular thought, by means of elections and constant public counsel, as to find arbitrariness of class spirit quite out of the question" (1987). Public office is a public trust and, as Thomas Jefferson so reminds us, past and present, "Where a man assumes a public trust, he should consider himself a public property" (1807/1824). From this foundational beginning through much of the twentieth century, public administrators were expected to carry out their duties in a manner that served the community, state, and nation with impartial deeds that were responsive to democratically elected masters while advancing the public interest. The result, for the most part, was what Jeremy Plant describes in Chapter 8 as "almost universal expectations for honest, disciplined, and disinterested administrative behavior."

This characterization of ethical competence may have withstood the test of time for decades, but the times change. As Plant notes, "There has never been a time when the issue of what constitutes ethical competence for professional public administrators has been of greater importance than the present." Plant's survey of recent definitions and discussions of ethical competence in the public administration literature lead him to conclude that responsible ethical competence requires three characteristics—selflessness, skill, and trustworthiness.

There is no single path for acquiring ethical competence in public administration or, for that matter, in any profession, says Plant. Rather, there are four basic strategies: (1) ethics education mostly provided by graduate university programs; (2) formal approaches embedded in laws, codes, and standards of conduct; (3) professional codes and associations; and (4) leadership-mentoring-exemplars. These strategies vary from formal to informal and, as noted in Chapter 1, involve a lifelong pursuit. Among these four strategies, Plant does not single out one as better or more effective than another, nor does he treat each as a necessary prerequisite for ethical competence. A cookie-cutter approach does not work. Individual administrators and aspiring administrators will have to find their own way. This discussion leads Plant to address in his own way the question of how ethical competence contributes to effective public service leadership.

How Does Ethical Competence Contribute to Effective Public Service Leadership?

Plant rephrases the question in the following way: "What is the goal of ethical competence and how do we measure success?" This question can be answered in part quite directly and easily—effective public service leadership is the goal. The hard part to answer is how we should measure success. Plant does not back away from an answer. "The measure of success," he asserts, "is trust." Leaders must draw on ethical competence, their own and others in their charge, to garner the trust of elected bosses, employees, colleagues, and community or nation. The absence of trust is surely a signal that ethical competence is missing. This conclusion, as the reader may recall from the description of the Sarasota County administrator's fall from grace in Chapter 1, is truly warranted.

Law

The ethical challenges facing social workers and public administrators in pursuit of ethical competence is no less daunting for lawyers who advise public officials and often play a key role in drafting legislation that has consequences for millions of citizens. Robert N. Roberts in Chapter 9 paints a trying picture of the work and life of lawyers in government. Although relatively few in number in government service when compared to the number in professional occupations, these attorneys have, in his judgment, a huge influence on the work of government. Their presence in government is complicated by today's skeptical public trust and lack of confidence in government writ large and even more so by the low esteem the public has for the law profession. Public opinion polling firms consistently find that the American public ranks the ethics of lawyers on the low end of the spectrum, along with business executives, stockbrokers, and car salespeople. Lawyers are not among the professionals who receive high ethical marks such as nurses, pharmacists, medical doctors, police officers, college teachers, and the clergy.

Identifying ethical competencies in the practice of law for those who hold positions of public trust is not an easy process, says Roberts. This is due in part to the divided loyalties that government attorneys experience and the transition in recent decades from a self-proclaimed view of lawyering as a client-centered private enterprise to lawyering as a business-commercial enterprise. Let's examine first the matter of the divided loyalties of lawyers.

Divided Loyalties

Lawyers in government and those who hold positions of public trust are socialized into the professional view that one's ethical obligations are to serve the client in a competent and impartial manner. At the same time, they are expected to advocate for and protect their clients' interests. While this role is fully consistent with the private practice of law, it becomes more problematic when the client is a public official or powerful government agency. How does one balance the twin pressures of providing defensible legal counsel while at the same time vigorously serving one's political superior? Alas, in recent years few lawyers in government have been successful at finding a balance. Rather, new recruits are expected to know the law (have technical competence), promote or advocate legal counsel that is responsive to political superiors, and subscribe to ideologically compatible positions with the prevailing political majority.

Commercialization

Another "sea change" in the law profession as Roberts sees it is the commercialization of law—not just in corporate America but in government as well. He documents in a persuasive manner how "prior to the commercialization of the practice of law, many lawyers viewed their most rewarding role as that of a trusted adviser who had the ability to help their clients avoid trouble, not simply get them out of trouble." The industrial age and the rise of the administrative state brought a new breed of lawyer who plied specialized knowledge and skills to meet the demand by corporate America and government for legal services. Specialization and commercialization went hand in hand. Yet, despite this development, the ethical worldview of lawyers stayed focused on the private attorney, not the government attorney. The uneasy ethical relationship that evolved early in the twentieth century finally motivated the American Bar Association (ABA) to put "a finger in a leaking dam," as Roberts notes. The ABA adopted the Canons of Legal Ethics in 1908, a move that began to place ethical boundaries around such matters as advertising one's services, soliciting clients, and handling funds owned by the client. However, by the turn of the twenty-first century, these restrictions had given way to a much more aggressive posture by lawyers in both private practice and government service. In addition, new issues such as leaving government service to work for a business firm (the revolving door) or taking up a lobbying position with an industry that was once under one's regulatory jurisdiction as a government lawyer have added considerable complexity to a lawyer's ethical worldview. Moreover, legal advocacy that fosters social change through law was launched in earnest in the 1960s, when lawyers became advocates for social justice (civil liberties and desegregation, for example) and consumer and environmental protection. The public interest law movement put an entirely new face on the law profession and brought to the fore many questions regarding the ethical responsibilities of lawyers inside and outside of government.

Competencies

This rather complicated picture of the pursuit of ethical competencies to meet an ever-changing future in a legal context brings full circle the question: "What are the ethical competencies for public service lawyers?" Roberts identifies four. The first, and most important, "is the recognition that public service ethics involves much more than complying with disciplinary ethics rules." Compliance-based ethics has come to define legal ethics. Moreover as Roberts asserts, "The preoccupation with compliance-based legal ethics rules fails to answer the questions of whether lawyers in general and government lawyers in particular need to develop ethical competencies not embodied in compliance-based ethics rules." The second competency is the need to develop civility. Many clients feel that lawyers should do whatever it takes to win, and this mindset has led to a breakdown of civility in the legal profession. "The ability of government lawyers to do their job in a civil and respectful manner is an ethical competence of importance for all lawyers and particularly for lawyers who work for the government," Roberts asserts.

The third ethical competency, according to Roberts, requires government lawyers to understand and act on the "basic constitutional doctrines that place limits on governmental interference in the lives of its citizens." The practice of seeing one's role as interpreting the law and the Constitution in conformity with one's ideological beliefs "has done serious damage to the credibility of government lawyers." Roberts argues that "government lawyers occupying nonpolitical positions should be excluded from the task of rendering opinions with obvious partisan or ideological bias."

The fourth competence is the ability to dissent, to avoid becoming merely a reliable instrument of the organization. "The fact that a government attorney may face serious consequences for dissenting makes it a true ethical dilemma." The ability to dissent from a practice or policy that could do significant damage to the lives of citizens and to the nation's democratic institutions is an essential ethical competence. Of course, the risks to the lawyer who dissents could be high, including harassment and/or termination of employment. But is this not the unique obligation of government attorneys—to prevent government from violating basic democratic and moral principles? Doesn't a government attorney have a higher duty to dissent when such violations are at hand? Roberts answers decisively and clearly—yes!

Nonprofits

The challenges facing lawyers, public administrators, and social workers in pursuit of ethical competence for public service leadership are equally challenging for nonprofit professionals and staff members. The nonprofit world is one of scarce resources, competition, and—increasingly—accountability; it is by no means a place of tranquility. The "third" sector, as nonprofits are sometimes described (after private and public), has become a vital, dynamic actor in governing and governance at all levels of government in the United States and abroad.

Barbara S. Liggett, the author of Chapter 10, documents the universe of ethical challenges and issues that nonprofit managers, staff, and volunteers confront. They include fiscal accountability, treatment of human capital, gifting and solicitation of funds, investment policies, and more. And, as she points out, no nonprofit organization "wants the words *misbehavior, fraud, discrimination, conflict of interest,* or *scandal* used in the same sentence describing the activities or the action of specific staff."

Liggett draws particular attention to the significant influence that the organizational context of human resource decision making brings to bear on the behavior of members of nonprofits. Misbehavior or ethical breaches are certainly acts of an individual or individuals, yet blame may be placed too narrowly on the specific person or persons involved. Rather, one should take a close look at the nonprofit organization's policies and practices to ensure that they are not somehow at the root of the misbehavior. She asks: "Does an organization create a culture of honesty or dishonesty by way of its policies and practices?" Whatever ethical competencies can be ascribed to members of nonprofits, they must include the capacity to have knowledge of the whole of human resources systems, including how they are linked to and dependent on each other for both paid staff and volunteers.

The author contends, "*Ethical competence* for members of nonprofit organizations means possessing the ability to use critical thinking with an understanding of (1) the nonprofit context; (2) the frameworks for determining right and wrong; (3) the recognition of the "whole" of human resources and nonprofit systems; and (4) a desire for fairness, equitable treatment, and respect for all persons, which results in the nonprofit making the right decisions as purveyors of the public good." Being able to view situations from multiple perspectives requires one to think like a board member, an executive director, a paid staff member, a volunteer, a donor, and more—a tall order to be sure!

Understanding ethical frameworks such as virtue ethics, duty, and consequential ethics is a must. In "an ideal world," Liggett explains, an ethically competent nonprofit manager would draw on all three approaches to yield effective decision making. "Knowing the options from the ethical frameworks allows us to talk about the competence needed for ethical decision making regarding human resources policies and practices in nonprofits."

Acquiring critical thinking skills enables one to reason through challenging ethical problems. While much has been written about critical thinking skills, their importance in ethical problem solving has not been as central as one might suspect. Liggett points to the lack of such reference in professional associations that have known influence in the nonprofit sector, among them the Independent Sector Code of Ethics for Nonprofit and Philanthropic Organizations, the Nonprofit Academic Centers Council, and the Nonprofit Leadership Alliance. Also missing from the list of competencies is the desire to be fair.

The author admits that the desire or passion for fairness is a challenging competency, especially to teach; in fact, it may be impossible to teach. However, it can be observed, and, as she argues, "the desire for fair, equitable, and respectful treatment of others might not be possible for some—but the obligation of treating others fairly may be present. Perhaps that is enough."

Given the key components of ethical competence for members of nonprofits, can they be evaluated? Yes, Liggett contends—through (1) observation of individuals possessing multiple perspectives, (2) knowledge of human resources systems and ethical frameworks, and (3) an organizational environment where all are treated fairly, equitably, and with respect.

7

Ethical Competence in Social Work

Frederic G. Reamer

Efforts to enhance social workers' ethical competence have matured dramatically in recent years. From modest beginnings in the late nineteenth century, when social work was inaugurated formally as a profession, social work has developed a rich intellectual framework designed to identify compelling ethical issues and dilemmas in the profession, develop tools for ethical analysis and decision making, and educate social work students and practitioners.

Social Work: A Brief Overview

Social work is a profession in which the primary mission is to enhance human well-being and to help people meet basic human needs, with particular attention to the needs of people who are vulnerable, oppressed, and living in poverty. Social workers assist individuals, families, couples, groups, organizations, communities, and the broader society. Social workers may be clinicians, case managers, administrators, policy analysts, social and political advocates, community organizers, or researchers. Key to social work's mission is its simultaneous focus on individual well-being in a social context and the well-being of society in general. One of social work's defining attributes is the attention that the profession's practitioners pay to societal forces that create, contribute to, and address problems in living.

Social work began as a formal profession in the late nineteenth century. It grew out of a wide range of efforts to assist people experiencing problems in living. These efforts included work by "friendly visitors" in the mid-1800s, among them (1) primarily middle- and upper-class women who volunteered to help indigent families; (2) charity organization societies, begun in the nineteenth century in Europe and the United States to provide services to the "worthy" poor and disabled; and (3) settlement houses, also begun in the nineteenth century in Europe and the United States, in which the staff lived in the communities where they worked, devoting much of their effort to problems related to housing, health care, employment and working conditions, and sanitation (Trattner 1998).

From these early attempts to help poor and vulnerable people, which have their historical roots in the English Poor Laws enacted between 1601 and 1834, social work has matured into a full-fledged profession with rigorous education, fields and methods of practice, and ethical standards. The first formal social work education program began in 1898.

Contemporary social work is practiced in a wide range of public- and private-sector settings such as schools, correctional facilities, hospitals, senior centers, hospice programs, outpatient mental health facilities and independent practices, community agencies, welfare agencies, child-welfare agencies, the military, policy offices in government agencies, and a wide range of residential facilities for people with mental illness, physical and developmental disabilities, and substance abuse problems.

The Evolution of Ethical Competence in Social Work

Ethical competence in social work has evolved significantly since the profession's formal inception in the late nineteenth century. Formal ethics education and codes of ethics did not exist during the first half century of social work's existence. Although ethical norms emerged during social work's early years, it took decades for them to be codified and taught. The earliest ethics literature and codes of ethics in social work were relatively simplistic, as were codes in every profession. Early ethical standards resembled affirmations, oaths, and pledges and, in contrast to contemporary codes, did not provide in-depth, comprehensive coverage of a wide range of complex ethical issues.

Ethical standards in social work have developed in stages (Reamer 2006a, 2006b). The first stage—the *morality period*—began in the late nineteenth century, when charity organization societies were common and social work was inaugurated formally as a profession. During this period, social work was much more concerned about the morality of the client than about the morality or ethics of the profession or its practitioners. Especially in England and the United States, practitioners who were concerned about vulnerable people focused on organizing relief and responding to the "curse of pauperism" (Paine 1880). This preoccupation often took the form of paternalistic attempts to strengthen the morality or rectitude of the poor whose "wayward" lives had gotten the best of them.

The rise of the settlement house movement in England and the United States in the early twentieth century marked a time when the aims and value orientations of many social workers shifted from concern about the morality or immorality of the poor to need for dramatic social reform and structural change designed to ameliorate a wide range of social problems—those related to housing, health care, sanitation, employment, poverty, and education. During the Progressive Era especially, social workers promoted social reforms and policies to enhance people and communities. All of this unfolded without clearly articulated ethical standards or codes of ethics, although an experimental code of ethics, published in 1920, has been traced to Mary Richmond, a pioneer in the field of social work (Pumphrey 1959). This was the first known attempt to formulate a social work code of ethics, a major step on the path toward ethical competence in the profession. Although several other social work organizations also formulated draft codes during these early years of the profession's history—for example, the American Association for Organizing Family Social Work and several chapters of the American Association of Social Workers—not until 1947 did the latter group, the largest organization of social workers of that era, adopt a formal code (Johnson 1955).

Concern about the morality of the client continued to recede somewhat during the next several decades of social work's evolution, as practitioners engaged in earnest attempts to create and refine their intervention strategies and techniques, training programs, and schools of thought. Over time, during this *values period,* concern about clients' morality was overshadowed by debate about the profession's future, that is, the extent to which social work would stress the cultivation of expertise in psychosocial and psychiatric casework, psychotherapy, social welfare policy and administration, community organization, or social reform. After a half century of development, the social work profession was moving into a phase characterized by several attempts to develop consensus about the profession's core values. This was especially prominent between the late 1950s and 1970s (Emmet 1962; Hugman 2003; Keith-Lucas 1963; Levy 1976; Pumphrey 1959; Teicher 1967; Younghusband 1967). Significantly, it was during this period, in 1960, that the National Association of Social Workers (NASW) in the United States ratified the first prominent social work code of ethics.

Social work codes of ethics were relatively brief and superficial in the 1960s. Typical was the 1960 NASW Code of Ethics, which consisted of a series of proclamations concerning, for example, every social worker's duty to give precedence to professional responsibility over personal interests; respect the privacy of clients; give appropriate professional service in public emergencies; and contribute knowledge, skills, and support to programs of human welfare. First-person statements (such as "I give precedence to my professional responsibility over my personal interests" and "I respect the privacy of the people I serve") were preceded by a preamble that set forth social workers' responsibility to uphold humanitarian ideals, maintain and improve social work service, and develop the philosophy and skills of the profession.

Ethical standards and ethics literature in social work matured significantly during a third historical period that focused on *ethical theory* and *decision making.* This period marked a turning point in the development of social workers' ethical competence. Until the late 1970s, social work literature and ethics codes focused primarily on the profession's core values and value base. Then the profession underwent another significant transition in its concern about values and ethics. The 1970s saw a dramatic surge of interest in the broad subject of applied and professional ethics, also known as practical ethics. Professions as diverse as medicine, nursing, law, business, journalism, engineering, social work, psychology, psychiatry, and criminal justice began to devote sustained attention to the subject. The literature on professional ethics burgeoned, as did academic coursework on the subject and continuing education. As professionals' understanding of ethical issues matured, a number of scholars and practitioners developed, for the first time, conceptually rich ethical decision-making protocols and guidelines. During this period, a number of social work authors focused explicitly on the application of ethical theories to real-life ethical dilemmas encountered by professionals (Banks 2003, 2006; Barsky 2010; Congress 2000, 2008; Dolgoff, Loewenberg, and Harrington 2008; Linzer 1999; Reamer 2006a, 2006b; Rhodes 1989). Not surprisingly, codes of ethics also matured during this period, reflecting this expanded understanding of ethical issues and greater ethical competence (Congress and McAuliffe 2006). For example, the NASW in the United States embarked on a complete overhaul of its existing code in an effort to reflect the remarkable growth of new knowledge related to professional ethics. The NASW Code of Ethics ratified in 1996 (and revised slightly in 2008) constituted a sea change in social workers' approach to ethics.

The remarkable growth of interest in professional ethics in the last three decades of the twentieth century, and professionals' expanded grasp of ethical challenges and understanding of the need for more sophisticated codes of ethics, was due to a variety of factors (Callahan and Bok 1980; Reamer 2006b). Complex and controversial technological developments in health care and other fields certainly helped to spark ethical debate and analysis involving such issues as termination of life support, organ transplantation, genetic engineering, psychopharmacological intervention, and test-tube babies.

Also, widespread publicity about scandals in government, especially in the United States, triggered considerable interest in professional ethics and the cultivation of more meaningful, instructive ethical standards. Beginning especially with Watergate in the 1970s, the public became painfully aware of various professionals and public officials who abused their authority. The media became saturated with disturbing reports of politicians, agency administrators, physicians, lawyers, clergy, nurses, pharmacists, and social workers, among others, who took advantage of the people they served. One by-product was professionals' growing awareness of the need for clearer ethical standards.

In addition, the professions' and the public's embrace of the language of rights—women's rights, prisoners' rights, children's rights, and so on—helped shape professionals' thinking about the need for more ambitious codification of ethical standards. Contemporary professionals also developed a much better appreciation of the limits of science and its ability to respond to the many complex moral and ethical questions that professionals face. Although for some time, particularly since the 1930s, science had been placed on a pedestal and widely regarded as the key to many of life's mysteries, modern-day professionals began to acknowledge that science cannot answer a variety of questions that are, fundamentally, ethical in nature (Sloan 1980).

Finally, the well-documented increase in litigation and malpractice in some nations, along with publicity about unethical professionals, has forced the professions to strengthen ethical standards that distinguish ethical and unethical behavior. Especially in the United States, social workers have experienced an increase in claims and lawsuits against practitioners, and a substantial portion of these complaints allege some form of unethical conduct (Houston-Vega, Nuehring, and Daguio 1997; Reamer 2001a, 2003).

This trend has led to the most recent phase in the development of ethical competence in social work, with its emphasis on *ethics risk management* (Reamer 2001a, 2003). This stage is characterized mainly by the significant expansion of ethical standards to guide practitioners' conduct and by increased knowledge concerning professional negligence and liability. More specifically, this period includes the development of more detailed, comprehensive codes of ethics and ethics-related regulatory standards. For example, the NASW Code of Ethics and many state licensing regulations now include specific guidelines concerning phenomena such as confidentiality, privacy, privileged communication, informed consent, conflicts of interest, boundaries, cultural competence, documentation, termination of services, collegial relationships, consultation, referral, practitioner impairment, practitioner incompetence, unethical conduct of colleagues, supervision, education and training, billing, administration, labor-management disputes, discrimination, solicitation of clients, evaluation, and social welfare, among others.

The Evolution of Ethical Standards

The evolution of ethical standards, especially in the form of codes of ethics, provides compelling evidence of professions' efforts to enhance ethical competence. One hallmark of a profession is its willingness to establish formal ethical standards to guide practitioners' conduct (Callahan and Bok 1980; Greenwood 1957; Hall 1968; Lindeman 1947). Ideally, ethical standards are created to help professionals achieve ethical competence by strengthening their ability to identify ethical issues in practice and provide meaningful guidelines to determine what is ethically acceptable and unacceptable behavior. Ethically competent practitioners are familiar with relevant ethical standards, keep current with changes in them, identify ethical standards that pertain to ethical dilemmas, explore ways to resolve conflicts among ethical standards, and apply ethical standards in their efforts to resolve ethical dilemmas.

In reality, codes of ethics serve various functions. Codes provide measuring rods when courts of law and licensing or other regulatory bodies assess whether a professional has complied with or departed from standards in the field. Employers may adopt a prominent code of ethics to provide its employees with a moral compass and set of guidelines. Further, codes provide an opportunity for a profession to announce to the public the nature of its mission, moral ideals and principles, and guidelines for proper conduct. Codes of ethics may be steeped in self-serving ideology or principled language designed primarily to protect the public. Thus, codes serve multiple purposes and have multiple aims (Bayles 1986; Brandl and Maguire 2002; Cooper 2006; Freeman, Engels, and Altekruse 2004; Kultgen 1982; Menzel 2007; Van Wart 2003).

Put succinctly, codes of ethics are designed to address three major issues (Jamal and Bowie 1995). First, codes address problems of moral hazard, or instances in which a profession's self-interest may conflict with the public's interest. Such conflicts can occur in a variety of ways. Examples include whether accountants should be obligated to disclose confidential information concerning financial fraud that their clients have committed, whether dentists should be permitted to refuse to treat people who have an infectious disease such as HIV/AIDS, whether physicians should be allowed to invest personally in laboratories or rehabilitation facilities to which they refer their own patients, and whether social workers should be expected to disclose to law enforcement officials confidential information about very serious crimes their clients have admitted committing.

Second, codes of ethics address issues of professional courtesy, that is, rules that govern how professionals should behave to enhance and maintain a profession's integrity. Examples include whether lawyers should be permitted to advertise and solicit clients, whether psychiatrists should be permitted to engage in sexual relationships with former patients, whether psychologists should be prohibited from soliciting colleagues' clients, and whether social workers should be expected to report colleagues who are impaired or who engage in unethical conduct.

Finally, codes of ethics address issues that concern professionals' duty to serve the public interest. For example, to what extent should public agency administrators be expected to disclose fraudulent activities in their agencies? Should physicians and nurses be expected to assist vulnerable people when faced with a public emergency? Should dentists donate a portion of their professional time to provide services to low-income people who do not have private dental insurance or a government-sponsored coverage? Should social workers provide pro bono services to people in need who have difficulty paying for assistance?

It is important to recognize that codes of ethics are political documents as well as guides to professional practice. In their purest form, codes of ethics provide professionals with moral inspiration, values, and ethical norms. In fact, codes of ethics also serve political purposes. Many codes are created by voluntary professional associations whose principal purpose is to promote the profession, along with serving the public. These associations may use their codes of ethics to regulate their members' ethical conduct, particularly when members of the public or clients allege ethical misconduct. In addition to using the code of ethics to protect the public, the profession also is using the code to protect itself. In this respect, codes of ethics can be self-serving documents, at least in part.

Further, codes such as the NASW Code of Ethics frequently are used even more explicitly for political purposes when they are incorporated formally into legislation and governmental regulations. Many legislative, licensing, and regulatory bodies adopt codes of ethics not to promote or protect the social work profession but, rather, to protect the public.

The NASW Code of Ethics:
A Case Study in Defining Ethical Competence

The NASW Code of Ethics has served as an influential model and resource for many codes of ethics around the world that attempt to codify ethical competence (Congress and McAuliffe 2006). NASW, the largest professional social work association in the United States, uses the NASW Code of Ethics to promulgate ethical standards for its members; NASW also uses the code to review and adjudicate ethics complaints filed against NASW members and assess members' ethical competence. NASW is a voluntary membership organization that has the authority to use the NASW Code of Ethics to discipline and sanction its members when they violate the code (for example, by imposing probation or membership revocation) or require members who violate the code to engage in some form of corrective action (such as ethics education, supervision, and consultation). NASW does not have authority over social workers' professional licenses; however, sanctioning by NASW could affect social workers' eligibility for malpractice and liability insurance and their right to use widely recognized NASW-sponsored credentials.

Many state licensing boards also use the NASW Code of Ethics to define ethical competence formally and promulgate and enforce ethical standards for licensed practitioners. Social workers can be disciplined and sanctioned by state licensing boards that draw on the NASW Code of Ethics. Many state licensing boards in the United States have formally adopted the NASW Code of Ethics, or portions of the code, and use its standards to review and adjudicate ethics complaints filed against licensed social workers and assess their ethical competence. A number of states have formally adopted the entire NASW Code of Ethics. In these states, social work licensing statutes and regulations refer explicitly to the NASW Code of Ethics, thereby incorporating the code into law. Other states excerpt and cite specific portions of the NASW Code of Ethics in their licensing statutes and regulations. Licensing boards that conclude that social workers violated these ethical standards have the authority to place licensees on probation, suspend or revoke a license to practice social work, or require licensees to engage in some form of corrective action (such as ethics education, supervision, and consultation). Social workers may be named as respondents in ethics complaints filed with NASW, state licensing boards, or both.

Finally, many public and private social service agencies have adopted the NASW Code of Ethics, or portions of the code, as agency policy, and they use the code's standards to guide and assess employees' ethical competence. Various agencies incorporate the NASW code into formal policies, which are approved by a board of directors and are then used to review and sanction employee conduct. In addition, many social service agencies seek accreditation by national organizations—such as the Joint Commission on Accreditation of Healthcare Organizations, the Council on Accreditation, and the Commission on Accreditation of Rehabilitation Facilities—and draw on NASW Code of Ethics standards to demonstrate their commitment to ethically competent practice.

The current NASW code includes four major sections. The first section, "Preamble," summarizes social work's mission and core values. This is the first time in NASW's history that its code of ethics has contained a formally sanctioned mission statement and an explicit summary of the profession's core values.

The second section, "Purpose of the NASW Code of Ethics," provides an overview of the code's main functions and a brief guide for dealing with ethical issues or dilemmas. The code identifies its five key purposes: (1) to set forth broad ethical principles that reflect the profession's core values and establish ethical standards to guide social work practice; (2) to help social workers identify relevant considerations when professional obligations conflict or ethical uncertainties arise; (3) to familiarize practitioners new to the field to social work's mission, values, and ethical standards; (4) to provide ethical standards to which the general public can hold the social work profession accountable; and (5) to articulate standards that the profession itself (and other bodies that choose to adopt the code, such as licensing and regulatory boards, professional liability insurance providers, and government agencies) can use to assess whether social workers have engaged in unethical conduct.

An important feature of the current NASW code is its overview of key resources that ethically competent social workers should consider when faced with difficult ethical decisions. These resources include ethical theory and conceptually based decision-making frameworks; social work practice theory and research; laws and regulations; agency policies; and other relevant codes of ethics. The code also encourages social workers to obtain ethics consultation, when appropriate, from an agency-based ethics committee, regulatory bodies, trained ethicists, knowledgeable colleagues, supervisors, or legal counsel.

Another key feature in this section of the NASW code is explicit acknowledgment that instances sometimes arise in social work in which the code's values, principles, and ethical standards conflict. The code does not provide a formula for resolving such conflicts and does not specify which values, principles, and standards are most important and ought to outweigh others in instances when they conflict. Furthermore, the code acknowledges that reasonable differences of opinion can and do exist among social workers with respect to the ways in which values, ethical principles, and ethical standards should be rank-ordered with the conflict.

The code's third section, "Ethical Principles," presents six broad ethical principles that inform social work practice, one for each of the six core values cited in the preamble: service, social justice, dignity and worth of the person, importance of human relationships, integrity, and competence. Each principle includes a brief annotation.

The code's final and most extensive section, "Ethical Standards," includes 155 specific ethical standards designed to guide social workers' conduct and provide a basis for adjudication of ethics complaints. This is the heart of the social work profession's attempt to define ethical competence (Reamer 2006a). The standards are divided into six sections concerning social workers' ethical responsibilities to clients, to colleagues, in practice settings, as professionals, to the profession, and to society at large. The introduction to this section of the code states explicitly that some of the standards are enforceable guidelines for professional conduct, and others are standards to which social workers should aspire (so-called aspirational, as opposed to enforceable, standards).

The NASW Code of Ethics is far more than an abstract document with scant practical application. Indeed, the code has multiple purposes and represents the profession's formal attempt to define ethical competence.

Articulating Social Work's Principal Mission, Values, Ethical Principles

Ideally, codes of ethics offer practitioners and the public a clear, compelling statement of a profession's primary aims and moral purposes. In principle, codes of ethics provide a moral touchstone for the profession and ethically competent practitioners.

Offering Guidance to Social Workers and Employers in Addressing Ethical Issues

The current NASW Code of Ethics, unlike earlier versions, includes extensive detail regarding a wide range of ethical issues and challenges. The code provides guidance regarding issues such as confidentiality, privacy, privileged communication, informed consent, conflicts of interest, boundaries, cultural competence, documentation, termination of services, collegial relationships, consultation, referral, practitioner impairment, practitioner incompetence, unethical conduct of colleagues, supervision, education and training, billing, administration, labor-management disputes, discrimination, solicitation of clients, evaluation, and social welfare, among others.

Ethically competent social workers demonstrate expertise concerning three kinds of issues: ethical mistakes, ethical dilemmas, and ethical misconduct. The framers of the NASW code consulted relevant literature on these issues, surveyed practitioners, and drafted standards reflecting ethical competence (Reamer 2003, 2006a, 2009).

The first category includes what can be defined as "mistakes" that social workers might make that have ethical implications. Examples include leaving confidential documents displayed in public areas in such a way that they can be read by unauthorized persons, failing to protect the privacy of electronic communications with or about clients, or forgetting to include important details in a client's informed consent documents. The second category includes issues associated with difficult ethical decisions—for example, whether to disclose confidential information, without client consent, to protect a third party from harm; whether to barter with low-income clients who want to exchange goods for social work services; whether to engage in social relationships with or hire former clients; or whether to terminate services to a noncompliant, yet vulnerable, client. The final category includes issues pertaining to social worker misconduct, such as exploitation of clients, boundary violations, or fraudulent billing for services.

Protecting Consumers from Ethically Incompetent Practice and Delineating Standards for Ethical Practice

The express purpose of licensing boards and regulatory boards is to protect the public from incompetent or unethical conduct by social workers. As discussed, many licensing boards draw explicitly or implicitly on the NASW Code of Ethics in order to enhance public protection. Licensing boards use these ethical standards to assess whether social workers have departed from professional standards in the event that a client or former client files a formal complaint. Licensed social workers who violate NASW code standards may be sanctioned. Also, NASW itself may sanction members who violate Code of Ethics standards, which is another form of consumer protection. In addition, courts of law draw on the profession's formal ethics standards when social workers are named in lawsuits alleging professional malpractice and negligence.

Providing Opportunities for Social Workers to Self-Govern Their Professional Behavior

The National Association of Social Workers uses the NASW Code of Ethics to evaluate and, when necessary, adjudicate ethics complaints filed against NASW members by clients or other parties. NASW may impose sanctions (for example, suspension, expulsion, notification of a licensing or regulatory body, publication of findings) or require various forms of corrective action (for example, consultation, supervision, training, continuing education) when there is evidence that practitioners do not possess ethical competence.

Protecting Social Workers from Ethics Complaints and Litigation

Codes of ethics also serve a preventive function. Social workers who fully understand prevailing ethical standards may be more likely to be ethically competent and less likely to engage in conduct that leads to ethics complaints and litigation.

Ethical Standards as a Risk-Management Tool

In recent years, formal ethical standards in social work have been used to reduce ethics-related risks in professional practice and minimize the likelihood of harm to clients and other parties. Social workers engage in high-risk behavior when they practice in a manner that is inconsistent with prevailing ethical and professional standards (Houston-Vega, Nuehring, and Daguio

1997; Reamer 2003; Strom-Gottfried 2007). Social workers can be held accountable for negligence and ethical violations in several ways. People who believe they have been harmed by incompetent social workers can file a negligence claim or lawsuit. Also, disgruntled parties can file formal complaints with social work organizations to which social workers belong and with licensing or regulatory bodies that govern social work practice. In these instances, the NASW Code of Ethics may be used as the standard for ethical conduct and assessments of ethical competence. In exceptional circumstances, criminal charges may be filed (for example, based on allegations of sexual misconduct or fraudulent billing of a government agency or private insurance company).

Voluntary membership organizations, such as NASW, typically process ethics complaints and evaluate ethical competence using a peer review model that includes members. The governing body may conduct a hearing during which the complainant, the respondent, and witnesses have an opportunity to testify. After hearing all parties and discussing the testimony, the organization may impose sanctions or require various forms of corrective action when there is evidence that the NASW Code of Ethics was violated by the practitioner.

Licensing and regulatory bodies also use formal procedures to process and review complaints against licensed social workers that raise questions about their ethical competence. Typically, the procedures involve a thorough review of the complaint, investigation, and, when warranted, a hearing conducted by a panel of colleagues (some boards include public members in addition to professional colleagues). In some jurisdictions, proceedings are conducted in a court of law.

Negligence claims or lawsuits filed against social workers typically allege that they engaged in malpractice in that they failed to adhere to specific standards of care. Often these formal complaints allege some form of ethical incompetence, for example, with regard to social workers' management of confidential information, professional boundaries, or conflicts of interest. The standard of care is based on what an ordinary, reasonable, and prudent social worker with the same or similar training would have done under the same or similar circumstances. Departures from the profession's standards of care—as reflected in the NASW Code of Ethics, related standards, literature, and expert testimony—may result from a social worker's acts of commission or acts of omission.

Ethically incompetent acts of commission can occur as a result of misfeasance or malfeasance. Misfeasance is the commission of a proper act in a wrongful or injurious manner or the improper performance of an act that might have been performed lawfully. Examples include disclosing clients' confidential information without authorization, providing substandard services to clients, and terminating services to clients prematurely. Malfeasance is the commission of a wrongful or unlawful act. Examples include becoming sexually involved with a client and billing insurance companies for services that social workers did not provide. An act of omission, also known as nonfeasance, occurs when a social worker fails to perform certain duties that ought to have been performed. Examples include failing to obtain clients' informed consent before providing services, or releasing confidential information and failing to inform clients about exceptions to their confidentiality rights.

Lawsuits that allege ethical incompetence that rises to the level of malpractice are civil suits, in contrast to criminal proceedings that might result when a social worker is charged with sexual assault of a client or fraudulent billing. Ordinarily, civil suits are based on tort or contract law, with plaintiffs (the party bringing the lawsuit) seeking some sort of compensation for injuries they claim to have incurred as a result of the social worker's negligence. Injuries that result from ethical incompetence may be economic (for example, lost wages that may result if the client is unable to work due to emotional impairment, or medical expenses associated with therapy that the client needs to help cope with the abuse); physical (for example, arising out of a sexual relationship between a social worker and client); and emotional (for example, depression suffered by a client who did not receive competent care from a social worker).

Of course, social workers who are accused of malpractice in civil litigation are presumed innocent until proven otherwise. In many jurisdictions, professionals are liable for their actions or inactions (sometimes known as errors or omissions) based on the legal standard of preponderance of the evidence, as opposed to the stricter standard of proof beyond a reasonable doubt used in criminal trials. In general, malpractice—including instances that result from ethical incompetence—occurs when four evidentiary elements are satisfied.

1. At the time of the alleged malpractice, a legal duty existed between the social worker and the client (or whatever party files the complaint)

This element is often the easiest to satisfy. Social workers assume a duty—known technically as a fiduciary duty—to clients once they agree to provide them with professional service. In contrast, a social worker who is asked for advice informally by a casual acquaintance whom the social worker just met at a social gathering, when the social worker was not working, would not have a formal duty of care to this acquaintance.

2. The social worker was derelict in that duty or breached the duty, either by commission or omission

Determining whether a social worker was derelict in the performance of a duty typically is more complex. Here questions may arise concerning the nature of the standard of care related to ethical competence in social work—that is, what is considered ordinary, reasonable, and prudent practice under the same or similar circumstances. In some instances, the standard of care is clear, as in cases related to fraudulent activity by agency administrators, sexual relationships between social workers and clients, or fraudulent documentation or billing. However, in many instances, social workers may disagree about the nature of the standard of care, as well as the relevance and application of formal ethical standards. The NASW code prohibiting inappropriate dual relationships between social workers and former clients serves as a good case in point: Some social workers might argue that this ethical standard prohibits a social work administrator from hiring former clients, as when a former client in a substance abuse treatment program applies for a job there as a case manager. Other social workers, however, might argue that in some circumstances hiring a former client would not be unethical and would not constitute an inappropriate dual relationship. Similarly, some social workers might argue that code-of-ethics provisions concerning clients' right to confidentiality prohibit a social worker who counsels an adolescent from sharing confidential information with the client's parents; others might argue that the social worker should respect the adolescent's right to privacy.

The fact that formal ethical standards can be interpreted differently by ethically competent practitioners is critically important. While some ethical standards are crystal clear (for example, with regard to sexual involvement with a client), others are necessarily vague and open to interpretation (for example, criteria for allocating scarce or limited agency resources).

Courts of law recognize that ethically competent professionals subscribe to various, sometimes conflicting, schools of thought, especially with respect to ethical standards. The idea that different schools of thought in a profession are permissible emerged primarily in medicine, when it became clear that physicians subscribed to different philosophies of practice, or schools, each with its own principal concepts, assumptions, and standards. Rather than try to determine which school of thought is "right," courts of law generally have acknowledged the legitimacy of different perspectives, so long as they are supported by a respectable minority of the profession. When it is difficult to determine whether a respectable minority of a profession endorses a particular school of thought, a judge is likely to explore whether the conduct that is in dispute falls within a reasonable range of views based on language in a prominent, recognized code of ethics (Reamer 2003).

3. The client suffered some harm or injury

Demonstrating harm or injury can also be difficult in social work. Unlike medicine, for example, where injuries resulting from malpractice are sometimes easy to document with x-rays or lab results, in social work the injuries alleged are often difficult to document empirically. In many instances, plaintiffs claim that they have experienced some form of emotional harm or injury, as opposed to some form of physical injury. In these cases, the plaintiff may have some difficulty substantiating the injury.

4. The harm or injury was directly and proximately caused by the social worker's dereliction of duty

Even plaintiffs who can document that they sustained some form of injury—emotional distress or depression, for example—may have difficulty demonstrating that the social worker's alleged dereliction of duty in the form of ethical incompetence, or departure from the ethics-related standard of care, was the direct and proximate cause of the injury. For example, a client who manifests symptoms of depression following a sexual relationship with a social worker may have struggled with depression before meeting the social worker; as a result, the preexisting condition (depression) may make it difficult to establish that the sexual relationship was the direct and proximate cause of the client's current depression.

Compelling Ethical Challenges: The Pursuit of Ethical Competence

Current social work literature and ethical standards address a wide range of ethical issues related to social workers' ethical responsibilities to clients, to colleagues, in practice settings, to the social work profession, and to the broader society (Banks 2003, 2006; Barsky 2010; Congress 2000, 2008; Dolgoff, Loewenberg, and Harrington 2008; Linzer 1999; Reamer 2006a, 2006b; Rhodes 1989). Some ethical standards provide enforceable guidelines for professional conduct; others are aspirational. As a group, these standards help to define ethically competent social work practice.

Client Rights

Especially since the 1960s, social workers have developed a keen understanding of clients' diverse rights, many of which were established by legislation, regulation, or court ruling and now are reflected in codes of ethics. These include rights related to confidentiality and privacy, release of information, informed consent, access to services, use of the least restrictive alternative, refusal of treatment, options for alternative services, access to records, termination of services, and grievance procedures.

Cultural and Social Diversity

One of the most significant developments in social work is the profession's increasingly substantial and nuanced grasp of diversity issues. Only in recent years have prominent ethics codes incorporated standards related to cultural competence, social diversity, and oppression.

Client Self-Determination and Professional Paternalism

The presumption in social work is that practitioners should promote and respect clients' rights to self-determination. Only recently have prominent social work codes of ethics acknowledged that instances arise when social workers may have a duty to override clients' rights to self-determination to protect clients from harming themselves or others. Interference with this right, taken in an effort to protect them from harming themselves, raises complex issues of professional paternalism.

Confidentiality, Privileged Communication, and Privacy

One of the most significant developments in the maturation of social work codes of ethics is the proliferation of standards pertaining to confidentiality, privileged communication, and privacy. For example, today's codes pay much more attention to these issues than earlier codes, particularly with respect to issues related to solicitation of private information from clients; disclosure of confidential information to protect clients from self-harm and protect third parties from harm; release of confidential information; disclosure of information about deceased clients; release of information to parents and guardians of minor clients; sharing of confidential information among participants in family, couples, and group counseling; disclosure of confidential information to media representatives, law enforcement officials, protective service agencies, and other social service organizations; protection of confidential written and electronic records, information transmitted to other parties through the use of computers, email, fax machines, telephones, and other electronic technology; transfer or disposal of clients' records; protection of client confidentiality in the event of a social worker's death, disability, or employment termination; precautions to prevent discussion of confidential information in public or semi-public areas; disclosure of confidential information to third-party payers; disclosure of confidential information to consultants; disclosure of confidential information for teaching or training purposes; and protection of confidential and privileged information during legal proceedings, for example, divorce proceedings, custody disputes, criminal trials, termination-of-parental-rights proceedings, and negligence lawsuits (Dickson 1998).

Informed Consent

Current ethical standards focus on informed consent requirements in a variety of circumstances, including release of confidential information, program admission, service delivery and treatment, videotaping, and audiotaping (Berg et al. 2001). Common elements included in ethics standards focus on social workers' duty to give clients specific details about the purpose of the consent, a verbal explanation, information about clients' rights to refuse consent and withdraw consent, information about alternative treatment options, and an opportunity to ask questions about the consent process.

Service Delivery

Ethical standards address social workers' duty to provide service and represent themselves as competent only within the boundaries of their education, training, license, certification, consultation received, supervised experience, or other relevant experience. They also focus on social workers' obligation to provide services in substantive areas and use practice approaches and techniques that are new to them only after engaging in appropriate study, training, consultation, and supervision from people who already possess competence in those practice approaches, interventions, and techniques.

Boundary Issues, Dual Relationships, and Conflicts of Interest

Literature on boundary issues in professional-client relationships has burgeoned in recent years, and this has influenced expanded content in ethics codes (Reamer 2001a; Syme 2003; Zur 2007). Contemporary ethics codes address issues related to financial or organizational conflicts of interest; sexual relationships with current and former clients; counseling former sexual partners; sexual relationships with clients' relatives or acquaintances; sexual relationships with supervisees, trainees, students, and colleagues; physical contact with clients; friendships with current and former clients; encounters with clients in public settings; attending clients' social, religious, or life cycle events; gifts to and from clients; performing favors for clients; the delivery of services in clients' homes; delivery of services to two or more people who have a relationship with each other (such as couples, family members); bartering with clients for goods and services; managing relationships in small or rural communities; self-disclosure to clients; and becoming colleagues with a former client.

Documentation

Ethical and risk-management standards related to documentation have also proliferated in recent years, particularly as they pertain to agency administration, assessment of clients' circumstances, planning and delivery of services, supervision, and accountability to clients, other service providers, funding agencies, utilization review staff, and courts of law (Kagle and Kopels 2008; Reamer 2005; Sidell 2011). Ethics standards focus on appropriate content in administrative and clients' records; clients' and other parties' access to records; and storage and retention of records.

Supervision

Ethics standards also focus on supervision issues, especially pertaining to supervisors' competence, documentation of supervision, and dual relationships between supervisors and supervisees. These issues are particularly important when ethics complaints and lawsuits against social workers raise questions about the quality of supervision they received.

Consultation and Referral

Occasionally ethical issues arise concerning social workers' consultation with professional colleagues and referral of clients to other professionals. As a result, ethics literature and standards address social workers' duty to be clear about when consultation with colleagues is appropriate and necessary and the procedures they should use to locate competent colleagues. Codes also address social workers' responsibility to refer clients to other professionals when they do not have the expertise or time to assist clients in need.

Dishonesty, Fraud, and Misrepresentation

A number of ethical standards in social work focus on social workers' duty to prevent dishonesty and fraud related to, for example, misrepresentation, documentation in case records, billing, and employment applications.

Termination of Services

Social workers face ethical risks when they terminate services improperly, as may occur when services are terminated prematurely, against a client's wishes, or when a social worker leaves an employment setting. Ethical standards provide procedural protocols and guidelines to ensure that services are terminated ethically.

Practitioner Impairment, Misconduct, and Incompetence

A significant percentage of ethics complaints are filed against social workers who meet the definition of impaired professional—that is, social workers who struggle as a result of substance abuse, mental illness, extraordinary personal stress, or financial or legal difficulties (Reamer 1992; Strom-Gottfried 2007). In addition, social workers sometimes encounter colleagues who are incompetent or engage in misconduct. Consequently, ethics codes include standards pertaining to social workers' duty to address their own and colleagues' impairment, incompetence, and misconduct.

Administration

Only in recent years have the social work literature and ethical standards acknowledged ethical challenges related to administration. Relevant ethical standards focus on resource allocation, management practices, performance evaluation and personnel practices, and social workers' commitment to employers (particularly when social workers believe that employers' policies, procedures, or administrative orders interfere with their ethical practice of social work). For example, the NASW Code of Ethics includes a number of specific standards that require agency and organization administrators to "advocate within and outside their agencies for adequate resources to meet clients' needs" (standard 3.07[a]), "advocate for resource allocation procedures that are open and fair" (standard 3.07[b]), "take reasonable steps to ensure that adequate agency or organizational resources are available to provide appropriate staff supervision" (standard 3.07[c]), and "take reasonable steps to provide or arrange for continuing education and staff development for all staff for whom they are responsible" (standard 3.08).

Evaluation and Research

Research and evaluation have become more prominent in social work, particularly with respect to clinical and program evaluation and evidenced-based practice. Codes of ethics now include extensive guidelines regarding the protection of human participants in research. These standards are particularly important in light of notorious abuse and exploitation of research and evaluation participants, as, for example, in the well-known Tuskegee and Willowbrook studies that exploited vulnerable research participants (Sales and Folkman 2000).

Social Welfare and Social Action

One of social work's distinguishing features is its explicit concern about broad social welfare, in addition to social workers' concern about individual well-being. The NASW Code of Ethics includes extensive standards pertaining to global social welfare, advocacy, social and political action, and preventing discrimination and exploitation.

Looking Ahead: Future Challenges

The evolution of social workers' ethical competence is one of the most remarkable developments in the profession's history. In little more than a century, social work has moved from rather moralistic, sometimes paternalistic, instincts to comprehensive, robust ethical standards that guide practice, protect the public, and regulate the profession. Codes of ethics have blossomed as they have expanded from relatively simplistic oaths to sophisticated documents replete with diverse ethical prescriptions, prohibitions, moral ambiguity, and nuance. Further, ethics education in social work has matured, moving from comparatively simplistic overviews of core professional values to conceptually rich discussions of complex ethical dilemmas and decision-making frameworks that draw on ethical concepts and theories (including the application of theoretical perspectives in moral philosophy such as deontology, teleology, utilitarianism, virtue ethics, and feminist ethics perspectives).

The maturation of ethical competence in social work has not occurred in a vacuum. These compelling developments reflect broader societal trends related to ethics and morality, the emergence of a discrete discipline focused on practical and professional ethics, and practitioners' deepening grasp of morally complex dimensions of professional practice. In the second decade of the twenty-first century, the net result is a worldwide collection of increasingly complex and influential ethics codes and frameworks for ethical analysis and decision making.

That said, social workers should not be lulled into a false sense that this more mature grasp of ethical issues addresses all challenging ethical issues in the profession and provides answers to all complex ethical dilemmas. Indeed, no ethical theory or code of ethics is a panacea. Realistically, ethics concepts and codes of ethics identify critically important ethical issues in the profession, set a moral tone, outline broad ethical principles, and provide practical guidance on a wide variety of ethical challenges. Ethical standards cannot resolve all ethical dilemmas; in fact, it is inevitable that ethical principles and standards will conflict on occasion, requiring social workers to think hard about which ethical duties and obligations take precedence. This is an inherent quality of true ethical dilemmas that resist easy solutions. In these instances, ethics concepts and codes of ethics provide a valuable inventory of pertinent principles and standards; however, ethically competent social workers understand that they must supplement these standards with a conceptually rich, nuanced analysis of pertinent ethical issues and moral judgment that incorporates relevant moral concepts and consultation.

As social workers now understand, ethics codes are living documents that require periodic revision to reflect new knowledge and ethical challenges. During social work's early years, the broad discipline of applied, practical, and professional ethics did not exist. Ethical decision-making protocols had not been created, and it took decades for the profession to begin to conceptualize about ethical dilemmas, apply ethics concepts and theories to ethical challenges, and develop rigorous ethical decision-making protocols. Moreover, social work's early pioneers could not have imagined some of the ethical challenges facing today's practitioners. In the late nineteenth and early twentieth centuries, what social worker could have imagined confidentiality and privacy issues that arise when practitioners provide counseling services using video conferencing and web-based chat rooms, send documents to third parties electronically, store records in computers, and talk with clients on wireless telephones? Social work's pioneers could not have anticipated litigation that challenges social workers' relationships with former clients or practitioners' decisions to disclose confidential information, without client consent, to a client's sexual partner in order to protect the partner from HIV infection. These and many other contemporary ethical challenges in social work teach us a compelling lesson: Forecasting the ethical challenges that the next generation of social workers will encounter is extraordinarily difficult, if not impossible. Technological developments, the emergence of novel social work interventions, and changes in the law are likely to require periodic re-examination and revision of social work's ethical frameworks and standards. This is at it should be. Ethical standards in the profession should always reflect social workers' perpetual growth of knowledge about the moral purposes of the profession and ways to assist people in need.

Social work's principal challenge as it moves forward is to ensure that its practitioners continue to seek ethical competence. Ethical competence in social work depends on four key educational goals that must be pursued during the course of professional education and post-graduate continuing education (Hastings Center 1980; Reamer 2001b).

Stimulate the Moral Imagination

Social work educators and agency administrators must identify opportunities to alert students and practitioners to the moral dimensions of the profession. Educators and administrators must ensure that social workers have the ability to identify ethical issues when they arise in the profession, especially those related to the profession's core values, conflicts between social workers' personal values and the profession's values, conflicts among professional duties and obligations, ethical decision making, and ethics-related risk management.

This knowledge is not automatic. Social workers must be deliberately taught about the anatomy of ethical issues and ways to examine them conceptually. Social workers should be encouraged to look actively for moral and ethical issues that are embedded in social work functions. Ideally, social workers will learn to raise critical questions about these issues and systematically apply ethics concepts and guidelines in their efforts to address them.

Develop Analytical Skills

There is a wide range of rich conceptual tools that social workers can use to analyze ethical issues arising in professional practice. Drawing on the long-standing intellectual frameworks created by moral philosophers and professional ethicists—including diverse theories of normative ethics such as deontology, teleology, virtue ethics, and feminist ethics—social workers can critically examine conflicts among values and ethical dilemmas in an effort to resolve these issues in a manner consistent with the profession's enduring ethical principles and standards. Thus, one of the major goals of ethics education promoting ethical competence should be to help social workers understand classic ethical theories and conceptual frameworks and apply them to the ethical dilemmas they encounter.

Elicit a Sense of Moral Obligation and Personal Responsibility

In the final analysis, social work is anchored in a deep-seated moral commitment to assisting vulnerable people who are experiencing problems in living. Debate throughout the profession's history concerning social work's mission and its practitioners' fundamental duties is rooted in the profession's core values and ethical framework. Ethics education must focus on the relationship between the moral dimensions of social work's mission and social workers' personal virtues, commitments, and sense of duty. Ultimately, social workers' decisions about the kind of work they do and the populations with which they work should be a function of practitioners' beliefs about both social work's moral purposes and their own.

Develop the Ability to Respond to Ethical Controversy and Ambiguity

Ethical issues often generate considerable and intense differences of opinion. Social workers sometimes question the value of ethical theory and analysis when even the most rigorous application of ethics concepts fails to produce clear answers to complex questions. Differences of opinion about the limits of clients' right to confidentiality and self-determination, ways to allocate limited resources, the appropriateness of paternalism, boundary issues, conflicts of interest, and the ethics of whistle-blowing can lead to some frustration for social workers who, understandably, yearn for clarity and clear, unequivocal moral guidance.

Furthermore, social workers sometimes find themselves embroiled in intense debate about the very meaning of ethical terms (*justice, fairness, right, wrong, good, bad, duty,* and *obligation*, among others), the derivation of ethical principles and standards, and ways of applying ethical guidelines to real-world ethical dilemmas. This fact of professional life should not lead us to conclude that discussions about ethics are futile and pointless, and that ethical relativism is the only realistic option. Disciplined, principled, and informed discussions of ethical issues can help ethically competent social workers clarify and challenge their own and one another's assertions and conclusions.

Social workers who seek ethical competence should be willing to acknowledge the inevitable ambiguity in many moral matters and the fact that true expert judgment in ethics is often elusive. Macklin's (1988) keen observation with respect to moral ambiguity in bioethics can be generalized to social work and other professions: "Rarely does bioethics offer 'one right answer' to a moral dilemma. Seldom can a philosopher arrive on the scene and make unequivocal pronouncements about the right thing to do. Yet, despite the fact that it has no magic wand, bioethics is still useful and can go a long way toward 'resolving the issues,' once that phrase is properly interpreted" (p. 52).

Social workers' earnest pursuit of ethical competence cannot guarantee a virtuous outcome, but it can greatly enhance the likelihood that practitioners will be cognizant of complex moral matters and explore their vitally important implications. Ultimately, we must have some confidence that social workers can cultivate sound moral instincts and, over time, develop the ability to grasp the complex ways in which ethical constructs and guidelines are germane to the compelling ethical dilemmas they encounter. Perhaps, as the moral philosopher Kass (1990) asserts, "in ethics, the true route begins with practice, with deeds and doers, and moves only secondarily to reflection on practice. Indeed, even the propensity to *care* about moral matters requires a certain *moral disposition*, acquired in practice, before the age of reflection arrives. As Aristotle points out, he who has 'the that' can easily get 'the why'" (p. 8).

References

Banks, S. 2003. From oaths to rulebooks: A critical examination of codes of ethics for the social professions. *European Journal of Social Work* 6: 133–144.

———. 2006. *Ethics and Values in Social Work*, 3d ed. Hampshire, England: Palgrave Macmillan.

Barsky, A. 2010. *Ethics and Values in Social Work: An Integrated Approach for a Comprehensive Curriculum.* New York: Oxford University Press.

Bayles, M. 1986. Professional power and self-regulation. *Business and Professional Ethics Journal* 5: 26–46.

Berg, J., P. Appelbaum, C. Lidz, and L. Parker. 2001. *Informed Consent: Legal Theory and Clinical Practice,* 2d ed. New York: Oxford University Press.

Brandl, P., and M. Maguire. 2002. Codes of ethics: A primer on their purpose, development, and use. *Journal for Quality and Participation* 25: 8–12.

Callahan, D., and S. Bok, eds. 1980. *Ethics Teaching in Higher Education.* New York: Plenum Press.

Congress, E. 2000. *Social Work Values and Ethics.* Chicago: Nelson-Hall.

———. 2008. Codes of Ethics. In *Encyclopedia of Social Work,* 20th ed., Vol. 1, ed. T. Mizrahi and L. Davis, 326–331. Washington, DC, and New York: NASW Press and Oxford University Press.

Congress, E., and D. McAuliff. 2006. Social work ethics: Professional codes in Australia and the United States. *International Social Work* 49: 151–164.

Cooper, T.L. 2006. *The Responsible Administrator: An Approach to Ethics for the Administrative Role,* 5th ed. San Francisco, CA: Jossey-Bass.

Dickson, D. 1998. *Confidentiality and Privacy in Social Work.* New York: Free Press.

Dolgoff, R., F. Loewenberg, and D. Harrington. 2008. *Ethical Decisions for Social Work Practice,* 8th ed. Belmont, CA: Brooks Cole.

Emmet, D. 1962. Ethics and the social worker. *British Journal of Psychiatric Social Work* 6: 165–172.

Freeman, S., D. Engels, and M. Altekruse. 2004. Foundations for ethical standards and codes: The role of moral philosophy and theory in ethics. *Counseling and Values* 48: 163–173.

Greenwood, E. 1957. Attributes of a profession. *Social Work* 2: 45–55.

Hall, R. 1968. Professionalization and bureaucratization. *American Sociological Review* 33: 92–104.

Hastings Center. 1980. *The Teaching of Ethics in Higher Education.* Hastings-on-Hudson, NY: Author.

Houston-Vega, M., E. Nuehring, and E. Daguio. 1997. *Prudent Practice: A Guide for Managing Malpractice Risk.* Washington, DC: NASW Press.

Hugman, R. 2003. Professional values and ethics in social work: Reconsidering postmodernism? *British Journal of Social Work* 33: 1025–2041.

Jamal, K., and N. Bowie. 1995. Theoretical considerations for a meaningful code of professional ethics. *Journal of Business Ethics* 1: 703–714.

Johnson, A. 1955. Educating professional social workers for ethical practice. *Social Service Review* 29: 125–136.

Kagle, J., and S. Kopels. 2008. *Social Work Records*, 3d ed. Long Grove, IL: Waveland Press.

Kass, L. 1990. Practicing ethics: Where's the action? *Hastings Center Report* 20(1): 5–12.

Keith-Lucas, A. 1963. A critique of the principle of client self-determination. *Social Work* 8: 66–71.

Kultgen, J. 1982. The ideological use of professional codes. *Business and Professional Ethics Journal* 1: 53–69.

Levy, C. 1976. *Social Work Ethics.* New York: Human Sciences Press.

Lindeman, E. 1947. Social work matures in a confused world. *The Compass* 28 (January): 3–9.

Linzer, N. 1999. *Resolving Ethical Dilemmas in Social Work Practice.* Boston: Allyn & Bacon.

Macklin, R. 1988. Theoretical and applied ethics: A reply to the skeptics. In *Applied Ethics and Ethical Theory,* ed. D. Rosenthal and F. Shehadi, 50–70. Salt Lake City: University of Utah Press.

Menzel, D. 2007. *Ethics Management for Public Administrators: Building Organizations of Integrity.* Armonk, NY: M.E. Sharpe.

Paine, R., Jr. 1880. The work of volunteer visitors of the associated charities among the poor. *Journal of Social Science* 12: 101–114.

Pumphrey, M. 1959. *The Teaching of Values and Ethics in Social Work Education.* New York: Council on Social Work Education.

Reamer, F. 1992. The impaired social worker. *Social Work* 37(2): 165–170.

———. 2001a. *Tangled Relationships: Managing Boundary Issues in the Human Services.* New York: Columbia University Press.

———. 2001b. *Ethics Education in Social Work.* Alexandria, VA: Council on Social Work Education.

———. 2003. *Social Work Malpractice and Liability: Strategies for Prevention*, 2d ed. New York: Columbia University Press.

———. 2005. Documentation issues in social work: Evolving ethical and risk-management standards. *Social Work* 50(4): 325–234.

———. 2006a. *Ethical Standards in Social Work: A Review of the NASW Code of Ethics,* 2d ed. Washington, DC: NASW Press.

———. 2006b. *Social Work Values and Ethics,* 3d ed. New York: Columbia University Press.

———. 2009. *The Social Work Ethics Casebook: Cases and Commentary.* Washington, DC: NASW Press.

Rhodes, M. 1989. *Ethical Dilemmas in Social Work Practice.* London: Routledge and Kegan Paul.

Sales, B., and S. Folkman, eds. 2000. *Ethics in Research with Human Participants.* Washington, DC: American Psychological Association.

Sidell, N. 2011. *Social Work Documentation*. Washington, DC: NASW Press.

Sloan, D. 1980. The teaching of ethics in the American undergraduate curriculum: 1876–1976. In *Ethics Teaching in Higher Education*, ed. D. Callahan and S. Bok, 1–57. New York: Plenum.

Strom-Gottfried, K. 2007. *Straight Talk About Professional Ethics*. Chicago: Lyceum.

Syme, G. 2003. *Dual Relationships in Counseling and Psychotherapy*. London: Sage.

Teicher, M. 1967. *Values in Social Work: A Reexamination*. New York: NASW.

Trattner, W. 1998. *From Poor Law to Welfare State: A History of Social Welfare in America,* 6th ed. New York: Free Press.

Van Wart, M. 2003. Codes of ethics as living documents. *Public Integrity* 5: 331–346.

Younghusband, E. 1967. *Social Work and Social Values*. London: Allen and Unwin.

Zur, O. 2007. *Boundaries in Psychotherapy: Ethical and Clinical Explorations*. Washington, DC: American Psychological Association.

8

Ethical Competence and Professionalism in Public Administration

Jeremy F. Plant

Public administration, as a field of practice and an academic discipline, has wrestled with the issue of ethical competence since its inception as a self-aware field in the late nineteenth and early twentieth centuries. Yet questions remain. What do we mean by ethical competence in the profession of public administration? What should be the focus of efforts to establish standards of ethical competence? Can we take a one-size-fits-all approach to ethical competence for professionals in public administration or tailor specific competencies to the work performed by a variety of professionals working in public and nonprofit organizations? Should our attention be only with those employed by government agencies or all those outside government engaged—in one way or another, through grants, contracts, and other arrangements—in public service activities? Once defined, how do we educate public administration professionals to be ethically competent? How do we measure competence—at the individual, group, organizational, or systemic level? Should the focus of ethical competence be on compliance with explicit standards of conduct and behavior, or should it stress public service values such as selflessness, commitment to excellence, civility, and honesty?

Public administration, like many other professional fields, is now focusing on competency-based courses and educational programs with measureable outcomes. The new guidelines for professional education in public policy and public administration adopted by the National Association of Schools of Public Affairs and Administration (NASPAA) require programs to identify specific learning outcomes and competencies for all courses and program objectives. There has never been a time when the issue of *what constitutes ethical competence for professional public administrators* has been of greater importance than the present.

In short, ethical competence raises issues that go to the heart of the professional life of the field of public administration and for which there are no easy answers. Public administration is a vast field of enterprise encompassing the work of government at all levels, nonprofit organizations, and, increasingly, a plethora of organizations and contractors doing the public's business through third-party administration of programs, public-private partnerships, and collaborative networks. Education in public administration aims to form a professional community that ranges from the individual working in a remote village in Ethiopia delivering aid to impoverished children to the top aide working for a member of Congress, and from a city budget director to a deputy police chief in Los Angeles, and on and on.[1] Public administration has wrestled with these issues of identity since its inception as a self-aware professional undertaking in the early years of the twentieth century. In recent years, the field has expanded to include more and more professional activities beyond its initial focus on career public servants in government agencies. At the same time, interest in ethics and ethical competence has become a major focus in the field, as Cooper and Menzel (2013) discuss in the introductory chapter of this book.

In this chapter, we begin by examining the efforts made by scholars and practitioners to wrestle with the complex and difficult question of defining ethics in public administration. Second is the issue of coverage: What are the boundaries of the field and profession of public administration, and what roles should be included in the discussion of ethical competence? This is followed by an examination of ways in which ethical competence can be conveyed and measured in actual administrative performance. The final section concludes the discussion by returning to the concept of *professional responsibility* as the foundation for ethically competent action for those engaged in serving the public. Operationalizing the idea of responsible conduct is derived from the idea of the *ethical checklist*, by which the ethically competent administrator can easily and reliably include ethical considerations into day-to-day decision making, from the most mundane and routine affairs to high-level decisions under stressful and crisis situations.

What Is Ethical Competence in Public Administration?

Ethical competence in public administration was first defined as *professional responsibility*. Carl Friedrich (1935) and John Gaus (1936) used the concept of administrative responsibility in the 1930s as the need of the public servant to understand how all elements of the work she is asked to perform have an ethical component. Responsibility, as Pennock (1960) pointed out, "has two primary meanings, or what I have called the core of meaning has two facets, (a) accountability and (b) the rational and moral exercise of discretionary power (or the capacity or disposition for such exercise), and . . . each of these notions tends to flavor the other" (p. 13). Responsible administrative conduct requires action and judgment, but action based on a firm foundation of knowledge and a commitment to evidence-based decisions, in the context of administrative authority accountable both to organizational and political superiors and to the professional peer community that stands ready to assess the factual, procedural, and ethical standards displayed.

When Friedrich and Gaus were developing the concept of professional responsibility, there was limited attention given to theories of administrative ethics in the literature and pedagogy of public administration (Cooper 2001). Since the 1970s, the field of public administration has been enriched by a robust discussion of the meaning of ethics and those specific competencies that should be considered essential for the ethical administrator. These range from extremely broad and general definitions to highly specific lists of competencies that the ethical administrator will internalize. Definitions can be found in the scholarly literature of the field but also in codes of conduct and ethics promulgated by professional associations and government jurisdictions. What are the commonalities and differences among the various definitions?

The most basic definition of ethical competence is simply *the capacity to recognize ethical issues,* as one reviewer of this chapter has helpfully pointed out. Finnish scholar Turo Virtanen (2000) takes a somewhat similar tack, arguing that ethical competence is "conforming to moral values and moral norms that prevail in a culture." While such short and general definitions are a useful place to begin, most writers on the subject have preferred to expand the definition. One approach has been to build upon the idea of moral reasoning and ethical judgment. Using this approach, as noted by Michael Macauley and Alan Lawton (2006), James S. Bowman and his colleagues argued that ethically competent administrators must understand and practice moral reasoning (interpreted as ethical reasoning here); be able to sort through competing values; and engage in prudent decision making. This requires the ability to engage in principled moral reasoning, recognize ethics-related conflicts, refuse to do unethical actions, and know how to apply ethical theory to concrete situations.

Katherine Denhardt (2009) approached the definitional issue from a different perspective—begin with an understanding of what we mean by *unethical behavior* and build out from there to develop a sense of what constitutes ethical competence. Noting that "the vast majority of ethical and competent behaviors go unnoticed, while unethical and incompetent behaviors make news," she concluded that "a description of an *unethical and incompetent public servant* might therefore begin:

- Fails to conform to approved standards of social or professional behavior for persons carrying out public duties, roles and responsibilities;
- Acts in a manner that is inadequate or unsuited to their role as a public administrator or leader." (2009, 1)

Denhardt's discussion hints at an issue that offers no easy answer: Is ethical competence related to general administrative competence? Is it unethical to knowingly assume a role for which you are not capable? She concludes her paper with a list of competencies that graduates of public administration degree programs should possess, including the following: the ability to understand and apply approved standards of social or professional behavior; the ability to develop qualities requisite for effective ethical action; and the ability to lead and manage in a manner that raises ethical awareness and competence in the broader organization or context.

Denhardt is in good company in arguing for a broader view of ethical competence. Most scholars writing on the subject have attempted to include not only a list of specific skills or competencies but also the view that the application of the skills must take into account the context in which action is taken. In a thoughtful paper presented at the 2009 Annual Conference of the National Association of Schools of Public Affairs and Administration in Arlington, Virginia, James Svara argued that "the choice of 'competence' as the focus for the development and support of ethical public administrators seems to cover only part of the territory. . . . Ethical public administrators must also have awareness, commitment, autonomy, courage, and an understanding of their distinctive context" (Svara 2009, 1).

In the introductory chapter to this volume, Terry Cooper and Donald Menzel (2013) take a similarly expansive view, noting,

> We cannot define competence apart from a set of specific competencies—skills, knowledge, and abilities to do things measured against a standard. Competencies would then be personal skills that reflect proficiency in:
>
> 1. identifying ethical problems and the issues that emerge from them,
> 2. reasoning about the principles involved in the problem and issues,
> 3. arriving at a decision that can be defended based on public service principles, and
> 4. balancing organization development and design to move organizations toward structures and cultures that are supportive of ethical conduct.

Most discussion of ethical competence in the literature of public administration has been based on examples drawn from administrative practice in the United States. In recent years, however, the discussion has been enriched by comparative examination of ethics in different national settings. To tie this development into the discussion of ethical competence, Raymond Cox (2009) approached the issue of defining ethical competence in a way that allowed for examination of specific aspects of competence in different national and cultural settings (cited in Paddock 2011). Cox utilized six skill areas that he concluded were inclusive of ethical competence: identification of problems, problem solving, advocacy, self-awareness and consensus building, subject matter knowledge, and attitude and commitment (cited in Paddock 2011).

While most discussions of ethical competence have come from the academic side of public administration, it is useful to note as well the definitions that come from professional associations. The International City/County Management Association (ICMA) has a long history of concern with ethical conduct and ethical competence, dating back to its first Code of Ethics in 1924. ICMA defines ethical competence in terms of integrity: personal, professional, and organizational (ICMA, 2008). The American Society for Public Administration (ASPA) established its Code of Ethics considerably later, in the early 1980s, with a significant revision to the present code in 1995. Although the ASPA code does not use the term *competence* as such, it identifies five areas in which the ethical administrator is expected to be competent: serving the public interest; respecting the Constitution and the law; demonstrating personal integrity; promoting ethical organizations; and striving for professional excellence.

What can we conclude from this discussion of some of the many definitions and discussions of ethical competence that can be gleaned from the public administration field? First, there is agreement that public administration is a field of action, and competence in the area of ethics requires informed action based on ethical awareness and knowledge. Second, there is an understanding that ethical competence is meaningful only in regard to the relevant setting in which administrative action is taken. This includes actions within and between organizations, interactions between administrators and the public (either in general or in dealings with individual citizens), and actions within the political environment. Third, and most problematic for those concerned with a bridge between theory and practice, there is a sense that ethical competence needs to include both cognition and affect—mind and heart. It is not enough simply to master a knowledge of ethics; rather, one must have personal qualities that fit with the requirements for public service. Among these qualities are the courage to act in the face of uncertainty or adversity; compassion and genuine concern for others; personal honesty and integrity; and a commitment to excellence and a willingness to strive for greater self-awareness and ethical autonomy. How to inculcate such a multifaceted sense of ethical competence is the big task for educators and professional associations. But first, other questions must be posed and answered: Who should be considered as relevant to the task? What roles do we include within the definition of public administration, and how does this influence the strategies we consider to develop greater ethical competence?

Who Should Be Included?

As the definition suggests, public administration as a profession is guided
by both a concern for knowledge, skills, and attitudes and abilities, as well
as values, and a commitment to the goal of a better and more just society.
Compared to other professions, it does not certify or license its membership
or require a particular graduate degree or course of study for entry (although
personnel systems and civil service requirements often specify educational or
professional criteria for employment). Also unusual is the context in which
the profession operates. Since the first steps were taken in the late nineteenth
century to professionalize the public service, political elites and the public
at large have wrestled with the tension between the need for professional expertise in government and the fear that expert bureaucrats would wrest power
from those in elective office (Karl 1976, 1987). As a result, a sort of balance
or middle ground has been established, with career professionals serving as
a middle group between nonprofessional workers below and politically appointed agents above. Professional judgment and action remain subordinate
to the dictates of the political institutions and those within the organizations
of governance who are their agents. Unlike those trained in business management or accounting or medicine or most other professions, those in the
profession of public administration cannot aspire to hold the top positions in
most public-sector organizations.[2]

The result has been a quandary from the outset as to what makes public
administration a true profession. Even setting its own standards for entry, or
exercising final say in disciplining its members, has been proscribed as tread-
ing on powers reserved for the people and their elected representatives. For
those adhering to traditional bureaucratic values, obedience to higher authority and its resulting behavior (serving loyally and impartially any political
superior) forms a core professional value. Others see this as an excuse for
career professionals to be morally mute and inattentive to ethical issues other
than obedience to legitimate authority. Yet a concern for ethics and ethical
conduct is part of the DNA of public administration, as a field of study or
discipline and as a profession.

A first cut at categorizing professionals in government service yields four
distinct professional groupings:

- *General Public Administration professionals.* This category includes those
  utilizing the traditional knowledge, skills, and values associated with MPA
  programs, in jobs that involve general management, budgeting, program
  planning and evaluation, human resource management, and other generalist
  job categories involving internal management concerns.

- *Public-sector professionals.* This grouping includes professionals with technical expertise in policy and program areas found only or predominantly in the public sector, including the military, public health, diplomacy, public safety and corrections, K–12 education, and other job categories that reflect the role of government in society.
- *Publicly employed professionals.* These professionals work for and in public-sector organizations but are members of professions that span the public and private sectors, such as government attorneys, accountants, physicians, scientists, and engineers. This is the largest of the groupings in numbers, and is increasingly found in state and local governments as well as the federal government.
- *At-will professionals.* Individuals in these roles owe their nontenured appointment to professional expertise and not political or partisan bases, and are not expected to be agents of elected officials in pursuing their agenda. Most in public service positions are employed in county and municipal government. However, one can include in addition to these government-based professionals those in leadership positions in nonprofit organizations. Public administration has embraced the nonprofit sector in recent years. Professional nonprofit and association managers are in many ways analogous to the at-will professionals found in local government, but larger nonprofit organizations may mirror the range of professions noted above in government service.

How can such a diverse and complex pattern of professional employment and engagement in public service occupations lead to a true profession of public administration? Can the field generate the sense of shared identity, cohesion, and *esprit de corps* needed by any profession to inculcate a sense of shared competencies?

The problem of professional identity and cohesion is exacerbated by the increasing presence and salience in public administration of actors not employed directly by public organizations whose work is largely or entirely delivering public service and goods through contractual relationships with government. This "third sector" represents a challenge in applying traditional notions of ethical competence in public administration. To whom are these individuals ultimately responsible, the public or the stockholders and managers of the companies that employ them? What is the meaning of professional responsibility for individuals whose work spans the public and private sectors? Is it the responsibility of educators and professional societies associated with public administration to reach out to government contractors, or vice versa? To date, public administration as a profession has not resolved the issues that result from having so much of the work of governance entrusted to organizations and individuals outside the traditional boundaries of the public sector and the professional life of public administration.

In a 1968 essay Dwight Waldo advised public administration to "act as if it is a profession" even if it lacked many of the attributes of more established professions such as law, medicine, and the ministry. He raised a number of critical questions for the field to consider. Should it emulate those established professions and work to develop clear standards for educating, testing, certifying, and disciplining its members, or accept a more loosely coupled sense of professional identity? Or is public administration too general or too diverse a field of action to form the basis of a single professional identity? If so, should it recognize the pluralism of its professionalism and embrace the range of professions found in public service careers and organizations? In the even more complex professional and organizational arrangement of contemporary governance, Waldo's admonition to act like a profession continues to make sense. In the following section of the chapter, four strategies commonly employed by professions to develop ethical competence: educational programs, formal codes of ethics, training programs, and leadership and mentoring activities.

What Strategies Are Available to Develop Ethical Competence in Public Administration?

Four basic strategies exist for developing ethical competence in any profession: professional studies in graduate university programs; statutes, codes of ethics, standards of conduct, and other formal statements of the "dos and don'ts" of personal behavior; training programs; and leadership, mentoring, and courageous decision making by ethical exemplars, individuals of integrity who point the way to ethical behavior within organizations. Despite its relative lack of cohesiveness compared to other professions, public administration employs all four strategies to develop ethical competence within its ranks.

Ethics Education

Ethics was a late-arriving topic in graduate public administration programs. The first courses devoted to public or administrative ethics appeared in the 1970s. Prior to that time, there was little in the way of literature in the field devoted to ethics around which to build a course, and the topic had little standing among educators in the field. A number of factors in the period between the late 1960s and the 1980s stimulated an interest in adding ethics to the standard MPA curriculum, including:

- a growing concern with the role of public administration in social equity and the role that individuals and organizations could and should play as advocates of a more just and equitable society;
- an interest among younger scholars in ethics, leading to a rapid development of the literature available to use in classes devoted to ethics or in which ethical issues were discussed;
- declining trust in government, triggered in part by the high-level abuses of the Watergate scandal; and
- a growing interest in professional ethics by associations and organizations, often with impact on graduate programs responding to demands by such parties for more attention to ethics in the curriculum.

More or less at the same time that ethics education was expanding exponentially in graduate public administration programs, the field was moving toward stricter accreditation standards, led by the association representing schools of public affairs and administration, the National Association of Schools of Public Affairs and Administration (NASPAA). NASPAA was formed in 1974 and moved to first roster and then formally accredit graduate masters-level programs in the field. For ethicists in the field, this represented a golden opportunity to advance the idea that ethics, and in particular a required course devoted to public administrative ethics, be part of every graduate degree program.

An alternative to the required course in ethics was the notion that ethics could be discussed as an element in courses concerned primarily with other topics–ethics as an element of budgeting, policy analysis, human resource management, and so on. Faculty with special expertise in ethics argued against this approach, saying it diluted the coverage of ethical concepts and issues and led to instructors without adequate knowledge of ethical theory and practice passing kernels of wisdom without the required knowledge. The issue has never gone away since it was raised at the time the first NASPAA MPA standards were promulgated, but accredited programs have never been required to do more than show coverage of ethics in the core curriculum. Whether this coverage is achieved through a dedicated course or via inclusion of ethics-related issues in other core courses has remained a program decision.

The most recent iteration of NASPAA standards puts an emphasis on the development of competencies and measurable outcomes. The 2009 NASPAA standards clearly and explicitly use the term *public service values* rather than *public service ethics* in identifying the set of expectations dealing with the normative focus of the program (NASPAA 2009). In the section that identifies the preconditions for accreditation review, the language is as follows:

The mission, governance, and curriculum of eligible programs shall demonstrably emphasize public service values. Public service values are important and enduring beliefs, ideals, and principles shared by members of a community about what is good and desirable and what is not. They include pursuing the public interest with accountability and transparency; serving professionally with competence, efficiency, and objectivity; acting ethically so as to uphold the public trust; and demonstrating respect, equity, and fairness in dealings with citizens and fellow public servants. (NASPAA 2009, p. 2)

Utilizing the concept of public service values rather than public ethics follows the continuing line of development of literature on *public values,* which has emerged in the past decade to challenge the existing field of *public ethics.* That this issue is more than a semantic one for the affected academicians relates back to the emphasis on performance and demonstrable competencies. If one takes the limited definition of "acting ethically" from the above statement, ethical competence is largely concerned with issues of public trust. Ethical conduct is seemingly separate from (1) professionalism, which becomes identified only with technical skills; (2) the pursuit of the public interest, which is seen again as a largely technical exercise of rules and accountability rather than the integrated approach favored by most writers in the field; and (3) behavior related to relationships, as identified in the section of the statement concerning respect, equity, and fairness. All these questions were once thought to constitute the field of public ethics, and are included in the American Society for Public Administration's ethics code (ASPA Code of Ethics, n.d.) and many of the writings in the field that take a holistic view of public ethics.

This creates a quandary for public administration ethicists. Do the new standards narrow the definition of ethical competence, or do they require ethicists to provide the range of competencies related to public values? The narrow definition seems to require attention largely to the issues most relevant to public trust: corruption prevention and efforts to avoid the appearance of wrongdoing. Will the possible separation of ethics from consideration of the other aspects of public values noted by NASPAA—accountability, professionalism, equity and fairness in interpersonal dealings—dilute the coverage to include largely formal or compliance-driven measures and behaviors? Will it reduce the role of ethics scholarship in NASPAA programs? For those in the ethics field who have pushed for years to require coursework focused on ethics and taught by qualified ethicists, many questions are raised by the way in which ethics is apparently subsumed under public values in the new guidelines. It certainly raises questions about how ethical competence stands in relation to other required competencies in the new performance- and competence-based approach to program design and delivery.

In addition to the argument over the role of ethics in the curriculum of MPA programs, there has been a healthy discussion of the proper approach to teaching ethics. Should the focus be on ethical theories such as consequentialism, deontology, virtue ethics, or democratic political theory? Should it focus on issues of corruption and violation of clear standards, or take a more aspirational view of how public administrators can advance positive social and political values? Should it stress personal integrity, or the development of organizational culture that values ethical behavior and individual ethical awareness?

As ethics has matured as an element in public administration education, the available literature to utilize in ethics courses has evolved from a highly theoretical or normative focus to a more practical approach—one that introduces the basics of ethical theory and builds upon them to develop knowledge, skills, and competence in handling typical ethical issues in the workplace. Two recent examples of such books are *The Ethics Primer for Public Administrators in Government and Nonprofit Organizations* by James Svara (2007) and the second edition of *Ethics Management for Public Administrators: Leading and Building Organizations of Integrity* by Donald Menzel (2012). Both books have a pedagogical focus, and, according to Svara (2007), they target "persons who occupy career leadership and staff positions in government and nonprofit organizations" (1). Both authors are concerned with the context in which ethical behavior is situated; Menzel notes, "The intellectual legacy of the great philosophers has spawned a blind spot in our understanding of contemporary ethical behavior. What has been largely overlooked is the *context* in which ethical decisions are made" (2012, 7).

Svara (2007) takes an even more competency-based approach in his primer. He first defines what he means by administrative ethics:

> Administrative ethics refers to well-based standards of right and wrong that prescribe what public administrators ought to do, in terms of duty to public service, principles, virtues, and benefits to society. (16)

Svara then adds this important qualification: the definition by itself is less important as an end than as a starting point in developing ethical competence.

> The challenge is to bring this definition forward in the consciousness of public administrators and to deepen and broaden the understanding of what it means. In other words, you are challenged to further develop your ethical judgment. (Svara 2007, 17)

Along with ethics primers such as the books by Svara and Menzel, classic works such as Terry Cooper's *The Responsible Administrator* (2012), multi-authored books, monographs on specific ethical concerns (O'Leary 2006), case examples, articles and symposia on ethics education, and short biographical sketches of exemplary public officials (Cooper and Wright 1992) are available to instructors of ethics in graduate programs, either to use as the basis for a separate class on ethics or as supplementary texts in more general courses in public administration. The literature in the field is now extensive and supports any of the approaches to ethics education chosen to convey ethics to students.

Formal Approaches to Ethics: Laws, Codes, and Standards of Conduct

Over the last few decades i the United States, the "ethics industry" (as it is sometimes derisively termed) has produced a raft of ethics laws, codes of ethics, standards of conduct, and other visible and formal artifacts that try to specify which behaviors are forbidden and which individuals should seek to achieve. The literature on this aspect of public ethics is considerable (Plant 2001). In this section of the chapter, the movement to formalize and codify ethics rules is examined, with specific examples presented for the different approaches used. Strengths and weaknesses of the compliance-based approach are then reviewed, and the impact of the formal approach to the development of ethical competence considered.

For many, both inside and outside government, the formal approach is *the* approach to ethics. It is the bread and butter of institutionalized ethics boards, commissions, agencies, and organizational compliance and audit units. It is often the public's definition of the ethical problem in public administration: real or apparent corruption by public officials that needs to be subject to a range of sanctions up to and including prosecution on corruption charges. While many in the academic field of public administration label such approaches the "low road" that demands only compliance, not ethical awareness and competence, political elites and the general public take a more positive view of efforts to constrain public administrators through laws, codes, and other formal mechanisms.

Formal approaches can be placed on a continuum whose poles are, on the one hand, approaches that require only strict compliance with clearly stated rules of conduct, and, on the other, those that express norms, aspirations, and internalized values without clear means or expectation of enforcement and discipline. Ethics laws are usually at or very close to the strict compliance side of the ledger. A review of state ethics laws reveals six major problems that they attempt to constrain:

- Real or apparent financial conflicts of interest
- Gifting of public officials by outside groups and individuals
- Relations with lobbyists
- Use of public office for private gain (defined usually more broadly than simply financial gain)
- Regulating relations with outside organizations to ensure fair treatment of all parties and prohibit preferential or corrupt activities
- Post-employment restrictions, especially relevant for those formerly employed in agencies that contract for goods and services with private-sector organizations.

Delaware's law is a good example of state laws of this sort. Title 29, Chapter 58, titled "Laws Regulating the Conduct of Officers and Employees of the State," begins with Subchapter I: State Employees', Officers' and Officials' Code of Conduct. Four points are made by the General Assembly in promulgating the law: (1) that "the conduct of officers and employees of the State must hold the respect and confidence of the people" and avoid conduct that violates public trust or creates a "justifiable impression" of misconduct; (2) that, "to ensure propriety and to preserve public confidence, officers and employees of the State must have the benefit of specific standards to guide their conduct and of some disciplinary mechanisms to guarantee uniform maintenance of those standards"; (3) that, in order to encourage individuals to assume public office, "the activities of officers and employees of the State should not be unduly circumscribed"; and (4) that "municipalities and towns adopt codes of conduct legislation at least as stringent as this act to apply to their employees and elected and appointed officials" (Del. Gen. Laws Ann. title 29, ch 58, §5802, 1990).

The code then proceeds to specifically prohibited practices: conflicts of interest, assisting private enterprises with respect to matters under consideration by the state government, giving preferential treatment to any persons, making governmental decisions outside official channels, disclosing confidential information, and granting or demanding sexual favors. Enforcement is delegated to the State Public Integrity Commission, consisting of a seven-member panel appointed for a seven-year term with nominal compensation of $100 per day of official performance of duties.

Delaware's law has been examined in detail not because it is unique or exemplary, but in fact the opposite—it represents the usual approach to ethics laws in the states and municipalities. It is heavy on proscription and lean on prescription. It is clearly a code of conduct based in law, not ethics, and it is imposed upon officials in the name of preserving the confidence of the public in the probity of government affairs. Its oversight is also quite representative of state ethics laws, with a quasi-judicial commission with multiple members somewhat connected to the political arena through gubernatorial nomination but also relatively independent through long terms of office and multiple members. The emphasis is solely on compliance; it is even couched as a "benefit" to employees that the standards are clear and the penalties plainly laid out. They are more the province of attorneys than ethicists.

Somewhere in the middle of the scale between strictly compliance based and strictly aspirational codes is the Standards of Ethical Conduct for Employees of the Executive Branch found in Part 2635 of the Code of Federal Regulations. The use of the term "ethical conduct" in the title is a clue that this code is more than a list of proscribed activities, as in the Delaware law. The preamble to the listing of principles is noteworthy in this regard:

> Public service is a public trust. Each employee has a responsibility to the United States Government and its citizens to place loyalty to the Constitution, laws and ethical principles above private gain. To ensure that every citizen can have complete confidence in the integrity of the Federal Government, each employee shall respect and adhere to the principles of ethical conduct set forth in this section, as well as the implementing standards contained in this part and in supplemental agency regulations. (Standards of Ethical Conduct for Employees of the Executive Branch 1989)

What follows is a list of 14 general principles that together provide a way for federal employees to behave ethically and in compliance with standards. The section also notes the need for ethical reflection, stating: "Where a situation is not covered by the standards set forth in this part, employees shall apply the principles set forth in this section in determining whether their conduct is proper."

The 14 principles that follow are divided almost equally into "dos and don'ts," although some of the principles include both sorts of statements conjoined, as in Principle 9, requiring employees to "act impartially and not give preferential treatment to any private organization or individual." The listing does not group the proscribed and prescribed principles but moves from one type to another in random fashion. Examples of the aspirational principles include such canons as "employees shall put forth honest effort in the performance of their duties" and "employees shall endeavor to avoid any actions creating the appearance that they are violating the law or the ethical standards set forth in this part." Principles prohibiting certain behavior include such statements as "employees shall not use public office for private gain" and "employees shall not knowingly make unauthorized commitments or promises of any kind purporting to bind the Government" (Standards of Ethical Conduct for Employees of the Executive Branch 1989).

Both the examples of statutory codes summarized here show a common problem of the one-size-fits-all approach to mandating ethics by law: they do not differentiate between the obligation of professional employees and those in positions that do not require specific skills and judgment. As a result, they have limited ability to guide the professional work of public administration. Instead, they form a foundation of compliance upon which professional organizations can erect more meaningful codes that apply general principles to the responsibilities of those in professional roles.

Professional Codes and Professional Associations

Codes of ethics that emanate from professional associations in some ways appear to be similar to ethics laws and regulations handed down from political institutions controlling public administration. Some writers in the field lump the two types of codes together as the "low road" of compliance-based ethics. But this conflation hides the basic fact that professional associations are voluntary and in many respects democratic. Codes are usually produced through the participation and assent of members, as has been the case with ICMA and more recently with the generalist association in the public administration field, the American Society for Public Administration. Professional codes also differ in being less legalistic in providing sanctions for violations—some do, others don't—and in being more open to change through the actions of the affected party itself, the community of professionals in a given field. They attempt to guide professional action by showing the connection between knowledge, skills, and abilities and ethical principles in the exercise of professional judgment and action. They express principles with the recognition that the essence of all professional activity is responsible action, with each particular situation unique in its details, requiring judgment, decisiveness, and often courage in understanding the values in play and the likely consequences of alternative courses to be taken. Van Wart (1996) provides a good summary of how professional codes differ from ethics laws and ethics training approaches:

> Unlike the narrow perspective of the short ethics-training class, professional codes of ethics are broader and include the aspirational aspects of right behavior, as well as the broad prohibitions. Although professional codes of ethics may lack in the technical specificities, they can counterbalance with a far richer sense of ethical behavior as both avoiding wrongdoing and pursuing right doing than that found in lengthy admonitions simply to avoid technical prohibitions. (527)

The issue, though, has been whether a single professional code can encompass the variety of professional identities contained within the public service and represented by the array of professional associations that promulgate codes and other statements of proper professional conduct and values. The quandary that professional associations create for public administration is the sheer number, variety, and nature of associations representing public professionals. The only true general purpose association in the field is ASPA, but it has been losing members to more specialized associations and cannot speak for the majority of professionals (or professional educators in public administration degree programs) Svara and Terry 2009). A recent study shows that at least nine other public official associations have greater numbers of members than ASPA Svara and Terry 2009, 1054). This does not take into account the professional associations that represent professionals employed both in government and in the private sector, many of which have codes of ethics and substantive discussions in professional conferences and exchanges of what it means to act responsibly and ethically.

ASPA's efforts to develop a code for its members and its actions as the profession's generalist association for the field of public administration illustrate the difficulties of crafting a code that covers the range of ethical principles that speak to the profession of public administration (PA). Although William Mosher—the individual who contributed most to the founding of ASPA and served as its first president—thought that a code of ethics was critical for any professional association (Plant 2009), it was not until the 1970s that ASPA began to seriously consider adopting a code of ethics. ASPA president Nesta Gallas appointed a number of leading ethicists to the newly formed Professional Standards and Ethics Committee in 1976. The committee published a workbook on ethics and wrote a code that was adopted as a set of principles by ASPA's National Council in 1981. In 1984, ASPA adopted a revised version of the principles as its first official Code of Ethics. The resulting code reflected the debate over what constituted professionalism in PA: Should it embrace all those in public service positions, or just those professional managers who were "pure" PA professionals? Could such a general code speak to the vast and varied audience of ASPA, which represents not only all the categories of professionals noted here but also academics and students? Could it help such a disparate group find added value in a code that was general and not specific in relating ethical concepts to the day-to-day work of administration?

ASPA has wrestled with these issues since the initial code was promulgated. The code was significantly rewritten in the mid-1990s (Van Wart 1996) around five major sources of ethical principles relevant to the work of public administration professionals: the public interest, the law (broadly defined), personal integrity, organizational interests, and professionalism. The grouping of specific points around these five sources of ethical principles was thought to provide ASPA members with a guideline for action in situations where values were in conflict or judgment was necessary to deal with vague laws, policies, and orders (Van Wart 1996, 532). It was adopted by ASPA's National Council in December of 1994.

Since its adoption, the ASPA code has received both high marks and criticism. Supporters of the code point out its combination of breadth—identifying five major sources of ethical principles as foundational—and its relative brevity and conciseness. Critics point to its lack of enforceable canons and the lack of a preamble or statement of purpose, giving little sense of how to relate the five separate sections around an overall vision of ethical conduct in professional conduct. ASPA also chose to eliminate the group that drafted the 1994 code, the Professional Ethics Committee, leaving no body within the association with the mandate to revise, update, or interpret the code.

Debate over the direction to take on the code continues within ASPA and, as of this writing, was being examined by an appointed task force for possible revision or complete rewriting. In addition to the specific wording, the task force is also wrestling with the question: What is the purpose of the code? Is it to speak only to ASPA members, in which case it lacks relevance to two of the three groups within the membership (students and academics)? Or is to be a statement of ethical conduct for all in the public service, whether members of ASPA or not, based on the professional roles individuals perform? If so, how can ASPA use it to connect with other professional groups and associations? How these questions are addressed has implications for the reworking of the code to serve perhaps a higher objective than simply guiding the conduct of the ASPA membership.

The at-will professional category has been among the most active, and one might argue the most effective, in incorporating ethics into the work and culture of the profession. As noted earlier, city managers were pioneers in recognizing the value of ethics as a mark of their fledgling profession. It is not too far from the mark to claim that the profession's identity has always been tied to its code of ethics. Decades later, other at-will groups moved to codify ethics, including chiefs of police and planners. In some cases, the code was designed not only to codify ethical behavior for the top level of the profession, but for those in related professional positions; for example, the code of the International Chiefs of Police is also the model for rank-and-file police officers in many jurisdictions.

At-will professions have three particular reasons for an abiding interest in ethical conduct by their members. First, they see a need to promote a sense of self-enforcing ethical conduct to justify the relatively unencumbered grant of power they receive from elected officials. It is a way to minimize obtrusive demands for accountability by pledging to enforce high standards of probity and ethical conduct. Second, codes help bind members of the group and provide a sense of common purpose and identity in lieu of formal licensing. Third, and in some ways both a cause and effect of the previous factors, is the presence of strong professional associations that organize the profession and provide a forum for code formation and enforcement.

Professional associations representing the professions found both inside and outside public administration present a more difficult setting for codifying or promulgating ethical standards for those working in governmental organizations. They are dominated by professionals outside government and their concerns, and in some instances provide a curious form of privatization in which government requires professionals working in public organizations to be members of the relevant professional association or accept the ethical code or canons adopted by such associations. Rarely found are examples of codes specific to work in the public sector, or even systematic attention to how the professional code works under the particular conditions of public-sector employment. This appears to be a fruitful area for further research, in the U.S. setting and also using comparative examples.

Ethics Training Programs

Ethics training is in many respects the orphan child of the ethics movement in public administration. It has received only modest attention in the literature (Hejka-Ekins 2001; Bowman et al. 2004; Menzel 2012), often as part of a discussion of how ethics is increasingly an aspect of the work of human resource managers in public and nonprofit organizations. Historically, *training* is a word that smacks of a lower order of instruction than most professionals consider appropriate to their role, certainly less likely than university coursework to relate ethical theory to professional responsibility. Training programs often stress the description of rules and steps needed to be in compliance. Svara (2007) notes,

> Effective training should address conditions within the organization—possibly guided by a climate survey—and include agency-specific cases. Simply providing drills on the content of law and regulations pertaining to employee conduct is a narrow approach that reinforces a rule-based orientation. It provides a useful foundation of knowledge, but it does not promote judgment and problem solving. (135)

As it relates to ethical competence for the profession, training raises two important and related questions: What do public managers need to know about effective ways to use ethics training to deal with the issues they consider most relevant to their agency? And what sort of training is needed for the professionals within the agency to build on their existing professional values and ethical orientation?

One aspect of ethical competence in addressing these questions is developing a good working relationship with the human resource managers in the organization. A quite robust literature has developed on how human resource management relates to public-sector ethics (Payne and Wayland 1999; Legge 2000; Palmer 2007). This interest reflects changes in the workforce and society that raise new and vexing issues—issues that public managers and human resource professionals should deal with as partners. The growing diversity of the workforce, along with the increased attention to workforce violence, harassment, drug abuse, homeland security, and related issues, has altered our view of how managers and human resource managers go about their work. Individuals within the organization are more likely than before to express discontent and dissent against the rule-bound nature of traditional organizations (O'Leary 2006).

Technology is also changing the way in which training can be delivered. Multimedia approaches can be used more readily than in the past, allowing organizational members to play out roles in group settings, observe situations involving ethics on their personal computers, and engage in both synchronous and asynchronous discussions with ethical exemplars. Trainers have a much greater range and variety of tools at their disposal, from YouTube to proprietary multimedia training programs.

In short, the ethically competent public manager needs to appreciate the value of training for the organization, know how to bring it most effectively into the organizational setting, and use it not simply as a how-to guide to comply with rules but as a way to expand the sense of ethical purpose and responsibility in the setting of the organization and its mission and work. In this sense, it complements the final strategy for enhancing ethical competence, leading by mentoring and example.

Leadership, Mentoring, and Exemplars

The final strategy we consider is the most subtle and least formal of the four: the exercise of leadership and the power of example. This strategy implies a dual set of relationships: (1) individuals in positions to influence the work of others act according to principled reasoning, and (2) those who form the organizational audience learn from the examples set by such individuals. Leadership can come from anyone and anywhere in an organization or network; it is not dependent on formal role so much as personal qualities of integrity, character, empathy for others, and good communication skills.

A great deal has been written in the literature of administrative ethics on the character- or virtue-based approach (Hart 1974; Cooper 1987; Cooper and Wright 1992; Dobel 1990; Garofalo and Geuras 1999; Cooper 2004). Svara (2007) includes it as one of the three approaches—along with consequentialism and deontology—that need to be kept in balance and, together, form the "ethics triangle."

A recurring theme in the discussion of character and virtue in the setting of public administration is the tension between the individual of integrity and the external goods valued by institutions and organizations. Organizations may actually bring ethical individuals to challenge formal authority (O'Leary 2006) or make it impossible for them to achieve high ethical standards by putting external goods—bigger budgets, control of programs, maintenance of hierarchical power—above the achievement not simply of the stated goals of the organization but of the search for excellence in the practices that represent the professional work of the institution. As Cooper (1992) points out,

> The keys to protecting the internal goods of practices from displacement by the external goods of institutions are the virtues of practitioners. These character traits must be cultivated by those who engage in the practice for two purposes: to support the pursuit of higher standards of the internal goods of the practice in its routine activity and to protect those internal goods from displacement by the external goods of host institutions. (328)

The cornerstone of making leadership effective in Cooper's approach is to understand two categories of leadership through which exemplars can achieve the goal of institutions supporting and not thwarting professional practices: moral processes and moral episodes. The former represents the work of leaders to invest the everyday work of the organization with a sense of moral purpose, a way of illustrating how ethical principles inform even the mundane elements of organization work. The second requires the ability to maintain one's ethical standards and act with courage and decisiveness in crises and confrontations that often involve high levels of risk, uncertainty, and dire consequences for failure.

Leadership theory assumes that formal positions of authority often enable leaders of character and integrity to have a broader field of action in which to influence others; however, a position of authority is not a precondition for the exercise of genuine leadership. As a strategy for developing ethical competence within organizations, individuals in positions of formal authority must be able to decentralize the exercise of leadership in two complementary ways. First, they need to be able to *delegate,* recognizing individual exemplars at all levels of the organization and appointing them to be mentors to others in the organization or team leaders in group activities. Second, they need to *toler-ate*. understanding that formal leadership need not necessarily be threatened or weakened by the exercise of informal leadership within the organization. Achieving ethical competence requires that individuals be afforded every reasonable opportunity to exercise judgment, so that they can deal later with situations that challenge them to act on ethical principles in highly charged situations. Along with the exercise of judgment and discretion is the need for individuals in organizations to see the role they play in achieving goals and objectives. This broadens their understanding of the way in which their work, humble as it may be, contributes to the public good. Nothing is so destructive of morale and the desire for excellence in professional practice within an organization than individuals in positions of authority taking sole credit for work done by others or by the organization functioning as a team. As one exemplar, John Gardner, once told me,

> As a leader you have two checkbooks. One is to write checks to cover the costs of your operations. This is based on your budget and is always inadequate. The second is the checkbook where you can credit others for the good work they have done. This one is unlimited or limited only by the choices you make to give credit where credit is due. When I was Secretary of Health, Education and Welfare we would book the largest auditorium in Washington and bring everyone in the department there for the signing of a law authorizing a major new program. It was my way of thanking them and letting them know they played a part in something of great national importance. (Personal communication 1985)

What Is the Goal of Ethical Competence and How Do We Measure Success?

The movement within graduate education toward clear learning objectives and measurable competencies has changed the way we define program mission, program activities, and assessment and evaluation of success. In no area of public administration is this more difficult than in determining clear learning outcomes and competencies in ethics. Ethics training, ethics laws and codes of ethics, and mentoring programs all share in one way or another the goal of imparting values, knowledge, skills, and abilities that can guide behavior toward preferred outcomes. How do we measure their effectiveness? Are we confident that we know the cause-and-effect relationships that influence how people choose to behave, or how organizations choose to invest time and resources into particular strategies to impart ethical competence?

Consider, for example, this question: How do we measure the effectiveness of a code of ethics? Is it to catch or discipline wrongdoers, or to stimulate individuals to aspire to higher goals and objectives? To use a play on words—is it to *proscribe* or *prescribe* behavior? If the former, then perhaps a measurable outcome is the number of individuals disciplined or relieved of duties. If it is the latter, the same measure may indicate failure, not success—the code failed to motivate and inspire people to do good. Or perhaps the measure is in fact irrelevant. Codes may have little impact on either stopping bad people from doing bad things or inspiring good people to "be all that they can be." Probably the most realistic outcome is somewhere in between: Individuals of all degrees of personal integrity may find the code useful in identifying ways of staying out of trouble.

The effectiveness of various ethics-building strategies can be assessed in many ways, but no single technique has enough demonstrated validity to allay doubts about the actual causal relationship between strategy and outcome. For instance, qualitative research can be used to ask individuals how effective they felt a particular approach to imparting ethical competence was. Survey research, focus groups, or interviews may be useful tools in this regard but have the usual liabilities of self-reporting, representativeness, and so on. Strictly cognitive approaches may be used, especially in educational and training exercises, but the test of ethical competence in any profession, including public administration, is not in *knowing what to do* but in *doing what needs to be done*. Professions are fields of action, not ivory towers of contemplation and reflection.

Other strategies can be viewed as useful measures of inputs but not outcomes. For example, attendance at training sessions, or meetings with designated professional mentors, or hits on URLs for agency or jurisdictional codes of ethics might provide supplemental information for managers, but they do not meet the criteria for real outcome measures. In and of themselves, these input measures do not predict how decisions will be made in the heat of the moment, but they provide some indicators of how ready individuals and organizations may be to understand and act upon ethical principles. They also may serve as a means of assessing specific ethical training and educational activities: After training on how to understand and implement a newly enacted ethics law, for example, was there a downturn in the number of complaints lodged, or the number of visits from organizational staff members to the manager to ask for explanation and interpretation of the statute?

The measure of success that is mentioned most frequently in regard to professional ethical competence is *trust*. Visible evidence of efforts to impart ethical reasoning to professionals is seen in all professions as a way in which the public is convinced of the value of the work of the profession and those it has certified as qualified to perform such activities. Licensed professions in particular ask the public to trust them above all others in performing a particular social role and reward them by limiting choices in several ways: the profession can decide who can perform the duties of the profession; set the qualifications to be a member of the professional community; monitor and, if needed, discipline those who fail to live up to the stated professional standards of conduct; and enjoy the economic benefits that come from having the exclusive right to act as professionals in a given arena of action.

Trust as an aspect of public administration has several dimensions. Most writers are concerned with the role that ethics can play in increasing trust—or reducing distrust—in government (Menzel 2012). As Menzel notes, "Closing the trust deficit between the public and government agencies is a legitimate and needed activity and one that ethics managers should embrace" (17). Trust also reduces transaction costs within and between agencies, between individuals, and between public officials and outside clients and regulated parties, although specific metrics of this "trust advantage" are hard to measure.

Trustworthiness is especially relevant to the multi-organizational approaches now considered the "new normal" for public administration. Whether it is through interagency programs, contracting and memoranda of understanding between public and private entities, networks, or public-private partnerships, more and more of the work of governance is done through arrangements that involve numerous organizations. Trust keeps things moving quickly and efficiently, with a minimum of formal arrangements needed to structure and regulate the interactions. For public administration professionals, this requires ethical competence to balance the need for efficient and effective networking arrangements with the primary ethical responsibility of advancing the public and not private or particularistic interests. Ethical competence specifically requires public officials to be able to identify and eliminate any real or apparent conflicts of interest, and sever connections if necessary—even if that might be considered disloyal or disruptive to erstwhile partners in collaborative undertakings. More fundamentally, it is the competence to develop networks based on trust and mutual understanding of the responsibility of all participants in governance to advance the public interest over and above the interests of the individual players.

What everyone desires is not going to come to pass: a perfect world in which corrupt practices are entirely purged, trust in governance activities is maximized, training and education allow individuals to maximize their capacity for ethical awareness and competence, and the profession of public administration becomes so cohesive and established that it can assume all those in the public service share the same values and behaviors. What is required is a sense of what is reasonable to consider as benchmarks of trustworthiness, integrity, knowledge, and appreciation of formal standards and controls. How to move forward on this objective requires all elements of the profession—those preparing professionals in degree programs, those responsible in human resource management offices for ethics training, those in the field actually implementing public programs, and those in higher management and policy positions overseeing operations, leading through example, and maintaining ties to other agencies and organizations—to establish performance measures that are not only reasonable given today's activities but also flexible enough to prepare for the inevitability of fundamental changes down the road.

Conclusion

As is the case with other professions, the ethical problem in public adminis-tration is not corruption or lack of compliance with rules and regulations. By any reasonable set of standards, public administration in the United States and other developed nations can proudly point to almost universal expectations for honest, disciplined, and disinterested administrative behavior. As pointed out by Roberts in Chapter 9 of this volume on ethical competence in the legal profession (Cooper and Menzel 2013), the pressing need is to constantly ramp up the aspirations of professional administrators to aim for ever-higher standards of personal and organizational excellence. In this regard, public administration professionals face some daunting constraints. Their profession is more a field of common professional activity than a unified and cohesive field such as law or medicine—although even those venerable examples are showing signs of fracture today. Recent developments have added to the complexity of administration by introducing alternatives to the traditional approach of state-determined and state-implemented programs. Public-private partnerships, contracting out, vouchers, privatization schemes—all such so-called "reforms" have added to the complexity of the way in which services are provided to the public.

Perhaps even more corrosive to the environment of public administration is the declining level of understanding and trust in government, both from political and social elites and the public at large. Ethical competence is both an independent and dependent variable in this regard. High levels of ethical competence, especially evidence of behavior that goes beyond compliance with rules to standards of excellence in public service and personal integrity, should provide an antidote to the cynicism and ideologically based criticism that characterizes much public discussion of governance today. Yet trust itself is a source of motivation, an energizer of otherwise complacent officeholders. How this dilemma can be resolved is an important test of any formula for ethical competence in public administration.

Professionalism, wherever it is found, requires a community of peers to flourish and function. In this regard, public administration seen as a general profession has been less able to establish and institutionalize itself than other, more established, professions such as law, medicine, and engineering. This is not necessarily a sign of weakness. Notions of professional responsibility and ethical conduct that relate general theories to the specifics of work-related duties are as vital for responsible and ethical public administration as is the general Code of Ethics of ASPA. What they represent, though, is a complicating factor in producing a clear sense of ethical competence for the field as a whole.

Surgeon and author Atul Gawande, in a fascinating book titled *The Checklist Manifesto* (2009), argues that

> all learned occupations have a definition of professionalism, a code of conduct. It is where they spell out their ideals and duties. The codes are sometimes stated, sometimes just understood. But they all have at least three elements. First is an expectation of selflessness: that we who accept responsibility for others—whether we are doctors, lawyers, teachers, public authorities, soldiers, or pilots—will place the needs and concerns of those who depend on us above our own. Second is an expectation of skill: that we will aim for excellence in our knowledge and expertise. Third is an expectation of trustworthiness: that we will be responsible in our personal behavior toward our charges. (182)

Professionalism, by Gawande's definition, has an ethical component that cannot be separated from the sense of identity assumed by any given profession. Selflessness, skill, and trustworthiness form a trinity of obligations for every profession to uphold. By combining a sense of craft—skills—with a set of values and attitudes—selflessness and trustworthiness—every profession must develop and operationalize a sense of ethical competence that is shared by its members and which helps to define what it is.

In the final analysis, responsible ethical competence in public administration requires what Dr. Gawande proposes: a checklist to follow when situations demand thoughtful and decisive action. The three characteristics of a profession—selflessness, skill, and trustworthiness—are the keys to the checklist for public administration as they are for other professions. The exercise of professional competence requires the character traits of humility and courage in the face of complex problems and the possibility of failure. An overly long list makes the checklist too cumbersome to be useful. An incomplete sense of competence heightens the likelihood of failure. What might this checklist for professionals in public administration include? Consider the following:

- What rules and regulations must I follow to be in compliance? Which of these are absolute and which may need to be broached based on a realistic sense of likely consequences?
- Do my organization, have the skills, discipline, and experience to make a decision? If not, to whom do I turn? Who needs to be enlisted and what professional skills and values do they bring to the situation?
- What distinguishes this situation from others I have encountered? What values are represented? Is it a routine event or something that raises issues of conflicting values?
- Who is helped and who is harmed by this decision? By what criteria are such determinations made?
- Have I clearly separated my personal interest and the interests of my organizations from the responsibility to serve the public good?
- How will I learn from this situation and make the experience useful for my own learning and that of the organization? How will I communicate the lessons to those who need to know?

The checklist approach does not suggest using an idealized version of the world as a basis for action. It is well grounded in Public Administration practice and mirrors the approach taken by the authors of the ASPA-sponsored workbooks on ethics dating back to the 1970s. It recognizes the wickedness of complex problems, the inability of even the best leaders to grasp patterns and prepare for new and unique situations. It accepts the likelihood of failure but requires the ethical public administrator to act responsibly and be accountable for outcomes. It takes a broad view of the capacity of individuals and organizations to learn from experience disciplined by foundational knowledge. It elevates the practice of the profession above self and organizational interest. As Robert Frost so beautifully wrote,

> Only where love and need are one,
> And the work is play for mortal stakes,
> Is the deed every really done
> For Heaven's and the future's sake. (Frost 1934).

Notes

I wish to thank my colleague Dr. Triparna Vasavada for her assistance in preparing the sections on professionalism, and my graduate assistants Mr. Timothy Golden and Ms. Blair Saul for their help in researching sources and proofreading the chapter.
    1. These examples represent just a few of the diverse professional and occupational backgrounds found in this semester's online MPA classes at Penn State Harrisburg and are chosen to show the enormous range of roles that fit into the profession of public administration.

2. Exceptions are those professionals, such as city and county managers, planning directors, police chiefs, and school superintendents, who report directly to elected leadership and not through a top layer of political appointees. In this chapter, we refer to them as a separate category of public administration professionals, "at-will professionals."

References

American Society for Public Administration. ASPA code of ethics. http://www.aspanet. org/public/ASPA/Resources/Code_of_Ethics/ASPA/Resources/Codeof_Ethics/ Code_of_Ethics1.aspx?hkey=acd40318-a945-4ffc-ba7b-18e037b1a858 (accessed August 30, 2012).

Bowman, J.S., J.P. West, E.M. Berman, and V.M. Van Wart. 2004. *The Professional Edge: Competencies in Public Service.* Armonk, NY: M.E. Sharpe.

Cooper, T.L. 1987. Hierarchy, virtue, and the practice of public administration. *Public Administration Review* 47(4): 320–328.

———. 1992. Conclusion: Reflecting on exemplars of virtue. In *Exemplary Public Administrators: Character and Leadership in Government,* ed. T.L. Cooper and N.D. Wright. San Francisco: Jossey-Bass.

———, ed. 2001. *Handbook of Administrative Ethics,* 2d ed. New York: Marcel Dekker.

———. 2004. Big questions in administrative ethics: A need for focused, collaborative effort. *Public Administration Review* 64(4): 395–407.

———. 2012. *The Responsible Administrator,* 6th ed. San Francisco: Jossey-Bass.

Cooper, T.L., and N.D. Wright, eds. 1992. *Exemplary Public Administrators: Character and Leadership in Government.* San Francisco: Jossey-Bass.

Cox, R.W. 2009. *Ethics and Integrity in Public Administration: Concepts and Cases,* 3d ed. Armonk, NY: M.E. Sharpe.

Del. Gen. Laws title 29, ch 58, §5802. Laws regulating the conduct of officers and employees of the state. 23 July 1990. http://delcode.delaware.gov/title29/c058 / sc01/index.shtml#5801(accessed August 30, 2012).

Denhardt, K.G. 2009. Ethical competencies for public administrators and leaders. Unpublished manuscript.

Dobel, J.P. 1990. Integrity in the public service. *Public Administration Review* 50(3): 354–366.

Friedrich, C.J. 1935. Responsible government service under the American Constitution. In *Problems of the American Public Service,* ed. C.J. Friedrich et al. New York: McGraw-Hill.

———. 1940. Public policy and the nature of administrative responsibility. *Public Policy* 1(1): 1–20.

———. 1960. The dilemma of administrative responsibility. In *Responsibility,* ed. C.J. Friedrich, 189–202. New York: The Liberal Arts Press.

Frost, R. 1934. Two tramps in mud time. In *Poetry X,* ed. Jough Dempsey. http:// poetry.poetryx.com/poems/290/ (accessed August 30, 2012).

Garofalo, C., and D. Geuras. 1999. *Ethics in the Public Service: The Moral Mind at Work.* Washington, DC: Georgetown University Press.

Gaus, J.M. 1936. The responsibility of public administrators. In *The Frontiers of Public Administration,* ed. J.M. Gaus, L.B. White, and M. Dimock. Chicago: University of Chicago Press.

Gawande, A. 2009. *The Checklist Manifesto: How to Get Things Right.* New York: Henry Holt.

Hart, D.K. 1974. Social equity, justice, and the equitable administrator. *Public Administration Review* 34(1): 3–11.

Hart, D.W. 1999. Ethics education in public affairs. *Journal of Public Affairs Education* 5(1): 67–76.

Hejka-Ekins, A. 2001. Ethics in in-service training. In *Handbook of Administrative Ethics,* 2d ed., ed. T.L. Cooper, 79–103. New York: Marcel Dekker.

International City/County Management Association. 2008. ICMA code of ethics with guidelines. http://icma.org/en/icma/ethics/code_of_ethics (accessed August 30, 2012).

Karl, B.D. 1976. Public administration and American history: A century of professionalism. *Public Administration Review* 36(5): 489–504.

———. 1987. The American bureaucrat: A history of a sheep in wolves' clothing. *Public Administration Review* 47(1): 26–34.

Legge, K. 2000. The ethical context of HRM: The ethical organization in the boundaryless world. In *Ethical Issues in Contemporary Human Resource Management,* ed. D. Winstanley and J. Woodall, 23–40. London: Macmillan.

Macaulay, M., and A. Lawton. 2006. From virtue to competence: Changing the principle of public service. *Public Administration Review* 66(5): 702–710.

Menzel, D.C. 2012. *Ethics Management for Public Administrators: Leading and Building Organizations of Integrity,* 2d ed. Armonk, NY: M.E. Sharpe.

Menzel, D.C., and T.L. Cooper. 2013. In pursuit of ethical competence. In *Achieving Ethical Competence for Public Service Leadership,* ed. Terry L. Cooper and Donald C. Menzel, 3–23. Armonk, NY: M.E. Sharpe.

National Association of Schools of Public Affairs and Administration. 2009, October 16. NASPAA standards 2009. http://www.naspaa.org/accreditation /standard2009/docs/NS2009FinalVote10.16.2009.pdf (accessed August 30, 2012).

O'Leary, R. 2006. *The Ethics of Dissent: Managing Guerrilla Government.* Washington, DC: CQ Press.

Paddock, S.C. 2011. Thinking globally about ethics. Review of *Ethics and Integrity in Public Administration: Concepts and Cases,* by R.W. Cox. *Public Administration Review* 71(2): 319–322.

Palmer, G. 2007. Socio-political theory and ethics in HRM. In *Human Resource Management: Ethics and Employment,* ed. A. Pinnington, R. Macklin, and T. Campbell, 23–34. Oxford, UK: Oxford University Press.

Payne, S.L., and R.F. Wayland. 1999. Ethical obligation and diverse value assumptions in HRM. *International Journal of Manpower* 20(5/6): 297–308.

Pennock, J.R. 1960. The problem of responsibility. In *Responsibility,* ed. Carl J. Friedrich, 3–27. New York: The Liberal Arts Press.

Plant, J.F. 2001. Codes of ethics. In *Handbook of Administrative Ethics,* 2d ed., ed. T.L. Cooper, 309–334. New York: Marcel Dekker.

———. 2009. Good work, honestly done: ASPA at 70. *Public Administration Review* 69(6): 1040–1049.

Standards of Ethical Conduct for Employees of the Executive Branch, 5 C.F.R. pt. 2635. 1989. http://ecfr.gpoaccess.gov/cgi/t/text/text-idx?c=ecfr&sid=eaab3e 76921028ab2de631c3f4b0f8a0&rgn=div5&view=text&node=5:3.0.10.10.9&id no=5 (accessed August 30, 2012).

Svara, J.H. 2007. *The Ethics Primer for Public Administrators in Government and Nonprofit Organizations.* Sudbury, MA: Jones & Bartlett.

———. 2009. The elements of administrative ethics. Paper presented at the NASPAA Annual Conference, Crystal City, VA, October.

Svara, J.H., and L.D. Terry II. 2009. The present challenges to ASPA as an association that promotes public professionalism. *Public Administration Review* 69(6): 1050–1059.

Van Wart, M. 1996. The sources of ethical decision making for individuals in the public sector. *Public Administration Review* 56(6): 525–533.

Virtanen, T. 2000. Changing competences of public managers: Tension in commitment. *International Journal of Public Sector Management* 13(4): 333–341.

Waldo, D. 1968. Scope of the theory of public administration. In *Theory and Practice of Public Administration: Scope, Objectives, and Methods,* ed. J.C. Charlesworth. Philadelphia, PA: The American Academy of Political and Social Science.

9

Ethical Competence for Public Service Lawyers

Robert N. Roberts

Like other public employees, the identification of important ethical competencies for lawyers in public service roles such as that of government attorney is not an easy process. With little debate, government lawyers must comply with traditional public corruption prohibitions that apply widely to all government employees. These include bribery, extortion, theft of government property, misuse of nonpublic information for private gain, and a spectrum of financial conflict-of-interest matters. Beyond traditional types of compliance-based or rule-driven ethics issues, government lawyers have a clear ethical obligation to take steps to ensure that their agencies and other government officials uphold constitutional and democratic values. Important democratic values include honesty and integrity, justice and due process, transparency and openness, efficiency and effectiveness, and civility. Yet, the evolution of modern legal ethics rules has had little to do with the development of the ethical competencies of lawyers inside or outside of government (Lerner 2006, 785). The need to protect consumers of legal services from unscrupulous lawyers drove the movement for stricter compliance-based ethics rules.

The preoccupation with compliance-based legal ethics rules fails to answer the questions of whether lawyers in general and government lawyers in particular need to develop ethical competencies not embodied in compliance-based ethics rules. Do public service lawyers employed by government have a higher ethical duty than other government employees to protect democratic institutions? Is it not sufficient for the government attorney to comply with legal ethics codes and government ethics rules that apply to all government employees? These are controversial questions. Much too often, elected and appointed government officials wrongly expect government attorneys to provide legal justifications for controversial actions taken by agencies and their employees and officials. And the leadership of government agencies rely on government lawyers to effectively defend agencies and their employees and officials from various types of legal challenges (Simon 2010, 827). Although government attorneys have a professional obligation to defend their clients to the best of their abilities, they also have an ethical obligation to protect the democratic values of our governmental institutions. No one should underestimate the challenges faced by attorneys who attempt to live up to both obligations.

This chapter identifies four ethical competencies that are needed for those trained in law to provide successful public service leadership: (1) awareness that public service ethics is more than complying with rules, (2) civility, (3) constitutional competence, and (4) the ability to engage in principled dissent. Certainly, to the dismay of many lawyers inside and outside of government, these competencies may place them in direct conflict with compliance-based ethics rules that place a high priority on serving clients and a much lower priority on serving the general welfare. This fact may help to explain the lack of attention by the legal community toward the development of ethical competencies (Lerner 2006, 781–792).

Beyond Compliance

The first ethical competency required of government attorneys is their recognition that public service ethics involves much more than complying with disciplinary ethics rules. The development of this competency, however, is easier said than done. The heavy emphasis placed on compliance-based ethics regulation as the preferred method of protecting public trust in government has had the unintended consequence of lowering ethical standards in government and the private sector. Because compliance-based ethics standards are set relatively low, one may come to believe that ethics simply involves complying with clearly defined rules. Ethics rules, then, are largely seen as black and white—without gray areas and ambiguity. The decision to adopt a black-and-white approach to legal ethics rules was driven by the practical need to meet minimum due process standards when moving to revoke the licenses of practicing lawyers. Yet, the adoption of minimum standards of conduct places pressure on lawyers inside and outside of government to comply only with the minimum rules rather than applying higher self-imposed standards of conduct (Nicolson 2005, 618).

A public prosecutor, for example, may face strong pressure to obtain convictions in order to increase his or her chances of reelection. Such pressures can have unmistakable effects on the pursuit of justice. Say the court appoints an inexperienced lawyer to represent an indigent defendant in a high-profile sexual assault case. The prosecutor recognizes there may be problems with how police officers obtained a search warrant to conduct a search of the suspect's house. Does the prosecutor have a moral obligation to point out potential problems with the search to defense counsel?[1]

Civility

Civility constitutes the second ethical competency that government lawyers need to develop. The American Bar Association's (ABA's) *Model Rules of Professional Conduct* effectively replaced "aspirational" guidelines with mandatory disciplinary rules. Like the evolution of public-sector ethics rules, the ABA embraced compliance-based ethics as the solution for the perceived decline in the ethics of the legal profession. The decision to adopt compliance-based ethics rules reflected the widely held belief that in order to restore public confidence in the legal community, the legal community needed to demonstrate its ability to discipline lawyers. An objective rather than subjective process was needed in order to make it possible to examine and follow through on investigations of attorney misconduct. The ABA argued the adoption of mandatory standards of conduct would make it easier for states to discipline attorneys.

The *Model Rules of Professional Conduct* consisted of eight sections: (1) the client-lawyer relationship, (2) the counselor, (3) the advocate, (4) transactions with persons other than clients, (5) law firms and associations, (6) public service, (7) information about legal services, and (8) maintaining the integrity of the profession (model rules of professional conduct). The *Model Rules* sought to protect clients from fraudulent actions by attorneys, maintain the confidentiality of communications between lawyers and their clients, and regulate conflicts of interest that often arise in large law firms. Again, to reemphasize, the *Model Rules* were much more relevant to the private practice of law than the ethical issues faced by the majority of government attorneys. And while the ABA had no authority to require states to adopt its guidelines, the majority of states did adopt the new ethical guidelines. State law also typically requires lawyers to complete a number of continuing legal education hours.

The completion of the transformation of legal codes of ethics from aspirational to disciplinary occurred in both the government and corporate arenas. The use of compliance-based ethics regulation permitted the establishment of administrative disciplinary systems that provided attorneys due process in determining whether they had violated specific prohibitions. The adoption of compliance-based ethics rules also had the advantage of limiting the ambiguity related to aspirational ethics guidelines. By the end of the 1980s, many states had established independent agencies to investigate and adjudicate alleged violations of the rules of professional conduct (ABA 2011; Wilkins 1992, 805). Due largely to the tradition of state courts handling the discipline of attorneys, state legislatures assigned the responsibility for the supervision of these new disciplinary agencies to the highest state court (Wilkins 1992, 805).

Not surprisingly, post-1980 legal disciplinary proceedings have many characteristics of a criminal trial. Full-time professional investigators conduct the investigations. Rules generally prohibit investigators and prosecutors from having any prior association with the disciplinary cases they have responsibility for investigating or prosecuting (Wilkins 1992, 805). Judgments regarding whether a lawyer has violated a rule of professional conduct are made solely "on the basis of evidence presented at a formal hearing. Lawyers accused of ethical violations are accorded a full panoply of due process protections" and often hire their own lawyers to defend themselves against the allegations (Wilkins 1992, 806).

Critics of compliance-based ethics rules argue that such rules do little to develop ethical competence. Instead, they send a message to the law profession that ethics simply involves complying with the rules and little else. In fact, one may make an argument that the *Model Roles* adopted by the American Bar Association are "deliberately amoral" (Lerner 2006, 786). Supporters of the *Model Rules*, however, counter that the ABA did not adopt those rules with the goal of ensuring the ethical competence of lawyers. They adopted the *Model Rules* to stop certain conduct that presented a direct threat to the clients of legal services. According to this line of reasoning, personal ideals have "no place in a legal document such as the *Model Rules*" (Lerner 2006, 786). In a world grown so large and complex, many consumers of legal services find it impossible to determine on their own the reputation of lawyers recommended by friends and associates. Enforcement of the *Model Rules* helps to provide consumers of legal services some assurance that lawyers engaging in conduct detrimental to the interests of their clients will be punished.

The ABA's *2009 Survey on Lawyer Discipline Systems* (2010c) found that disciplinary agencies investigated 75,221 complaints against licensed attorneys and dismissed 37,762 complaints after investigation. The survey found that during 2009, disciplinary agencies charged 5,502 lawyers with disciplinary violations (ABA 2010c, Chart I). The same year saw disciplinary agencies publicly sanction 5,009 lawyers and privately sanction 1,760 lawyers (ABA 2010c, Chart II). Penalties included public reprimand (929); public probation (458); public suspensions for noncriminal conduct (2,824); public suspension for criminal conduct (507); voluntary disbarment (356); and involuntary disbarment (441) (ABA 2010c, Chart II). The data indicates that most lawyers experience little difficulty complying with these minimum standards due to the fact that they rely on "lowest common denominator standards" (Nicolson 2005, 618).

The criticisms of the *Model Rules of Professional Conduct* relate to the behavior of private rather than government lawyers. Critics of the *Model Rules*, for example, argue the rules failed to deal adequately with the lack of effective legal representation for poor and indigent Americans (Stephens 2004, 71). Rule 6.1, Voluntary Pro Bono Public Service, states that "Every lawyer has a professional responsibility to provide legal services to those unable to pay. A lawyer should aspire to render at least (50) hours of pro bono public legal services per year" (ABA 2010a, 2010b). A number of states encourage licensed attorneys to provide a specific number of hours of pro bono services— Alaska, Connecticut, Delaware, Indiana, Kansas, Maine, Michigan, Missouri, Nebraska, New Hampshire, New Jersey, North Carolina, Ohio, Oklahoma, Pennsylvania, Rhode Island, South Carolina, South Dakota, Tennessee, West Virginia, and Wisconsin (ABA 2010b). On the other hand, only a small number of states require licensed lawyers to pay a specific dollar amount or percentage of their income into a fund to pay for legal representation for indigent clients if they fail to provide pro bono services. These include the District of Columbia, Florida, Massachusetts, Mississippi, Nevada, New Mexico, Utah, and Wyoming (ABA 2010b). No state requires attorneys to provide pro bono legal services (Cooper and Humphreys 1995/1996, 940). Pro bono service enables those trained in law to appreciate the trials and tribulations of those in need and is likely to contribute to a greater sense of civility among lawyers. Although one may make an argument that pro bono service does not enhance the ethical competence of lawyers, one may also make an equally persuasive argument that by requiring or encouraging lawyers to engage in such services, they may feel compelled to confront moral issues related to the legal system. A lawyer who normally represents upper-class clients may be forced to recognize that clients from poor backgrounds receive much less favorable treatment. Consequently, a pro bono lawyer may face the prospect of having to devote much more time and energy defending an indigent client than a wealthy client who is already likely to receive the benefit of the doubt or preferential treatment.

Interestingly, a number of critics argue that the *Model Rules* make it more difficult for government lawyers to protect the public interest and public trust from unethical conduct by government agencies and officials. Rule 1.6 is absolutely clear. "A lawyer inside or outside of the government must keep the client's secrets unless the lawyer believes disclosure is necessary to prevent his or her client from committing a criminal act the lawyer believes is likely to result in imminent death or substantial bodily harm" (Radack 2003, 130). Although some states have adopted a modified version of the rule to permit disclosure of criminal conduct that does *not* involve a threat of imminent death or immediate harm, the fact remains that the confidentiality rule ties the hands of many lawyers, including government lawyers (Radack 2003, 130–131).

The adoption of the *Model Rules* has done little to deal with the "breakdown of civility in the legal profession" (Cooper and Humphreys 1995/1996, 935).

Popular media idealizes take-no-prisoners lawyers who make use of the legal process to beat down their opponents. Many clients expect their lawyers to do whatever it takes to win. In fact, the most effective lawyers are those who are able to settle disputes without litigation. The ability of government lawyers to do their job in a civil and respectful manner is an ethical competence important for all lawyers and particularly for lawyers who work for the government.

Experienced lawyers learn the hard way that there are other ways to resolve disputes besides "litigation, liens, demand letters, subpoenas, and so on" (Miller and Kremski 2009, 236). Many lawyers have either forgotten how or are afraid it may be perceived as a sign of weakness to attempt to resolve disputes through "a simple phone call with a polite request," which "may obtain better results for a client than years of litigation" (Miller and Kremski 2009, 236). Some lawyers have lost the art of preventive law, where "the legal counselor seeks to avoid controversy and prevent litigation by offering the client the services of a thoughtful adviser, a careful planner, and a skilled negotiator" (Re 1994, 119). Ethical competence for government attorneys requires that they develop the ability to negotiate and compromise rather than view the law solely as an adversarial process with only winners and losers.[2]

Constitutional Competency

Constitutional competency is the third ethical competency that government lawyers must possess to perform their jobs effectively. The term *constitutional competency* refers to an understanding of basic constitutional doctrines that place limits on governmental interference in the lives of its citizens (Rosenbloom, Carroll, and Carroll 2000). Model Rule 3.8, for instance, prohibits government prosecutors from attempting "to achieve her ends of justice through unjust means" (Williams 1999, 3444). Government attorneys "have an obligation of fidelity to the U.S. Constitution and the laws of the United States" (Wendel 2009, 1335). Broadly, this means that government attorneys must represent the interests of all Americans and not members of particular groups who may hold values and beliefs similar to their own.

The practice of some government lawyers who interpret the law and the Constitution to conform to their ideological beliefs or the ideological beliefs of their government employers has done serious damage to the credibility of government lawyers (Wendel 2009, 1336). Expecting career government lawyers, in their official capacity, to refrain from becoming directly involved in partisan or ideological battles may be naïve. The option may be exceptionally difficult when faced with a choice between providing an argument their employer wants and possibly losing their job. It seems logical that government lawyers occupying nonpolitical positions should be excluded from the task of rendering opinions with obvious partisan or ideological bias. Instead of presenting one side of the argument in a memorandum, an attorney should have the ability to present both sides of an argument in a fair and unbiased manner.

Ability to Engage in Principled Dissent

The ability to dissent in principle without retribution constitutes the fourth ethical competency government lawyers need to develop. According to Thompson, "Conventional theory and practice of administrative ethics holds that administrators should carry out the orders of their superiors and the policies of the agency and the government they serve" (1985, 555–556). According to this theory, when individuals accept government positions, they fully understand that they should not allow their moral concerns to interfere with the performance of their official duties as assigned by their superiors. The ideal administrator is an entirely reliable instrument of the organization. She never injects personal values into her implementation of the goals of the organization (Thompson 1985, 556).

From the perspective of adherents to the "ethic of neutrality," the ideal administrator learns to follow orders. If one accepts the argument that government attorneys have a unique obligation to act to prevent government from violating basic democratic and moral principles, then the government attorney has a higher duty to oppose policies that arguably have a legitimate possibility to do significant damage to the lives of citizens and to the nation's democratic institutions.

The development of a capacity to dissent does not mean that the government attorney has an obligation to dissent only when he may be confident that he will not be retaliated against for his conduct. The fact that a government attorney may face serious consequences for dissenting makes doing so a true ethical dilemma. Therefore, a government attorney, like all government employees, must carefully weigh the risks and benefits of dissent and the methods he uses to express disapproval of an action proposed or taken by his organization. Dissent can take many forms (Thompson 1985, 556–561). It may involve raising an objection with the attorney's immediate supervisor. It may involve going over the head of the supervisor to higher level officials. It may involve resigning in protest. It may involve going public and risking retaliation. And it may even require leaking a story to the press. The most difficult decision of all comes when dissent forces a government attorney to breach her duty of confidentiality and face the possibility of disbarment.

The Role of the ABA in Advocating Ethical Competence[3]

In 1908, the American Bar Association adopted the Canons of Legal Ethics (Tucker et al. 1922, 254–260). The Canons focused almost exclusively on the practice of law by private-sector attorneys. Of particular significance, the ABA did not have any authority to enforce the new Canons. For the Canons to have any impact, each state had to incorporate the recommendations into their standards of conduct for attorneys licensed to practice within their boundaries. Critics of the Canons argue they were motivated by an effort of "WASP lawyers" to make it difficult for urban immigrant lawyers to practice law "by not allowing advertising, public indication of a specialty, and solicitation" of clients (Backof and Martin, Jr. 1991, 100). From this perspective, the Canons had much more to do with market control than policing the ethical conduct of lawyers. On the other hand, defenders of the Canons argue that they constituted a sincere effort to protect the profession from lawyers concerned primarily with making money rather than with practicing law competently, professionally, and ethically.

The Canons were designed to establish minimum legal competencies for lawyers practicing in the United States. Of particular significance, the Canons sought to professionalize the practice of law by prohibiting lawyers from taking a personal position on the merits of cases. Canon 15 stated that it was "improper for a lawyer to assert in argument his personal belief in his client's innocence or in the justice of his cause" (Tucker et al. 1922, 256). To effectively represent a client, then, a lawyer needed to detach his personal beliefs or values from the merits of the client's case. Taking into consideration the fact that the Canons were directed primarily at the private sector, the provision sought to ensure that all clients would receive the best effort from their attorney—even unpopular clients.

Of equal significance, the Canons of Legal Ethics sought to sharply restrict advertising by lawyers. The drafters viewed advertising by lawyers as unseemly and contributing to a significant increase in the pursuit of fraudulent claims. Canon 27 stated that "the publication or circulation of ordinary simple business cards, being a matter of personal taste or local custom, and sometimes of convenience, is not per se improper. But solicitation of business by circulars or advertisements, or by personal communications or interviews, not warranted by personal relations, is unprofessional" (Tucker et al. 1922, 258). In adopting a broad prohibition against the direct solicitation of clients by lawyers, the drafters of the Canons reflected a belief that good lawyers did not need to advertise. Lawyers needed to rely upon referrals from satisfied clients rather than advertising. The advertising ban also reflected a belief that advertising had the ability to deceive potential clients into believing a lawyer was qualified to handle their case. The authors of the Canons rejected the argument that advertising made it much easier for potential clients to compare the services various lawyers might be able to provide. In the wake of the adoption of Canon 27, advertising bans became a fixture of the practice of law in the United States.

From the perspective of the ABA, Canon 11 was probably the most important of all. It called for the exclusion from the practice of law any attorney who engaged in clearly corrupt conduct. Clients often entrusted their lawyers with large amounts of money. This made it fairly easy for a corrupt lawyer to defraud a client. Such conduct sullied the reputation of all lawyers. Therefore, Canon 11 required that "money of the client or other trust property coming into the possession of the lawyer should be reported promptly, and except with the client's knowledge and consent should not be commingled with his private property or be used by him" (Tucker et al. 1922, 256). To this day, defrauding a client is regarded as one of the most serious ethical breaches a lawyer and in almost all states will result in disbarment. Not surprisingly, Canon 11 had little relevance to government lawyers who never charged clients for their services.

Growing concern that a new generation of lawyers filed meritless claims to extort payments from defendants led the ABA to attempt to deal with the problem. Canon 30 prohibited lawyers from using the judicial process to harass or injure the opposing party or pursue a meritless claim. "The lawyer must decline to conduct a civil cause or to make a defense when convinced that it is intended merely to harass or to injure the opposite party or to work oppression or wrong. But otherwise it is his right, and, having accepted retainer, it becomes his duty to insist upon the judgment of the Court as to the legal merits of his client's claim," stated the Canon (Tucker et al. 1922, 259). Yet, the Canons provided little guidance on how to distinguish between meritorious and unmeritorious cases. Again, the provision had little relevance to government lawyers.

Despite growing concern over the lack of legal representation for indigent criminal defendants, the ABA failed to act on the growing problem of indigent clients not being able to obtain competent representation in criminal or civil matters. The failure of the Canons to deal with the issue of providing adequate representation for indigent individuals constituted the most significant omission of the new ethical guidelines. Canon 4 stated that "a lawyer assigned as counsel for an indigent prisoner ought not to ask to be excused for any trivial reason, and should always exert his best efforts in his behalf" (Tucker et al. 1922, 255). Yet, the Canons did not propose to impose a pro bono service representation requirement on attorneys.

The adoption of the Canons of Ethics by many states did not usher in a new renaissance for the legal profession. The ABA had hoped the adoption of the Canons might help to restore public trust in the integrity of the legal profession. The Great Depression, however, placed even greater pressure on the profession. Competition between lawyers for clients led to sharp declines in fees charged by lawyers. Fee wars threatened the livelihood of lawyers and threatened to devalue legal services. To stop the downward spiral in legal fees, many state bar associations adopted minimum fee schedules for lawyers (Powell 1985, 285). States also enacted much stricter laws against the unauthorized practice of law.[4]

Ethical Failure

Because public opinion of legal ethics continued to decline through the 1960s, the ABA turned again to compliance-based ethics as a way to restore public trust in the legal profession, not as a remedy for the actions of unethical lawyers. To the contrary, many supporters of the stricter legal ethics rules rejected the idea that the rules are responsible for ensuring the integrity or ethical competence of lawyers (Lerner 2006, 785–786) Legal ethics rules were needed to protect consumers of legal services, not to ensure the personal integrity of members of the legal profession. The expansion of the scope of legal ethics rules did not lead to a greater degree of ethical competence by members of the legal profession.

Much like the situation that had prevailed in 1905, the ABA viewed the new Code of Ethics as vital to reversing the downward public perception of lawyers by the American people. Many Americans had come to associate the practice of law with so-called "whiplash" lawyers who sought to turn minor slip-and-fall accidents or automobile accidents into large paydays for themselves and, to a lesser degree, for their clients. Lawyers came to be regarded as "greedy and self-serving" (Petrowitz 1979, 1275). Conservatives accused progressive lawyers of tying the hands of police officers by pressing for the expansion of the rights of criminal defendants, and of trying to destroy the free enterprise system by filing countless frivolous lawsuits. Liberals blamed greedy lawyers for shielding big business from accountability for putting dangerous products on the market and otherwise jeopardizing the lives of countless Americans through unethical business practices.

In 1969, the ABA adopted the Code of Professional Responsibility. Again, the new ethics code focused on the private rather than the public practice of law. The new ethics code marked a major departure from the Canons of Legal Ethics. Besides incorporating traditional aspirational guidelines, the Code included new enforceable disciplinary rules (Frankel 1976, 877; Hall and Clark 2002, 278). When the ABA proposed the new

Code of Professional Responsibility, it recognized that the rules would have little impact without effective enforcement. Enforcement rested with each state.

In 1970, with the ink barely dry on the Code of Professional Responsibility, an ABA blue ribbon committee, chaired by the then-sitting U.S. Supreme Court Justice Tom Clark, issued a report highly critical of lawyer discipline in the United States (Wolfram 2002, 217). Through the 1960s, the discipline of lawyers by bar associations and the courts was a hit-or-miss proposition. Courts, not bar associations, typically had the responsibility for the discipline of attorneys for ethics violations. And the effectiveness of the disciplinary system varied from state to state. It is important to realize, however, that the establishment of a much more comprehensive discipline system was never viewed as a marker on the road to greater ethical competence among lawyers. In fact, ethical competence had little to do with the promulgation of the *Model Rules*. Rather, the goal was to put in place a system that would punish certain types of conduct generally agreed upon as detrimental to the effective representation of a client.

The Clark Committee identified 36 problems with state lawyer disciplinary systems. The most important finding of the committee was that "disciplinary action [was] practically nonexistent in many jurisdictions; practices and procedures [were] antiquated; [and] many disciplinary agencies ha[d] little power to take effective steps against malefactors" (Devlin 1994, 369). To deal with this problem, the Clark Committee recommended that states replace decentralized disciplinary systems with formal systems much like those used to investigate and discipline other professionals (Devlin 1994, 369–374). Decentralized disciplinary systems—typically managed by state courts—relied heavily upon volunteer lawyers to conduct investigations of alleged disciplinary violations (Devlin 1994, 369).

To deal with the lack of professionalism in the conduct of legal ethics investigations and the inconsistent treatment of disciplinary cases, the Clark Committee called for the establishment of permanent legal disciplinary agencies with adequate funding to investigate allegations of misconduct, along with adequate authority to discipline lawyers. To hold the feet of state governments and bar associations to the fire, the committee report warned that unless state bar associations threw their full support behind the professionalization of lawyer discipline systems, it was likely that appropriate legislative bodies would put in place a system that had non-lawyers play major roles in the discipline of lawyers (Powell 1986, 40).

If the Clark Committee report were not enough to raise serious questions about the effectiveness of lawyer disciplinary systems, two Supreme Court decisions from the 1970s would significantly increase the difficulty of regulating the ethical conduct of attorneys. In *Goldfarb v. Virginia State Bar* (1975), the Supreme Court held that the "minimum-fee schedule for lawyers published by the Fairfax County Bar Association and enforced by the Virginia State Bar" constituted a restraint of trade under the Sherman Act (Powell 1985, 285). The decision freed lawyers to compete for business on price. As a result of this decision, "intraprofessional competition for the provision of personal legal services greatly increased and the costs of certain routine legal services such as title examinations, uncontested divorces and the preparation of wills declined markedly" (Powell 1985, 285).

Bates and O'Steen v. State Bar of Arizona (1977) struck down a blanket ban on advertising by lawyers by holding that Arizona's "disciplinary rule serve[d] to inhibit the free flow of commercial information and to keep the public in ignorance" (p. 365).

Within a short time of the *Bates and O'Steen v. State Bar of Arizona* decision, courts also placed limits on the ability of state legislatures and state bar associations to prohibit lawyers from advertising on television. On the other hand, in *Ohralik v. Ohio State Bar Association* (1978), the Supreme Court upheld the constitutionality of a state ban on the in-person solicitation of clients by lawyers.

Bates and O'Steen had a profound impact on the practice of the law in the United States. The decision permitted lawyers to tap a much larger market for all types of legal services. The combination of the end to minimum pricing regulations for lawyers and the lifting of the ban on advertising by lawyers removed two of the major barriers lawyers faced in competing aggressively for business. Critics of the deregulation of lawyer fee structures and advertising argued it provided an incentive for lawyers to engage in unethical practices in order to attract clients.

Legal Education and Ethical Competencies

Professional responsibility courses taught in law schools "focus for the most part on the ethics of lawyers as governed by the *Model Rules*" (Sturm and Guiner 2007, 537). Yet, many law schools and continuing education courses that focus on professional responsibility "neither encourage students to address the conflicts between their personal and their professional identities, nor provide sustained opportunity for self-reflection" (Strum and Guiner 2007, 537). The fact that all states require licensed lawyers to take legal ethics continuing education courses (Weeman, Regan, Jr., and Gillers 2007, 325) does not mean that law schools and legal continuing education programs prepare attorneys who practice law in government agencies with a satisfactory level of ethical competence. The drafters of the *Model Rules* never intended those rules to ensure the ethical competence of members of the legal profession (Lerner 2006, 783–784).

It is not surprising that teaching law students about how to comply with the *Model Rules* does little to develop the ethical competence of lawyers inside or outside of government (Lerner 2006, 785). Instead of preparing law students or lawyers to deal with difficult ethical issues, the *Model Rules* "were written to create a mere legal code that gave boundaries of permissible conduct and [to] codify the obligations already imposed on lawyers by other areas of the law" (Lerner 2006, 785). Much more serious, using the *Model Rules* as the foundation of law school and continuing legal training ethics courses effectively gives law students and practicing lawyers permission to ignore broader ethical issues and dilemmas that certainly occur in the professional practice of law.

Critics of legal ethics training programs argue that such courses fail to prepare lawyers to deal with serious ethical choices. Prior to the commercialization of the practice of law, many lawyers viewed their most rewarding role as that of a trusted adviser who had the ability to help clients avoid trouble, not simply get them out of trouble. Clients hired lawyers to help keep them from stepping on legal landmines. Lawyers who viewed themselves as advisers had few problems telling their clients what they did not want to hear—that sometimes they might not be able to get the outcome they wanted.

At the same time, lawyers who enter government service find themselves unprepared to deal with the ethical implications of public policy formulation and implementation. "If the ethical sensibilities of the [government] lawyer remain dull, it is cause for concern because the management of governmental organizations, like its corporate counterpart, commonly look to lawyers, in the absence of governmental or corporate chaplains, for counsel on ethical matters as well as 'purely legal' matters" (Wollan, Jr. 1978, 108). One may make an argument that government lawyers face the problem of divided loyalties much more frequently than private-sector attorneys. Does the government lawyer owe primary loyalty to their government client or to broader constitutional and democratic values? Does the government lawyer have a higher obligation than other public employees to avoid even the appearance of impropriety in her private financial affairs? Does the government lawyer have a greater ethical obligation than other government employees to protest arguably immoral actions by governments and their officials?

Instead of throwing up their hands and walking away from the battle, a number of legal ethics scholars contend that law schools have the ability to structure legal ethics courses that truly prepare law students for the dilemmas they will face as practicing lawyers. Some law schools have moved in recent decades "beyond mere tinkering with the way professional responsibility is taught," attempting instead to significantly broaden the scope of ethics education to include ethical decision making as an essential part of being an effective lawyer (Wolfson 1995, 299).

In 1984, for instance, Loyola Law School, located in Los Angeles, California, required all students to take a course dealing with client interviewing, client counseling, and legal negotiation (Wolfson 1995, 299). Arguing that the vast majority of ethical issues facing lawyers arise "in the context of the representation of a client" (Wolfson 1995, 299), the course integrates common types of ethical issues that lawyers face when interviewing and counseling clients and conducting negotiations. Throughout the course, "the emphasis is continually on the interconnection between ethics and skills necessary to deal effectively with a client" (Wolfson 1995, 299). Advocates of the "by doing" model of legal ethics education argue that until law students actually face real-life ethical problems related directly to representing a client, they will fail to understand the importance of their personal integrity in the practice of law.

Without debate, the simulation approach to legal ethics education makes sense. Taught in small sections, law students find themselves in simulated interviewing sessions, conducting legal research into the problems faced by their clients, and then advising those clients on how to proceed. However, law courses that require students to participate in simulated client interviewing and counseling sessions may find it difficult to replicate the actual practice of law. As a result, it may be necessary to strongly encourage law students to participate in internal law school clinics in order to adequately prepare them for the practice of law (Tarr 2009, 1013). Yet, to require all law schools to offer courses that attempt to simulate the practice of law or to require that all law students participate in internal law clinics is probably neither financially nor administratively possible.

Consequently, a number of legal ethics scholars and studies of legal ethics education argue that integration of the teaching of ethics into all three years of the law school curriculum constitutes the best way to enhance the ethical reasoning skills of future lawyers. *Educating Lawyers: Preparation for the Profession of Law*, prepared by the Carnegie Foundation for the Advancement of Teaching (Sullivan et al. 2007), for instance, argues that the teaching of ethics and professionalism must be integrated into the entire legal curriculum.

Drake University Law School in Des Moines, Iowa, is one institution that has adopted an integrated approach to legal ethics education (Weresh 2007, 25–28). In a two-semester legal research and writing course, students study foundational legal ethics rules: the importance of professionalism in serving as an advocate, and the essential role of personal integrity and character in legal practice (Weresh 2007, 25). To reinforce the lessons learned in the classroom, all first-year law students must attend a series of lectures that explore (1) ethics, moral character, and bar admission, (2) professionalism and electronic communication, and (3) character and ethical decision making (Weresh 2007, 25–28). The third orientation lecture "integrates concepts of ethical decision making developed by the Joseph and Edna Josephson Institute of Ethics" (Weresh 2007, 25–28). The Josephson Institute believes that all citizens including lawyers and other professionals have a moral obligation to adhere to ethical standards that go beyond rules of conduct established by law or regulation.

In addition to the legal research and writing course and the ethics lecture series, first-year law students at Drake participate in a series of field trips that bring them into direct contact with justices of the state's appellate and supreme court. During small group sessions, "justices [attempt to] reinforce the notion of professionalism" (Weresh 2007, 25–28). Finally, the first-year ethics orientation program requires students to complete the First-Year Trial Practicum (FYTP). Law students observe an actual jury trial conducted on campus with the collaboration of the law school, the judiciary, and members of the Iowa bar. Students are provided the opportunity to "observe the trial from jury selection through verdict" (Weresh 2007, 25–28). The practicum also allows students to "debrief trial counsel, members of the jury, and the judge" (Weresh 2007, 25–28).

Clearly, law schools have the ability to expand the scope of legal ethics training in order to "go beyond the rules of conduct and consider the demands of personal conscience"; the right training at the university level can, indeed, increase the sensitivity of law students to the difficult moral dilemmas they are bound to face in practice (Spaeth, Jr., Perry, and Wachs 1995, 157–158). It is possible to develop legal ethics courses that require law students and practicing attorneys to work through common types of ethical dilemmas faced by attorneys working inside and outside of government. The stories do not always have to be based on real-life cases but may be developed to demonstrate common types of ethical problems faced by lawyers in government or private-sector practice (Spaeth, Jr., Perry, and Wachs 1995, 159–160).

Government Lawyers and Ethical Competencies Revisited

To succeed, efforts to persuade law schools and continuing legal education programs to shift the focus of ethics training from rule compliance to ethical decision making must overcome the widespread belief among legal educators that they lack the ability to shape the personal value and belief systems of those who decide to embark on a legal career. At the very least, legal ethics education has the ability to prevent lawyers from cheating or violating the trust of clients.

Ethics scholars concerned about the integrity of government lawyers face an even more difficult problem when confronting the issue of persuading government attorneys to exercise personal moral judgment in carrying out their official duties.

Thompson argues that "conventional theory and practice of administrative ethics holds that administrators should carry out the orders of their superiors and the policies of the agency and the government they serve" without allowing personal beliefs or values to interfere (1985, 556). The so-called ethic of neutrality, argues Thompson, requires that the administrator "serve as a completely reliable instrument of the goals of the organization, never injecting personal values in the process of furthering these goals" (Thompson 1985, 557). Consequently, a government lawyer has a professional obligation to come up with the most effective legal argument to support a policy adopted by his agency—even if the lawyer has strong personal moral objections to the policy. Lerner argues that the teaching of political and ethical theory in law school could help address the "shortcomings in the legal ethics curriculum" (Lerner 2006, 787). "Authors and thinkers, from ancient Greece to the present day," argues Lerner, "have dealt with topics such as the proper role of the state, what makes an action moral and immoral, the existence (or non-existence) of justice, what justice is if it exists" as well as a vast array of other ethics issues and dilemmas (2006, 786).

A number of public service ethics scholars argue that all public administrators should develop a high level of "constitutional competence" (Rosenbloom, Carroll, and Carroll 2000). Despite this fact, relatively few master's of public administration programs require students to take courses in administrative law, the legal environment of public administration, or constitutional civil rights (Roberts 2008, 361–381). And it is impossible to determine how other public administration courses treat constitutional competence issues. Although law schools routinely require first-year law students to take some type of constitutional law course, no guarantee exists that graduates are sufficiently informed of constitutional law and civil liberties. Despite this fact, compelling arguments exist that government lawyers have a higher duty to guard against violations of established constitutional or statutory rights and to disclose governmental misconduct. First, they are sworn to uphold the law. Second, they frequently occupy positions that "give them privy to high-level deliberations" (Morse 2010, 432). Third, their knowledge of the law often "enables them to identify government misconduct and illegal activity" (Morse 2010, 432). Fourth, government clients often rely heavily upon their advice on constitutional issues. This places government lawyers in the difficult position of having to decide whether or not "to stretch the law to accommodate their bosses' actions" (Morse 2010, 432). Yet, the *Model Rules of Profes-*

sional Conduct significantly complicates the ability of government lawyers to publicly oppose arguably unconstitutional conduct by their agencies by constraining "government lawyers from making unauthorized disclosures" (Morse 2010, 422). A government lawyer who achieves a high level of constitutional competency may find himself with few legal options to publicly oppose the action or policy.

Not surprisingly, the competency of principled dissent is directly related to the competencies of recognizing that legal ethics involves more than just complying with carefully drafted ethics rules and the moral obligation of government lawyers to protect basic constitutional rights. Law schools and continuing legal education programs simply do not offer courses on how government lawyers may engage in principled dissent. And public service ethics scholars and legal ethics scholars have written relatively little on the subject of government lawyers serving as public or secret whistle-blowers (O'Leary 2005; Morse 2010, 421–454; Thompson 1985, 555–561). Government lawyers frequently find themselves bound by client confidentially and statutory secrecy requirements (Morse 2010, 434–435). Even if client confidentiality rules and secrecy laws do not apply, the 2006 U.S. Supreme Court decision in *Garcetti v. Ceballos*, 547 U.S. 410 (2006), has effectively stripped all government employees of any First Amendment protection to publicly disclose matters of public concern in the course of performing their official duties (Wiese 2010, 509–529).

Thompson argues that the acceptance of the ethic of neutrality makes administrative ethics impossible. Consequently, principled dissent is vital to achieving administrative ethics. Thompson also argues that those government employees who consider becoming dissenters must assess the costs and potential benefits of four types of dissent (1985, 557). These include (1) official protests within the organization, (2) "protest[ing] outside the organization while otherwise performing their jobs satisfactorily," (3) open obstruction of policy within an organization, and (4) covert obstruction, including leaking information in violation of the law (Thompson 1985, 558).

Conclusion

No easy solution exists for declining public confidence in the legal profession as a whole. As of this writing, government lawyers find themselves subject to extensive and carefully drafted rules of conduct, but these rules fail to deal with some of the most serious ethical dilemmas typically faced by lawyers in government positions. Unlike private attorneys, government lawyers have a special responsibility to protect democratic and constitutional values. One may make a strong argument that government lawyers face increasing pressure to view their role as advocates for partisan or ideological positions. They also face increased pressure to prevail in legal disputes much like their private-sector counterparts. To persuade government attorneys that they have a higher moral obligation than other government employees to protect democratic values is an exceptionally difficult task; however, it is not an impossible task. Ethics education has the ability to help government lawyers develop the ability to work through difficult ethical dilemmas and develop ethical competencies that will enable them to do their jobs while fostering public trust in government.

It is easy to understand why law schools and continuing legal education programs have avoided expanding the scope of legal ethics education. It is problematic to send law school graduates into the legal profession and urge them to exercise independent judgment that may directly conflict with their ethical obligations under legal ethics rules. The major objectives of legal ethics education is to keep lawyers from getting disciplined or disbarred and not condoning conduct that might produce such a result—even though such conduct might benefit society as a whole. By urging government lawyers to develop these ethical competencies, one must recognize the possibility that lawyers will find themselves forced to choose between complying with ethics rules and serving the greater good.

Is ethical competence achievable for public service lawyers? Yes, if they can learn to think and act beyond compliance, acquire civility in their professional life, become constitutionally informed, and acquire the ability to engage in principled dissent.

Notes

1. A November 2009 Gallup Poll on honesty/ethics in professions (Gallup 2009) painted a less than rosy ethical picture for the legal profession. Only 13 percent of those surveyed rated the ethics of lawyers as very high. Those surveyed rated only business executives (12 percent), advertising practitioners (11 percent), senators (11 percent), insurance salespeople (10 percent), members of Congress (9 percent), stockbrokers (9 percent), HMO managers (8 percent), and car salespeople (6 percent) lower (Gallup 2009). On the other end of the ethical scale, those surveyed gave high marks to the ethics of nurses (83 percent), pharmacists (66 percent), medical doctors (65 percent), police officers (63 percent), engineers (62 percent), dentists (57 percent), college teachers (54 percent), and clergy (50 percent). In 2005, only 18 percent of those surveyed rated the ethics of lawyers very high (referenced in Gallup 2009). A July 2008 Harris Organization poll found the occupations with the greatest prestige included firefighters (62 percent), scientists (57 percent), doctors (56 percent), nurses (54 percent), military officers (51 percent), teachers (51 percent), police officers (44 percent), ministers (41 percent), and engineers (39 percent) (Harris Poll 2009). On the other hand, only 26 percent of those surveyed believed that lawyers have very great prestige.

The survey also reported that from 1977 to 2008, the number of those surveyed who believed that being a lawyer had very great prestige had gone down by 10 percentage points.

In 1950, it was estimated that 212,605 lawyers were licensed to practice law in the United States (Segal and Fei 1953, 114). In 2008, according to the American Bar Association, 1,180,386 licensed lawyers practiced law in the United States (ABA 2009). From 1950 through 2010, the population of the United States grew from roughly 151 million to just under 309 million. In 2000, 73 percent of lawyers were male and 27 percent were female. Lawyers were distributed between private and public sectors in the following proportions: private practice accounted for 74 percent of lawyers; governments employed 8 percent of lawyers; private industry employed another 8 percent; the judicial branch employed 3 percent; and educational institutions and public defender agencies employed about 1 percent each (ABA 2009). In 2000, 48 percent of lawyers were solo practitioners, 15 percent worked in firms with two to five lawyers, 6 percent worked in firms with 11 to 20 lawyers, 6 percent worked in firms with 21 to 50 lawyers, 4 percent worked in firms with 51 to 100 lawyers, and 14 percent worked in firms with 101 or more lawyers (ABA 2009).

2. Even though the number of government lawyers remained small, as the administrative state grew so did the responsibilities of lawyers. As professionals, in theory, government lawyers had the responsibility to tell their clients bad news as well as good news. After World War II, as judicial review of the administrative state increased, government lawyers increasingly found themselves forced to deliver bad news to their clients. Governments no longer could ignore the Fifth and Fourteenth Amendment procedural due process rights of citizens subject to governmental action. An increasing number of interest groups on the right and left side of the political spectrum were quite willing to go to court to challenge administrative actions.

The growth of the administrative state also led to much greater concern over whether powerful special interests had succeeded in persuading significant numbers of government employees to do their bidding instead of representing the public interest.

Good government groups doubted the ability of government employees to resist the overtures of special interests. Instead of relying primarily on the personal integrity of career public servants to do the right thing, governments found themselves under strong pressure to rely much more heavily upon rule-driven ethics programs (Reynolds, Jr. 1995, 126–128). During the 1960s and 1970s, governments adopted a new generation of rule-driven ethics regulations that applied to all government employees, including government lawyers. The new set of disciplinary ethics rules had a very limited objective. They did not attempt to ensure that government employees acted morally. They only sought to prevent government employees from becoming involved in financial conflicts of interest that might weaken public confidence in their impartiality and objectivity (Huddleston and Sands 1995, 141).

3. The Development of the ABA's Canons of Ethics: Putting a Finger in a Leaking Dam: During the colonial period, admittance to the bar required an individual to complete an apprenticeship or clerkship with an established lawyer. The length of a required apprenticeship varied from colony to colony (Katcher 2006, 339). From the post-Revolutionary War years through the 1820s, only individuals from the upper class had the academic preparation to pursue the practice of law. Consequently, members of the legal profession did not see an overriding need for a formal system

to discipline unethical lawyers. Peer pressure had the ability to ensure that lawyers complied with generally accepted ethical standards.

Beginning in the early 1830s, an "anti-elitist ethos," directly related to the emergence of Jacksonian democracy, led to the elimination of most formal training requirements for becoming a practicing lawyer (Devlin 1994, 365). A number of states permitted individuals to study the law by themselves and then take an oral or written exam. During the same period, many local and state bar associations went out of existence, due largely to the widespread belief that members of the upper class had used them to limit the number of lawyers, thereby reducing competition and protecting the power of the upper class (Devlin 1994, 365). Not surprisingly, lowering the barriers to legal practice led to a flood of new lawyers who found themselves forced into fierce competition to make a living.

During the 1860s and 1870s, a backlash against the perceived lowering of standards for entry into the practice of law led to a call by established lawyers to reestablish local and state bar associations in an effort to reassert some control over those entering the legal profession (Backof and Martin, Jr. 1991, 99). In particular, established lawyers grew particularly alarmed over new lawyers aggressively soliciting clients. Scholars continue to debate whether economic self-interest or legitimate concern over the state of the profession led to efforts to fight back against the "rising tide of commercialism" in the practice of law (Drinker 1955, 38).

By the turn of the twentieth century, however, major changes in the practice of law forced the ABA to carefully examine the ethical responsibilities of members of the profession (Carle 1999, 6–7). The industrial revolution and the growth of large corporations greatly increased the demand for lawyers with specialized skills. Corporate law quickly became a recognized subfield. Specialized law firms emerged to meet the growing demand for legal services from corporations (Carle 1999, 7). As a result, an increasing number of lawyers began to work directly for corporations or for law firms hired by corporations. Many of these lawyers would play a key role in making use of the law and the judicial system to help corporations and trusts amass vast economic wealth and power; for instance, corporate lawyers used the courts to block strikes by labor unions, to justify the use of the police and military to break strikes, and to arrest and imprison labor leaders (Hodson and Sullivan 2008, 133). Courts would routinely issue injunctions against labor stoppages. Not surprisingly, the legal profession became closely associated with protecting powerful economic interests and doing little to help the common people. Many Americans came to regard lawyers as "hired guns" willing to sell their services to the highest bidder.

From about 1900 to 1920—the last two decades of the Progressive Era—a major backlash developed against the legal profession and the use of the courts to block progressive reforms. In 1905, President Theodore Roosevelt spoke before the American Bar Association "and condemned corporate lawyers for helping their clients evade regulation" (Carle 1999, 7). At the same time, established lawyers grew alarmed over a new breed of lawyers who actively sought out clients in the alleged pursuit of frivolous lawsuits. Many of these lawyers were said to come from "immigrant backgrounds and low socioeconomic classes" (Carle 1999, 8). To lawyers from largely Protestant backgrounds, the members of this new class of lawyers were only interested in making a fast buck—even if it meant engaging in illegal or unethical conduct. Consequently, the combination of growing corporate law firms and growing numbers of lawyers with immigrant backgrounds "were seen by some to destroy the professional harmony the bar had enjoyed and contribute to the bar's declining status" (Backof and Martin, Jr. 1991, 100).

4. The Canons of Ethics did not envision the law becoming an instrument of social change. Through much of American history, those with property and wealth used the law to protect private property rights. Courts rarely expanded individual civil liberties.

With little hope of persuading Congress to outlaw segregation, during the 1930s the NAACP established its own legal department. In 1940, the Legal Defense Fund became an independent organization with the mission of making use of the courts to confront segregation. Instead of waiting for clients to come to them, attorneys for the Legal Defense Fund actively sought out clients to challenge segregation laws across the South in transportation, schools, public accommodations, and so on. Even before the U.S. Supreme Court issued its landmark decision in *Brown v. Board of Education* (1954), striking down the constitutionality of segregated schools systems, lawyers working for the NAACP Legal Defense Fund were seeking out clients to challenge the enforcement of laws requiring the segregation of public transportation and public accommodations. After *Brown*, the NAACP filed hundreds of lawsuits seeking the full implementation of the Court's decision. The Legal Defense Fund did not even try to maintain the fiction that lawyers never solicited clients.

The 1960s saw civil liberties lawyers launch a much broader crusade for social change. Instead of waiting for the states to deal with the pervasive problem of inadequate representation for indigent defendants, for instance, civil liberties lawyers turned to the federal courts for relief. At the beginning of the 1960s, no uniform system existed for providing legal representation for indigent defendants. Legal aid societies in cities such as New York sought to provide legal counsel for indigent defendants. Many courts relied upon the practice of court-appointed counsel. The patchwork system for providing indigent criminal defendants with legal representation still left many of those defendants without legal assistance. In the landmark case of *Gideon v. Wainwright* (1963), the Supreme Court held that indigent defendants in serious felony cases had a constitutional right to counsel. Then, in *Miranda v. Arizona* (1966), the high court held that anyone arrested for a crime was entitled to legal representation paid for by the government if they lacked the resources to pay for their own defense. Yet, poor Americans continued to lack legal representation in a wide range of civil matters.

In 1965, Congress established the Office of Economic Opportunity (OEO). To the dismay of many state bar associations, the OEO took the controversial step of establishing legal aid clinics to help poor citizens with their civil legal problems (Carle 1999, 104). Many legal aid lawyers viewed their role as one of advocating for the poor rather than simply providing legal assistance for traditional civil matters (Erlanger 1978, 253–254). This included bringing suit against governments for violating the statutory and constitutional rights of their poor clients. Controversial lawsuits brought by OEO lawyers against government bodies and agencies for alleged violations of the rights of their clients led to open warfare between state and local governments and OEO lawyers (Letter to the editor, *ABA Journal* 1972, 374–375).

In April 1972, after Vice President Spiro Agnew sharply criticized suits brought by OEO legal services lawyers against state and local government, ABA president Leon Jaworski vigorously defended the conduct of OEO lawyers. "The propriety of legal services lawyers instituting suits against the government officials or institutions is an issue which has been considered by the Congress and by the American Bar Association. Such suits were found to be within the legislative mandate governing the program and the dictates of the lawyer's professional responsibility. In the last analysis, it is the courts which must decide these issues and the record indicates that many of these suits have been decided in favor of the poor," stressed Jaworski (Letter to the editor, *ABA Journal* 1972, 375).

References

ABC News. 2007. Attorney general Gonzales resigns. August 27. http://abcnews. go.com/TheLaw/Politics/story?id=3421219&page=1 (accessed January 2, 2011).
American Bar Association. 2009. Lawyer demographics. ABA Section of Legal Education & Admissions to the Bar. Compiled by the ABA Market Research Department. http://new.abanet.org/marketresearch/PublicDocuments/Lawyer_Demographics. pdf (accessed November 20, 2010).
————. 2010a. *Model Rules of Professional Conduct.* http://www.americanbar.org/ groups/professional_responsibility/publications/model_rules_of_professional_ conduct/model_rules_of_professional_conduct_table_of_contents.html.
————. 2010b. Policies—state pro bono ethics rules. http://www.abanet.org/legalser-vices/probono/stateethicsrules.html (accessed December 2, 2010).
————. 2010c. *2009 Survey on Lawyer Discipline Systems,* ABA Standing Committee on Professional Discipline. http://www.americanbar.org/content/dam/aba/migrated/ cpr/discipline/2009sold.authcheckdam.pdf (accessed December 15, 2010).
————. 2011. *Directory of Lawyer Disciplinary Agencies 2011–12.* http://www. abanet.org/cpr/regulation/directory.pdf.
Backof, Jeanne F., and Charles L. Martin, Jr. 1991. Historical perspectives: Development of the codes of ethics in the legal, medical, and accounting professions. *Journal of Business Ethics* 10(2): 99–110.
Bates and O'Steen v. State Bar of Arizona, 433 U.S. 350. 1977.
Brown v. Board of Education of Topeka, 347 U.S. 483. 1954.
Carle, Susan D. 1999. Lawyer's duty to due justice: A new look at the history of the 1908 canons. *Law & Social Inquiry* 24(1):1–44.
Clark, Kathleen. 2008. Government lawyers and confidentiality norms. *Washington University Law Review* 85: 1034–1091.
Cooper, N. Lee, and Stephen F. Humphreys. 1995/1996. Beyond the rules: Lawyer image and the scope of professionalism. *Cumberland Law Review* 26: 923–941.
Devlin, Mary M. 1994. The development of lawyer disciplinary procedures in the United States. *Journal of the Professional Lawyer* 15: 359–387. http://www. americanbar.org/content/dam/aba/migrated/cpr/pubs/devlin.authcheckdam.pdf (accessed December 10, 2010).
Drinker, Henry S. 1955. Legal ethics. *Annals of the American Academy of Political and Social Science* 297: 37–45.
Erlanger, Howard S. 1978. Lawyers and neighborhood legal services: Social background and impetus for reform. *Law & Society Review* 12(2): 253–274.
Frankel, Charles. 1976. Review: Code of professional responsibility. *University of Chicago Law Review* 43(4): 874–886.
Gallup. 2009. Honesty/ethics in professions. Graph. http://www.gallup.com/poll/1654/ honesty-ethics-professions.aspx.
Garcetti v. Ceballos, 547 U.S. 410. 2006.

Gideon v. Wainwright, 372 U.S. 335. 1963.

Goldfarb v. Virginia State Bar, 421 U.S. 773. 1975.

Hall, Kermit, and David Scott Clark. 2002. *The Oxford Companion to American Law.* New York: Oxford University Press.

Harris Poll. 2009. Firefighters, scientists and doctors seen as most prestigious occupations. News release, August 4. http://new.abanet.org/marketresearch/PublicDocuments/harris_poll.pdf.

Hodson, Randy, and Teresa A. Sullivan. 2008. *The Social Organization of Work*, 4th ed. Belmont, CA: Wadsworth.

Huddleston, Mark W., and Joseph C. Sands. 1995. Enforcing administrative ethics. *Annals of the American Academy of Political and Social Science* 537: 139–149.

Katcher, Susan. 2006. International conference on legal education reform: Legal training in the United States: A brief history. *Wisconsin International Law Journal* 24: 335–375.

Lerner, Gabriel. 2006. Current development 2005–2006: How teaching political and ethical theory could help solve two of the legal profession's biggest problems. *Georgetown Journal of Legal Ethics* 19: 781–793.

Letter to the editor. 1972. Opinion & comment: Legal services buffeted. *ABA Journal* 58: 374–375.

Miller, Nelson, and Victoria Kremski. 2009. Who is the customer and what are we selling? Employer-based objectives for the ethical competence of law school graduates. *Journal of the Legal Profession* 33: 223–238.

Miranda v. Arizona, 384 U.S. 436. 1966.

Morse, Mika C. 2010. Note: Honor or betrayal? The ethics of government lawyer-whistleblowers. *Georgetown Journal of Legal Ethics* 23(2): 421–452.

Nicolson, Donald. 2005. Making lawyers moral? Ethical codes and moral character. *Legal Studies* 25(4): 601–626.

Ohralik v. Ohio State Bar Association, 436 U.S. 447. 1978.

O'Leary, Rosemary. 2005. *The Ethics of Dissent: Managing Guerrilla Government.* Washington, DC: CQ Press.

Petrowitz, Harold C. 1979. Some thoughts about current problems in legal ethics and professional responsibility. *Duke Law Journal* 1979(6): 1275–1290.

Powell, Michael J. 1985. Developments in the regulation of lawyers: Competing segments and market, client, and government controls. *Social Forces* 64(2): 281–305.

————. 1986. Professional divestiture: The cession of responsibility for lawyer discipline. *American Bar Association Research Journal* 11(1): 31–54.

Radack, Jesselyn. 2003. The government attorney whistleblower and the rule of confidentiality: Compatible at last. *Georgetown Journal of Legal Ethics* 17: 125–143.

Re, Edward D. 1994. The causes of popular dissatisfaction with the legal profession. *St. John's Law Review* 68: 85–136.

Reynolds, Harry W., Jr. 1995. Educating public administrators about ethics. *Annals of the American Academy of Politics and Social Science* 537: 122–149.

Roberts, Robert. 2008. Teaching law in public administration programs. *Journal of Public Affairs Education* 14(3): 361–381.

Rosenbloom, David H., James D. Carroll, and Jonathan D. Carroll. 2000. *Constitutional Competence for Public Managers: Cases and Commentary.* Itasca, IL: F.E. Peacock.

Segal, Robert M., and John Fei. 1953. The economics of the legal profession. *ABA Journal* 39: 110–116.

Simon, Roy. 2010. The ethics of lawyers in government: Foreword. *Hofstra Law Review* 38: 825–833.

Spaeth, Edmund B., Jr., Janet G. Perry, and Peggy B. Wachs. 1995. Teaching legal ethics: Exploring the continuum. *Law and Contemporary Problems* 58(3/4): 153–172.

Stephens, Helynn. 2004. Price of pro bono representations: Examining lawyer's duties and responsibilities. *Defense Counsel Journal* 71(1): 71–78.

Sturm, Susan, and Lani Guinier. 2007. The law school matrix: Reforming legal education in a culture of competition and conformity. *Vanderbilt Law Review* 60(2): 515–553.

Sullivan, William M., Anne Colby, Judith Welch Wegner, Lloyd Bond, and Lee S. Shulman. 2007. *Educating Lawyers: Preparation for the Profession of Law*. San Francisco: Jossey-Bass.

Tarr, Nina W. 2009. Ethics, internal law school clinics, and the training of the next generation of poverty lawyers. *William Mitchell Law Review* 35(3): 1011–1055.

Thompson, Dennis. 1985. The possibility of administrative ethics. *Public Administration Review* 45(5): 555–561.

Tucker, Henry St. George, et al. 1922. The canons of ethics for lawyers adopted by the American Bar Association. *Annals of the American Academy of Political and Social Science* 101: 254–260.

Weeman, Lauren A, Milton C. Regan, Jr., and Stephen Gillers. 2007. Twenty years of legal ethics: Past, present, and future. *Georgetown Journal of Legal Ethics* 20(2): 321–346.

Wendel, W. Bradley. 2009. Symposium: Government lawyers, democracy, and the rule of law. *Fordham Law Review* 77: 1333–1361.

Weresh, Melissa. 2007. An integrated approach to teaching ethics and professionalism. *The Professional Lawyer* 18(2): 25–28.

Wiese, Tyler. 2010. Seeing through the smoke: The "official duties" in the wake of *Garcetti v. Ceballos*. *ABA Journal of Labor and Employment Law* 25(3): 509–529.

Wilkins, David B. 1992. Who should regulate lawyers? *Harvard Law Review* 105(4): 799–887.

Williams, Lesley E. 1999. Note: The civil regulation of prosecutors. *Fordham Law Review* 67: 3441–3479.

Wolfram, Charles W. 2002. Toward a history of the legalization of American legal ethics—II: The modern era. *Georgetown Journal of Legal Ethics* 15: 205–229.

Wolfson, Michael E. 1995. Professional responsibility as a lawyering skill. *Law and Contemporary Problems* 58(3/4): 297–304.

Wollan, Laurin A., Jr. 1978. Lawyers in government—"The most serviceable instruments of authority." *Public Administration Review* 38(1): 105–112.

10

Ethical Competence
in Nonprofit Organizations
A Human Resources Perspective

Barbara S. Liggett

With more than 1.8 million nonprofit organizations representing a diverse group of employers in the United States, there are substantial opportunities for ethical and unethical decision making (White 2010). Nonprofits span the arts, education, faith-based organizations, health care, human services, recreation, and social services organizations that typically offer services not provided by the public or private sectors. Additionally, nonprofits increasingly are forming alliances or collaborating with other sectors in meeting the needs of the public.

Decisions for nonprofits, like their public and private counterparts, arise in many managerial scenarios and activities such as governance, fiscal accountability, physical location and capacity, human capital, legal, gifting, customer/client services, political activity, and investment policies (Boucher and Hudspeth 2008; Rhode and Packel 2009; Wells and Gill 2007). Additionally, attention has been given to nonprofit fraud (Greenlee et al. 2007) and whistle-blowing (Harshbarger and Crafts 2007). While one could focus on a myriad of decision areas and the ethical competencies to make decisions, the essence of this chapter is the internal management arena of the organization as an entity driven by its human resources policies and practices. These policies and practices can create a culture that allows the nonprofit's paid staff and volunteers to be ethical—or not.

Nonprofits exist because employees and volunteers work together to provide services in a community. Without the human capital to provide services, the nonprofit organization cannot exist. No nonprofit organization wants the words *misbehavior, fraud, discrimination, conflicts of interest,* or *scandal* used in the same sentence describing the activities or the actions of specific staff. Such words, though, are used by the media more often than any nonprofit desires.

Throughout this chapter, the reader will be drawn to think about individuals' behaviors, the organizational context for the behaviors, and the need for specific competencies among individuals so the nonprofit can demonstrate its core values of integrity, honesty, fairness, openness, respect, and responsibility as charged by the Independent Sector Code of Ethics (Independent Sector 2004).

Ethical competence for members of nonprofit organizations means possessing the ability to use critical thinking with an understanding of (1) the nonprofit context; (2) the frameworks for determining right and wrong; (3) the recognition of the "whole" of human resources and nonprofit systems; and (4) a desire for fairness, equitable treatment, and respect for all persons, which results in the nonprofit making the right decisions as purveyors of the public good. This chapter also describes several influential professional and educational associations' perspectives on ethical competence and discusses a means to develop and evaluate ethical competence. And, as detailed later, the ethical framework of beneficiaries and the consequences of ethical decision making will be discussed as well.

From the Individual to the Organization

Most attention on unethical behavior focuses on the individual, with a nonprofit's governing board or executive director forced to decide whether to punish or terminate staff members or volunteers. Such decisions cause turmoil for the organization and are exacerbated when the media publicizes the wrongdoing on the front page of the local newspaper. The blame for the misbehavior is typically put squarely on the individual (Greenlee et al. 2007; Harshbarger and Crafts 2007), but it may be too narrowly placed when it is assigned to an executive director, staff member, or volunteer; the nonprofit's policies and practices also may be a source for the cause of an individual's misbehavior. The following questions offer useful insights into how a nonprofit's management philosophy affects staff performance.

1. Does an organization create a culture of honesty or dishonesty by way of its policies and practices? This question speaks to the context of organization culture.
2. What are examples of ethical dilemmas within the nonprofit's human resources systems? These are the settings for the decisions requiring critical thinking about the ethical frameworks.
3. What are ethical competencies needed for resolving the dilemmas? This question draws us into identifying the knowledge, skills, and attitudes and abilities individuals need for resolving dilemmas, as well as the organization's responsibility for creating a culture with its policies and practices that allows an individual to act ethically.

These questions provide opportunities to reflect on how nonprofits treat the human capital in their organizations. Such reflection is a response to the call by Rhode and Packel (2009) for organizations to examine the factors that influence moral conduct, to recognize that a person's ethical reasoning and conduct can be affected by organizational structures and norms, and to explore the ethical issues that arise in charitable organizations with the goal of finding the best ways to promote ethical behavior.

(Un)ethical Behavior in Nonprofits

The Ethics Resource Center's *National Nonprofit Ethics Survey*, conducted in 2007, reported that 55 percent of those working in the nonprofit sector observed misconduct in their organizations (2008). Such misconduct consisted of six distinct types: discrimination, sexual harassment, misuse of confidential information, lying to stakeholders, improper hiring, and safety violations. All of these forms of misconduct typically are referenced in documentation provided by the nonprofit organization and in state and federal laws.

In a 2010 survey conducted by the author, of 16,760 board members, paid staff, and volunteers in 1,784 small- and medium-sized U.S. nonprofit organizations, 76 percent were identified as engaging in problematic human resources practices that could foster "weak or diminished ethical behavior." Sixty-one percent (10,224) of the respondents noted the existence of a code of conduct and some familiarity with state and federal laws, but 84 percent (8,587) questioned if there was enough understanding of how and why certain policies existed. Thirty-three percent reported disagreeing with the established policies and practices, but they had not asked about specific human resources policies and practices for fear of "causing trouble."

So, we know misconduct happens. Is the employee responsible? Or are there infrastructures or systems in place that create vulnerabilities for ethical lapses? Perhaps it is a combination of both. Early in the popular Broadway musical *Wicked* (Schwartz 2003), based on the book by Winnie Holzman and the novel by Gregory Maguire, Glinda the Good Witch poses the questions: "Are people born wicked? Or do they have wickedness thrust upon them?" *Wicked* may be a strong word for the organizational context, but, in reality, whether we play a semantic game with *misconduct, misbehavior, wrongdoings,* or *wickedness,* we are talking about doing or not doing the right thing in an organization. How do we know and do what is right? These are provocative questions worth pondering as we examine nonprofit organizations.

Domains of Ethical Competence

One way to know and do what is right is to have a set of competencies, identified by domains for ease in classification. By using four domains, we can

Figure 10.1 **Domains and Competencies**

Domain 1: Context
1. Ability to identify the differences in staff and volunteers—their motivations, needs, availability, work approaches, and interest in the organization's mission.
2. Ability to recognize pressures on the organization and utilize skills to react appropriately, resolve conditions creating pressures, and create means to prevent pressures from occurring.
3. Know and comply with the applicable laws, plus recognize referents other than law that have an impact on decision making in the nonprofit.
4. Know and apply the codes of conduct that apply to the nonprofit for staff, volunteers, and the organization entity.
5. Ability to create effective human resources policies and practices in multiple areas.
   a. Design job tasks that meet the organization's needs and are satisfying for those doing the tasks.
   b. Design and use effective recruiting systems for staff and volunteers.
   c. Determine appropriate benefits and recognition programs for staff and volunteers.
   d. Design effective performance management systems that allow for development of staff and volunteers.
   e. Provide training and development to improve and affirm an individual's knowledge and skills appropriate to the mission of the nonprofit, with effective relationship building.

Domain 2: Frameworks for Right and Wrong
6. Ability to differentiate among a variety of frameworks for making decisions and apply the appropriate framework for the situation needing a decision.

Domain 3: The "Whole" of Human Resources Systems and Connections to Other Systems Within and Outside the Organization
7. Ability to integrate human resources systems activities for maximum benefit, with development of boundary spanning and border crossing to systems within the nonprofit and external to the nonprofit.

Domain 4: Desire To Do What Is Ethical
8. Ability to know and do what is right by:
   a. Analyzing competing values and perspectives and demonstrating fairness in decision making.
   b. Considering options but always providing equitable treatment across the nonprofit.
   c. Showing respect to others in all situations, relationships, and oral and written communications.

group specific competencies needed for creating the ethical nonprofit and its human resources setting. The specific competencies, once identified, can then be placed in the world of observation by those in the nonprofit and by those served by the nonprofit. Once observed, individuals and the organizations can evaluate the specific competencies. Figure 10.1 provides the overview for the domains and competencies.

Figure 10.2 **Nonprofit Organization (NPO) Ethical Competence**

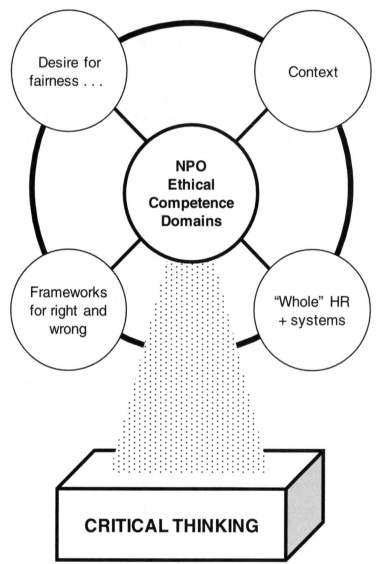

The four domains suggested in this chapter are context, frameworks for right and wrong, "whole" HR with linkages to other systems, and a desire for fairness, ethical treatment, and respect for others. The domains, portrayed in Figure 10.2, are situated on the foundation of critical thinking. Critical thinking, as the foundation, is discussed first.

Critical Thinking: The Foundation of the Domains

Much has been written about critical thinking skills at all levels of education. McPeck (1981) addressed critical thinking from the framework of philosophy of education, but scholars in other disciplines have also entered into the critical thinking discussion. Elaine Englehardt (2010) referenced a study from the American Philosophical Association for the purpose of finding consensus among nearly 50 American critical thinking experts. The study, known as *The Delphi Report*, provides the following description of critical thinking: "We understand critical thinking to be purposeful, self-regulatory judgment which results in interpretation, analysis, evaluation and inference as well as explanation of the evidential, conceptual, methodological, criteriological or contextual considerations upon which that judgment is based" (Facione 1990, 2). Critical thinking is a tool of inquiry, with the critical thinking skills used to "become self-attuned to the persuasive everyday pitfalls of moral judgment: moral intolerance, self-deception, and uncritical conformity" (Paul 1992, 32). Kennedy and Malatesa (2010, 163), in their request for public administration students to do more than be familiar with a code of ethics, ask students to learn "how to recognize circumstances (old and new) that pose ethical dilemmas." Englehardt (2010) and Paul (1992) are clear that strong critical thinking skills assist practitioners in moral reasoning. Others such as Bazerman and Tenbrunsel (2011) have recently continued this plea for critical thinking when addressing knowledge of ethical fading and bounded ethicality required to assist in moral reasoning.

Assuming critical thinking skills aid moral reasoning, the foundation for an individual's ethical competence is the ability to think critically. Some have developed the skill with an evolutionary process throughout the individual's education and life experiences. Some need instruction in how to think critically. When deciphering how we acquire critical thinking, Englehardt (2010), with reference to McPeck (1981), calls the "teaching how" of critical thinking new territory. Englehardt provides course development suggestions with intentionality to course content and course process, building on Paul and Elder's (2008) model of letting the students know how the course is designed with an introduction in the syllabus or at the first class session. Such an introduction might say:

> This class is going to be different from any class you have taken thus far because the emphasis will be on actively developing your thinking. Everything we do in this class will be designed to help you become better and better at thinking within (ethics and your profession). You will therefore not be asked to memorize information rotely. Instead you will be required to internalize information by using it actively in every class and in class

assignments. Each day we will be attempting to improve your thinking (in thinking related to this discipline). . . . You must be introduced to the fundamentals of sound thinking. Then you must regularly practice those fundamentals. Therefore I will design every class day with the primary purpose of helping you develop your (ethical) thinking, or reasoning skills. (Paul and Elder 2007, 15)

It is not unusual to use case studies or share life experiences as part of the thinking critical toolkit in the academic classroom. The best approach, though, when reflecting on policies and procedures in an organization, involves the creation of a probing model of questioning as part of the analysis. Why did such and such happen? How do you know? Why is that of importance? And, of course, who are the beneficiaries of the decisions? What are the consequences? What process did you use to identify these beneficiaries and consequences? When one thinks about this approach, one realizes that this type of critical thinking was part of almost every person at a young age. It was the first type of questioning that occurred at the age of four to six years old, when a child asked, Why? The "why" question may have irritated the parents, but it marked the first approach to knowing what was happening in the child's world. If the parent suppresses questions of why, a piece of the critical thinking process can be lost. Only with intentionality to the why approach and practice of using the "why" question can critical thinking occur.

Critical thinking practice can also occur outside the classroom. Employees and volunteers in a nonprofit can be encouraged to ask the "why" question. Meetings can be set up where there is always time for questioning. Such encouragement can create a culture of thinking about issues in a different way. Just imagine if, for every new policy or practice, there was a vetting process or time frame where employees and volunteers were invited to ask questions, including, Why are we doing this? Why should we not do this? Who benefits from the decision? What are the consequences?

Critical thinking is the foundation for ethical decision making and provides the platform for the domains and the competencies.

Context with Specific Competencies Identified (Domain 1)

Context of the decisions includes factors common to all organizations and factors unique to nonprofit organizations. To understand the context for human resources decisions, one can look at the staff composition and its multiple perspectives, pressures within the mission-driven focus of the nonprofit organization, the legal "plus" view, codes of conduct, and policies and practices (see Figure 10.3).

Figure 10.3   **Competence in Context**

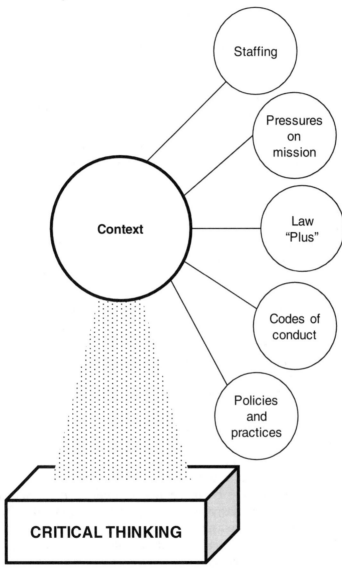

Competency 1: Identify Differences

Identifying differences is a competency needed in all managerial decision making. Because human resources decisions drive the outcomes of an organization's activities, ethical decision making needs to be part of all human resources functions. Many human resources policies and practices present ethical challenges for public, for-profit, and nonprofit organizations. Ethical decision making related to human resources systems and issues in nonprofits has an added layer of complexity, given the inclusion of a large number of volunteers in addition to the paid staff. The cast of volunteers in a nonprofit is unparalleled in either the public or for-profit sectors. It is common for nonprofits to have more volunteers than paid staff to meet the mission of the organization. It is essential to recognize the differences in multiple staffing, and thus multiple perspectives. *The first competency in creating the nonprofit ready for fulfilling its mission is the ability to identify the differences in staff and volunteers—their motivations, needs, availability, work approaches, and interest in the organization's mission.*

Competency 2: Recognize Pressures

The nonprofit organization's mission is important when considering human resources decisions. Ethics Resource Center President Patricia Harned is often referenced as stating nonprofits are different from a lot of organizations because they are mission driven and exist to address a social need not met by other entities. But, that said, nonprofits also regularly face a tremendous amount of pressure. The Ethics Resource Center acknowledges that, quite often, where there is pressure there are also pressures to compromise the standards to do the job. With a variety of pressures on the nonprofit and its individuals, a necessary competency is the ability to identify pressure when it is occurring. Additionally, one needs the skills for appropriately reacting to, resolving, and preventing those pressures from reoccurring. *This pressure recognition—with appropriate reaction, resolution, and preventions skills—is Competency 2.*

Pressures to provide services, meet stakeholders' expectations, and satisfy employees and volunteers with limited financial resources may motivate a nonprofit organization to ignore proper human resources policies, practices, and procedures. The financial pressures of the nonprofit organization can serve as catalysts for decisions about human capital (employees and volunteers). The financial pressures, though, can be mitigated with other strategic measures if the decision makers in the nonprofit organization have the ethical competence to understand and manage human resources challenges.

Competency 3: Know the Law "Plus"

Some organizations and staff cling narrowly to a legal framework for making decisions. The legal framework may take the form of state and federal laws, collective bargaining contracts, or other contracts. Astute nonprofit organization board members and managerial employees soon realize that there is more to decision making than quoting a law. After all, laws are routinely tested in the courts, resulting in numerous interpretations and changes in application over time. To complicate the use of a legal framework for decision making is the acknowledgment that not everything that happens in an organization has a referent in law. And, generally, ethicists view the law as the moral minimum; conduct cannot simply be judged by its legality. *Competency 3, then, is knowing and complying with the applicable laws, but also knowing there is more than the legal referent for decision making. Consider this the law "plus" competency.*

With so many articles, books, surveys, and media accounts of workplace ethics issues, the emphases are generally on the paid staff or the volunteer board members of the organization. The staff employee who is assigned to do the work and expected to be compensated in return, is often the focus of accounts about misbehavior or misconduct. The typical scenario, at its most basic, is that a rule or law is not followed. An offensive action is committed. A staff volunteer occasionally is part of the media blitz, especially when the volunteer's actions affect a vulnerable population, like children or the elderly. The volunteer is usually "unassigned" or "not called in for service." The management of the nonprofit organization includes the board of directors and the employees in managerial positions such as the executive director, the controller, a program director, a human resources director, or someone assigned to keep an "eyes and ears watch" on the staff. Indeed, much of what has been written about staff behavior and the ethical framework for decision making by the staff focuses on the individual—the nonmanagement employee or voluteer or the manager—who erred.

Competency 4: Use the Code of Conduct

A current and often referenced ethical compass is an organization's mission statement, accepted values, or code of conduct that should include the organization's position on ethical behavior. The code of conduct is a basic ingredient in creating ethical expectations for members of the organization. The written code may be published in the employee or volunteer handbook, posted on the organization's website, or hung on a wall in a nonpublic break room or at the entrance to the organization's offices. Staff may have been briefed about the organization's mission or values or even the code of conduct in an orientation session. Such codes usually reference items of service (client/customer first), integrity, use of the organization's resources, conflicts of interest, timeliness, and treatment of others. And, when the code is violated, someone is caught and punished—perhaps even finding his or her name on the front pages of the local newspaper. More often than not, the employee is simply "let go," and there is speculation about the "scandalous act"—not realizing the organization itself may have been responsible for a portion of the behavior. It is always easier to blame the individual than the entirety of an organization. Knowing the organization's formal code is by itself not sufficient. Those in the nonprofit also need the ability to apply the code in the design and implementation of the organization's policies and practices and in the monitoring of affiliated individuals' behavior. *The knowledge of a code of conduct and the ability to effectively apply the use of the code to individuals and the organization entity is Competency 4.*

Competency 5: Create Effective Human Resources Policies and Practices

While it may be easy to list violations of code or to point to an individual whose ethical compass is awry, this chapter asks you, the reader, to focus on the competency of creating policies and practices in the nonprofit has they pertain to staff—both the employee and the volunteer—so the nonprofit is an ethical culture. Certain policies and practices, long held as accepted human resources modus operandi, can be the cause of unethical behavior. A look at the possibilities for conflicts of interest leads to questions about who benefits from and who is harmed by a specific decision, policy, or practice. It is this duet of benefits and consequences that can provide an ethical framework for decision making. Who benefits from the policies and practices? Equally important, who does not benefit? And what are the consequences of the policies and practices? Surrounding these questions is another set of questions. What type of ethical compass or standard created the policy or practice? If an organization could change its policies and practices from situations that tempt staff to be unethical to situations promoting ethical and appropriate behavior, would the organization and thus the employees engage in ethical practices and behaviors? *Competency 5 requires the ability to create human resources policies and practices that create an ethical culture and promote ethical behavior.*

There are many human resources activities, each with its own policies, practices, and procedures. Selected for consideration in this chapter are activities with a variety of vested participants and decision opportunities ripe for ethical vulnerability. What follows are examples of challenges within human resources policies and practices and the competencies to address those challenges in specific functions to aid in the understanding of Competency 5. All of the challenges present issues of who benefits from the decision and what the consequences of the decision are. Because human capital in an organization revolves around job tasks, we start with the issue of job design in the nonprofit organization.

Competency 5a: Job Design. Determining what needs to be done—the tasks—for the organization to deliver its service is one of the first decisions. Related to the question of what needs to be done is the question of how the work or tasks will be organized and who will do the work. If too much work is assigned, employees and volunteers may ignore certain tasks or skimp on the quality of the attempted task. If the tasks are combined into single jobs requiring a combination of knowledge, skills, and abilities, it may prove to be impossible to find a competent individual with the necessary combination of skills to perform the tasks. And, if some tasks are seen as more interesting or more rewarding, these tasks will likely be completed at the expense of other more mundane or unrewarded (but necessary) tasks. *Competency 5a is the skill to design the work tasks in ways that are effective for the mission of the nonprofit and are doable, interesting, creative, and fair for those doing the tasks.*

In the nonprofit sector, the job design issue is compounded by the availability of human capital and the placement of the human capital into jobs of paid staff or volunteer staff (Bowman 2009; Hartenian 2007; Shannon 2009; Handy, Mook, and Quarter 2008). In the early days of nonprofit organizations, either all tasks were given to volunteers because there was no paid staff or the less complex work was often handed off to the volunteers. Twenty-first century workers and volunteers in nonprofit organizations have a wide variety of knowledge and skills. Tasks may be assigned to paid staff or volunteers. The decision of job design and job assignment is wrought with ethical challenges—both for those in the organization and those served by it. (Einolf 2009; Sundeen, Garcia, and Raskoff 2009; Handy and Greenspan 2009; Tang, Morrow-Howell, and Hong 2009; Brudney and Meijs 2009; Kreutzer and Jager 2011).

Compounding the issue of perception of value is the demographics of the paid staff and volunteer groups. If the volunteers are always the very young or the very old, or females, or the minority by race (or any other social identity category), one could ask why certain groups are not receiving the benefit of being placed in a paid position. The consequence of selective demographics for job tasks could set the foundation for discrimination charges among paid staff and disappointment among volunteers. Decisions at the ethical base are quickly thrown into a legal framework, with the potential for financial ramifications as well as a negative view of the organization by the volunteers.

Competency 5b: Recruitment Process. A second challenge for human resources practices is the recruitment of persons to do the organization's work. Where and how an organization recruits sends the message of who is to be included in the provision of services and who has an opportunity to be part of the nonprofit organization. When a nonprofit uses only word-of-mouth advertising or internal communications, the organization may get more staff but it is likely that the new staff will mirror the existing staff. The opportunity for new approaches and a broader range of visibility will be lost. Service recipients will end up seeing the "same faces." If an organization lists job postings only in the local newspaper, the readers of that newspaper are likely to be the only respondents. Those without access to a newspaper, or those without the habit of reading the newspaper, will lose out on the opportunity to apply for the work. And, according to media reports, younger generations and lower socioeconomic status groups are generally not regular readers of print media. An organization can determine its pool of potential paid staff and volunteers by where it decides to get the word out (including the use of social media sources) about paid and volunteer opportunities. The decisions about where and how to recruit has consequences. *The ability to make "good" recruitment process decisions is Competency 5b.*

Competency 5c: Benefits Design. Competency 5c is having the knowledge and skill of proper benefit design for the nonprofit's mission and the staff's satisfaction. Besides an employee's pay, the benefits package is of primary interest to the employee and the prospective employee. Most employees expect health care coverage, as well as some paid time off in the form of vacation pay or sick pay. These two areas raise questions of what is right and wrong—for both the organization and the employee.

1. Health care plans. Nonprofits have a variety of health care plans that may have been selected based on a board member's experience or the executive director's needs for himself/herself or for recruiting and retaining staff. The design of the health care plan is critical in meeting the needs of the employees and the needs of the organization for a human capital development purpose as well as for financial responsibility. A plan with no provision or minimal provision for family coverage may upset employees who need family coverage; conversely, a plan with provision for family coverage may upset employees who do not need family coverage.

2. Paid time off. Employees expect to have some time off, in the form of vacation or sick pay. Nonprofit organizations that require an employee to declare the reason for an absence from the workplace may force a worker into making a "less than truthful" declaration. If an employee has exhausted all her vacation time and an opportunity comes for tickets to baseball's opening day or a daughter's ballet debut at school, the employee may be tempted to call in sick, attend the event, and hope her supervisor will not be present at the same event. One could ask why the organization needs to know the reason for absence from work. Either the employee is present at work or the employee is not present. It should not be necessary to force the declaration. If an organization is concerned about time away from work, it makes more sense to declare a certain number of days available as time away from work with no specific purpose stated. That way, an employee would not have to resort to lying—which can cause some consequences for the employee's well-being and perceptions about the workplace.

Competency 5d: Performance Management. The area of performance management is not exempt from the discussion of ethical competence. The phrase *performance management* juxtaposes an organization's performance with an employee's performance. Joan Pynes (2011) puts the attention on nonprofit organization effectiveness and program measurement, noting the 1994 work of Hatry et al. stating that certain norms should guide all evaluators in organizational performance management. Pynes (2011,149) recognizes that "new cultural and social changes are affecting nonprofits," noting that the values of employees have changed and nonprofits need to "audit their human resources functions to ensure they are free from bias." Pynes's earlier work (2009) includes employee performance evaluations as integral to organizational performance management and draws attention to some of the ethical issues in the use of performance appraisals. Employee performance management in the public and private sectors is one of the few human resources systems with a record of research and publishing focusing on questions of right and wrong actions from the employee as well as right and wrong actions from the organization, apart from a mandatory legal framework (Fletcher 2001; Perrin 1998; Cheverton 2007; Kaplan 2001).

Without reference to the nonprofit sector, Werbel and Balkin (2010, 323) examine the linkages between rational choice theory and the design of human resource performance systems as factors shaping "organizational routines associated with misconduct." Their emphases on organization-specific situational factors—the proportion of performance-contingent, individual-incentive compensation in relation to base pay; discontinuous incentives; outcome-based performance evaluations versus behavior-based performance evaluations; linkages between supervisor's and employee's performance outcomes; and multiple and diverse sources of appraisals—point to the unintended negative consequences of performance management systems. The ability to design and integrate effective performance management systems is also a competency. *Performance management design is Competency 5d.*

The work of Werbel and Balkin supports the work of Kidder (2005), noting employee misconduct is influenced by both situational factors and individual components. Martin and Cullen (2006), in their meta-analysis, suggest that perceptions of ethical climate can be predictors of ethical behavior. This combination of authors, with Galang, Elsik, and Russ (1999) reminds one of the Glinda question from *Wicked:* "Are people born wicked? Or do they have wickedness thrust upon them?" The answers: yes and yes. Both employees and organizations are responsible for behavior and the ethical competence to address difficult situations in the nonprofit arena. Performance management is part of the responsibility package.

Design features of certain incentive systems are likely to create employee behavior that becomes misconduct. Consider, for example, a nonprofit with job assignments in fundraising that rewards fundraisers for dollars generated or the number of new donors contacted. If the emphasis is on the outcomes with no control for the methods to reach those outcomes, an employee might resort to creative gimmicks, gifting, and/or service provision to acquire dollars and donors. While codes of conduct from fundraising professionals (AFP 2008) note the inappropriateness of specific incentives plans for employee performance rewards systems, the temptation for nonprofit survival may create schemes or creative recognition for successful fundraisers. Or, consider the nonprofit that rewards its employees based on numbers of clients served, without consideration for the quality of service provided. The employee may benefit in the form of a pay increase, but the recipient of the service may be jeopardized by a lack of quality in the service provided. Such a consequence would not be acceptable.

Competency 5e: Training and Development Plus Labor Relations. Competency 5e is the ability to implement effective training and development activities for both employees and volunteers and to create harmonious labor relations. When an organization selects some paid staff and volunteers but ignores others for specialized training and development, a message is sent about who is valued in the nonprofit and/or who is "deficient" and needs special attention. Either perception can be problematic. An ethical organization determines and makes transparent to all the principles and criteria for training and development opportunities, as well as its philosophy in labor relations. In addition to who receives training and development is the question of what the content should be—specific operational processes or content with transference across the nonprofit organization and to other nonprofit organizations. And, in the labor relations arena comes the question of collaborative or confrontational approaches to the work environment. The answers to these questions may be predicated on available finances but is more likely based on the value the nonprofit organization places on its human capital—again, beneficiaries and consequences.

Frameworks for Right and Wrong (Domain 2)

There are more than enough ethical challenges in the human resources systems of nonprofit organizations to keep the designers and implementers of such systems busy reflecting on what is right and what is wrong for a given organization and the ethical competencies needed to excel in the nonprofit environment. Frameworks can provide the boundaries for critical thinking.

Competency 6. Discerning the Different Frameworks
and Applying the Correct One

Disciplines of inquiry, codes, laws, position papers, personal experiences, and expert views combine to form frameworks for understanding behavior. The specific frameworks about ethical decision making assist in organizing thoughts about ethical behavior. Thus, it is recommended that those interested in doing what's right and avoiding what's wrong have some sense of the variety of frameworks for determining right and wrong (Kennedy and Malatesa 2010; Walton, Stearns, and Crespy 1997). The classical ethical frameworks of beneficiaries/consequences, duty, and virtue are recognized approaches, useable for the practitioner on a personal and organizational basis (see Figure 10.4).

One framework for determining right and wrong is the practice of identifying beneficiaries and consequences. This approach includes the legal, financial, and societal foci and is linked to the duties of the organization and the virtues perceived as part of moral theory in practical ethics.

Part of the thinking about beneficiaries and consequences includes asking who benefits from a particular policy and describing the consequences. Then, moving forward, we again must ask who might feel the impact of the consequences. In a nonprofit, the "who" could be any one of the following: the board of directors or any one board member, the executive director, the employees, the volunteers, the service-recipients, the donors, an interested service provider (health care insurance organization, employment agency, legal counsel, and so on), and any other stakeholder or partnering entity (a private or governmental entity engaged in a shared service provision with the nonprofit organization). Sometimes the conflicts of beneficiaries are not readily apparent; other times they are obvious. When a board member suggests a certain health care plan and it happens to be the business of the board member to sell health care plans, the suggestion may benefit the board member but

Figure 10.4   **Frameworks for Right and Wrong**

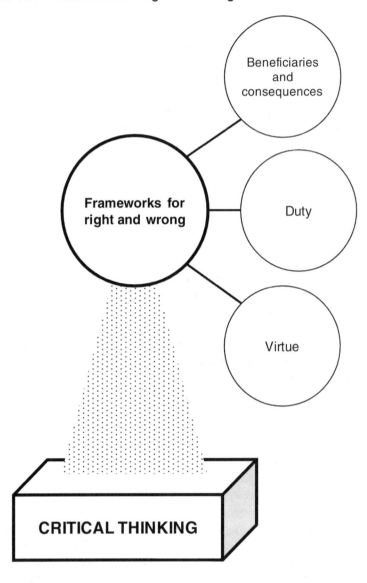

not be in the best interest of the nonprofit. The nonprofit would need a way to objectively determine the best plan for the organization. Creating an objective analysis becomes a regular activity of the ethically competent person and the organization. The competency of understanding benefits and consequences, as described next, brings us back to the foundation of critical thinking.

The consequences question puts the attention on the individual and organization, too, but with an added time horizon and a linking or network for the organization. Decisions come with both immediate and long-term impacts. The ethical approach is to consider both. The multi-perspective becomes part of our context domain: Does a decision about how and where to advertise have an impact on financial resources? Does a decision about benefit practices affect financial resources? Does a decision about job design create a certain culture in the organization of usefulness and value of volunteers and employees? Does a compensation plan create possible scrutiny by the donors? The answer to all of these questions is "of course." No decision stands alone. No decision is void of consequences. The test is to identify the consequences for each decision, and then make the best possible decision based on that consideration.

The beneficiaries and consequences model is compatible with the classical ethical frameworks found in much of the ethics literature and outlined by the Center for Ethical Deliberation (2010). There is more to examining human resources decisions than just looking at beneficiaries and consequences. The beneficiaries and consequences approach, though, is the first step in deliberating about ethical treatment of the staff. This approach draws attention to the likely outcomes of the various courses of action one could choose. If this is not enough, two other classical frameworks could be utilized: (1) the duty framework focuses on the obligations we have in various kinds of situations, and (2) the virtue framework draws attention to the character traits that motivate people to act in various ways. The duty framework manifests itself through actions; the virtue framework reveals what an individual's actions show about his character.

The virtue framework is very personal, with attention to the individual, and not easily generalizable to the organization as a whole—other than to the values statements of the organization. The duty/obligation approach, often rooted in law, can be too narrow, but admittedly is easier to test. The beneficiaries and consequences approach is an understandable and useable approach for nonprofits and can efficiently and effectively guide human resources decisions. In an ideal world, all three approaches would be used together to yield effective decision making. Knowing the options from the ethical frameworks allows us to talk about the competence needed for ethical decision making regarding human resources policies and practices in nonprofits.

How to distinguish right from wrong is learned in a variety of places—the classroom, the home, the court of law, the religious institution, the workplace, the volunteer setting, and through everyday encounters. It seems reasonable for the academic approach to provide an introduction to the classical ethical frameworks, minimally in a single course early in a student's program of study, but better yet in every course. If a university program (such as public or nonprofit administration and leadership) required all faculty to understand several approaches to ethical decision making and then to incorporate those approaches in all courses, what a difference could be made in the classroom or when moving out of the classroom and into the workplace. Think of the conversations that would occur when faculty grappled with ethical frameworks prior to incorporating them into courses. This approach would be more than an ethics issue across the curriculum; this approach could result in a laboratory of ethics for the faculty.

Outside the classroom and in the nonprofit organization, the introduction to classical ethical frameworks for decision making should be part of every board of directors' orientation session and employee and volunteer training and development sessions. *The ability to understand and differentiate among a variety of frameworks and apply the appropriate framework for the situation needing a decision is Competency 6.*

The "Whole" of Human Resources Systems and Connections to Other Systems Within and Outside the Organization (Domain 3)

Competency 7: Integrate Human Resources Systems and Link to Other Systems

To study and understand only one or a few parts of human resources systems in organizations limits the ability to use and examine any one part, let alone all, of the human resources activities in an organization. An HR representative with a less-than-sufficient understanding of compensation practices is unqualified to advise workers in an organization about employment policies. Making decisions about training and development or labor relations without understanding job design or recognition systems can lead to useless content and wasted time for employees and volunteers. The web of systems in the organization (human resources, finance, facilities, external relations, political, history) is critical to seeing a big picture about the employees, the volunteers, and their relationship to the mission of the nonprofit organization. Big picture thinking is necessary. Only when boundary spanning occurs does the nonprofit human resources system operate effectively and efficiently. *The ability to understand and integrate the "whole" human resources system with the development of boundary spanning and border crossing to systems within and outside the nonprofit is Competency 7* (see Figure 10.5).

Academic programs preparing nonprofit administrators must include the entirety of human resources systems and related issues and networks in course requirements. Programs allowing students to meet their human resources requirements with selected courses only in employment matters or only in

Figure 10.5 **Whole HR and Systems**

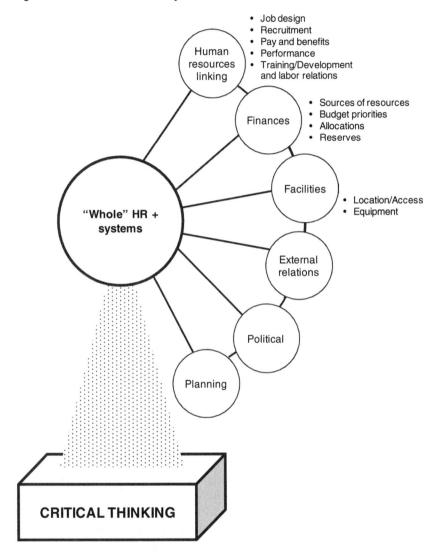

training and development or only in compensation or only in volunteer recruitment are lacking the synergy among the components of human resources required to understand the decision making affecting employees and volunteers in the nonprofit organization.

Administrators in nonprofit organizations must recognize that human resources systems are not only about paid employees. Volunteers, as part of the human capital in the nonprofit organization, must also be factored into the understanding of how an organization best provides its services to its clients. Orientations for volunteers where critical thinking techniques are used to explain codes of conduct, frameworks for ethical decision making, multiple perspectives, basic analytical tools, and the roles and responsibilities of paid staff and volunteers in their service to the organization and its service recipients are the beginning step for productive volunteer experiences. Orientation alone is not enough. Volunteers, like paid staff, need opportunities to renew their understanding of ethical decision making and to share their applications of what they have learned.

Desire for Fairness, Equitable Treatment, and Respect for All Persons (Domain 4)

The final domain is the most difficult one to describe; especially tricky is specifying the "how" of the competencies (see Figure 10.6).

Determining the desire for fairness, equitable treatment, and respect for all persons is difficult to identify, teach, and measure. We all know people who stand up for a cause or who at some point in time advocate for a person or a group of people. We may even observe those who generally put others ahead of themselves or question how people are viewed and treated in an organization. However, to have the desire for fairness, equitable treatment, and respect for all persons is complex beyond any ordinary means of education and measurement. This desire for fairness, equitable treatment, and respect for all persons is the very heart of ethics and the foundation for human resources decision making in nonprofit organizations.

The desire to do what is ethical is difficult (perhaps even impossible) to teach, but it is easy to measure by observation. One approach to teaching this desire is to create a classroom exercise or conduct a class for an entire semester in an unorthodox way—one in which the student takes on the persona of another and does not refer to himself in any way. The student must always be in someone else's situation—walking in "the other person's shoes" for the entire course. I have used this assignment for roles in gender, age, client, provider, staff, volunteer, policymaker, and policy beneficiary with the result of "aha" moments in the classroom and significant changes in perspective and development of ethical competence, as measured through pre- and post-course delivery. Students often make a point of mentioning on the course evaluations the difficulty and value of being in "the other person's shoes for a long period of time" (meaning a semester) as the way to test one's drive for fairness and respect.

Outside the classroom and into the nonprofit organization, the taking on of another persona for a day or week or month might be useful. What if the

Figure 10.6 **Desire for Fairness**

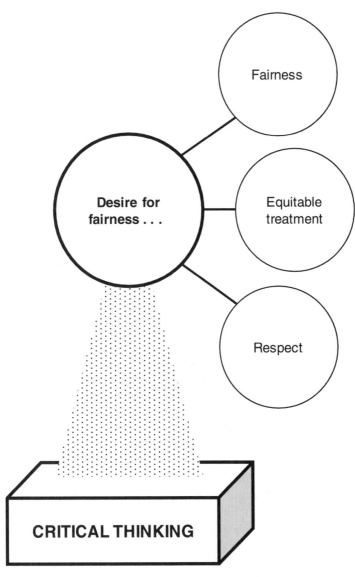

board members were asked to be the direct service providers? What if the paid staff were asked to take on the volunteers' activities? What if volunteers were asked (and paid) to take on the paid employees' tasks? Simulation experiences in training board members, paid employees, and volunteers may help in the development of desire for fairness. Such a desire is difficult to foster in a self-obsessed society and necessitates practice in looking out for others and valuing the community over the individual. *This domain of desire requires Competency 8, the ability to know and do what is right as evidenced by the following actions: analyzing competing values and perspectives and then demonstrating fairness in decision making; considering options but always providing equitable treatment across the nonprofit; and showing respect to others in all situations, relationships, and oral and written communications.* Competency 8 may be the most difficult to accomplish and measure. The desire for fair, equitable, and respectful treatment of others might not be possible for some—but the obligation of treating others fairly may be present. Perhaps that is enough.

Comparisons of Perspectives on Ethical Competence

Examining existing codes or statements on ethics in organizations with known influence on the nonprofit sector can test one's interest in the desire for fairness, equitable treatment, and respect as well as the other components of ethical competence. What is not obvious in the statements or codes is the need for, and consistent use of, critical thinking and the actual desire to be fair, provide equitable treatment, and show respect to others as part of ethical competence. Perhaps these are assumed. Rhode and Packel (2009) remind us of the four crucial factors influencing ethical conduct: moral awareness, moral decision making, moral intent, and moral action. Ethical competence becomes evident only when an individual or the nonprofit deliberately fosters moral awareness and moral decision making and places uncompromising value on fairness and equitable treatment, such that moral intent and moral action occur.

Perhaps it is beneficial at this point to take a look at several codes of ethics for comparison to the model presented in this chapter. On January 29, 2004, the Independent Sector Board of Directors approved a Code of Ethics for Nonprofit and Philanthropic Organizations (Independent Sector 2004). Pertinent to this chapter for individuals as well as the organization are the following:

All staff, board members and volunteers of Independent Sector act with honesty, integrity and openness, . . .

[The organization] promotes a working environment that values respect, fairness and integrity. . . .

The board . . .
• Ensures that its members have the requisite skills and experience to carry out their duties; . . .

- Has a conflict of interest policy; . . .
- Is responsible for the hiring, firing and regular review . . . and ensures that the compensation of the chief executive officer is reasonable and appropriate; . . .
- Ensures that the organization promotes working relationships with board members, staff, volunteers, and program beneficiaries that are based on mutual respect, fairness and openness; [and]
- Ensures that the organization is fair and inclusive in its hiring and promotion policies and practices for all board, staff and volunteer positions. . . .

[The organization] is knowledgeable of and complies with all laws, regulations and applicable international conventions. . . .

[The organization] . . .
- Compensates staff, and any others who may receive compensation, reasonably and appropriately. . . .

[The organization] has a policy of promoting inclusiveness, . . . its staff, board and volunteers reflect diversity, [and it] takes meaningful steps to promote inclusiveness in its hiring, retention, promotion, board recruitment and constituencies served. . . .

The Independent Sector Code of Ethics creates a template for observing evidence of ethical behavior with an emphasis on the roles of the board and the organization. The preface to the Code notes "an organization is defined by the people who work for it, and that those people, board members, executive leaders, staff, and volunteers must demonstrate their ongoing commitment to the core values of integrity, honesty, fairness, openness, respect, and responsibility . . . [and] values must be supported by high ethical standards . . . [such as] fostering discussion on ethical issues, promoting transparency" and so on. What is missing from this code is the "how" in reference to maintaining integrity, honesty, fairness, openness, respect, and responsibility. The model proposed for ethical competence in this chapter provides some of the "how"—engaging in critical thinking, using context, understanding frameworks for right and wrong, analyzing beneficiaries and consequences, integrating the "whole" of human resources with connection to other systems, and although difficult to measure, having a real desire to be fair, equitable, and respectful.

From the education perspective, the Nonprofit Academic Centers Council (NACC), a membership association of academic centers and programs at accredited colleges and universities that focuses on the study of nonprofit organizations, provides curricular guidelines for graduate study with inclusion of the need to address ethics and values, including:

- the teaching of foundations and theories of ethics as a discipline and as applied in order to make ethical decisions;
- standards of codes of conduct that are appropriate to professionals and volunteers;
- the role, value, and dynamics of volunteerism in carrying out the work;
- issues of supervision and human resource management systems and practices relevant to both paid and unpaid employees; and
- the dimensions and dynamics of individual and organizational diversity within the nonprofit sector and their implications for effective human resource management. (NACC 2007)

The NACC's curricular guidelines address parts of the model proposed in this chapter with attention given to selected context, frameworks for right and wrong, and the integration of HR activities. What is not identified is the need for critical thinking.

The Nonprofit Leadership Alliance (formerly American Humanics), in its list of competencies (prior to 2012) identified for undergraduate programs in nonprofit youth and human services management, calls attention to "foundation competencies," including a focus on personal attributes ("the importance of ethical behavior") and professional and development competencies in human resource development, supervision, and effective decision making. Again, this set of competencies includes ethical behavior, but without specific definition of what is meant by the activities being measured. It references the whole of HR and maybe one could infer that effective decision making utilized critical thinking. As the Nonprofit Leadership Alliance revises its competencies in 2012, it is expected to be more complete in describing the type of behavior that can be expected when competencies are measured.

Other organizations with nonprofit education initiatives such as the American Society for Public Administration (ASPA), the National Association of the Schools of Public Affairs and Administration (NASPAA), and the Association for Research on Nonprofit Organizations and Voluntary Action (ARNOVA) also have codes of ethics or provide commentary on ethics and ethical competence. The National Association of Social Workers addresses broad areas of ethical decision making by specifying ethical responsibilities to clients, colleagues, practice settings, professionals, the social work profession, and society (NASW 2008). Similarly, the American College of Healthcare Executives (ACHE) widens the code with ethical responsibility of the individual extending to the profession, patients, the organization, other employees, and the community/society (ACHE 2011). Executives in the fields of social work and health care place emphasis on the individual accountability and ethical competencies needed in their professions.

In contrast to several organizations' codes and guidelines for ethical competence, this chapter includes the components of critical thinking and desire for fairness, equitable treatment, and respect as necessary components for ethical competence. These are difficult components. It is easier to teach critical thinking than desire, but both are necessary.

Evaluation of Ethical Competence

Ethical competence makes itself known. One can test understanding of context, knowledge of ethical frameworks, and the "whole" of human resources systems. One can see and hear evidence of competence in individuals and in nonprofits where the "why" question is utilized. A desire to treat others with respect will be made known in behavior. Observation by others becomes the means of evaluation of competencies identified in any individual. The individual's declaration—"I am an ethical decision maker"—means nothing without verification by others. Bazerman and Tenbrunsel (2011, 22) affirm the verification need because "people behave in ways that may be inconsistent with their own personal values." Their notion that we experience gaps between who we believe ourselves to be and who we actually are is related to the problem of "bounded awareness" (2011, 7). Observation by others provides the reality check. The very concept of ethics is community oriented. The ethical decision maker of human resources decisions in the nonprofit organization will create an organization where all staff are treated fairly, equitably, and with respect—and the staff (employees and volunteers) know it, believe it, and live it. Complaints about staff will be minimal. Service-recipients will receive what they need, when they need it, in accordance with the resources available to the organization. The mission is accomplished. Misconduct and misbehaviors? Well, that's easy. In the perfect world, they don't exist! And, of course, there are the results of no litigation, no bad press, and an abundance of those wanting to work for and volunteer in the organization. Donors' dollars pour in because there is confidence that the organization knows what it is doing and why it exists. A focus on ethical decision making by individuals in mission-delivering nonprofits will create ethical organizations with ethical human resources policies and practices. In addition, ethical nonprofits will foster ethical behavior in paid staff and volunteers in nonprofits.

Conclusion

In this chapter, individual behaviors and the organizational context of nonprofit organizations were explored to understand the need for ethical competence. Examples of problematic human resources policies and practices were provided. A preference for the benefits/beneficiaries and consequences decision-making process was used. Domains of competence were identified, among them understanding context, utilizing frameworks for determining right and wrong, knowing the "whole" of human resources systems, and desiring fairness, equitable treatment, and respect for all persons. Critical thinking stands as the foundation for all the domains. This framework is individual-focused, but it becomes the framework of the organization as the individuals in the aggregate become the organization. The individual has an impact on the organization, and the organization has an impact on the individual.

These components were compared with recommendations from the Independent Sector, the Nonprofit Academic Centers Council, the Nonprofit Leadership Alliance, the National Association of Social Workers, and the American College of Healthcare Executives. While many of the components are similar in the comparison, this chapter places the focus on the need for critical thinking among all in the nonprofit organization and the a priori need for a desire to be fair, equitable in treatment of staff and volunteers, and respectful to all. It is acknowledged that ethical competence is learned to varying degrees in a variety of settings, with the caveat expressed by Rhode and Packel (2009) that people vary in their capacity for moral judgment and moral behavior. It is also acknowledged that there is a need for additional study of ethical competence in nonprofits, especially in the area of moral intent on the part of individuals and the nonprofits. It is the hope of the author that this chapter piques the interest of those trying to understand and practice ethical competence in nonprofit organizations with the goals of improved decision making, fairness to the organization's paid staff and volunteers, and outstanding provision of services to the public.

References

American College of Healthcare Executives (ACHE). 2011. *ACHE Code of Ethics.* Amended November 14. http://www.ache.org/abt_ache/code.cfm.
Association of Fundraising Professionals (AFP). 2008. *Code of Ethical Principles and Standards.* Report, revised October. Arlington, VA: AFP. http://www.afpnet.org/files/ContentDocuments/CodeOfEthicsLong.pdf.
Bazerman, M.H., and A.E. Tenbrunsel. 2011. *Blind Spots: Why We Fail to Do What's Right and What to Do About It.* Princeton, NJ: Princeton University Press.

Boucher, T., and S. Hudspeth. 2008. *Ethics and the Nonprofit.* Report, December. Wilton, CT: Commonfund. http://www.commonfund.org/InvestorResources/Publications/White%20Papers/Ethics%20and%20the%20Nonprofit.pdf (accessed September 5, 2011).

Bowman, W. 2009. The economic value of volunteers to nonprofit organizations. *Nonprofit Management and Leadership* 19(4): 491–506.

Brudney, J.L., and L.C.P.M. Meijs. 2009. It ain't natural: Toward a new (natural) resource conceptualization for volunteer management. *Nonprofit and Voluntary Sector Quarterly* 38(4): 564–581.

Center for Ethical Deliberation. 2010. Overview of the CED Guided Deliberation Process. http://mcb.unco.edu/ced/frameworks/.

Cheverton, J. 2007. Holding our own: Value and performance in nonprofit organisations. *Australian Journal of Social Sciences* 42(3): 427–436.

Einolf, C.J. 2009. Will the boomers volunteer during retirement? Comparing the baby boom, silent, and long civic cohorts. *Nonprofit and Voluntary Sector Quarterly* 38(2): 181–199.

Englehardt, E. 2010. *Critical Thinking and Ethics Across the Curriculum.* Paper presentation May 20, Western Michigan University, Kalamazoo, MI.

Ethics Resource Center. 2008. *National Nonprofit Ethics Survey: An Inside View of Nonprofit Sector Ethics, 2007.* Report. Arlington, VA: Ethics Resource Center. http://www.ethics.org/files/u5/ERC_s_National_Nonprofit_Ethics_Survey.pdf (accessed September 4, 2010).

Facione, P.A. 1990. *Critical Thinking: A Statement of Expert Consensus for Purposes of Education Assessment and Instruction—Executive Summary.* American Philosophical Association Delphi Research Report and ERIC Doc. No. ED315423. Millbrae, CA: The California Academic Press.

Fletcher, C. 2001. Performance appraisal and management: A multi-level analysis. *Journal of Occupational and Organizational Psychology* 73: 473–487.

Galang, M.C., W. Elsik, and G.S. Russ. 1999. Legitimacy in human resources management. In *Research in Personnel and Human Resource Management,* ed. G.R. Ferris, 41–79. Stamford, CT: JAI Press.

Greenlee, J., M. Fischer, T. Gordon, and E. Keating. 2007. How to steal from a nonprofit: Who does it and how to prevent it. *The Nonprofit Quarterly* (Winter): 28–32.

Handy, F., and I. Greenspan. 2009. Immigrant volunteering: A stepping stone to integration. *Nonprofit and Voluntary Sector Quarterly* 38(6): 956–982.

Handy, F., L. Mook, and J. Quarter. 2008. The interchangeability of paid staff and volunteers in nonprofit organizations. *Nonprofit and Voluntary Sector Quarterly* 37(1): 76–92.

Harshbarger, S., and A. Crafts. 2007. The whistle-blower: Policy challenges for nonprofits. *The Nonprofit Quarterly* (Winter): 36–41.

Hartenian, L.S. 2007. Nonprofit agency dependence on direct service and indirect support volunteers. *Nonprofit Management and Leadership* 17(3): 319–334.

Hatry, H.P., K.G. Newcomber, and J.S. Wholey 1994. Conclusion: Improving evaluation activities and results. In *The Handbook of Practical Program Evaluation,* ed. J.S. Wholey, H.P. Hatry, and K.E. Newcomber, 590–601. San Francisco: Jossey-Bass.

Independent Sector. 2004. *Code of Ethics for Nonprofit and Philanthropic Organiza-*

tions. http://www.independentsector.org/code_of_ethics (accessed December 20, 2010).

Kaplan, R.S. 2001. Strategic performance measurement and management in nonprofit organizations. *Nonprofit Management and Leadership* 11(3): 353–370.

Kennedy, S.S., and D. Malatesta. 2010. Safeguarding the public trust: Can administrative ethics be taught? *Journal of Public Affairs Education* 16(2): 161–180.

Kidder, D.L. 2005. Is it "who I am," "what I can get away with," "or what you've done to me"? A multi-theory examination of employee misconduct. *Journal of Business Ethics* 57: 389–398.

Kreutzer, K., and U. Jager. 2011. Volunteering versus managerialism: Conflict over organizational identity in voluntary organizations. *Nonprofit and Voluntary Sector Quarterly* 40(4): 634–661.

Liggett, B. 2010. *Problematic HR practices in U.S. nonprofit organizations.* Working Paper.

Martin, K.D., and J.B. Cullen. 2006. Continuities and extension of ethical climate theory: A meta-analytic review. *Journal of Business Ethics* 69: 175–194.

McPeck, J.E. 1981. *Teaching Critical Thinking.* New York: Routledge.

National Association of Social Workers (NASW). 2008. Code of ethics of the National Association of Social Workers. http://www.naswdc.org/pubs/code/code.asp (accessed September 6, 2011).

Nonprofit Academic Centers Council (NACC). 2007. *Curricular Guidelines for Undergraduate Study in Nonprofit Leadership, the Nonprofit Sector and Philanthropy.* Cleveland, OH: NACC. http://www.naccouncil.org/pdf/UnderGradCG07.pdf.

Nonprofit Leadership Alliance (NLA). 2012. *Competency Listing.* Kansas City, MO. http://www.nonprofitleadershipalliance.org/cnp/Our Core Competencies.pdf (accessed September 2, 2012).

Paul, R.W. 1992. *Critical Thinking: What Every Person Needs to Survive in a Rapidly Changing World.* Santa Rosa, CA: Foundation for Critical Thinking Press.

Paul, R., and L. Elder. 2007. *A Miniature Thinker's Guide for Those Who Teach on How to Improve Student Learning: 30 Practical Ideas.* Dillon Beach, CA: Foundation for Critical Thinking Press.

———. 2008. *The Miniature Guide to Critical Thinking: Concepts and Tools.* Dillon Beach, CA: Foundation for Critical Thinking Press.

Perrin, B. 1998. Effective use and misuse of performance measurement. *American Journal of Evaluation* 18(3): 367–381.

Pynes, J. 2009. *Human Resources Management for Public and Nonprofit Organizations.* San Francisco: Jossey-Bass.

———. 2011. *Effective Nonprofit Management.* Armonk, NY: M.E. Sharpe.

Rhode, D.L., and A.K. Packel. 2009. Ethics and nonprofits. *Stanford Social Innovation Review* 7(3): 29–35.

Schwartz, S. 2003. *Wicked.* Music and lyrics. Book by Winnie Holzman. Based on the novel *Wicked: The Life and Times of the Wicked Witch of the West,* by Gregory Maguire. New York: HarperCollins, 1995. http://web.archive.org/web/20070316231057/libretto.musicals.ru/text.php?textid=566&language=1 (accessed August 21, 2010).

Shannon, C.S. 2009. An untapped resource: Understanding volunteers aged 8–12. *Nonprofit and Voluntary Sector Quarterly* 38(5): 828–845.

Sundeen, R.A., C. Garcia, and S.A. Raskoff. 2009. Ethnicity, acculturation, and volunteering to organizations. *Nonprofit and Voluntary Sector Quarterly* 38(6): 929–955.

Tang, F., N. Morrow-Howell, and S. Hong. 2009. Inclusion of diverse older populations in volunteering: The importance of institutional facilitation. *Nonprofit and Voluntary Sector Quarterly* 38(5): 810–827.

Walton, J.R., J.M. Stearns, and C.T. Crespy. 1997. Integrating ethics into the public administration curriculum: A three-step process. *Journal of Policy Analysis and Management* 16(3): 470–483.

Wells, J.T., and J.D. Gill. 2007. Assessing fraud risk. *The Nonprofit Quarterly* (Winter): 33–84.

Werbel, J., and D.B. Balkin. 2010. Are human resource practices linked to employee misconduct? A rational choice perspective. *Human Resource Management Review* 20: 317–326.

White, D. 2010. *The Nonprofit Challenge: Integrating Ethics into the Purpose and Promise of Our Nation's Charities.* New York: Palgrave Macmillan.

Part IV

Conclusion

11

The Road Ahead

Donald C. Menzel and Terry L. Cooper

*Skeptics will reply that courses in moral reasoning have
no impact on behavior, but this criticism seems
overdrawn. To be sure, no instruction can suffice
to turn a scoundrel into a virtuous human being.*

—Former Harvard University President Derek Bok
(1971–91 and 2006–7)

The idea and ideal of achieving ethical competence for public service leadership is not wishful thinking. It is, as noted at the outset of this book, a challenging lifelong pursuit. You might say that after reading and thinking about ethical competence in business, social work, law, public administration, and the world of nonprofits, you've discovered that the challenge is indeed real. But still, you wonder how to get started on the path to ethical competence. You have already taken the first step with your motivation to acquire ethical competence.

Next Steps

Before moving forward, let's remind ourselves what the terminology surrounding competence means. *Competence* is a noun that can be qualified by an adjective, e.g., she has a moderate (or low or high) level of competence to run an organization. *Competent* indicates that one has achieved a sufficient level of competence to meet the standards for a profession, practice, craft, or trade that is typically certified by the granting of a license, passing an exam, completing an apprenticeship, receiving an academic degree, or some combination of these.

Competency is a much trickier word that has crept into our vocabulary without much consensus about its meaning; therefore, it is used in various, often conflicting, ways. In this volume, we reserve this term for references to sets of specific skills, knowledge, and attitudes that are components of *competence*, among them (1) the ability to perceive ethical problems; (2) the possession of ethical analysis skills; (3) a knowledge of ethical theories; (4) an understanding of how organization design encourages or impedes ethical decision making and conduct; (5) the strength of character to act on one's ethical conclusions; and (6) the holding of positive attitudes toward the importance of ethical conduct. The most appropriate use in this context would be references to *competencies* that are necessary to have some degree of *competence* and ultimately to be deemed *competent* in a practice, profession, craft, or trade. One might use *competency* appropriately to refer to a competency-based approach to ethics training, for example. Generally, this word has been overused in recent discourse and more often than not is used inappropriately.

To relate this terminology to the context of our book, the National Association of Schools of Public Affairs and Administration (NASPAA) is not proposing to determine the *competence* of graduates, but it is concerned in the accreditation process with whether or not certain *competencies*—i.e., specific skills, knowledge, traits, and attitudes that are identified as essential components of *competence*—are being taught or cultivated. Since there is no universal exam for the field, such as the bar exam or the medical board exams, to certify that one is *competent* in public administration (PA), NASPAA is taking the development of these *competencies* that are components of *competence* to be sufficient indicators that graduates have acquired sufficient *competence* to be deemed *competent* in practice.

What more do we need to know about departing on this journey? First, let's recall the roots of ethical behavior, especially as they pertain to the study and practice of public administration. The early roots, of course, are home, family, church, school, and friends. This is not to dismiss the possibility of ethics as an innate quality, but it is to suggest that, as one progresses to adulthood, the "rights" and "wrongs" become more plentiful and, all too often, confusing. And, when we become aspiring professionals, our values are not really formed until we begin professional education and then professional practice.

Philosophers of ethics have long recognized these challenges and have formulated ethical frameworks such as virtue theory, deontological (duty/ principles) doctrine, and teleological (instrumentalism, also referred to as consequentialism) doctrine to help one make sense out of ethical dilemmas. Indeed, James Svara (2007) asserts that public administrators rely heavily on these frameworks that he labels the "ethics triangle."

Among the contributors and the chapter diversity in this book, there is certainly a consensus that ethical competence requires one to have knowledge of these important frameworks, along with the capability, if not the courage, to act on them when that moment arrives, as surely it will in the life of a professional administrator. Thus, a significant starting point is knowledge and awareness.

Second, beyond the early stages of learning to be ethical, one must know the norms and the dos and don'ts of her particular field of work. The chapters on social work, law, and public administration highlight the diversity of context and its importance in framing the parameters of ethical competence. Perhaps Thomas Jefferson who is reported to have remarked—"When a man assumes a public trust he should consider himself a public property"—characterizes an essential competency boundary in public affairs and administration. Yet, there is no single boundary size that fits all professions and practices. Thus, it is the responsibility of the individual to know the ethical boundaries of her occupation.

Of course, these boundaries are not just out there hovering over professionals like a spaceship. Rather, they are taught and learned in a variety of ways, one of which is through formal education. Schools of public affairs and administration, social work, law, and more are the usual custodians of the learning that contributes to ethical competence. While there remains much debate about how the custodians carry out their responsibilities via dedicated courses or across the curriculum programs, there is no debate about the wisdom of accepting this responsibility. Indeed, to ensure that the work gets done in a consistent and high-quality manner, NASPAA began more than three decades ago to develop standards for managerial competence that included ethical competence.

These starting points for the departure on the journey to ethical competence are just that in the career of public service professionals. Along the route, there are "pauses" that are also essential.

Pauses

There are many pauses—opportunities to stop and take stock—in the journey to achieving ethical competence. Most stops are planned, but on occasion an unplanned stop, if not a jolt, can occur. Interestingly, there is evolving evidence that the ethical learning and experiential processes one encounters do little, perhaps nothing, to change a fundamentally unethical person into an ethical person. There is a burgeoning literature that asserts individuals who want to be unethical cannot be taught to be ethical (see Shu, Gino, and Bazerman 2011; Haidt 2001; Butterfield, Treviño, and Weaver 2000; Tetlock and Lerner 1999). Rather, organizational reward and punishment processes can only episodically influence unethical behavior. A few of these studies have linked the propensity to act unethically with a lower

278 DONALD C. MENZEL AND TERRY L. COOPER

level of ethical reasoning on Kohlberg's scale. Most important, men and women who want to be people of integrity and pursue ethically competent professional careers need reinforcement from time to time. Thus, pauses are helpful in this regard. There are four noteworthy pauses to consider: ethics training opportunities; professional association membership; the unexpected ethical dilemma; and yes, exercising one's moral imagination, perhaps through daydreaming.

Ethics Training

There are a growing number of ethics sensitivity and reasoning training opportunities provided by local and state governments, university institutes, state associations of public administrators, private consultants, and professional membership organizations such the International City/County Management Association (ICMA) and the National Association of Social Workers (NASW). The training varies in content and medium, with some putting an emphasis on "how to stay out of trouble," i.e., know the rules, regulations, and laws. This "gotcha" approach is a "low road" approach. Others put an emphasis on equipping individuals with the reasoning to learn how to avoid and resolve ethical quandaries. This "high road" approach is becoming increasingly popular among all providers (see Menzel 2012). While person-to-person, small group training is commonplace, there has been a rapid expansion of web-based, online ethics training. The effectiveness of online training is arguable, although a similar statement might be made about face-to-face training. Assessments of the effectiveness of ethics training (online or otherwise) is an under-researched area. Still, there is little doubt that ethics training is growing and can be an important pause for professionals in public service who seek reinforcement (see Menzel 2012).

Professional Associations

Associations such as the ICMA and NASW are at the forefront of reinforcing the ethical values and behaviors of their members. This is typically done through the development and implementation of a code of ethics that the membership embraces. And in these two associations, the members are more than empty receptacles where ethical values are lodged. Rather, the members are advocates of ethical behavior, and there is wide agreement that ethical competence is necessary to carry out their work as public service leaders (see Chapter 7 by Frederic Reamer).

Another professional association with a more homogeneous membership is the American Bar Association (ABA). Lawyering, of course, is a multifaceted enterprise, and as Roberts points out in Chapter 9, it is quite challenging for those in the employ of public agencies to be able to know when they or their colleagues are ethically competent practitioners. The ABA and law schools along with the 50 states promote legal competence that typically subsumes ethical competence. Still, both legal and ethical competence are defined in part when a would-be lawyer sits for the bar exam. Failure to pass the bar exam can be interpreted as incompetency.

The practice of law as suggested above can take place in the private sector, government, or quasi-public service realm in the form of contracted work done by city attorneys in smaller communities. Critics of lawyers' ethical behavior point to the commodification of law that often confounds the meaning of ethical competence in public sector agencies at local, state, and federal levels of government in the United States. Who, Roberts asks, is the public service lawyer's client? The employing agency? The public? These troubling questions do not lend themselves to easy answers.

Some professional associations lack a homogeneous membership and are therefore challenged in different ways to provide and reinforce ethics values essential to the achievement of ethical competence. One association discussed at some length in this volume is the American Society for Public Administration (ASPA), an umbrella association with membership that includes professionals in diverse fields, students, and university faculty who teach public administration (see Chapter 8 by Jeremy Plant). ASPA was founded in 1939 at the height of the New Deal to build a professional workforce in government. In 1981, ASPA's National Council adopted a set of moral principles. Three years later, the Council approved a Code of Ethics that was subsequently revised in1994. ASPA members are not required to adhere to the Code; they are given the option to sign or not sign a statement on the membership application that "I have read and agree with ASPA's Code of Ethics." Given the uncertainty of the Code's place in the life of the membership, there is no meaningful enforcement mechanism for members who may be accused of unethical behavior.

Nonetheless, ASPA offers its members many opportunities to reinforce their ethical worldviews through conferences, workshops, webinars, journals such as *Public Integrity* and *Public Administration Review*, and participation in the ASPA Section on Ethics (see ASPA 2012).

Unexpected Pauses

Have you ever been accused of doing something unethical? Hopefully not, but it can happen . . . and if it does, most everything comes to a stop in your "normal" day-to-day life. If the accusation is sufficiently serious and you hold a position of public trust, you may find yourself sitting before an ethics commission or some other body in your community or state that is charged with enforcing local or state ethics rules. Recall the case in Chapter 1 about the county administrator who was accused by a citizen of violating the city's charter when she "gave" herself a pay raise? Months dragged by while the county commission wrestled with her case and in the end fired her for cause. The implications and insinuations made by the local media and by authors of letters to the editor were, no doubt, difficult for the administrator to endure. The state ethics commission concluded that there was "probable cause" she had violated the county charter when she did not bring the matter of the pay raise to her commission bosses. In response, the administrator appealed the findings to an administrative law judge, who in turn ruled that she had not "willfully and corruptly"—meaning with wrongful intent—misused her office. The judge recommended to the state ethics commission that the case be dismissed, but that did little to alleviate the sting of local media reports (*Tampa Bay Times* staff 2012; Varian 2012).

This pause is not the kind one wants to experience. There are other experiential pauses, less onerous, that can foster ethical learning and contribute to becoming more ethically competent. For example, one can unknowingly and unwittingly act in a manner that presents the appearance of unethical behavior. Appearances matter in public life, and a competent ethical administrator must always have his antenna sensitized for those instances and circumstances that appear troublesome. Easier said than done? Without question, but even if an appearance of wrongdoing does occur, it can be a wake-up call on the road to ethical competence.

Daydreaming

Terry L. Cooper (2012) in his multiple editions of *The Responsible Administrator* suggests that readers exercise their moral imaginations to project the possible consequences of available alternatives when making an ethical decision. While one or two alternatives might dominate your feelings and imagination, it is essential, Cooper advises, to consider the full range of alternatives.

Daydreaming is a form of imagination that might be drawn on to enhance one's skill in making a decision that has the "best" outcome, namely one that is ethical beyond question. Annie Murphy Paul (2012) points out that daydreaming isn't a waste of time, as it is most often thought to be. Rather, "this kind of introspection is crucial to our mental health, to our relationships, and to our emotional and moral development."

Is it not so?

Arriving . . .

So the journey to ethical competence can be a long and challenging one in which the destination always seems just beyond the reach of the most determined traveler. What matters the most: the destination or the journey—or both? And herein lies the rub—we can keep track of the journey, but we have great difficulty knowing when we have arrived. The pursuit of ethical competence for public service leadership, as noted early in this book, is a lifelong quest. It is entwined with the commitment to professionalism and standards of performance and behavior. Professionals and their associations are necessarily challenged to continuously raise the bar. Put differently, the destination is not fixed but ever changing, driven by a commitment to higher standards of performance and greater ethical expectations.

In the first few pages of this book, we cautioned readers that our knowledge of ethical competence in public service—what it is, how to achieve it—is quite limited in both theory and practice. Indeed, as the chapters in this volume document, understanding ethical competence for public service leadership is a work in progress. These chapters, individually and collectively, provide helpful markers for the road ahead. Don't take any detours. Be sure to take time to pause once in a while to catch your breath, then full speed ahead.

References

American Society for Public Administration (ASPA). 2012. ASPA's ethics section. http://www.aspaonline.org/ethicscommunity/.

Bok, D. 1986–87. Ethics, the university, & society. In *The President's Report, 1986–87, Harvard University,* 15–17. http://www.drbachinese.org/vbs/publish/225/vbs225p015e.pdf (accessed June 5, 2012).

Butterfield, K.D., L.K. Treviño, and G.R. Weaver. 2000. Moral awareness in business organizations: Influences of issue-related and social context factors. *Human Relations* 53: 981–1018.

Cooper, Terry L. 2012. *The Responsible Administrator: An Approach to Ethics for the Administrative Role,* 6th ed. San Francisco: Jossey-Bass.

Haidt, J. 2001. The emotional dog and its rational tail: A social intuitionist approach to moral judgment. *Psychological Review* 108: 814–834.

Jefferson, T. 1807/1824. *A Winter in Washington.* Memoir in two volumes by Margaret Bayard Smith. New York: E. Bliss and E. White.

Menzel, D.C. 2012. *Ethics Management for Public Administrators: Leading and Building Organizations of Integrity,* 2d ed. Armonk, NY: M.E. Sharpe.

Paul, Annie Murphy. 2012. Why daydreaming isn't a waste of time. *Mind/Shift,* June 1. http://blogs.kqed.org/mindshift/2012/06/why-daydreaming-isnt-a-waste-of-time/.

Shu, L.L., F. Gino, and M.H. Bazerman. 2011. Dishonest deed, clear conscience: When cheating leads to moral disengagement and motivated forgetting. *Personality and Social Psychology Bulletin* 37: 330–349.

Svara, James H. 2007. *The Ethics Primer for Public Administrators in Government and Nonprofit Organizations.* Sudbury, MA: Jones & Bartlett.

Tampa Bay Times staff. 2012. Judge recommends clearing former Hillsborough administrator Pat Bean in ethics case. June 4. http://www.tampabay.com/blogs/baybuzz/content/judge-recommends-clearing-former-hillsborough-administrator-pat-bean-ethics-case.

Tetlock, P.E., and J.S. Lerner. 1999. The social contingency model: Identifying empirical and normative boundary conditions on the error-and-bias portrait of human nature. In *Dual Process Models in Social Psychology,* ed. S. Chaiken and Y. Trope. New York: Guildford.

Varian, B. 2012. Bean closer to clear record. *Tampa Bay Times,* June 5, 1B.

Index

Italic page references indicate tables and figures.

ABA, 160, 220, 225–227, 278–279
Abbott Laboratories, 78
Abrams, Frank, 72
Academy of Management, 84
Accountability, 27
Accusations of unethical behavior, 279–280
ACHE, 266–267
Ackerman, R.W., 75
Administration, ethical challenges in social
    work profession, 181
American Bar Association (ABA), 160, 220,
    225–227, 278–279
American College of Healthcare Executives
    (ACHE), 266–267
American Philosophical Association, 247
American Society for Public Administration
    (ASPA), 8, 119, 193, 198, 203–205,
    213, 279
Analytical skills, developing, 184
Aristotle, 96–99, *99*, 101–102, 106, 108
ASPA, 8, 119, 193, 198, 203–205, 213, 279
Assertions of students, questioning
    immediacy, 107–108
    omniscience, 104
    overview, 102–104
    reductionism, 105–107
Attaining ethical competence
    caution about, 281
    first step, 275
    moral development and, 134–135
    next steps, 275–277
    overview, 275
    pauses to stop and take stock
        accusations of being unethical, 279–280
        daydreaming, 280
        ethics training programs, 278
        overview, 277–278
        professional associations, 278–279
    question about, 52
    satisfactory level of, 10–11, 51–52
    strategies for
        ethics education, 196–200
        ethics training programs, 206–207

Attaining ethical competence
    strategies for *(continued)*
        laws, codes, and standards of conduct,
            200–203
        leadership, mentoring, and exemplars,
            207–209
        overview, 158, 196
        professional codes and associations,
            203–206
Attuned social performance, 75–76, 79–83, *80*
Audit, ethics, 80
Awareness of opinion, 103

Bailey, Stephen K., 11, 13
Bakker, F.G.A., 52
Balkin, D.B., 255–256
Barnard, C.I., 132
Bastiaens, Theo J., 30–31
Bates and O'Steen v. State Bar of Arizona
    (1977), 229
Baucus, M.S., 60
Bauer, R.A., 75
Bazerman, Max H., 17, 247, 267
Beck-Dudley, C.L., 60
Benefits design in nonprofit profession,
    254–255
Berghofer, Desmond, 6
Best practices, 80
Blind spots, ethical, 17
Boards of directors, 85
Bok, Derek, 275
Boundary approach, 35–36
Boundary issues, 179–180
Bourdieu, Pierre, 132
Bowman, James S., 34, 52
British Petroleum, 83
Brown, M.E., 58
Burke, James, 56, 82
Burkhalter, Bart, 44
Business profession
    attuned social performance in, 75–76,
        79–83, *80*
    best practices in, 80
    boards of directors in, 85
    codes of ethics in, 81

Business profession *(continued)*
  committees reflecting social responsibility
    in, 85
  corporate social responsibility in, 71–75, 85
  discovery leadership in, 73–76, 79–83, *80*
  documentation in, 74
  ethical competence in
    implications for research and practice,
      83–86
    overview, 27–28, 71, 86
  ethics audit in, 80
  ethics hotline in, 79–80
  executive compensation in, 85
  forums and, industry-wide, 80
  hiring practices in, 85
  ideal typing to model executive leadership
    in, 74–76
  legal standards in, 81
  myopic leadership in, 73, 75–79, *77*
  neglectful social performance in, 76–79, *77*
  ombudsperson in, 80, 85
  organizational structure in, 85
  reporting systems in, anonymous, 79–80
  stakeholders in, 82

Canons of Legal Ethics, 160, 225–227
Capitalism, 71
Center for Ethical Deliberation, 259
"Change orders" practice, 16
Cheng, Mei-I., 31–32
Cho, Chung-Lae, 18
City managers, 155
Ciulla, Joanne B., 19
Civility, 160, 220–223
Clark Committee, 228–229
Clark, Tom, 228
Client rights in social work profession,
  177–178
Client self-determination in social work
  profession, 178
Code of Ethics (ASPA), 193, 198, 213, 279
Code of Ethics for Nonprofit and
  Philanthropic Organizations
  (Independent Sector Board of Directors),
  264–265
Code of Ethics (ICMA), 12, 193
Code of Ethics (NASW), 165, 167, 169–173,
  181
Code of Professional Responsibility (ABA),
  227–228
Codes of conduct, 100
Codes of ethics. *See also specific name*
  in attaining ethical competence, 200–203
  in business profession, 81

Codes of ethics *(continued)*
  in nonprofit profession, 264–267
  in normative ethics, 8
  in public administration profession, 193
  in social work profession, 165, 168–169
Collaborative leadership, 18–19
Commercialization in law profession, 159–160
Committee for Economic Development
  (CED), 72
Committees reflecting corporate social
  responsibility, 85
Communication about ethics, 61–62
Compensation, business executive, 85
Competence. *See also* Ethical competence
  behavior versus, 42
  as concept, 30–32
  in context
    grounding in organization theory and
      behavior, 8
    knowledge of normative foundations of
      public administrative ethics, 7–8
    overview, 6–7
  core, 31
  defining, 5, 29–32, *30*, 275–276
  general, 32, 36
  incompetence versus, 41
  individual-level, 31, 35
  knowledge of organization development and
    design approach, 8–9
  organizational-level, 31, 35
  as personal characteristic, 31
  purpose of, 32
  specific, 32, 36
  subcompetencies, 38–41
  as task characteristic, 31
  work-oriented perspective of, 31, 35
  worker-oriented perspective of, 31–32, 35–36
Competency models and definitions, 43–44,
  275–276
Compliance-based ethics, 160, 219–221, 227
Confidentiality issues, 178–179
Conflicts of interest, 179–180
Constitutional doctrine and competency,
  160–161, 223–224
Consultation in social work profession, 180
Context with specific competencies identified
  create effect human resources polices and
    practices, 252–257
  identify differences, 249–250
  know the law "plus," 250–251
  overview, *245, 246, 248, 249*
  recognize pressures, 250
  use code of conduct, 251–252
Contingencies, 123–124

Cooper, Merri-Ann, 44
Cooper, Terry L., 33, 51–53, 64–65, 107–108, 123–126, 139, 190, 192, 200, 208, 280
Core competence, 31
Corporate social responsibility, 71–75, 85
Corporate social responsiveness, 75
Council on Economic Priorities, 84
Cox, Raymond, 192–193
Critical thinking, *246*, 247–248, *249*
Critique of public administration code of ethics, performing, 119–120
Cullen, J.B., 256
Culture, organizational, 7, 161–162

Dainty, Andrew R.J., 31–32
Darley, J.M., 132
Daydreaming, 280
De Schrijver, Annelies, 25–26
Decision making, ethical, 25, 43, 96–99, *99*, 101–102, 125–126
Defining Issues Test (DIT), 7, 42, 144
Delaware law, 201–202
Delegating, 208–209
The Delphi Report, 247
Denhardt, Kathryn, 11, 191–192
Denhardt, Robert, 7
Descriptive ethics, 33
Design approach, 8–9
Dickson, M.W., 145
Disbarment, 224
Disciplinary agencies, 170, 174, 220–221, 228. *See also specific name*
Discovery leadership, 27–28, 73–76, 79–83, *80*, 85–86
Dishonesty, 180
Dissent, 161, 224
DIT, 7, 42, 144
Diversity in social work profession, cultural and social, 178
Divided loyalties in law profession, 159
"Do no harm" concept, 155
Documentation issues, 74, 180
Dolph, K., 131
Domains of ethical competence in nonprofits
    context with specific competencies identified
        create effective human resources policies and practices, 252–257
        identify differences, 249–250
        know the law "plus," 250–251
        overview, *245, 246*, 248, *249*
        recognize pressures, 250
        use the code of conduct, 251–252
    critical thinking, *246*, 247–248, *249*
    fairness, *245, 246*, 262–264, *263*

Domains of ethical competence in nonprofits *(continued)*
    frameworks for right and wrong, *245, 246*, 257–260, *258*
    human resources systems and their connections, *245, 246*, 260–262, *261*
    overview, 243–246, *245, 246*
Drake University Law School, 231–232
Dual relationships in social work profession, 176, 179–180

Educating Lawyers (Carnegie Foundation for the Advancement of Teaching), 231
Education. *See* Ethics education
Elder, L., 247–248
Elsik, W., 256
Englehardt, Elaine, 247
Enron, 54
Epstein, E.M., 72
Equitable treatment, *245, 246*, 262–264, *263*
Eriksson, S., 5
Errors of omissions, 175
Ethic of neutrality, 224
Ethical behavior, role modeling, 59–60, 63
Ethical blind spots, 17
Ethical competence. *See also* Attaining ethical competence; *specific profession*
    boundary approach to, 35–36
    case for, 42–44
    as concept, 33–35
    defining, 5–6, 9, 29–30, 35, 51–52, 92
    ethical issues and, ability to recognize, 191
    ethical leadership and, 52–54, 64–65
    ethics education for, 91–93
    framework, overview, 36, *37*, 38–42
    "high road"/"integrity-based," 10, 207–208
    integrating pedagogical methods and, 11, 91–92, 95–96, 127–129
    leadership and, 19–20, 25–28
    as lifelong process, 3, 17, 64–65
    "low road"/"compliance-driven," 10, 123, 200, 203
    measuring
        moral development and, 144–146, *146*, 158
        in public administration profession, 209–212
    Menzel's five attributes of, 9, *10*, 115, 117, 119–120, 125
    mini-case presentations and, 92
    operationalizations of, 43
    organizational structure and culture and, 7–8
    overview, 20–21, 25–29, 44–45
    "possessing," 34

Ethical competence *(continued)*
  public administration competence and, 131
  questions central to, 3, 5
  strengthening, 64–65
Ethical controversy and ambiguity, responding
    to, 185–186
Ethical decision making, 25, 43, 96–99, *99*,
    101–102, 125–126
Ethical, defining and "being," 29, 33–34
Ethical fading, 17
Ethical imagination, 123–124
Ethical incompetence
  in public administration profession, 191–192
  in social work profession, 173–175
Ethical issues, ability to recognize, 191
Ethical leadership
  achievements of, 62–64
  defining
    leader-follower relationship, 26, *55*,
        57–58, 64
    moral manager, *55*, 58–62
    moral person, 54–57, *55*
    overview, 54–55, *55*
    varied ways, 51–52
  ethical competence and, 52–54, 64–65
  features of, 52–54
  overview, 27, 51, 65–66
  side effects, positive, 63–64
Ethical reasoning. *See* Moral development
Ethical reinforcement, 60–61
Ethical role modeling, 59–60, 63
Ethical textbook, selecting, 111–113
Ethical theory and decision making period in
    social work profession, 165–166
Ethical thought, introducing conflicting
    schools of, 116–119
Ethics. *See also* Codes of ethics
  age-old concept of, applying to modern
      society, 6
  audits, 80
  communication about, 61–62
  compliance-based, 160, 219–221, 227
  descriptive, 33
  hotlines, 79–80
  interest in professional, 166
  laws, 200–203
  normative, 7–8, 33
  public service, 197–198
  virtue theory, 116
Ethics education. *See also* Integrated
    pedagogical methods; *specific school*
  assertions of students, questioning
    immediacy, 107–108
    omniscience, 104

Ethics education
  assertions of students, questioning *(continued)*
    overview, 102–104
    reductionism, 105–107
  code of ethics, critiquing, 119–120
  effective ethics, elements of, 142
  for ethical competence, general, 91–93,
      138–144, *140, 141, 143*, 196–200
  ethics courses, 11
  failure to provide ethics and, 131
  influences, 145
  knowledge of students, assisting with what
      they do not know, 108–110
  for moral development, 138–144, *140, 141,
      143*
  provisional statement of ethics, writing,
      113–115, *114*
  for public administration profession,
      196–200
  for public service lawyers, 229–232
  question in ethics, overarching, 139
  schools of ethical thought, introducing
      conflicting, 116–119
  success markers
    increased sensitivity and responsiveness,
        123–125
    overview, 120
    standing for something, 125–127
    transition to principled reasoning,
        120–123
  textbooks, selecting, 111–113
  training programs, 79, 206–207, 230, 278
Ethics hotline, 79–80
"Ethics industry," 200
Ethics laws, 200–203
Ethics Resource Center, 244, 250
Ethics training programs, 79, 206–207, 230, 278
Ethics triangle, 276
Evaluation in social work profession, 181–182
Example, power of, 207
Executive compensation in business
    profession, 85
Executive leadership, ideal typing for
    modeling, 74–76
Exemplars, 207–209

Fading, ethical, 17
Fair Labor Association, 84
Fairness, *245, 246*, 262–264, *263*
Finer, Herman, 11
Florida Department of Law Enforcement
    (FDLE), 15
Florida Ethics Commission, 15
Follower-leader relationships, 26, *55*, 57–58, 64

Forums, industry-wide business, 80
Foucault, M., 132, 135
Four-Component Model, 25, 34, 38, 43
Frameworks for right and wrong, *245*, *246*,
    257–260, *258*
Fraud, 180
Frederick, W.C., 72
Friedman, Milton, 72
Friedrich, Carl, 11, 190–191
Friedrich-Finer debate (1940–41), 11

Galang, M.C., 256
Garcetti v. Ceballos (2006), 234
Gardner, John, 209
Gaus, John, 190–191
Gawande, Atul, 213
General competence, 32, 36
Gilligan, Carol, 121–122
Gilman, Stuart, 11
Goldfarb v. Virginia State Bar (1975), 229
Goss, Robert P., 11
Government attorneys. *See* Public service
    lawyers
Grojean, M., 60
Gulf of Mexico oil spill, 83
"Gut check," 122

Harned, Patricia, 250
Harrison, D.A., 58
Health care plans in nonprofit profession, 254
Health care profession and ethical
    competence, 5, 51
Hegelsson, G., 5
Hejka-Ekins, A., 11, 132
Heres, Leonie, 26–27
Hermeneutical suspicion, 112
"High road"/"integrity-based" ethical
    competence, 10, 207–208
Hillsborough County (Florida), 13–15, 17–18
Hiring practices, 85, 254
Hoeglund, A.T., 5
Hotlines, ethics, 79–80
Huberts, L.W.J.C., 52, 61
Human resources policies and practices in
    nonprofit profession
    benefits design, 254–255
    integrating and linking, *245*, *246*, 260–262,
        261
    job design, 253
    labor relations, 256–257
    overview, 252–253
    paid time off, 254–255
    performance management, 255–256
    recruitment processes, 254

Human resources policies and practices in
    nonprofit profession *(continued)*
    training and development, 256–257

ICMA, 8, 12–13, 119, 155, 193, 203, 278
Ideal typing, 74–76
Imagination
    ethical, 123–124
    moral, 184
Immediacy, 107–108
Incompetence, 41, 181
Independent Sector Board of Directors, 264
Independent Sector Code of Ethics, 243
Individual-level competence, 31, 35
Individual rights, 137–138
Informed consent, 179
Integrated pedagogical methods
    classroom activities
        critiquing public administration code of
            ethics, 119–120
        introducing conflicting schools of ethical
            thought, 116–119
        overview, 110–111
        selecting textbooks, 111–113
        writing provisional statement of ethics,
            113–115, *114*
    classroom culture
        assisting students in knowing what they
            do not know, 108–110
        integrating theoretical with technical,
            98–100, 106
        overview, 95–98
        questioning students' assertions,
            102–108
        temptations to avoid, 100–102
    ethical competence and, 11, 91–92, 95–96,
        127–129
    mini-case presentations and, 106–107
    overview, 11, 91–92, 95–96, 127–129
    standing for something, 125–127
    success markers
        increase in sensitivity and
            responsiveness, 123–125
        overview, 120
        transition to principled reasoning, 120–123
Integrity, 12
International Chiefs of Police code, 205
International City/County Management
    Association (ICMA), 8, 12–13, 119, 155,
    193, 278

Jacobs, Richard M., 91–92
Jefferson, Thomas, 157
Job design in nonprofit profession, 253

Johnson & Johnson, 56, 82–83
Jormsri, P., 51–52
Jurkiewicz, Carole L., 7, 59, 92–93, 132, 145
Justice theory, 116

Kak, Neeraj, 44
Karsing, Edgar D., 34
Kass, L., 186
Kavathatzopoulos, Iordanis, 6, 34–35, 52
Kennedy, John F., 131
Kennedy, S.S., 247
Kidder, D.L., 256
Knowledge
   of organization development and design
      approach, 8–9
   of students, assisting with what they do not
      know, 108–110
Knowledge, skills, and attitudes and abilities
      (KSAs), 25, 31, 33, 36, 38
Kohlberg, Lawrence, 7, 42, 92–93, 124–125,
      132, 134–138, 142–144, 278
KSAs, 25, 31, 33, 36, 38

Labor relations in nonprofit profession, 256–257
Lamboo, M.E.D., 61
Larkin, G.L., 51
Lasthuizen, Karin, 26–27, 61, 63
Law profession. *See also* Public service
      lawyers
   advertising in, 229
   advocacy in, 160
   Canons of Legal Ethics and, 160, 225–227
   civility in, 160
   Code of Professional Responsibility and,
      227–228
   commercialization in, 159–160
   compliance-based ethics in, 160
   constitutional doctrines in, 160–161
   disbarment in, 224
   dissent in, 161
   divided loyalties in, 159
   ethical competence in, 158–161
   litigation against social work profession,
      173–175
   "whiplash" lawyers and, 227
Laws, ethics, 200–203
Lawton, Alan, 191
Lay, Ken, 54
Leader-follower relationship, 26, 55, 57–58, 64
Leadership. *See also* Ethical leadership
   case studies
      failed, 13–15
      implications, 17–18
      successful, 15–17

Leadership *(continued)*
   collaborative, 18–19
   delegating and, 208–209
   discovery, 27–28, 73–76, 79–83, *80*
   ethical, 19–20
   ethical competence and, 19–20, 25–28
   ideal typing for modeling executive, 74–76
   moral episodes and, 208
   moral processes and, 208
   myopic, 27, 73, 75–79, *77*
   as strategy for developing ethical
      competence in public administration
      profession, 207–209
   theory, 208
Legal duty in social work profession, 175–176
Legal standards in business profession, 81
Legal versus ethical acts, 17
Lerner, Gabriel, 233
Lewis, Carole, 11
Licensing and regulatory bodies in social work
      profession, 170, 174, 220–221, 228
Liggett, Barbara S., 161–162
Light, Paul, 3
Likert scale, 114–115
Lind, George, 42
Litigation against social work profession,
      173–175
"Low road"/"compliance-driven" ethical
      competence, 10, 123, 200, 203
Loyola Law School, 231
Lycan, A., 131

Macauley, Michael, 191
Macklin, R., 185
Maesschalck, Jeroen, 25–26
Malatesta, D., 247
Malfeasance in social work profession,
      174–175
Malpractice in social work profession,
      175–177
Management, competence-based, 26
Mansfield, Richard S., 43–44
Martens, Rob L., 30–31
Martin, K.D., 256
McPeck, J.E., 247
Measuring ethical competence
   moral development and, 144–146, *146*, 158
   in public administration profession, 209–212
Meno, 103–105, 107
Mentoring, 207–209
Menzel, Donald C., 9, *10*, 34, 51–53, 64–65,
      95–96, 102, 112–113, 115, 119–120,
      123, 125, 190, 192, 199–200
Messick, Samuel, 42

Milgram, Stanley, 7
Mini-case presentations
    ethical competence and, 92
    integrating pedagogical methods and,
        106–107
    responsiveness and, increased, 123–124
    schools of ethical thought, introducing
        conflicting, 117–118, *118*
    sensitivity and, increased, 123–124
    standing for something and, 126
Misconduct, 181
Misrepresentation, 180
Model Rules of Professional Conduct (ABA),
    220–223, 228–230, 233–234
Moore, David R., 31–32
Moral awareness, 34, 43
Moral character, 26, 34
Moral courage, 56, 64
Moral development
    attaining ethical competence and, 134–135
    ethical competence in public sector
        profession and, 134–138
    ethics education for, 138–144, *140*, *141*, *143*
    individual rights and, 137–138
    Kohlberg's stages of, 7, 42, 92–93, 124–125,
        134–138, 142–144
    measuring ethical competence and,
        144–146, *146*, 158
    overview, 92–93, 131–132, 146–148
    pedagogical influence and, 92
    "right" and, defining, 132–134
    social contract and, 137–138
    social system and, 135–137
    universal ethical principles and, 136–138
Moral episodes, 208
Moral imagination, 184
Moral judgment, 34
Moral Judgment Test (MJT), 42
Moral manager, *55*, 58–62
Moral motivation, 34, 40
Moral obligation, 184–185
Moral person, 54–57, *55*
Moral processes, 208
Moral reasoning, 43. *See also* Moral
    development
Moral sensitivity, 38–39, 43
Mosher, William, 204
MPA curriculum, 100, 138, 196–197, 199
Myopic leadership, 27, 73, 75–79, *77*

NACC, 265–266
NASPAA, 189, 197–198, 276
NASW, 156, 165, 167, 169–173, 181, 266,
    278

National Association of Schools of Public
    Affairs and Administration (NASPAA),
    189, 197–198, 276
National Association of Social Workers
    (NASW), 156, 165, 167, 169–173, 181,
    266, 278
National Council (ASPA), 279
National Nonprofit Ethics Survey (Ethics
    Resource Center), 244
Neglectful social performance, 76–79, *77*
Negligence claims, 173–174
Nestlé's sales of infant formula, 78
Noddings, Nel, 121–122
Nonprofit Academic Centers Council
    (NACC), 265–266
Nonprofit Leadership Alliance (formerly
    American Humanics), 266
Nonprofit profession. *See also* Domains of
    ethical competence in nonprofits
    code of conduct in, using, 251–252
    codes of ethics in, 264–267
    culture in, 161–162
    ethical competence in
        evaluation of, 267
        overview, 161–162, 243, 268
        perspectives on, comparing, 264–267
    human resources policies and practices,
        creating
        benefits design, 254–255
        job design, 253
        labor relations, 256–257
        overview, 252–253
        paid time off, 254–255
        performance management, 255–256
        recruitment process, 254
        training and development, 256–257
    Independent Sector Code of Ethics, 243
    individual behavior and, 243–244
    legal framework in, knowing, 250–251
    misbehavior in, 161–162
    National Nonprofit Ethics Survey and, 244
    overview, 242–243
    pressures in, recognizing, 250
    unethical behavior in, 244
Normative ethics, 7–8, 33
Nursing profession and ethical competence,
    5, 51

Office of Government Ethics, 6
Ohralik v. Ohio State Bar Association (1978),
    229
Ombudsperson, 80, 85
Omissions, errors of, 175
Omniscience, 104

Operationalizations of ethical competence, 43
Opinions, wrong versus right, 102–104, 134
Organization behavior, 8
Organization development, 8–9
Organization theory, 8
Organizational culture, 7, 161–162
Organizational design approach, 124
Organizational integrity, 12
Organizational-level competence, 31, 35
Organizational structure, 7–8, 85

Packel, A.K., 264
Paid time off in nonprofit profession, 254–255
Paine, L.S., 60
Paternalism, professional, 178
Paul, Ann Murphy, 280
Paul, R., 247–248
Pauperism, early responses to, 164
Pennock, J.R., 190
Performance management in nonprofit
    profession, 255–256
Personal integrity, 12
Personal responsibility, 184–185
Piaget, J., 137
Plant, Jeremy, 157–158
Plato, 97, 102, 122
Practitioner impairment in social work
    profession, 181
Principled reasoning, transition to, 120–123
Principles of Ethical Conduct, 12–13
Privacy issues, 178–179
Privileged communication issues, 178–179
Professional associations, 203–206, 278–279.
    See also specific name
Professional codes, 8, 12, 81, 165, 168–169,
    200–203, 203–206. *See also specific name*
Professional Ethics Committee, 205
Professional integrity, 12
Professional paternalism, 178
Professional responsibility in public
    administration profession, 190
Progressive Era in social work profession,
    164–165
Provisional statement of public administration
    ethics, writing, 113–115, *114*
Public administration profession
  city managers in, 155
  Code of Ethics in, 193
  collaborative leadership in, 18–19
  competence in, 131
  discovery leadership in, 85–86
  ethical competence in
      attaining satisfactory level of, 10–13, *10*
      defining, 5–6

Public administration profession
  ethical competence in *(continued)*
      effective leadership and, 158
      ethical leadership and, 65
      evidence of, 134
      goal of, 209–212
      literature on, 3, *4*, 5
      measuring success of, 209–212
      overview, 157–158, 189–193, 212–214
      roots of competence and, 131
  ethical decision making in, 96–99, *99*
  ethical incompetence in, 191–192
  ethical theory with practice, 100–101
  normative foundations of ethics in, 7–8,
      106
  practical matters, avoiding focusing strictly
      on, 101
  practical mindset of ethics in, 98–102
  professional responsibility in, 190
  professionals in, categorizing, 194–195
  public service ethics in, 197–198
  public service values in, 197–198
  strategies to develop ethical competence in
      ethics education, 189, 196–200
      ethics training programs, 206–207
      exemplars, 207–209
      laws, codes, and standards of conduct,
          200–203
      leadership, 207–209
      mentoring, 207–209
      overview, 196
      professional codes and associations,
          203–206
  technological developments and, 207
Public policy, 73, 84
Public prosecutors. *See* Public service lawyers
Public service ethics, 197–198
Public service lawyers
  Canons of Legal Ethics and, 225–227
  civility and, 220–223
  Clark Committee and, 228–229
  Code of Professional Responsibility and,
      227–228
  compliance and, going beyond, 210
  compliance-based ethics and, 219–221, 227
  constitutional competency and, 223–224
  disbarment and, 224
  dissent and, principled, 224
  ethical competence and
      ABA's role in, 225–227
      overview, 160–161, 218–219, 234–235
      revisiting, 232–234
  ethical failure and, 227–229
  ethics education for, 229–232

Public service lawyers *(continued)*
  Model Rules of Professional Conduct and,
    220–223, 228–230, 233–234
Public service values, 197–198
Pynes, Joan, 255

Rachels, James, 111–112
Rawls, John, 116
Reamer, Frederic G., 155–157
Reasoning, ethical. *See* Moral development
Recruitment process in nonprofit profession,
  254
Reductionism, 105–107
Referrals in social work profession, 180
Regulation of rules and codes, 220–221
Rehearsal of defenses, 124
Reinforcement, ethical, 60–61
Reporting systems, anonymous, 79–80
Research in social work profession, 181–182
Respect for all persons, *245, 246,* 262–264, *263*
Response to opinion, 103
Responsiveness, 75, 123–125, 185–186
Rest, James, 25, 33–35, 38–39, 42–43
Rhode, D.L., 264
Richmond, Mary, 156, 165
Ricoeur, Paul, 112
Rigas, G., 34–35, 52
Right, defining, 132–134
Right opinion, 102–104
Roberts, R., 60
Roberts, Robert N., 158–161, 279
Rohr, John, 11
Role modeling, ethical, 59–60, 63
Rules, 38, 40–41, 221
Russ, G.S., 256

Sanghi, Seema, 32
Sarasota County (Florida), 15–18, 56
Self-reinforcing cycle, 54
Sensitivity, 38–39, 43, 123–125
Service delivery in social work profession, 179
Settlement house movement, 164
Sherman Act, 229
Six, F.E., 52
Smith, Adam, 71
Social action, 182
Social contract, 71–72, 137–138
Social system and moral development,
  135–137
Social welfare, 182
Social work profession
  administration in, 181
  boundary issues in, 179–180
  client harm or injury in, 177

Social work profession *(continued)*
  client rights in, 177–178
  client self-determination in, 178
  codes of ethics in, 165, 168–169
  complaints against, 173–174
  confidentiality in, 178–179
  conflicts of interest in, 179–180
  consultation in, 180
  contemporary, 164, 167
  dishonesty in, 180
  diversity in, cultural and social, 178
  documentation in, 180
  dual relationships in, 176, 179–180
  errors of omissions in, 175
  ethical competence in
    evolution of, 164–167
    future challenges to, 182–186
    overview, 155–157
  ethical incompetence in, 173–175
  ethical standards in
    evolution of, 167–169
    as risk-management tool, 173–177
  ethical theory and decision making period
    in, 165–166
  ethics risk-management in, 167, 173–177
  evaluation in, 181–182
  fraud in, 180
  future challenges facing, 182–186
  historical perspective, 163–164
  incompetence in, 181
  informed consent in, 179
  legal duty in, 175–176
  licensing and regulatory bodies in, 170, 174
  litigation against, 173–175
  malfeasance in, 174–175
  malpractice in, 175–177
  misconduct in, 181
  misrepresentation in, 180
  overview, 163–164
  practitioner impairment in, 181
  privacy in, 178–179
  privileged communication in, 178–179
  professional paternalism in, 178
  in Progressive Era, 164–165
  referral in, 180
  research in, 181–182
  service delivery in, 179
  settlement house movement in, 164
  social action and, 182
  social welfare and, 182
  supervision in, 180
  technological developments in, 183
  termination of services in, 181
  values period in, 165

Socrates, 102–105, 107, 122
Specific competence, 32, 36
Sprinthall, Norman, 7, 42
Stakeholders, 82
Standard Oil of New Jersey, 72
Standards, 38
Standards of conduct, 200–203. *See also specific type*
Standards of Ethical Conduct for Employees, 202
Standing for something, 125–127
State Public Integrity Commission, 201
Stenberg, Carl W., 18
Stewart, Debra, 7, 42
Stewart Sprinthall Management Survey (SSMS), 7, 42
Stoof, Angela, 30–31
Subcompetencies, 38–41
Supervision in social work profession, 180
Svara, James, 192, 199–200, 206, 208, 276
Swanson, Diane L., 27–28, 73, 75

"Talk the walk," 20, 26, 57
Technical and theoretical, integrating, 98–100, 106
Technological developments, 183, 207
Tenbrunsel, Ann E., 17, 247, 267
Termination of services in social work profession, 181
Textbook, selecting ethical, 111–113
Theoretical and technical, integrating, 98–100, 106
Thompson, Dennis, 12, 224, 233–234
Thought, introducing conflicting schools of ethical, 116–119
Tolerance, 134, 209
Training and development in nonprofit profession, 256–257
Training programs, 206. *See also* Ethics training programs
Transnational corporations, 84. *See also specific name*
Treviño, Linda K., 19–20, 58
Trust, 19, 158, 210–211, 219, 222, 227
Tuskegee studies, 182
2009 Survey on Lawyer Discipline Systems (ABA), 221
Tylenol tampering scandal, 56, 82–83

Unethical behavior, 27
United Nations Global Compact, 84

Universal ethical principles, 136–138
U.S. Supreme Court, 229. *See also specific case name*

Value attunement. *See* Attuned social performance
Value-myopic leadership. *See* Myopic leadership
Value-receptive discovery leadership. *See* Discovery leadership
Values period in social work profession, 165
Values, public service, 197–198
Van Wart, Montgomery, 18–19, 203
Vershoor, C.C., 145
Virtanen, Turo, 6, 191
Virtue ethics theory, 116

Wakenhut, R., 42
Waldo, Dwight, 196
"Walk the talk," 20, 26, 53–54, 57, 80–81
Watergate scandal, 166
Weber, Max, 74
Weick, K.E., 76
Werbel, J., 255–256
Wharton, Joseph, 72
"Whiplash" lawyers, 227
Whistleblower literature, 7
Whitbeck, Caroline, 9
White, Richard, 7
Whitton, Howard, 34
Willowbrook studies, 182
Wilson, Woodrow, 157
Winnecott, Donald W., 104
Work-oriented perspective of competence, 31, 35
Worker-oriented perspective of competence, 31–32, 35
World Health Organization, 78
Wright, Deil S., 18
Wrong opinion
  immediacy, 107–108
  omniscience, 104
  reductionism, 105–107
  right opinion versus, 102–104
  surmounting, 108, 112

Yankelovich, Daniel, 103, 126

Zimbardo, Philip, 7

About the Editors and Contributors

Terry L. Cooper is the Maria B. Crutcher Professor in Citizenship and Democratic Values at the University of Southern California Sol Price School of Public Policy. Cooper's research focuses on civic engagement and public ethics. He is the director of the USC Civic Engagement Initiative and the author of *The Responsible Administrator: An Approach to Ethics for the Administrative Role,* 6th ed. (Jossey-Bass, 2012) and *An Ethic of Citizenship for Public Administration* (Prentice Hall, 1991). In addition, Cooper is the editor of the *Handbook of Administrative Ethics,* 2d ed. (Marcel Dekker, 2001) and the coeditor of *Exemplary Public Administrators* (Jossey-Bass, 1992). He has published numerous articles in scholarly journals, including *Public Administration Review, Administration & Society,* and the *American Review of Public Administration.* His current research is on the homeowner association movement in China as an emerging expression of civil society in that country.

Annelies De Schrijver has a master's degree in criminology (Ghent University, Belgium) and a master's degree in quantitative analysis for the social sciences (Hogeschool-Universiteit Brussel, Belgium). As of 2012, she held the position of doctoral researcher for the Research Foundation Flanders at the Leuven Institute of Criminology, KU Leuven (University of Leuven, Belgium), focusing on a quantitative longitudinal project about police integrity at the Belgian police academies.

Leonie Heres is a PhD candidate and member of the research group Quality of Governance at the Department of Governance Studies, VU University Amsterdam. She holds a bachelor's degree in Public Administration and Organization Sciences and a master's degree in Social Science Research. Her primary research interests are leadership in the public and private sectors, organizational ethics, and organizational behavior. Several of her recent articles have been accepted for publication in the *International Journal of Leadership Studies, Public Management Review,* and *Journal of Change Management.* Her website address is www.leonieheres.com.

Richard M. Jacobs is a professor of education and counseling and a professor of public administration at Villanova University. A native of Chicago, Jacobs served for nearly two decades as a teacher and administrator in middle and secondary schools. He began his affiliation with Villanova University in 1991, earning the rank of associate professor in 1996, tenure in 1998, and full professor in 2006. Jacobs studied higher educational administration during the 1996 and 1997 academic years as assistant to the president of Merrimack College in North Andover, Massachusetts. In 1994, Jacobs was selected as the 12th U.S. Catholic Conference Seton-Neumann laureate. His current research interests include organization theory and leadership ethics.

Carole L. Jurkiewicz is the Woman's Hospital Distinguished Professor of Healthcare Management and the Kearney Jolly Endowed Professor at the E.J. Ourso College of Business, Louisiana State University. Her work centers on organizational performance as a function of employee ethicality and organizational culture. She has published over a hundred books, scholarly articles, and chapters in the areas of organizational and individual performance, ethics, power, and leadership. Jurkiewicz brings to her academic career many years of experience as a government consultant and an executive in private and nonprofit organizations.

Karin Lasthuizen is an associate professor of governance studies and a senior member of the research group Quality of Governance at the Department of Governance Studies, VU University Amsterdam. She is an expert in research on leadership and ethics in public-sector organizations and teaches ethics courses to undergraduate and postgraduate students at VU University. Recent writings by Lasthuizen have been published in *Public Management Review, Public Administration, Sociological Methods and Research,* and the *International Journal of Leadership Studies.* Her website address is www.lasthuizen.com.

Barbara S. Liggett is the director of the School of Public Affairs and Administration and an associate professor at Western Michigan University (WMU). She previously served WMU as the executive adviser for quality in the Office of the President and as the associate vice president for human resources in the Office of the Vice President for Business and Finance. Prior to her university appointments, Liggett was the director of management analysis in Genesee County, Michigan, and a salary administrator for City National Bank in Detroit. Her expertise is in public and nonprofit organizations' human resource systems and leadership. Her consultation practice throughout the United States, Egypt, Guatemala, Japan, Kuwait, and the People's Republic of China is extensive and focuses on organization system changes for improved workplace relations and productivity. She has published in the *American Review of Public Administration, ASQ Higher Education Brief, Public Integrity, Public Voices,* and *Perspectives.* Her media productions include *Comparable Worth: Issues* for the National Organization for Women and *An Equitable Salary: How You Can Help* for Hay Associates, Chicago. She is certified as a mediator in Conflict Dynamics Profiling and also as a Senior Professional in Human Resources (SPHR) through the Human Resource Certification Institute.

Jeroen Maesschalck studied public administration and philosophy at Ghent University, Belgium, and at the London School of Economics and Political Science, UK. He holds a PhD in social sciences from the KU Leuven (University of Leuven, Belgium) and serves there as an associate professor and the director of the Leuven Institute of Criminology in the Faculty of Law. He is also a research fellow in Integrity of Governance at the Free University of Amsterdam. His teaching and research interests lie in the fields of public administration ethics and management/policymaking in the criminal justice system. He also teaches qualitative research methods. His publications include articles in *Public Integrity, Public Administration, Administration and Society, International Public Management Journal,* and the *American Review of Public Administration.*

Donald C. Menzel is president of Ethics Management International and emeritus professor of public administration, Northern Illinois University. He served as the 2005–6 president of the American Society for Public Administration. He holds a PhD from Pennsylvania State University, a master's degree from Miami University (Ohio), and a bachelor's degree in mathematics from Southern Illinois University. Menzel served in the U.S. Air Force from 1962 to 1967 as a navigator/bombardier on B-52s. His most recent books are *Ethics Moments in Government: Cases and Controversies* (Taylor & Francis, 2010), *The State of Public Administration: Issues, Challenges, and Opportunities* (coedited with Harvey L. White; M.E. Sharpe, 2011), and *Ethics Management for Public Administrators: Leading and Building Organizations of Integrity,* 2d ed. (M.E. Sharpe, 2012). He is working on an interactive ebook titled *The New China: Myths and Realities.* His website address is ethicalmgt.com.

Jeremy F. Plant is professor of public administration and public policy and interim chair of the iMPS in Homeland Security program at Penn State University, where he has taught since 1988. Plant's research centers on the areas of administrative ethics, homeland security, and transportation policy and administration. His writings have appeared in such academic journals as *Public*

Administration Review, American Review of Public Administration, Review of Policy Research, Public Integrity, Journal of Urban Affairs, International Journal of Public Administration, Public Works Management & Policy, and several others. Plant has written two books, nearly 30 journal articles, and 20 chapters in multi-authored books. He has presented more than 70 conference papers on a variety of topics and has authored numerous reports to sponsors. He is a founding member and former chair of the American Society for Public Administration's (ASPA's) Section on Ethics and Section on Transportation Policy and Administration, and currently serves on the executive committee of each. Plant has been appointed to several task forces and committees by the Commonwealth of Pennsylvania, ASPA, and the National Association of Schools of Public Affairs and Administration, and is a frequent commentator on politics and public policy in print and electronic media.

Frederic G. Reamer is a professor in the graduate program of the School of Social Work, Rhode Island College. His research and teaching have addressed a wide range of human service issues, including mental health, health care, criminal justice, public welfare, and professional ethics. Reamer received his PhD from the University of Chicago and has served as a social worker in correctional and mental health settings. Since 1992, he has served on the Rhode Island Parole Board. Reamer is the author of many books and articles on the subjects of professional ethics and other topics. His recent books include *Boundary Issues and Dual Relationships in the Human Services,* 2d ed. (Columbia University Press, 2012); *Social Work Values and Ethics,* 3d ed. (Columbia University Press, 2006); *The Social Work Ethics Casebook* (NASW Press, 2009); and *Heinous Crime: Cases, Causes, and Consequences* (Columbia University Press, 2005).

Robert N. Roberts has taught at James Madison University since 1982. He is the author of *White House Ethics* (Greenwood, 1988) and *Ethics in U.S. Government: An Encyclopedia of Investigations, Scandals, Reforms, and Legislation* (Greenwood, 2001); coauthor with Marion T. Doss, Jr., of *From Watergate to Whitewater: The Public Integrity War* (Praeger, 1997); and coauthor with Scott John Hammond of *Encyclopedia of Presidential Campaigns, Slogans, Issues, and Platforms* (Greenwood, 2004). Articles by Roberts have appeared in the *Public Administration Review, International Journal of Public Administration, Public Integrity, PS: Political Science & Politics, Politics & Policy,* and the *Review of Public Personnel Administration.* Roberts has taught administrative law and legal environment of public administration courses since the early 1980s. He holds a BA, an MPA/JD, and a PhD in public administration from Syracuse University.

Diane L. Swanson is a professor of management and Edgerley Family Chair in Business Administration at Kansas State University, where she chairs the Ethics Education Initiative. She also holds teaching appointments at Benedictine University and the Graduate School of Credit Management hosted at Dartmouth College. Recognized in several *Who's Who* bibliographical indices, Swanson has published widely on corporate social responsibility, value-based leadership, and ethics education, including the books *Toward Integrative Corporate Citizenship,* coauthored with Dr. Marc Orlitzky (Palgrave, 2008), *Advancing Business Ethics Education,* coedited with Dr. Dann Fisher (Information Age Publishing, 2008), and *Toward Assessing Business Ethics Education,* also coedited with Fisher (Information Age Publishing, 2011). Her 1999 article in *Academy of Management Review* was awarded best article by the International Association for Business and Society in conjunction with *California Management Review*. Swanson served as an associate editor for the award-winning multivolume *Encyclopedia of Business Ethics and Society* and as an editorial board member for the *Academy of Management Review, Business Ethics Quarterly, Asia Pacific and Globalization Review*, and *Business & Society*.